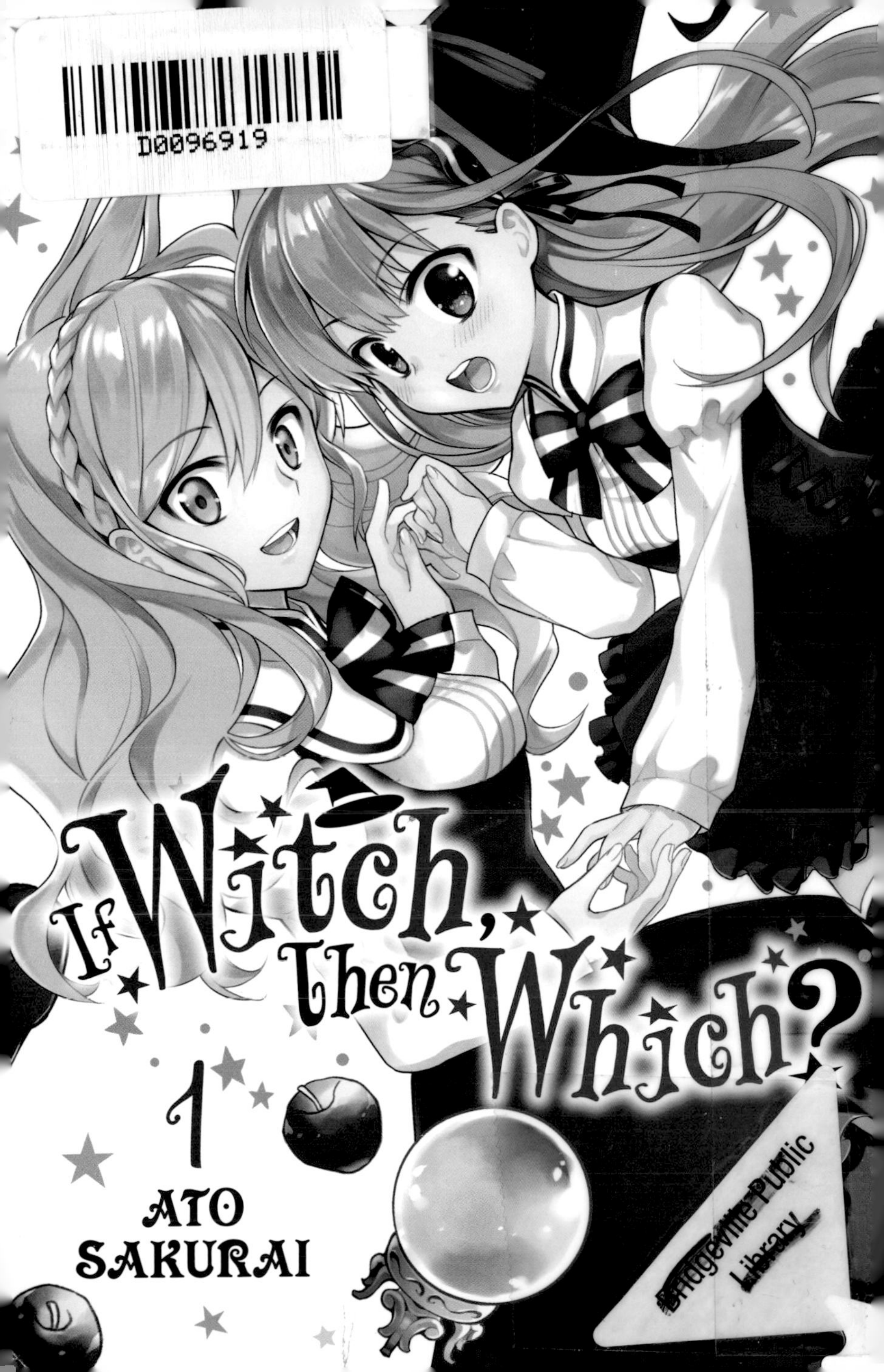
If Witch, Then Which?
1
ATO SAKURAI

If Witch, Then Which?

1 Ato Sakurai

Translation: **CALEB D. COOK** ★ Lettering: **BIANCA PISTILLO**

MAJO RABA MAJO REBA Vol. 1
©2019 Ato Sakurai/SQUARE ENIX CO., LTD.
First published in Japan in 2019 by SQUARE ENIX CO., LTD.
English translation rights arranged with SQUARE ENIX CO., LTD. and Yen Press, LLC through Tuttle-Mori Agency, Inc.

English translation ©2020 by SQUARE ENIX CO., LTD.

Yen Press
150 West 30th Street, 19th floor
New York, NY 10001

Visit us at yenpress.com
facebook.com/yenpress
twitter.com/yenpress

The

The

Library of Congress Control Number: 2020940350

ISBNs: 978-1-9753-1621-1 (paperback)
978-1-9753-1622-8 (ebook)

10 9 8 7 6 5 4 3 2 1

WOR

Printed in the United States of America

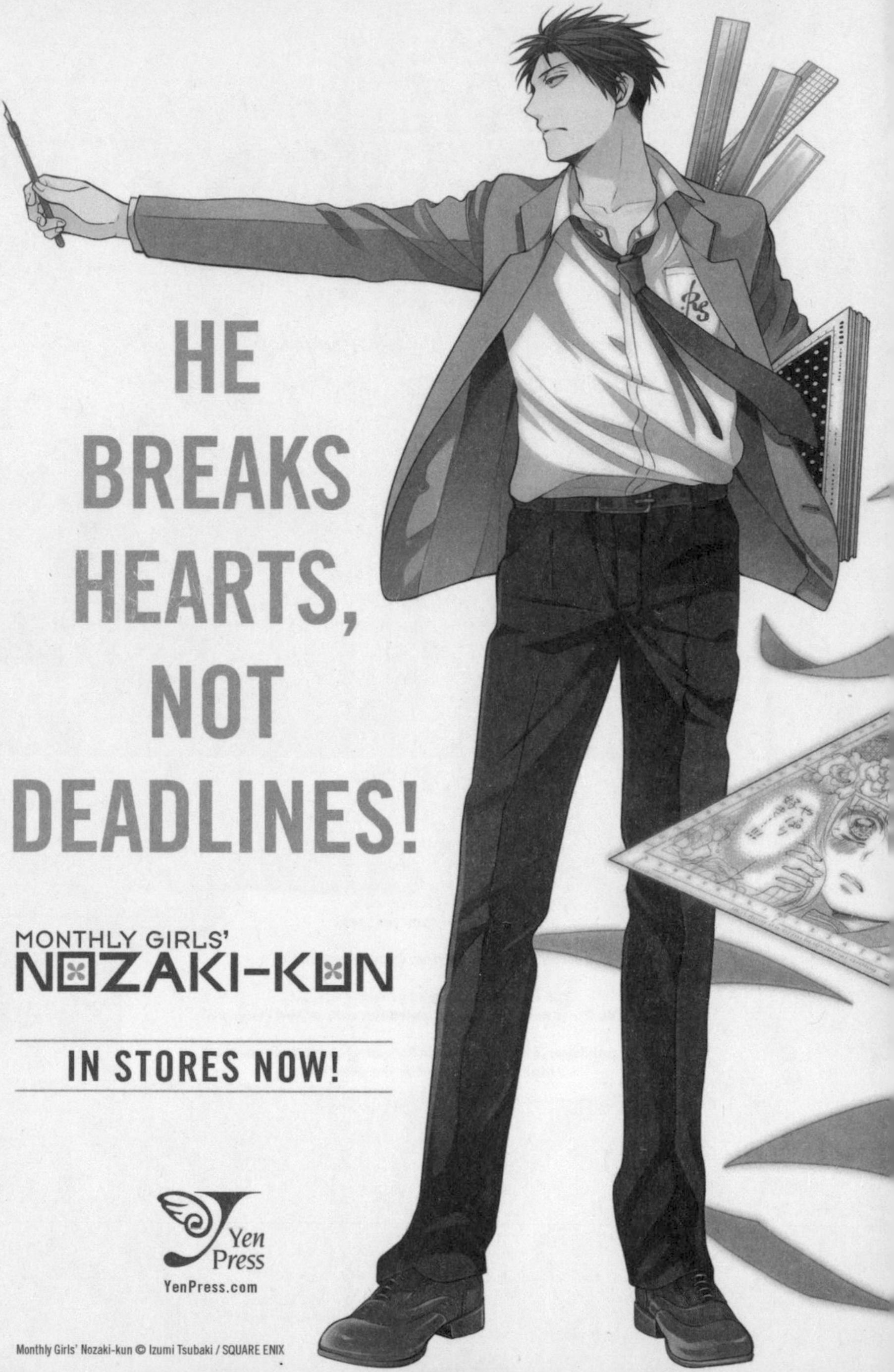

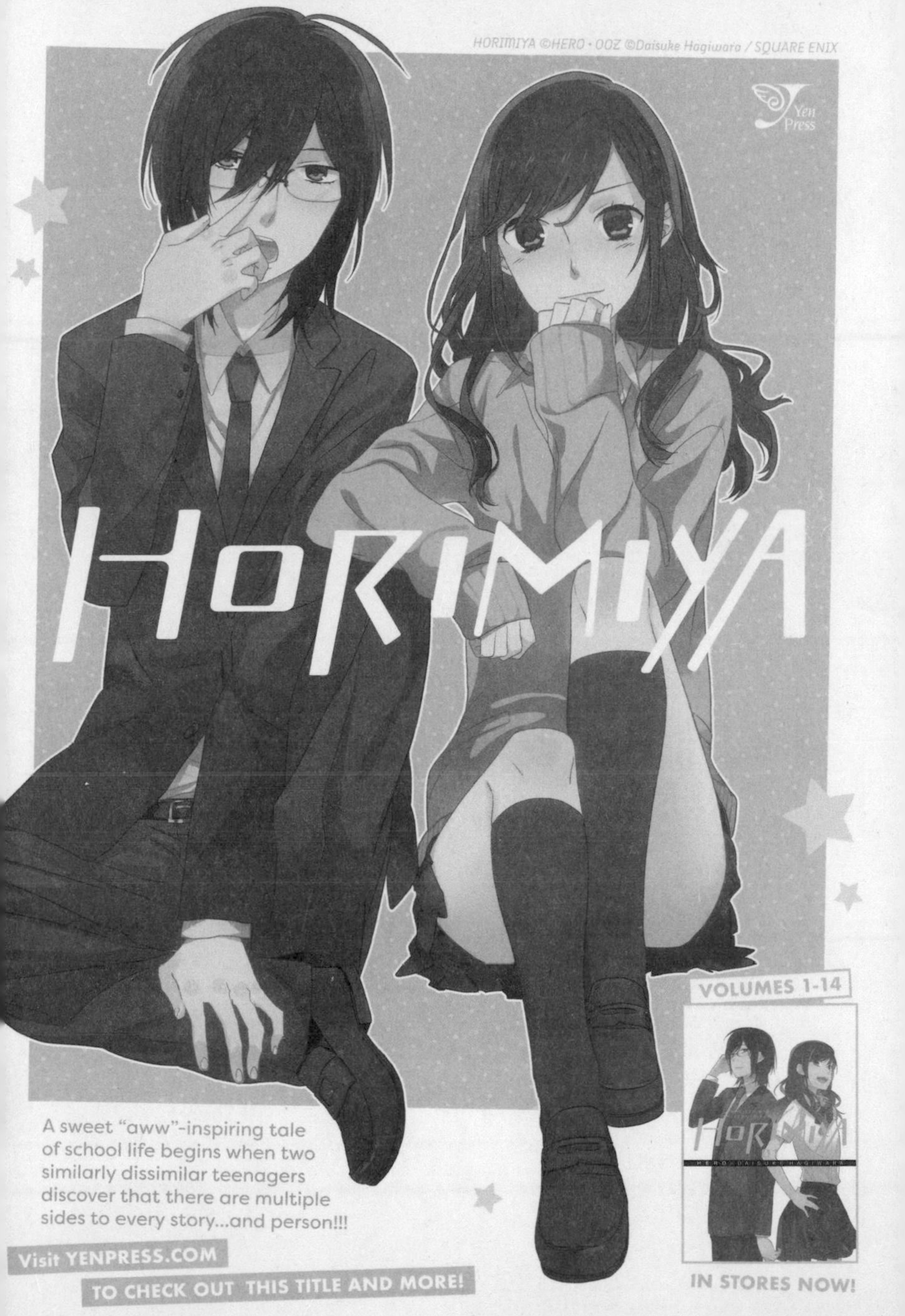
HORIMIYA ©HERO • OOZ ©Daisuke Hagiwara / SQUARE ENIX
Yen Press
HORIMIYA
VOLUMES 1-14
HORIMIYA
IN STORES NOW!
A sweet "aww"-inspiring tale of school life begins when two similarly dissimilar teenagers discover that there are multiple sides to every story...and person!!!
Visit YENPRESS.COM
TO CHECK OUT THIS TITLE AND MORE!

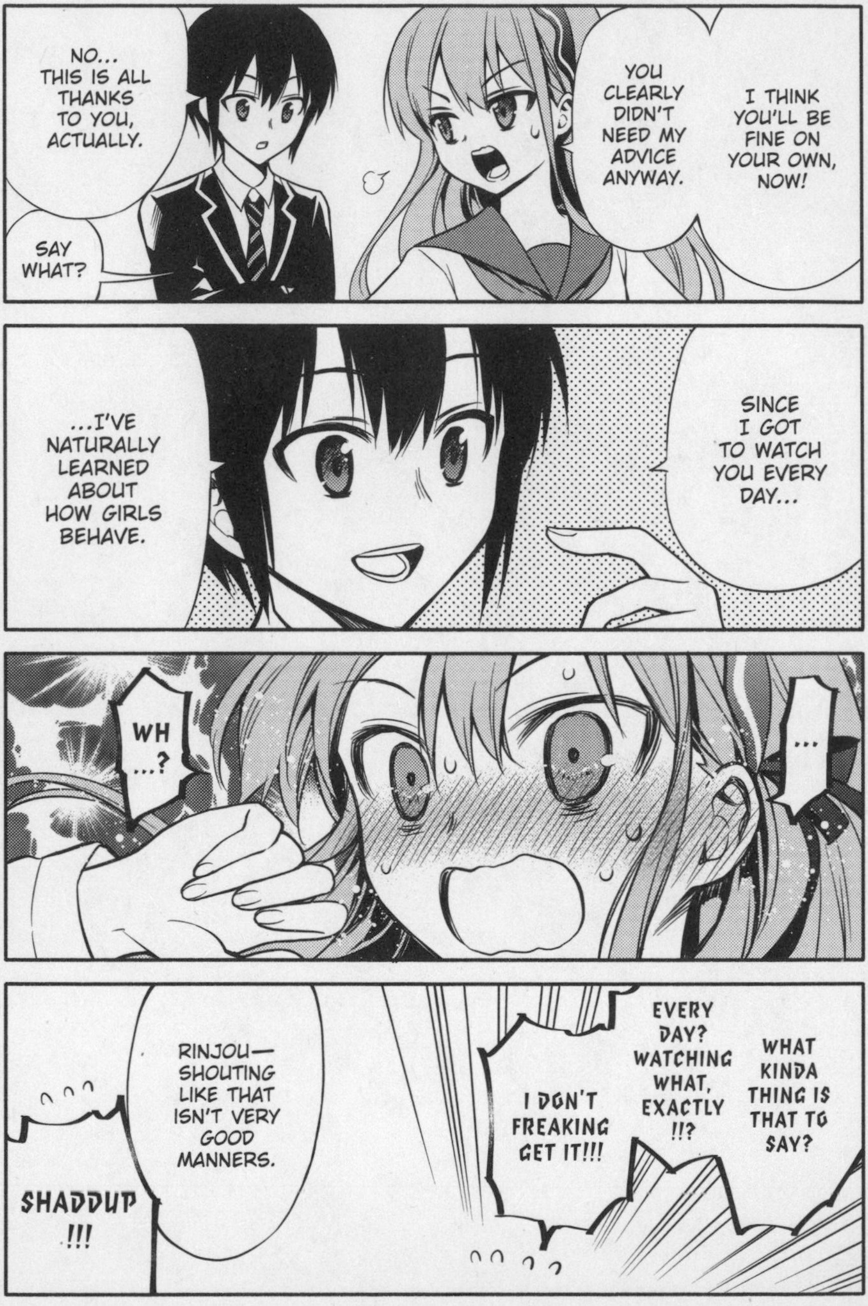
I THINK YOU'LL BE FINE ON YOUR OWN, NOW!
YOU CLEARLY DIDN'T NEED MY ADVICE ANYWAY.
NO... THIS IS ALL THANKS TO YOU, ACTUALLY.
SAY WHAT?
SINCE I GOT TO WATCH YOU EVERY DAY...
...I'VE NATURALLY LEARNED ABOUT HOW GIRLS BEHAVE.
...
WH...?
WHAT KINDA THING IS THAT TO SAY?
EVERY DAY? WATCHING WHAT, EXACTLY!!?
I DON'T FREAKING GET IT!!!
RINJOU—SHOUTING LIKE THAT ISN'T VERY GOOD MANNERS.
SHADDUP!!!

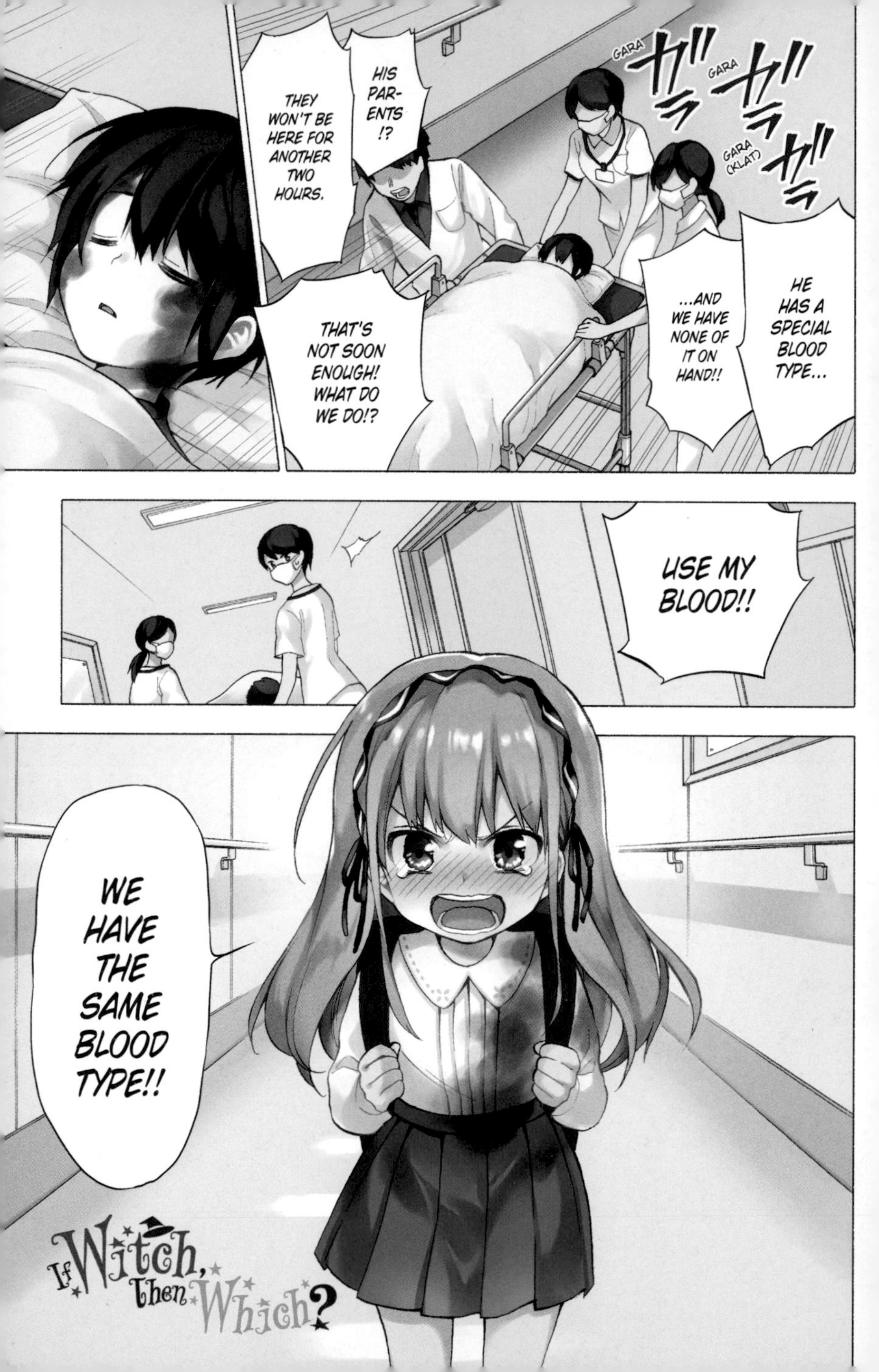
ガラ GARA
ガラ GARA
ガラ GARA (KLAT)
HE HAS A SPECIAL BLOOD TYPE...
...AND WE HAVE NONE OF IT ON HAND!!
HIS PAR-ENTS !?
THEY WON'T BE HERE FOR ANOTHER TWO HOURS.
THAT'S NOT SOON ENOUGH! WHAT DO WE DO!?
USE MY BLOOD!!
WE HAVE THE SAME BLOOD TYPE!!
If Witch, then Which?

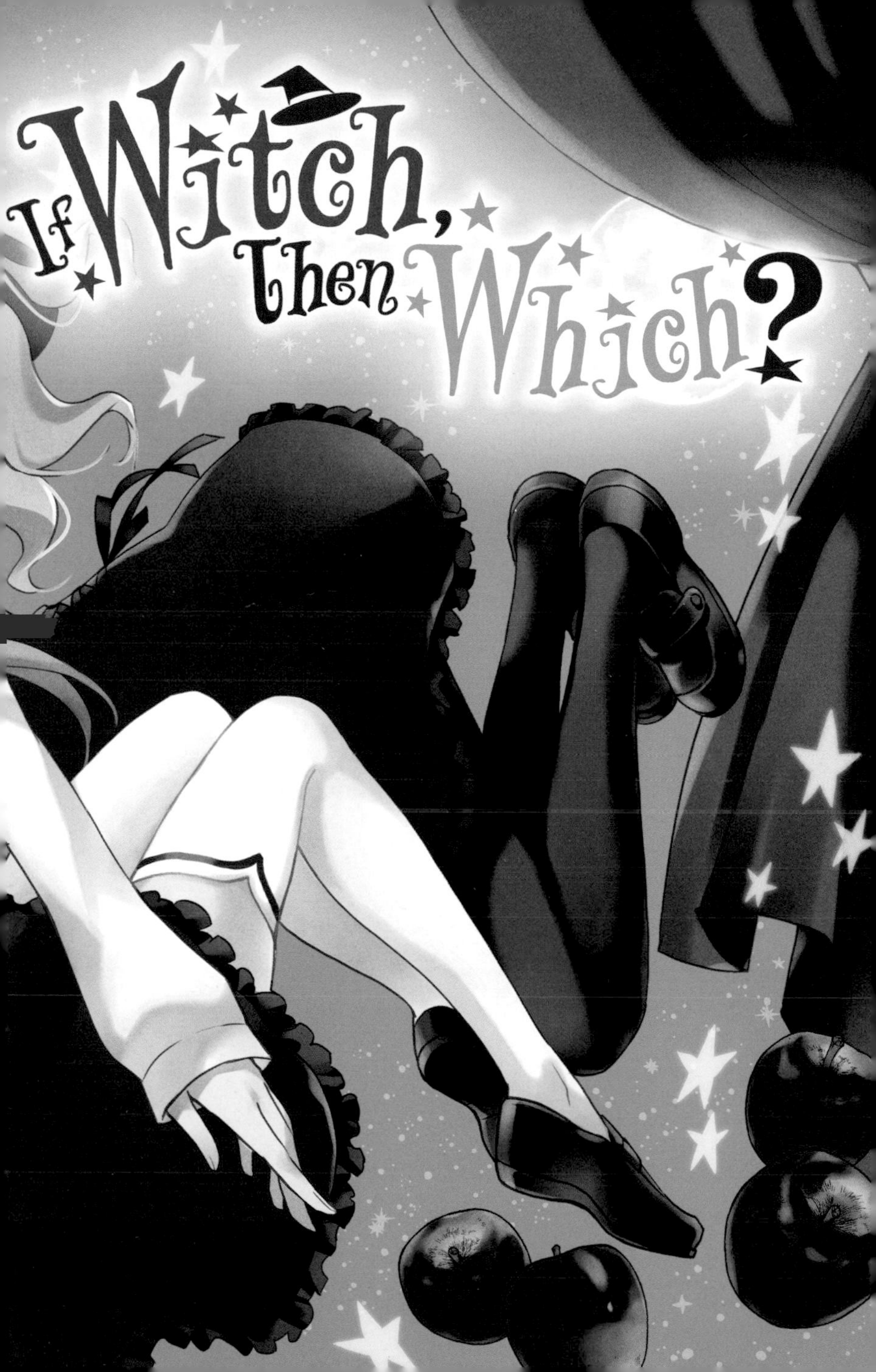
If Witch, Then Which?

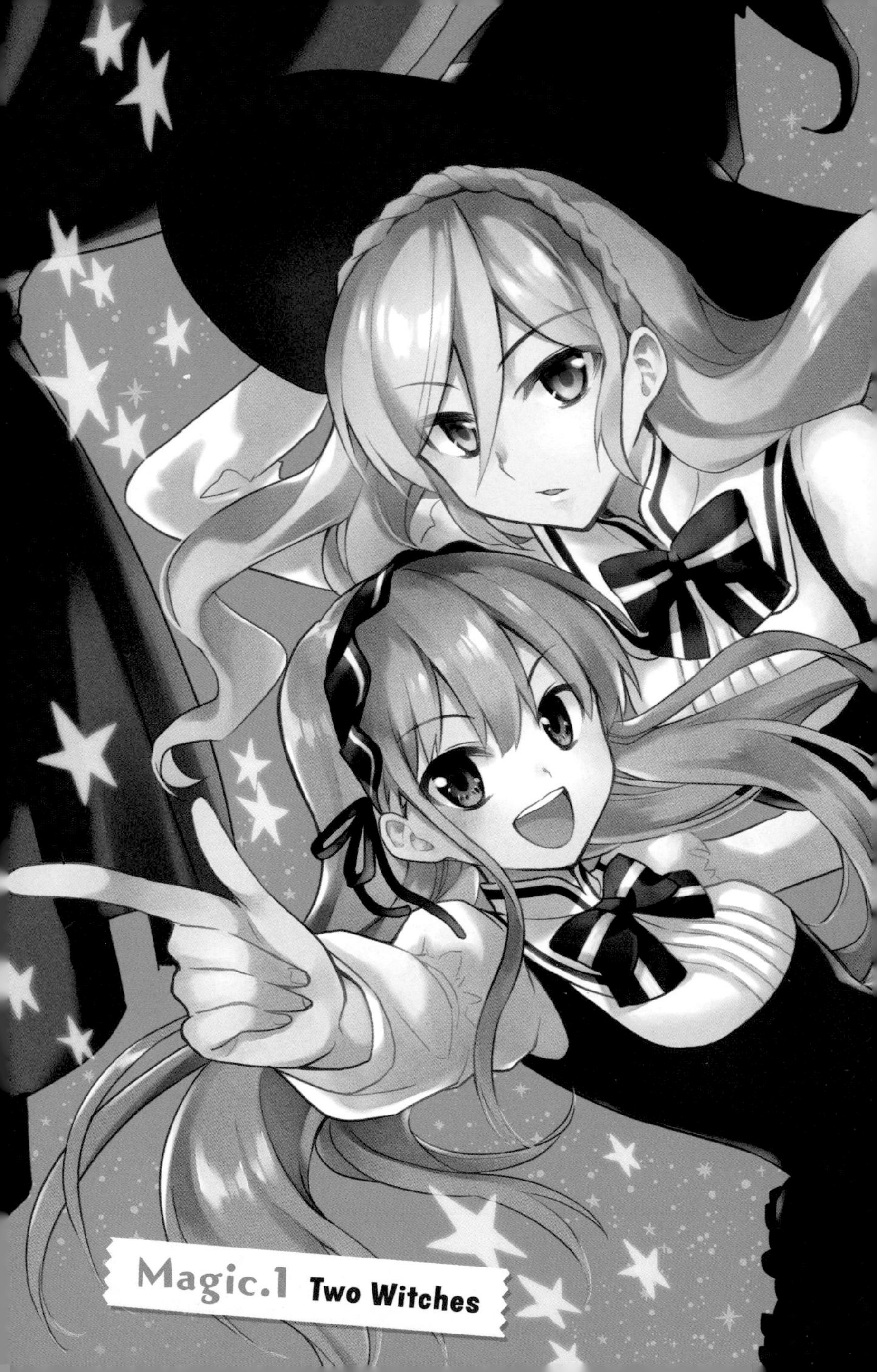

Magic.1 Two Witches

Contents

Be my minion !!!

IF WITCH,
THEN WHICH?

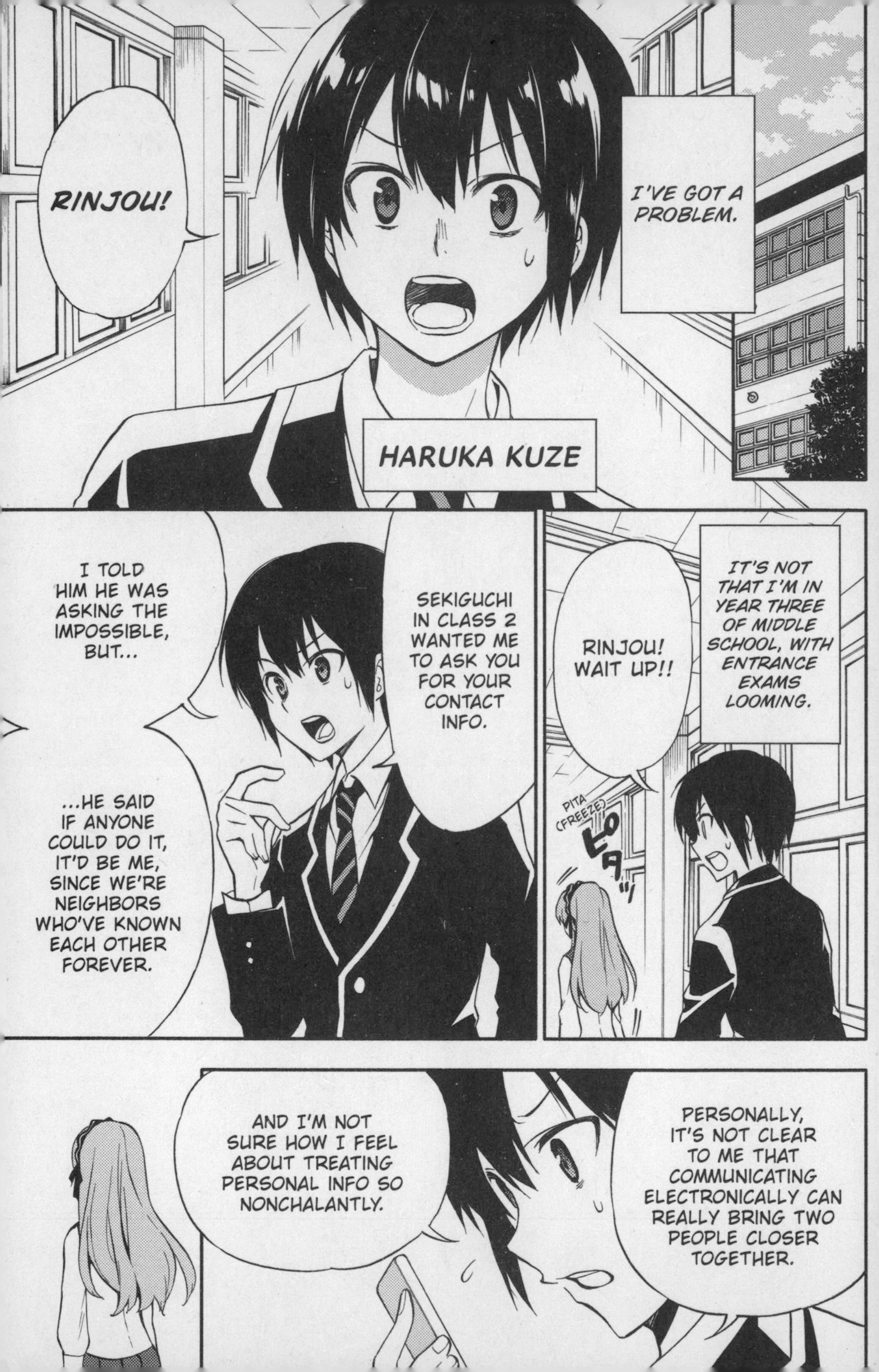
I'VE GOT A PROBLEM.
RINJOU!
HARUKA KUZE
IT'S NOT THAT I'M IN YEAR THREE OF MIDDLE SCHOOL, WITH ENTRANCE EXAMS LOOMING.
RINJOU! WAIT UP!!
PITA (FREEZE)
SEKIGUCHI IN CLASS 2 WANTED ME TO ASK YOU FOR YOUR CONTACT INFO.
I TOLD HIM HE WAS ASKING THE IMPOSSIBLE, BUT...
...HE SAID IF ANYONE COULD DO IT, IT'D BE ME, SINCE WE'RE NEIGHBORS WHO'VE KNOWN EACH OTHER FOREVER.
PERSONALLY, IT'S NOT CLEAR TO ME THAT COMMUNICATING ELECTRONICALLY CAN REALLY BRING TWO PEOPLE CLOSER TOGETHER.
AND I'M NOT SURE HOW I FEEL ABOUT TREATING PERSONAL INFO SO NONCHALANTLY.

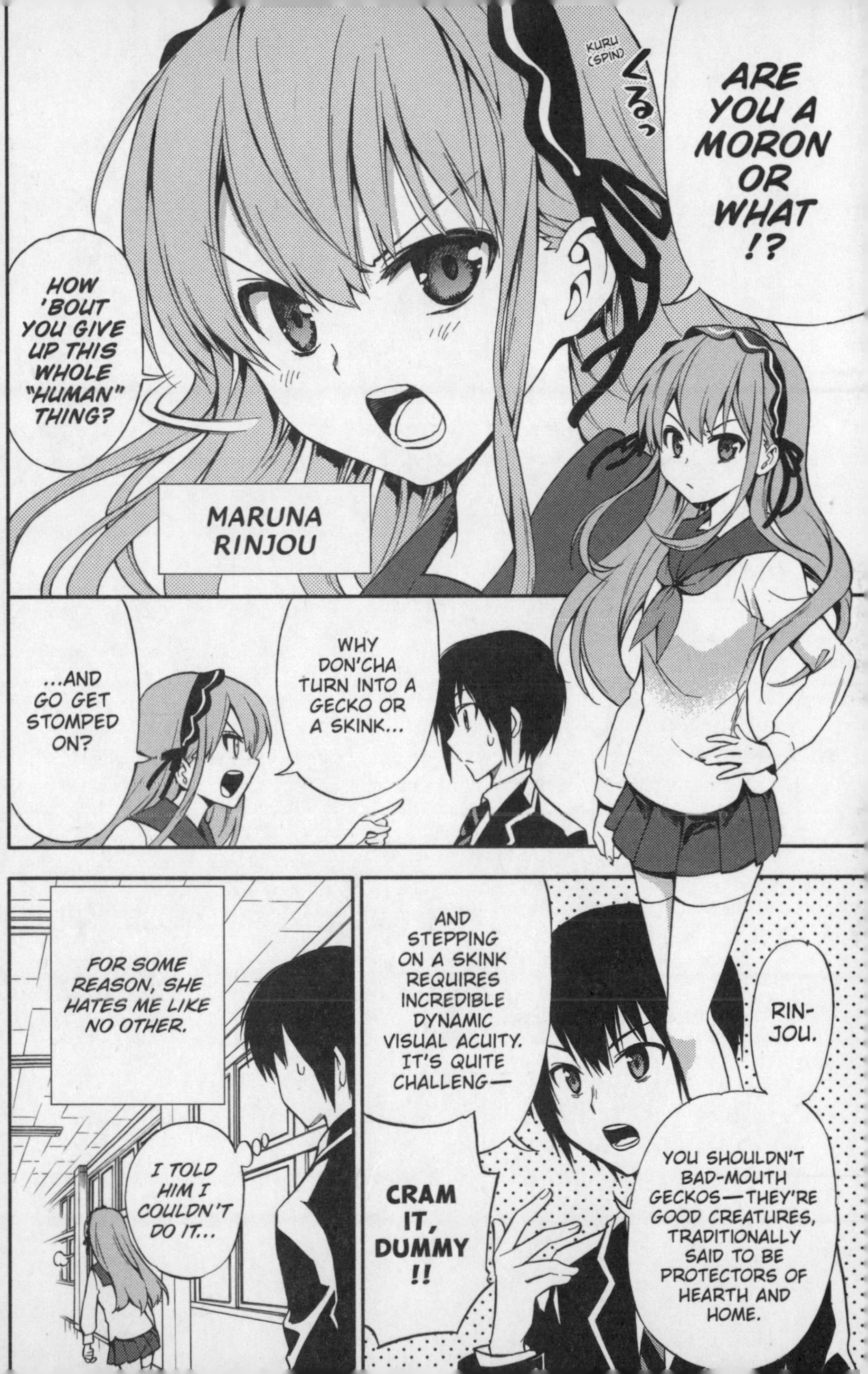
KURU (SPIN)
ARE YOU A MORON OR WHAT!?
HOW 'BOUT YOU GIVE UP THIS WHOLE "HUMAN" THING?
MARUNA RINJOU
WHY DON'CHA TURN INTO A GECKO OR A SKINK...
...AND GO GET STOMPED ON?
RIN-JOU.
YOU SHOULDN'T BAD-MOUTH GECKOS—THEY'RE GOOD CREATURES, TRADITIONALLY SAID TO BE PROTECTORS OF HEARTH AND HOME.
AND STEPPING ON A SKINK REQUIRES INCREDIBLE DYNAMIC VISUAL ACUITY. IT'S QUITE CHALLENG—
CRAM IT, DUMMY!!
FOR SOME REASON, SHE HATES ME LIKE NO OTHER.
I TOLD HIM I COULDN'T DO IT...

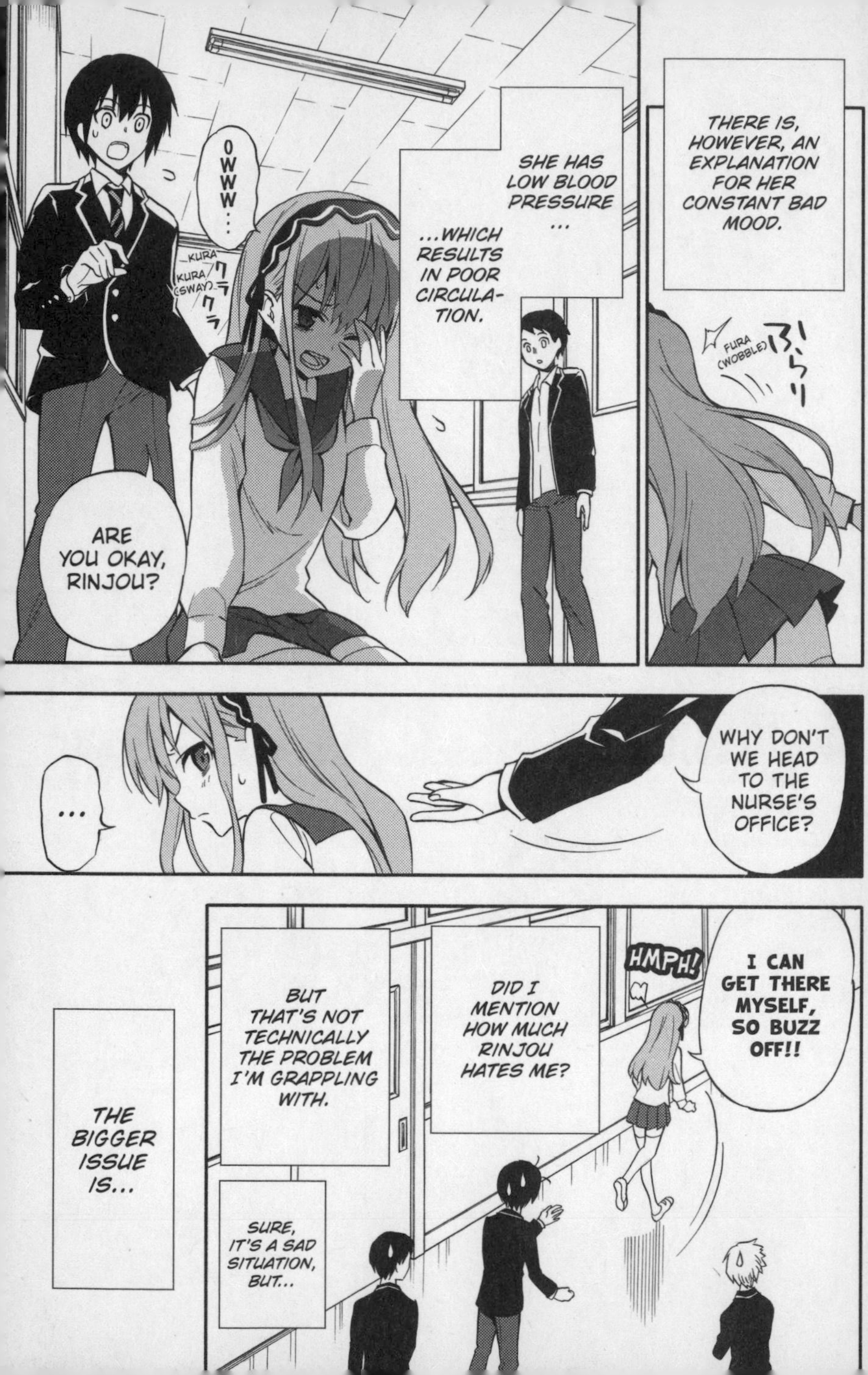
THERE IS, HOWEVER, AN EXPLANATION FOR HER CONSTANT BAD MOOD.
FURA (WOBBLE)
SHE HAS LOW BLOOD PRESSURE ...
...WHICH RESULTS IN POOR CIRCULATION.
OWWW...
KURA KURA (SWAY)
ARE YOU OKAY, RINJOU?
WHY DON'T WE HEAD TO THE NURSE'S OFFICE?
...
HMPH!
I CAN GET THERE MYSELF, SO BUZZ OFF!!
DID I MENTION HOW MUCH RINJOU HATES ME?
SURE, IT'S A SAD SITUATION, BUT...
BUT THAT'S NOT TECHNICALLY THE PROBLEM I'M GRAPPLING WITH.
THE BIGGER ISSUE IS...

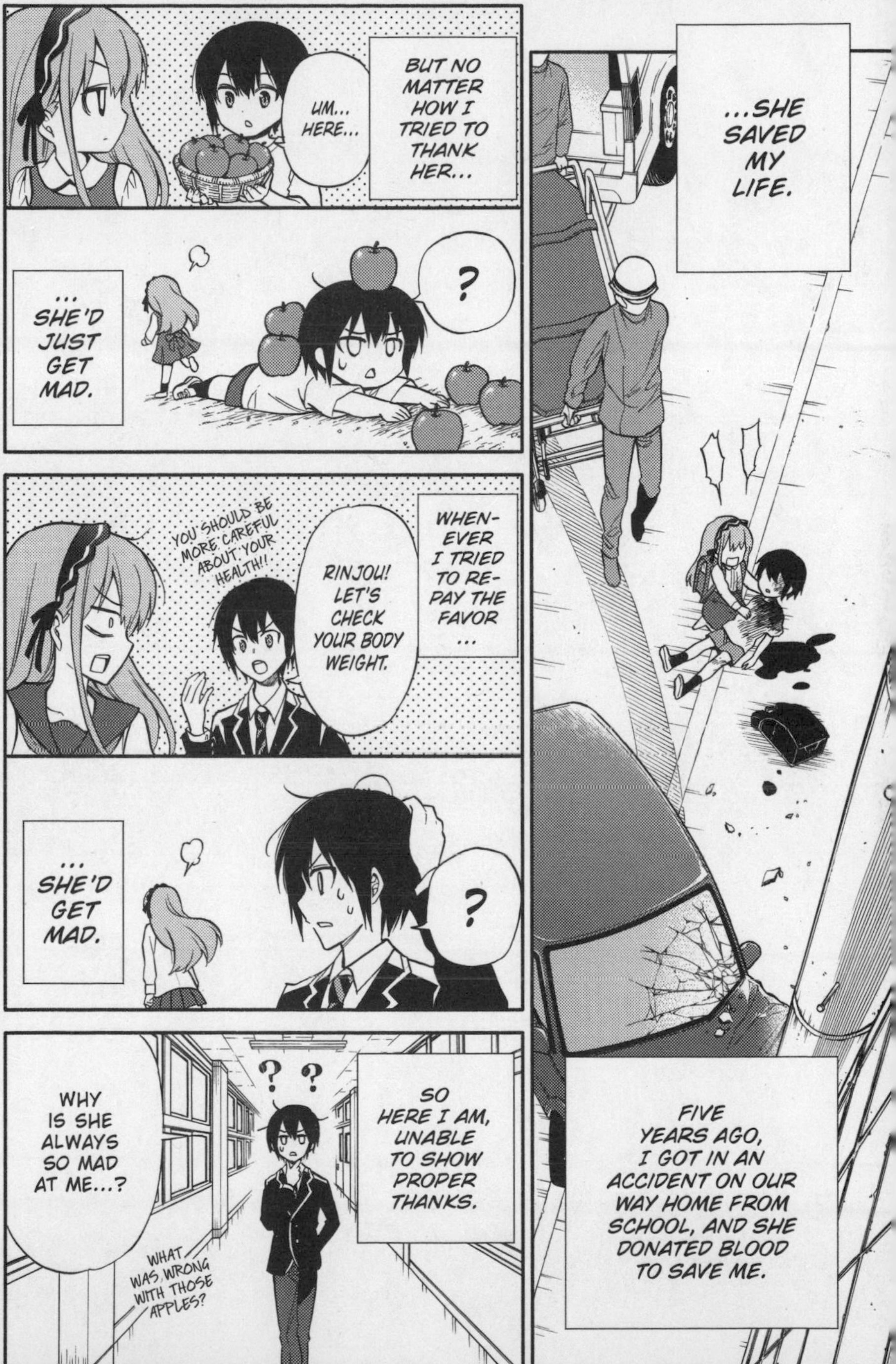
...SHE SAVED MY LIFE.
FIVE YEARS AGO, I GOT IN AN ACCIDENT ON OUR WAY HOME FROM SCHOOL, AND SHE DONATED BLOOD TO SAVE ME.
BUT NO MATTER HOW I TRIED TO THANK HER...
UM... HERE...
?
... SHE'D JUST GET MAD.
WHEN-EVER I TRIED TO RE-PAY THE FAVOR...
RINJOU! LET'S CHECK YOUR BODY WEIGHT.
YOU SHOULD BE MORE CAREFUL ABOUT YOUR HEALTH!!
?
... SHE'D GET MAD.
SO HERE I AM, UNABLE TO SHOW PROPER THANKS.
?
?
WHY IS SHE ALWAYS SO MAD AT ME...?
WHAT WAS WRONG WITH THOSE APPLES?

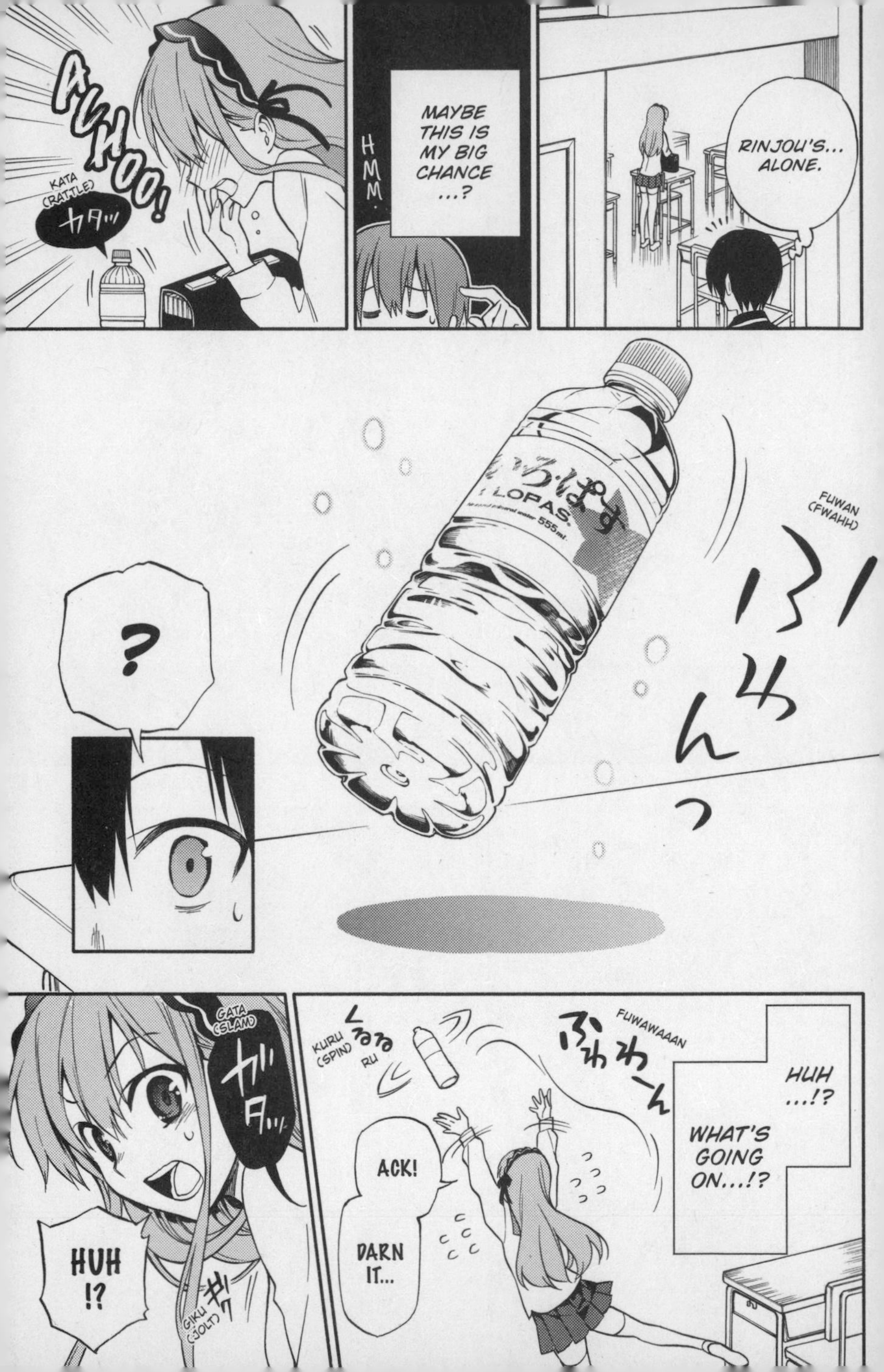
RINJOU'S... ALONE.
MAYBE THIS IS MY BIG CHANCE ...?
HMM.
AWHOO!
KATA (RATTLE)
カタッ
FUWAN (FWAHH)
ふわんっ
I LOPAS.
555ml
?
HUH ...!?
WHAT'S GOING ON...!?
FUWAWAAAN
ふわわーん
KURU (SPIN)
くるる
RU
ACK!
DARN IT...
GATA (SLAM)
ガタッ
HUH !?
GIKU (JOLT)
ギクッ

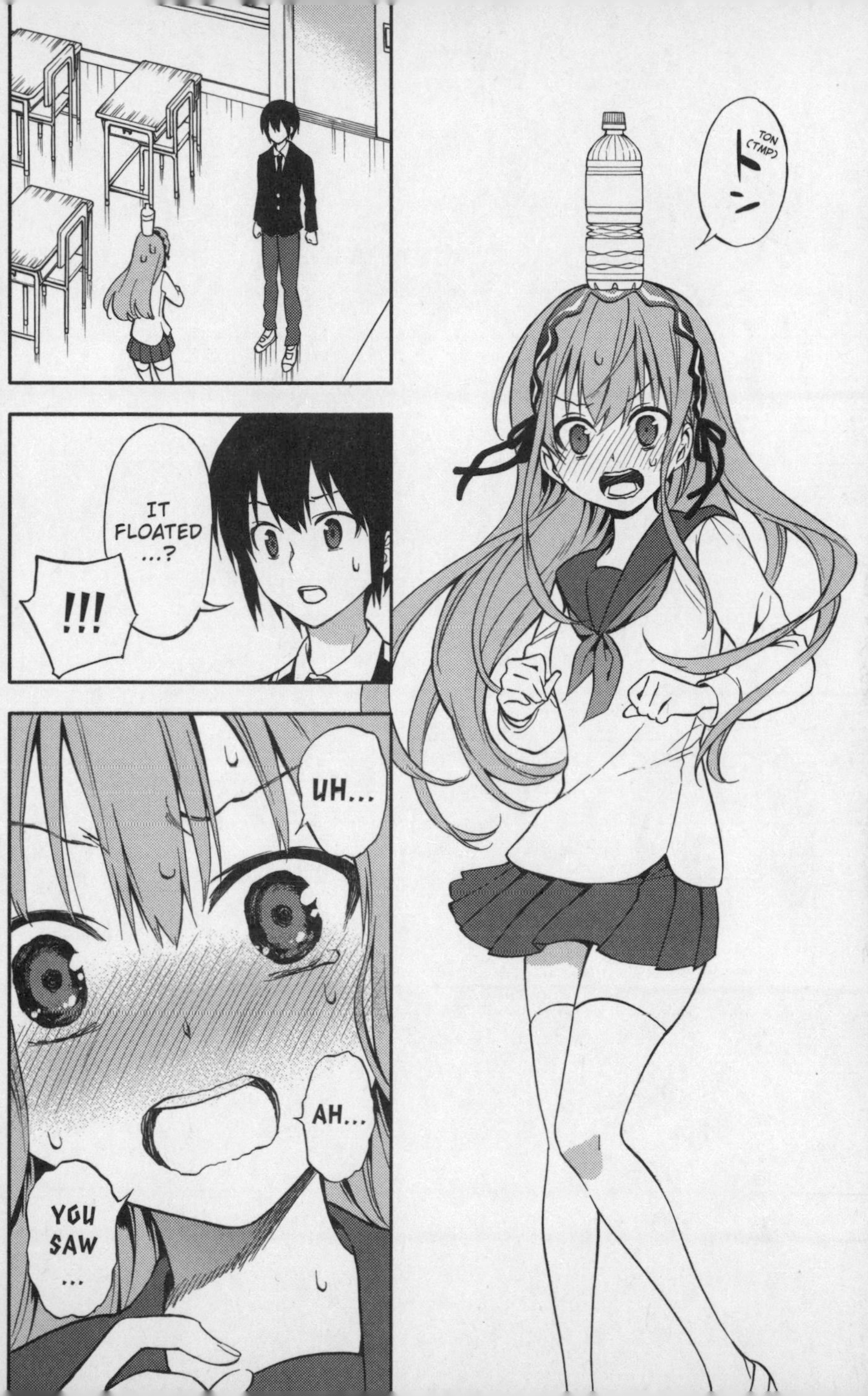
トン
TON (TMP)
IT FLOATED ...?
!!!
UH...
AH...
YOU SAW ...

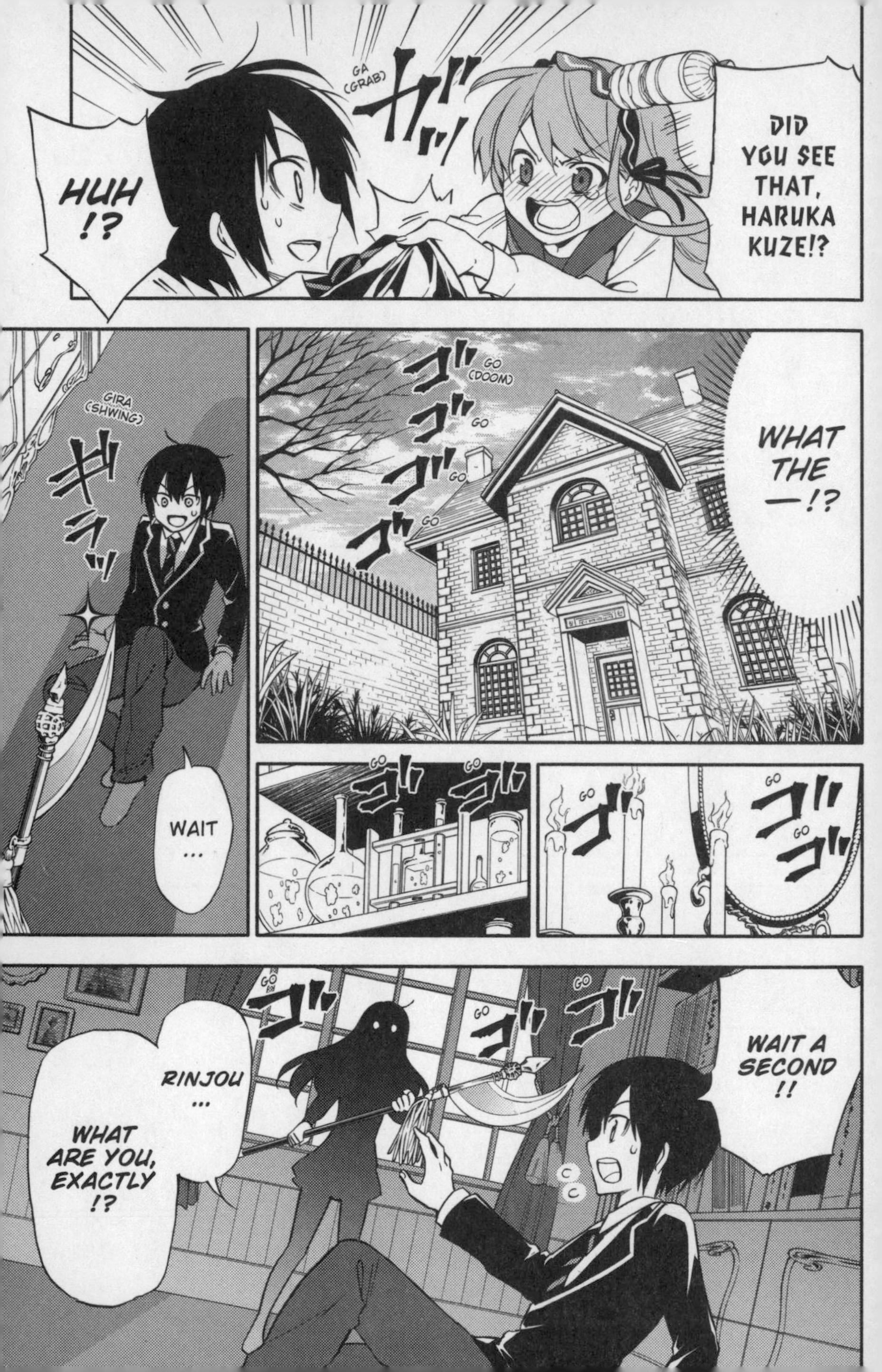
DID YOU SEE THAT, HARUKA KUZE!?
GA (GRAB)
HUH !?
WHAT THE—!?
GO (DOOM)
GO
GO
GO
GO
GO
GO
GO
GO
GIRA (SHWING)
WAIT ...
WAIT A SECOND !!
GO
GO
GO
RINJOU ...
WHAT ARE YOU, EXACTLY !?

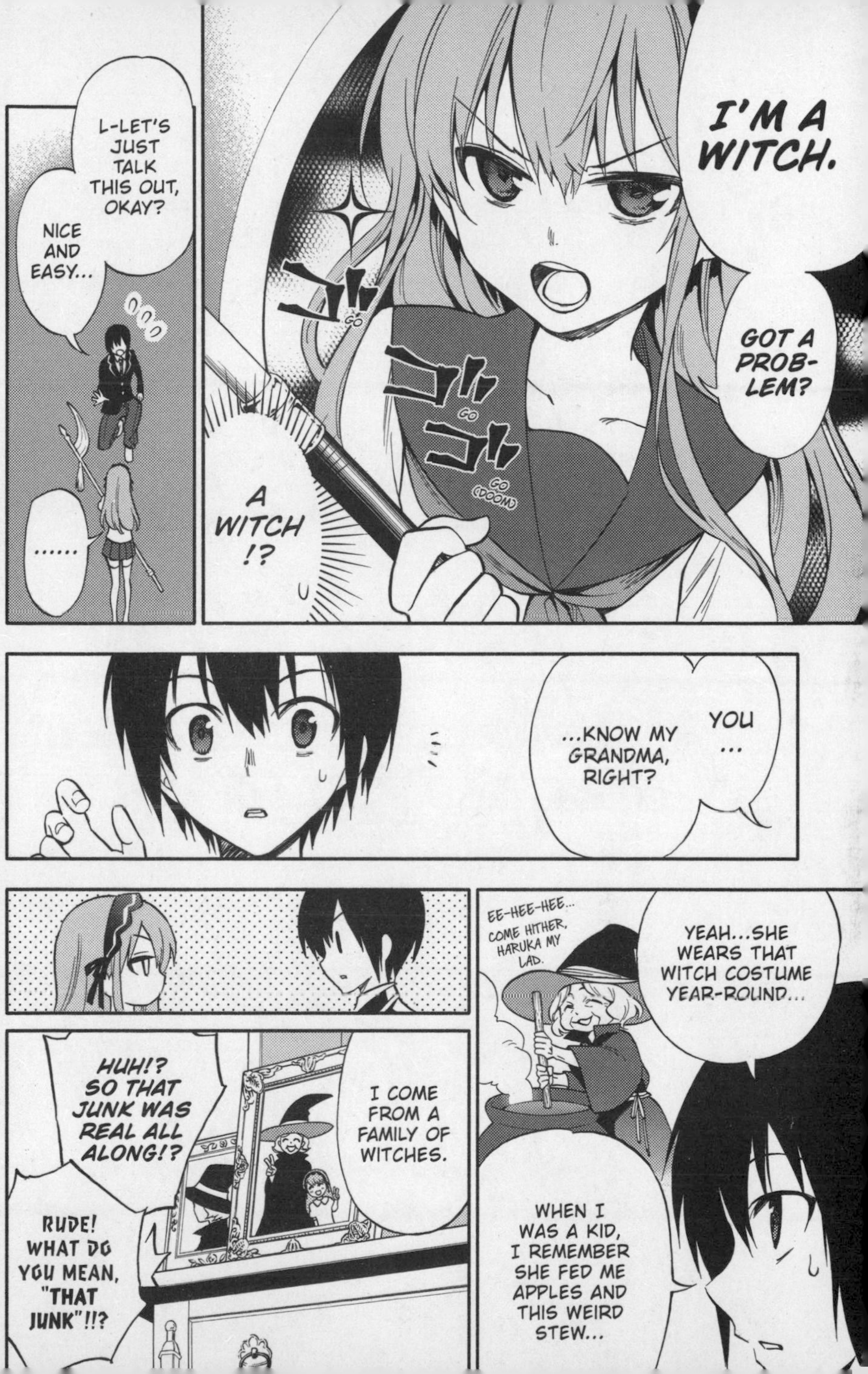
I'M A WITCH.
GOT A PROB-LEM?
GO
GO
GO (DOOM)
A WITCH !?
L-LET'S JUST TALK THIS OUT, OKAY?
NICE AND EASY...
......
YOU ...
...KNOW MY GRANDMA, RIGHT?
YEAH...SHE WEARS THAT WITCH COSTUME YEAR-ROUND...
EE-HEE-HEE... COME HITHER, HARUKA MY LAD.
WHEN I WAS A KID, I REMEMBER SHE FED ME APPLES AND THIS WEIRD STEW...
I COME FROM A FAMILY OF WITCHES.
HUH!? SO THAT JUNK WAS REAL ALL ALONG!?
RUDE! WHAT DO YOU MEAN, "THAT JUNK"!!?

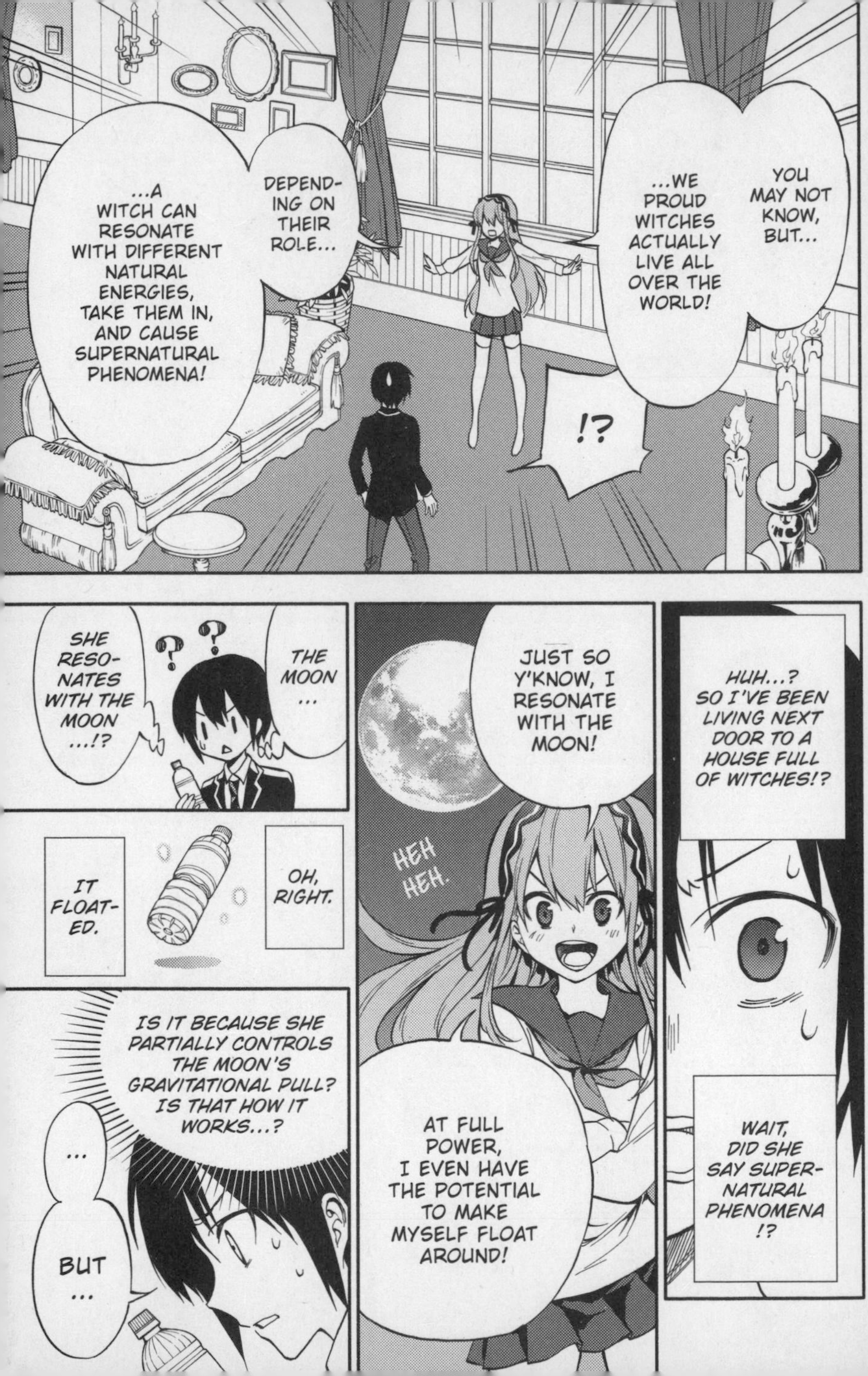

YOU MAY NOT KNOW, BUT...
...WE PROUD WITCHES ACTUALLY LIVE ALL OVER THE WORLD!
!?
DEPEND-ING ON THEIR ROLE...
...A WITCH CAN RESONATE WITH DIFFERENT NATURAL ENERGIES, TAKE THEM IN, AND CAUSE SUPERNATURAL PHENOMENA!
HUH...? SO I'VE BEEN LIVING NEXT DOOR TO A HOUSE FULL OF WITCHES!?
WAIT, DID SHE SAY SUPER-NATURAL PHENOMENA!?
JUST SO Y'KNOW, I RESONATE WITH THE MOON!
HEH HEH.
AT FULL POWER, I EVEN HAVE THE POTENTIAL TO MAKE MYSELF FLOAT AROUND!
THE MOON...
SHE RESO-NATES WITH THE MOON...!?
OH, RIGHT.
IT FLOAT-ED.
IS IT BECAUSE SHE PARTIALLY CONTROLS THE MOON'S GRAVITATIONAL PULL? IS THAT HOW IT WORKS...?
...
BUT...

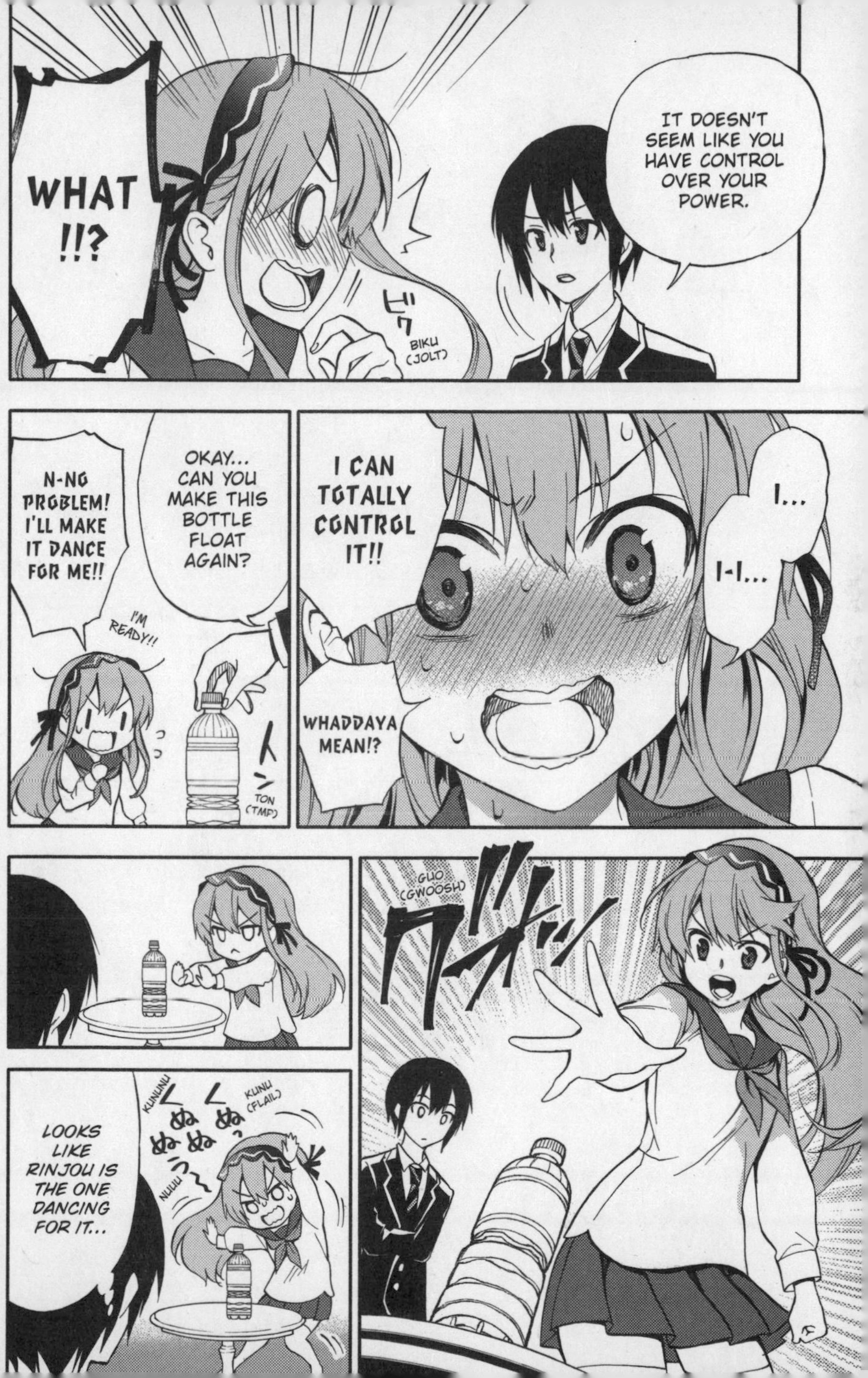
IT DOESN'T SEEM LIKE YOU HAVE CONTROL OVER YOUR POWER.
BIKU (JOLT)
WHAT!!?
I...
I-I...
I CAN TOTALLY CONTROL IT!!
WHADDAYA MEAN!?
OKAY... CAN YOU MAKE THIS BOTTLE FLOAT AGAIN?
N-NO PROBLEM! I'LL MAKE IT DANCE FOR ME!!
I'M READY!!
TON (TMP)
GUO (GWOOSH)
KUNU (FLAIL)
KUNUNU
NUUUU
LOOKS LIKE RINJOU IS THE ONE DANCING FOR IT...

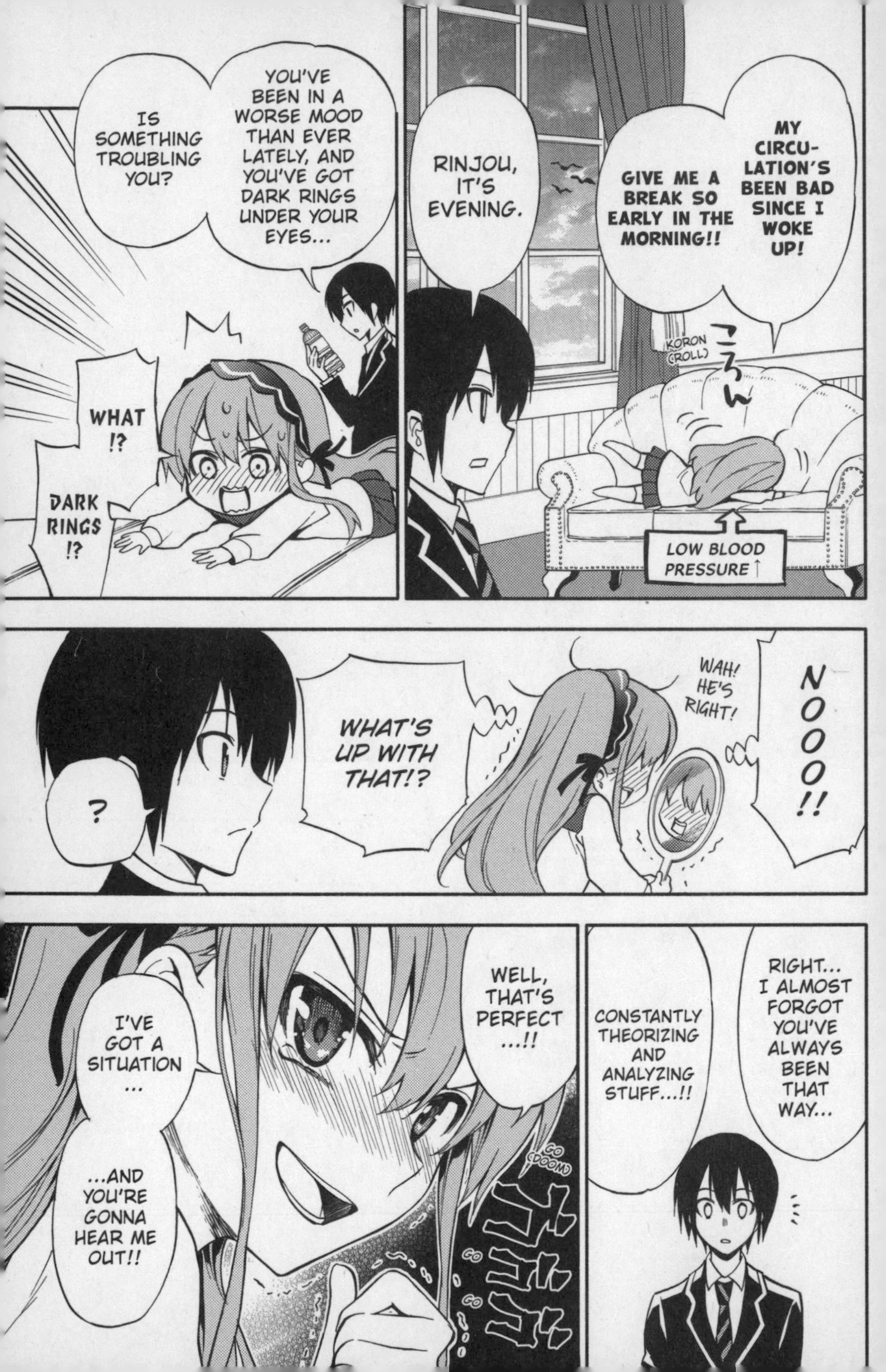

MY CIRCULATION'S BEEN BAD SINCE I WOKE UP!
GIVE ME A BREAK SO EARLY IN THE MORNING!!
KORON (ROLL)
ころん
LOW BLOOD PRESSURE ↑
RINJOU, IT'S EVENING.
YOU'VE BEEN IN A WORSE MOOD THAN EVER LATELY, AND YOU'VE GOT DARK RINGS UNDER YOUR EYES...
IS SOMETHING TROUBLING YOU?
WHAT!?
DARK RINGS!?
NOOOO!!
WAH! HE'S RIGHT!
WHAT'S UP WITH THAT!?
?
RIGHT... I ALMOST FORGOT YOU'VE ALWAYS BEEN THAT WAY...
CONSTANTLY THEORIZING AND ANALYZING STUFF...!!
WELL, THAT'S PERFECT...!!
GO (DOOM)
I'VE GOT A SITUATION...
...AND YOU'RE GONNA HEAR ME OUT!!

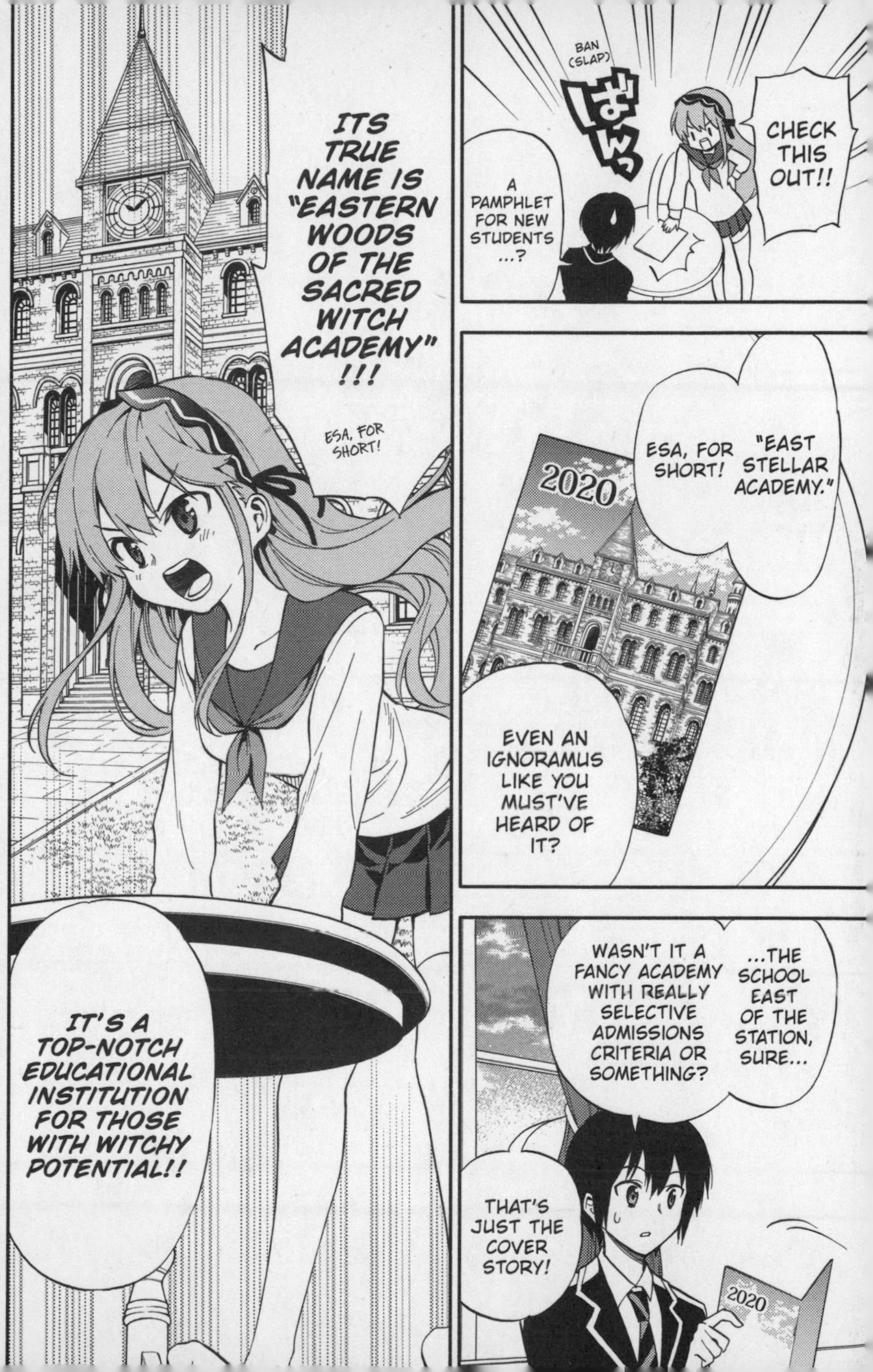
BAN (SLAP)
ばんっ
CHECK THIS OUT!!
A PAMPHLET FOR NEW STUDENTS ...?
"EAST STELLAR ACADEMY."
ESA, FOR SHORT!
2020
EVEN AN IGNORAMUS LIKE YOU MUST'VE HEARD OF IT?
...THE SCHOOL EAST OF THE STATION, SURE...
WASN'T IT A FANCY ACADEMY WITH REALLY SELECTIVE ADMISSIONS CRITERIA OR SOMETHING?
THAT'S JUST THE COVER STORY!
2020
ITS TRUE NAME IS "EASTERN WOODS OF THE SACRED WITCH ACADEMY"!!!
ESA, FOR SHORT!
IT'S A TOP-NOTCH EDUCATIONAL INSTITUTION FOR THOSE WITH WITCHY POTENTIAL!!

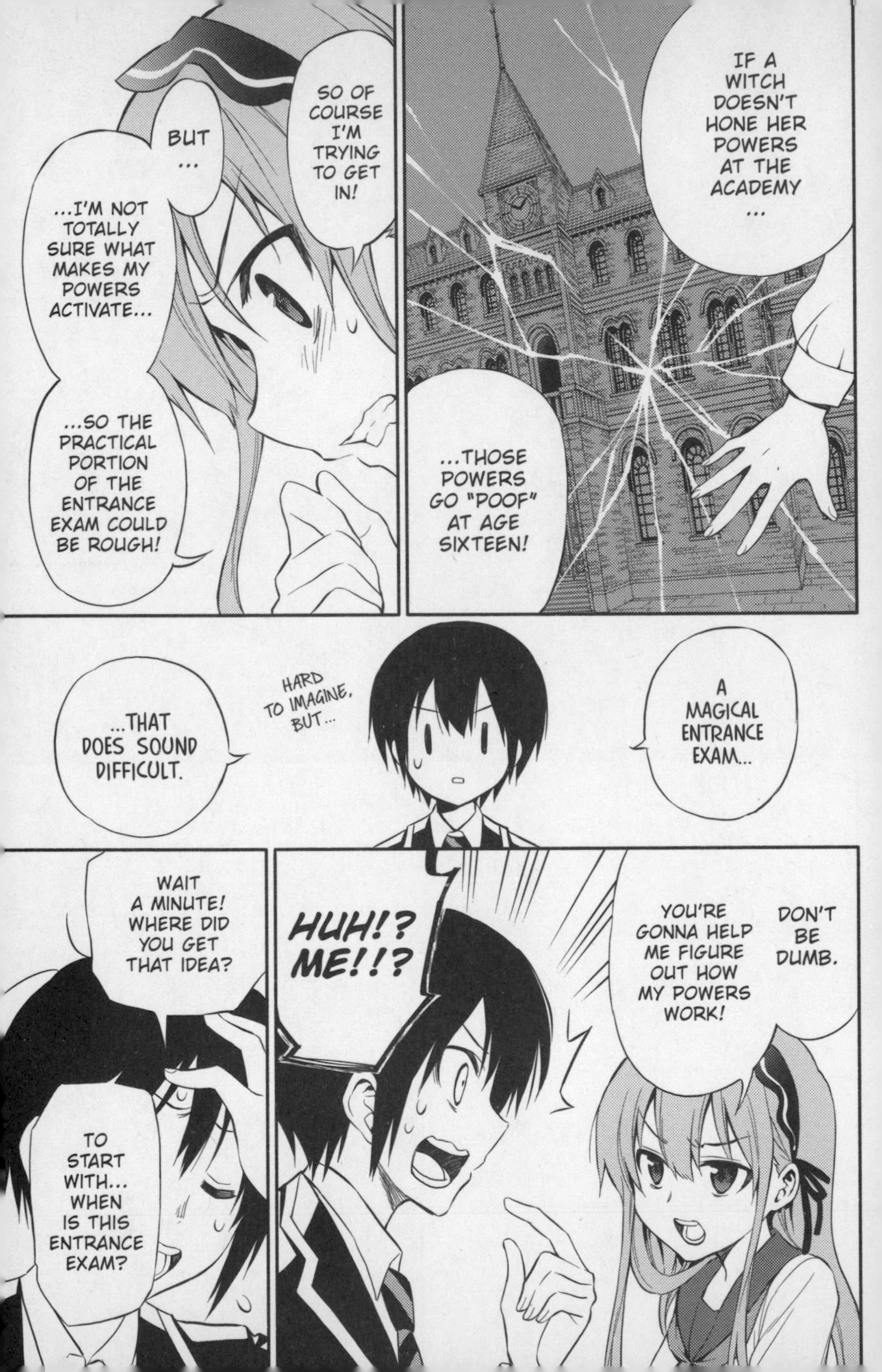
IF A WITCH DOESN'T HONE HER POWERS AT THE ACADEMY ...
...THOSE POWERS GO "POOF" AT AGE SIXTEEN!
SO OF COURSE I'M TRYING TO GET IN!
BUT ...
...I'M NOT TOTALLY SURE WHAT MAKES MY POWERS ACTIVATE...
...SO THE PRACTICAL PORTION OF THE ENTRANCE EXAM COULD BE ROUGH!
A MAGICAL ENTRANCE EXAM...
HARD TO IMAGINE, BUT...
...THAT DOES SOUND DIFFICULT.
DON'T BE DUMB.
YOU'RE GONNA HELP ME FIGURE OUT HOW MY POWERS WORK!
HUH!? ME!!?
WAIT A MINUTE! WHERE DID YOU GET THAT IDEA?
TO START WITH... WHEN IS THIS ENTRANCE EXAM?

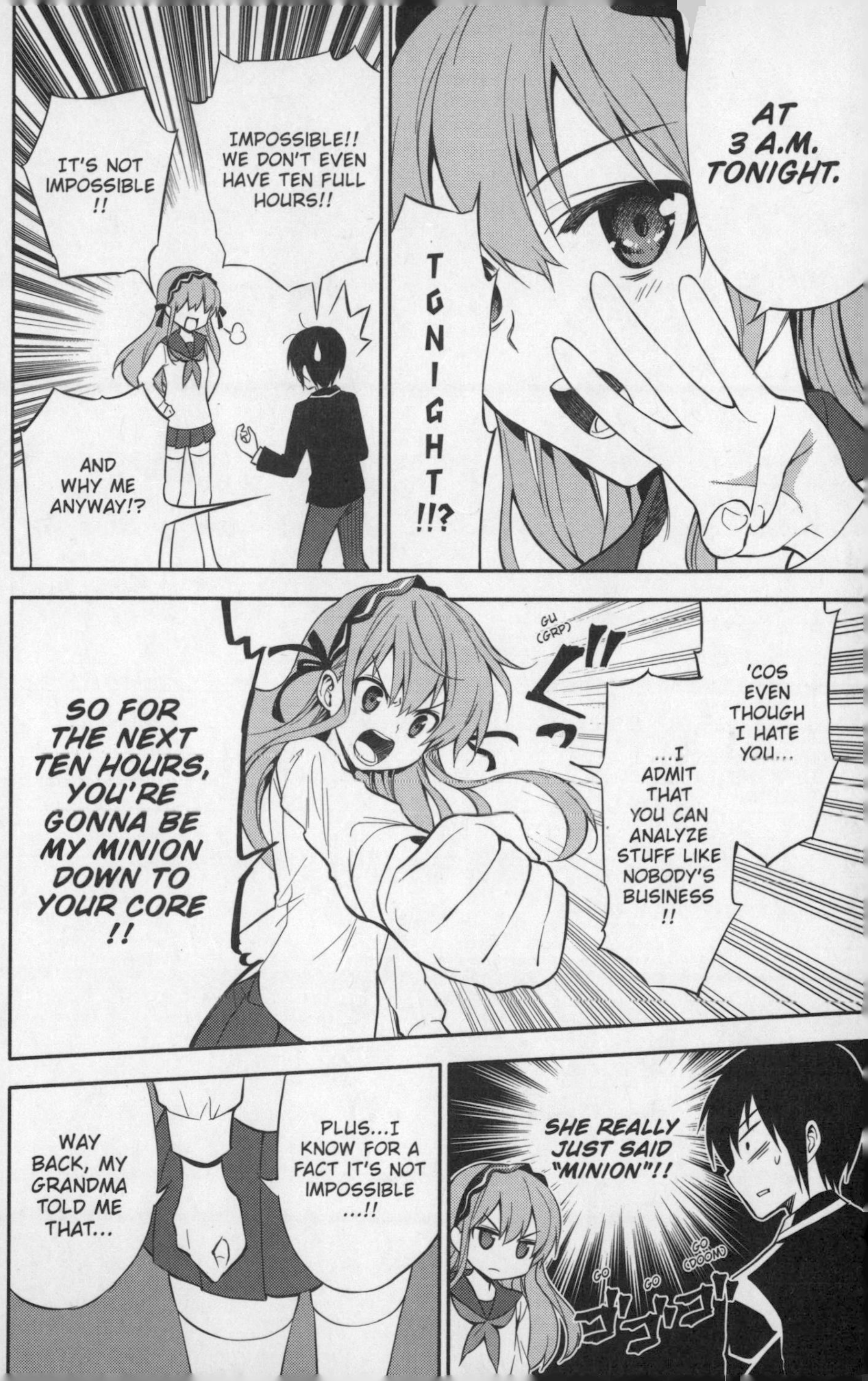
AT 3 A.M. TONIGHT.
TONIGHT!!?
IMPOSSIBLE!! WE DON'T EVEN HAVE TEN FULL HOURS!!
IT'S NOT IMPOSSIBLE!!
AND WHY ME ANYWAY!?
GU (GRP)
'COS EVEN THOUGH I HATE YOU...
...I ADMIT THAT YOU CAN ANALYZE STUFF LIKE NOBODY'S BUSINESS!!
SO FOR THE NEXT TEN HOURS, YOU'RE GONNA BE MY MINION DOWN TO YOUR CORE!!
SHE REALLY JUST SAID "MINION"!!
GO (DOON)
GO
GO
PLUS...I KNOW FOR A FACT IT'S NOT IMPOSSIBLE...!!
WAY BACK, MY GRANDMA TOLD ME THAT...

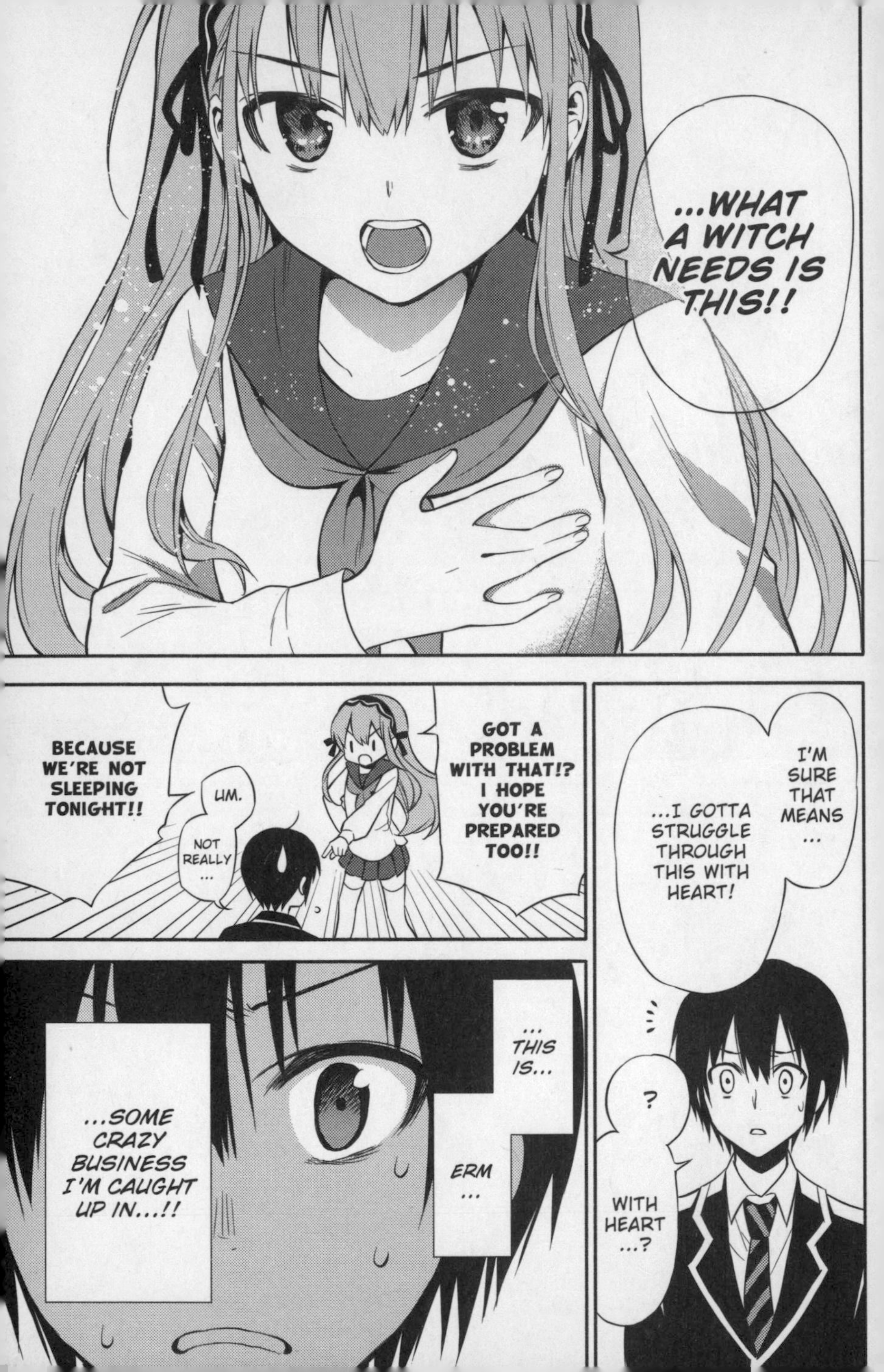
...WHAT A WITCH NEEDS IS THIS!!
I'M SURE THAT MEANS ...
...I GOTTA STRUGGLE THROUGH THIS WITH HEART!
?
WITH HEART ...?
GOT A PROBLEM WITH THAT!? I HOPE YOU'RE PREPARED TOO!!
UM.
NOT REALLY ...
BECAUSE WE'RE NOT SLEEPING TONIGHT!!
... THIS IS...
ERM ...
...SOME CRAZY BUSINESS I'M CAUGHT UP IN...!!

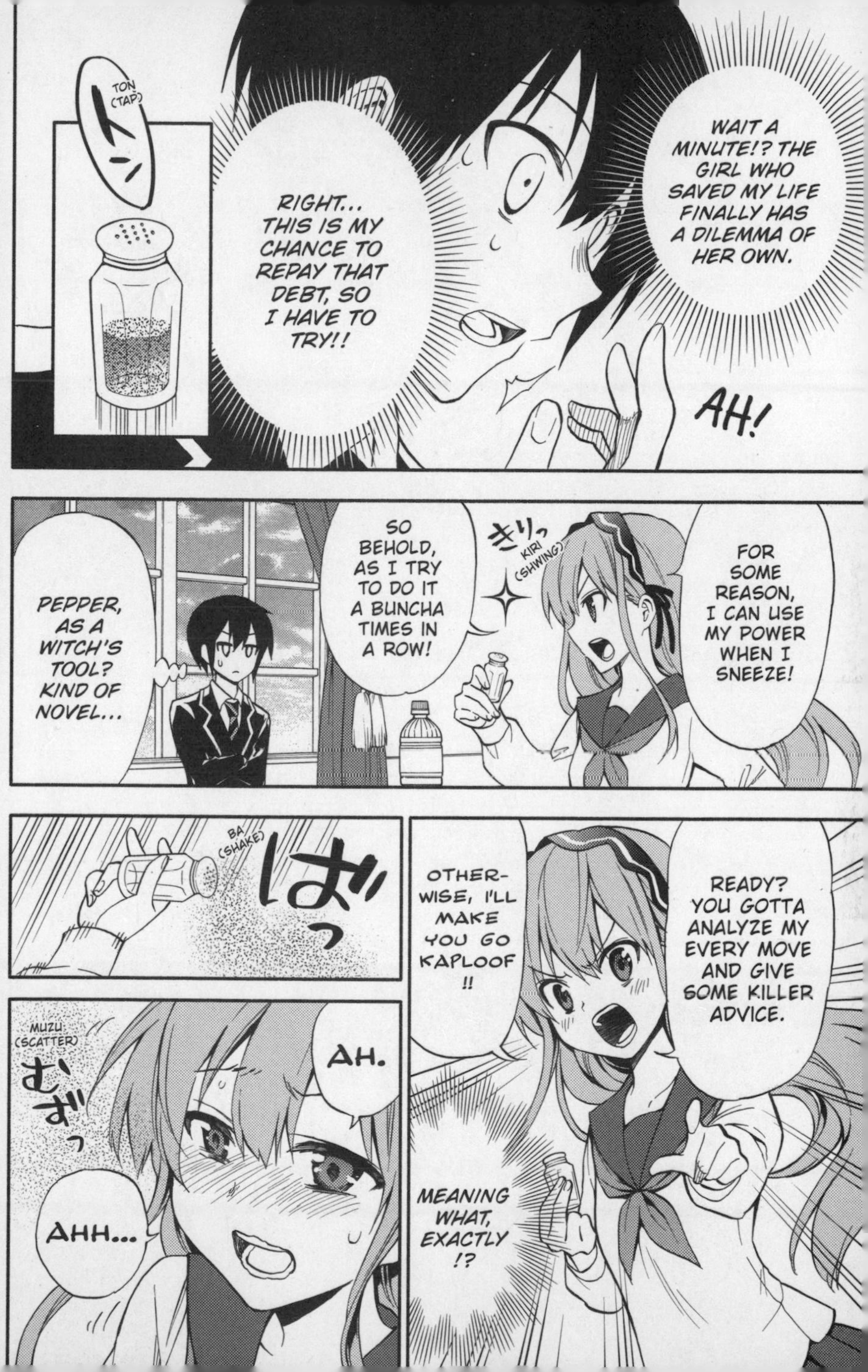
WAIT A MINUTE!? THE GIRL WHO SAVED MY LIFE FINALLY HAS A DILEMMA OF HER OWN.
AH!
RIGHT... THIS IS MY CHANCE TO REPAY THAT DEBT, SO I HAVE TO TRY!!
TON (TAP)
FOR SOME REASON, I CAN USE MY POWER WHEN I SNEEZE!
きりっ
KIRI (SHWING)
SO BEHOLD, AS I TRY TO DO IT A BUNCHA TIMES IN A ROW!
PEPPER, AS A WITCH'S TOOL? KIND OF NOVEL...
READY? YOU GOTTA ANALYZE MY EVERY MOVE AND GIVE SOME KILLER ADVICE.
OTHER-WISE, I'LL MAKE YOU GO KAPLOOF!!
MEANING WHAT, EXACTLY!?
BA (SHAKE)
ばっ
AH.
MUZU (SCATTER)
むずっ
AHH...

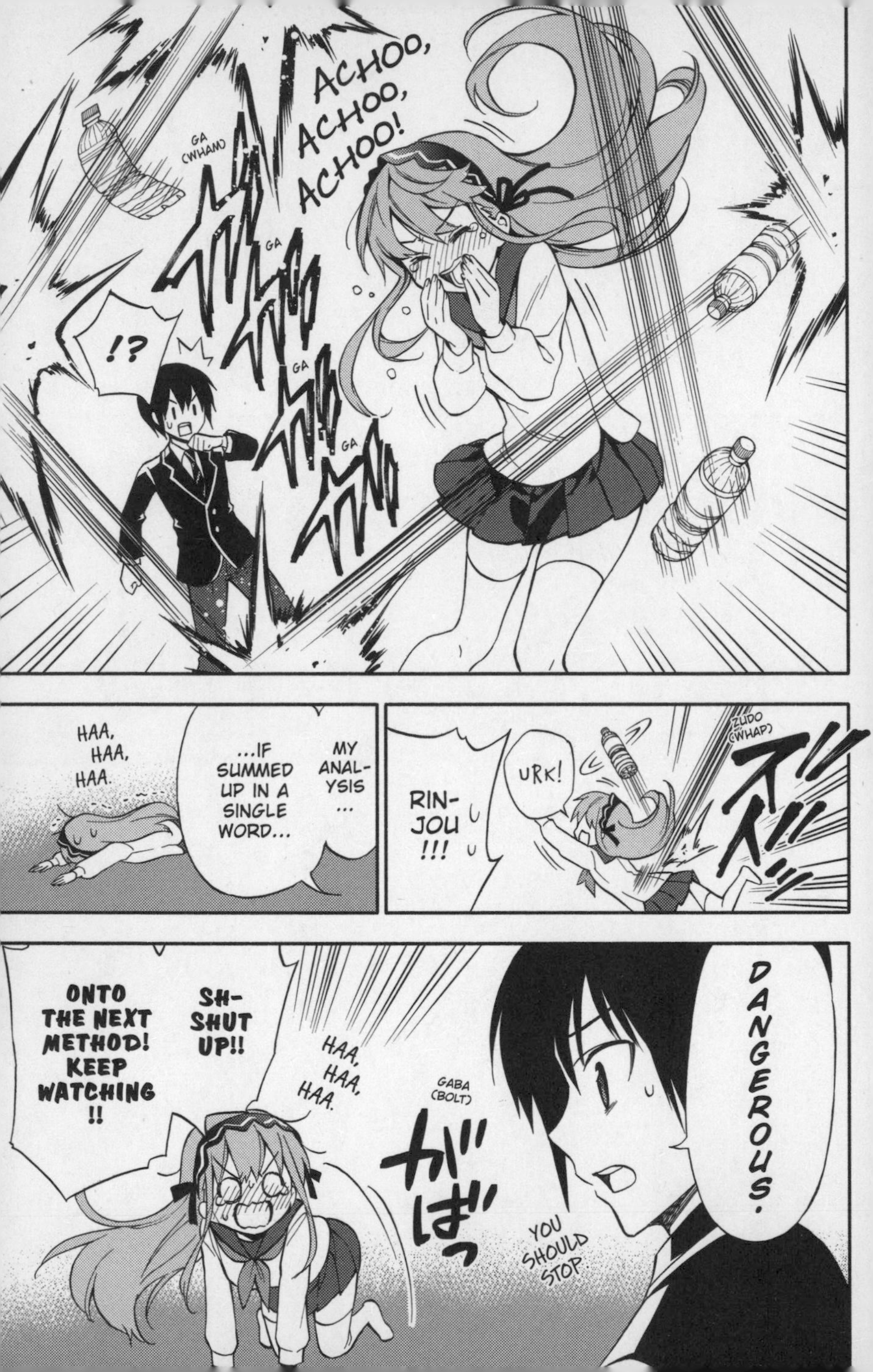
ACHOO, ACHOO, ACHOO!
GA (WHAM)
GA
!?
GA
GA
ZUDO (WHAP)
URK!
RIN-JOU!!!
MY ANALYSIS...
...IF SUMMED UP IN A SINGLE WORD...
HAA, HAA, HAA.
DANGEROUS.
YOU SHOULD STOP.
GABA (BOLT)
HAA, HAA, HAA.
SH-SHUT UP!!
ONTO THE NEXT METHOD! KEEP WATCHING!!

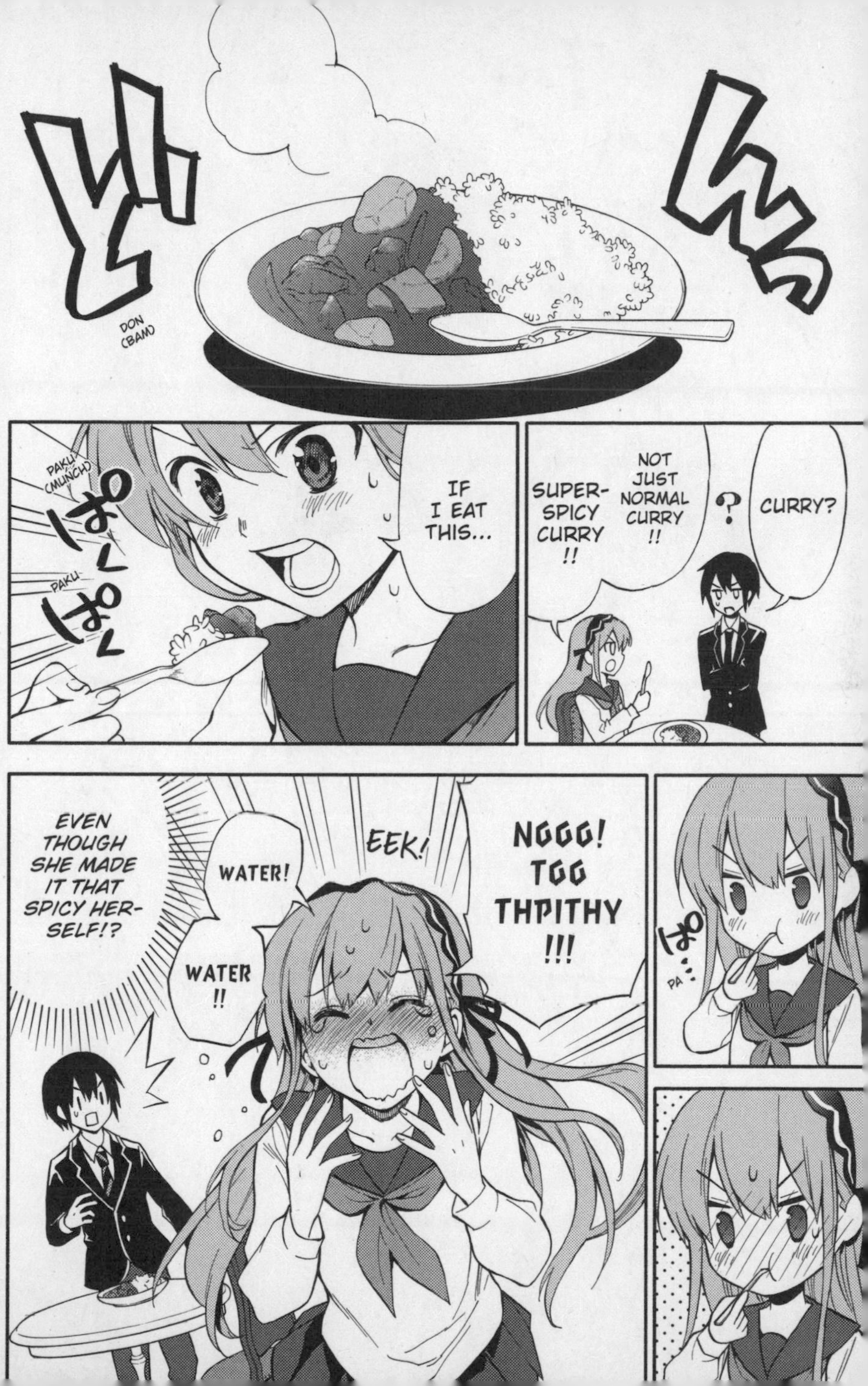
どん
DON (BAM)
CURRY?
?
NOT JUST NORMAL CURRY !!
SUPER-SPICY CURRY !!
IF I EAT THIS...
ぱくぱく
PAKU (MUNCH)
PAKU
ぱ…
PA
NOOO! TOO THPITHY !!!
EEK!
WATER!
WATER !!
EVEN THOUGH SHE MADE IT THAT SPICY HER-SELF!?

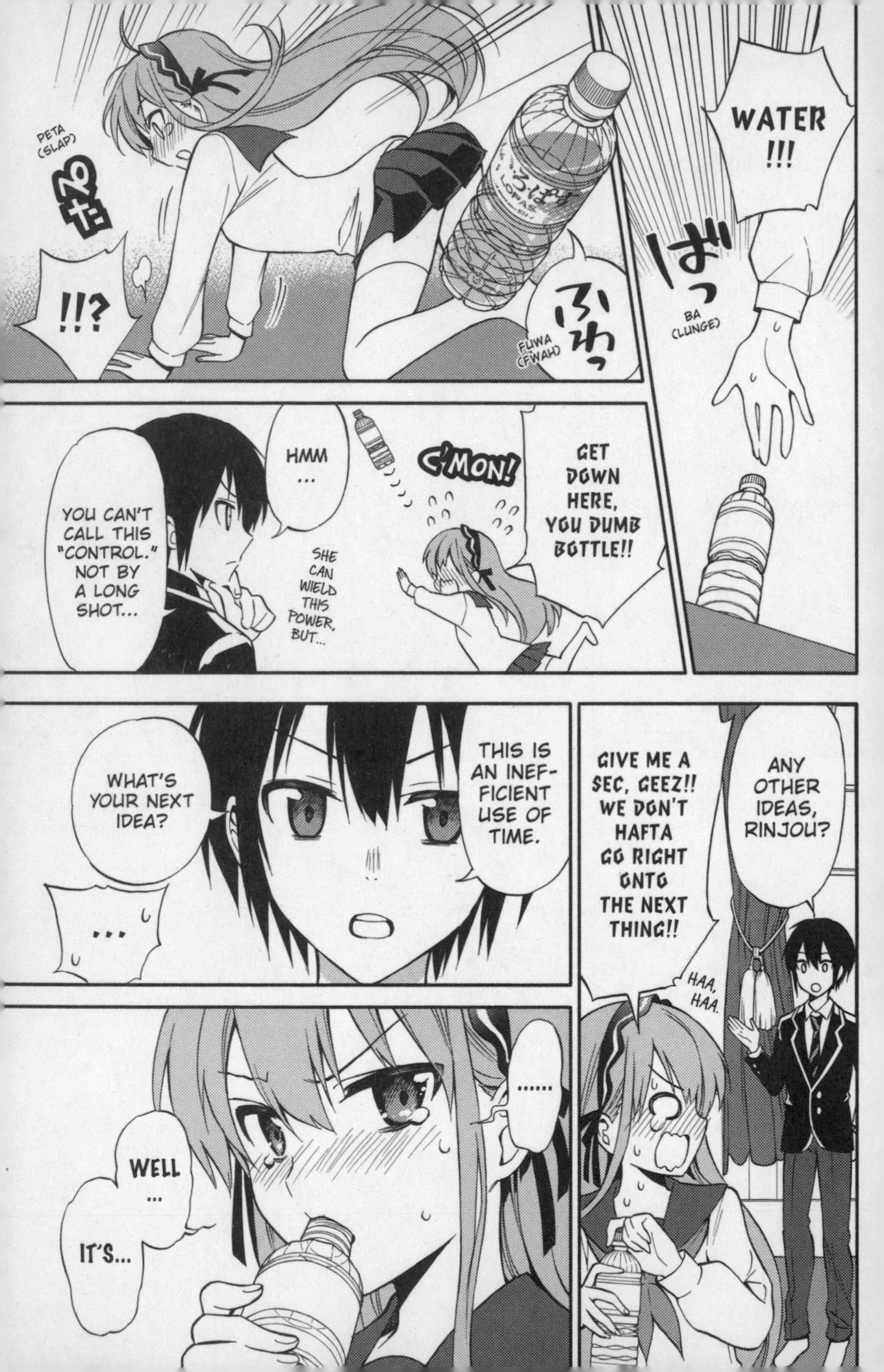
WATER!!!
ばっ
BA (LUNGE)
ふわっ
FUWA (FWAH)
ぺた
PETA (SLAP)
!!?
GET DOWN HERE, YOU DUMB BOTTLE!!
C'MON!
HMM...
SHE CAN WIELD THIS POWER, BUT...
YOU CAN'T CALL THIS "CONTROL." NOT BY A LONG SHOT...
ANY OTHER IDEAS, RINJOU?
GIVE ME A SEC, GEEZ!! WE DON'T HAFTA GO RIGHT ONTO THE NEXT THING!!
HAA, HAA.
THIS IS AN INEF-FICIENT USE OF TIME.
WHAT'S YOUR NEXT IDEA?
...
......
WELL... IT'S...

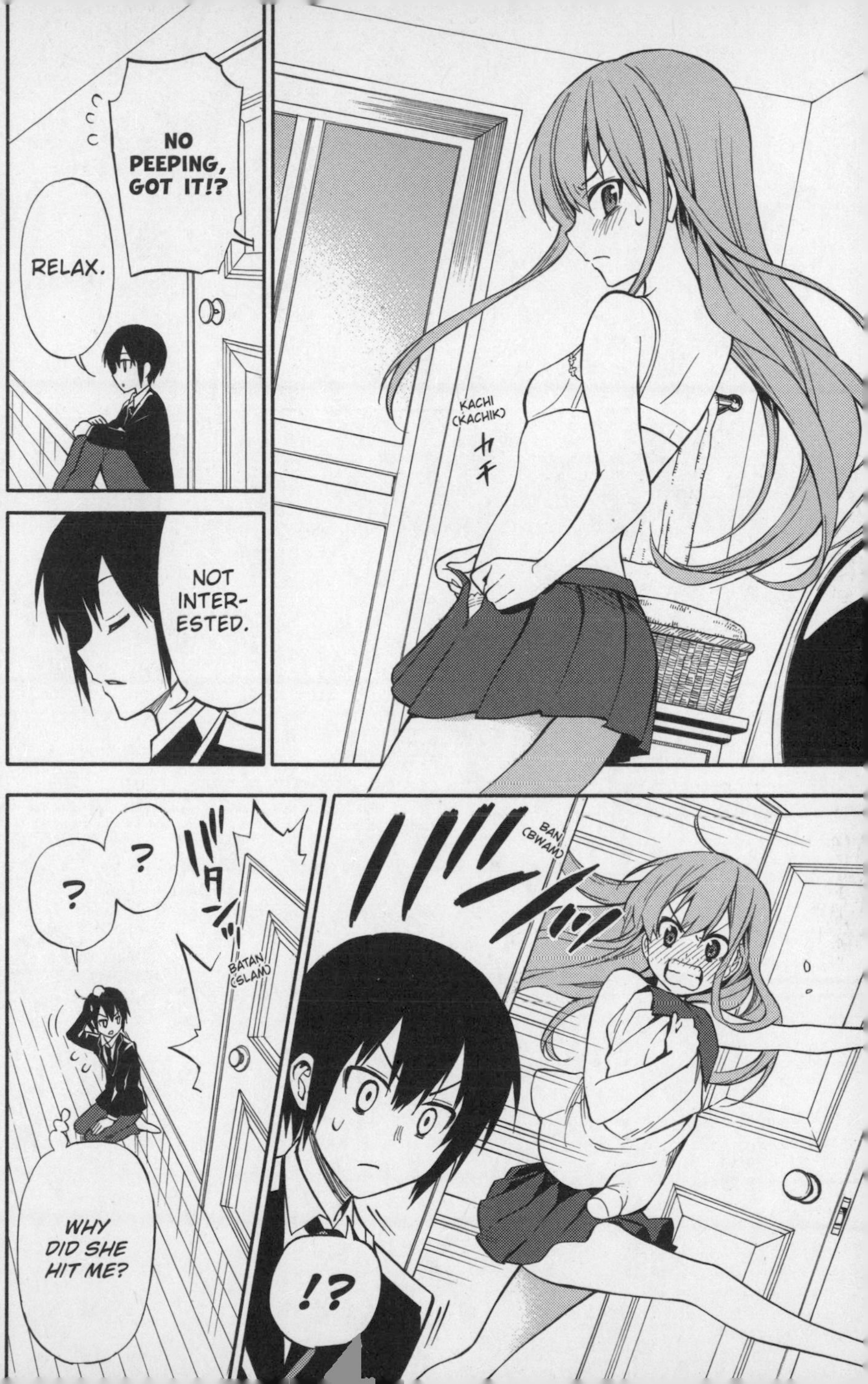
KACHI (KACHIK)
カチ
NO PEEPING, GOT IT!?
RELAX.
NOT INTER-ESTED.
BAN (BWAM)
バン
!?
バタン
BATAN (SLAM)
? ?
WHY DID SHE HIT ME?

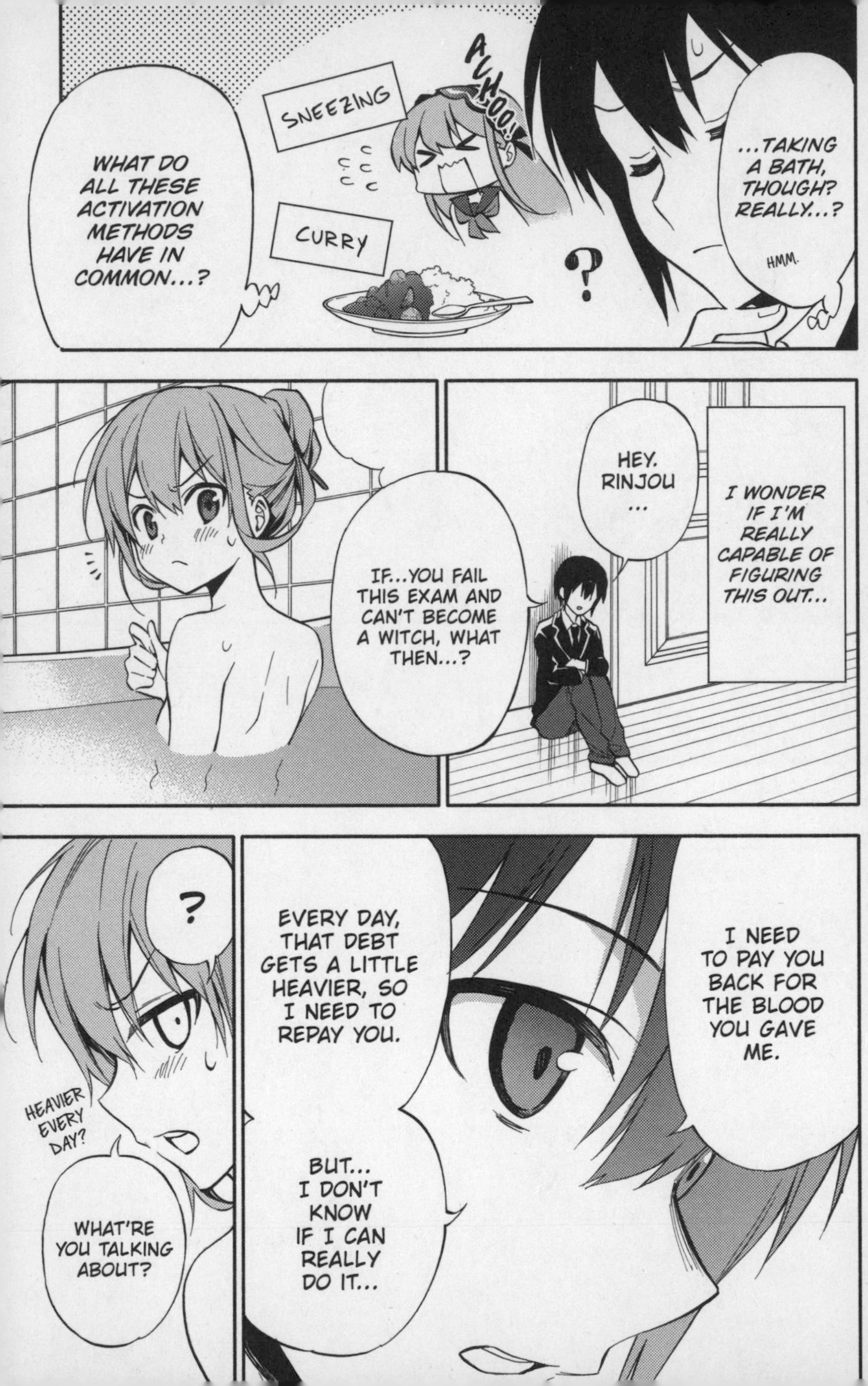
...TAKING A BATH, THOUGH? REALLY...?
HMM.
AHCHOO!
SNEEZING
CURRY
WHAT DO ALL THESE ACTIVATION METHODS HAVE IN COMMON...?
I WONDER IF I'M REALLY CAPABLE OF FIGURING THIS OUT...
HEY. RINJOU...
IF...YOU FAIL THIS EXAM AND CAN'T BECOME A WITCH, WHAT THEN...?
I NEED TO PAY YOU BACK FOR THE BLOOD YOU GAVE ME.
EVERY DAY, THAT DEBT GETS A LITTLE HEAVIER, SO I NEED TO REPAY YOU.
BUT... I DON'T KNOW IF I CAN REALLY DO IT...
?
HEAVIER EVERY DAY?
WHAT'RE YOU TALKING ABOUT?

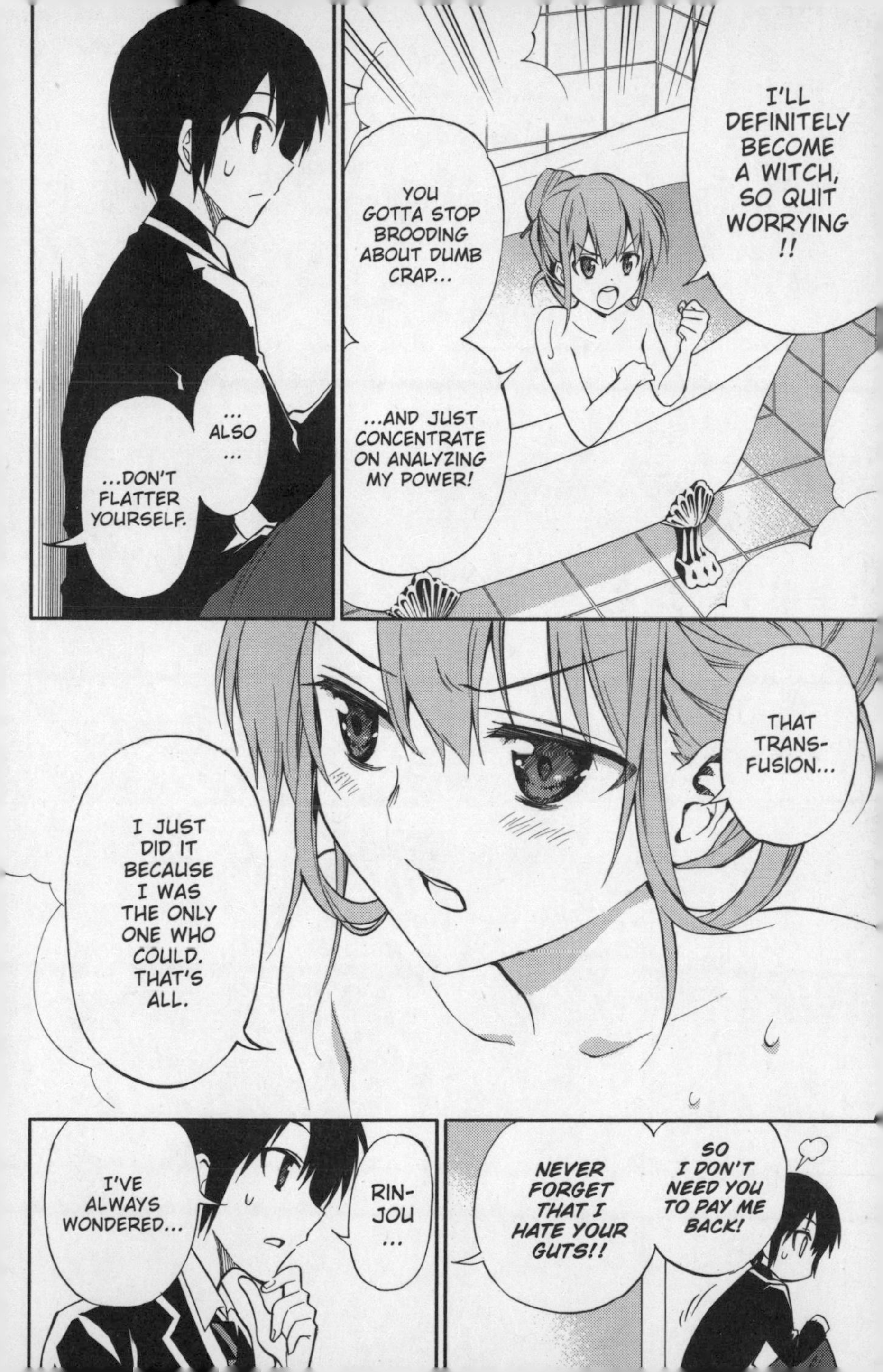
I'LL DEFINITELY BECOME A WITCH, SO QUIT WORRYING!!
YOU GOTTA STOP BROODING ABOUT DUMB CRAP...
...AND JUST CONCENTRATE ON ANALYZING MY POWER!
...ALSO...
...DON'T FLATTER YOURSELF.
THAT TRANS-FUSION...
I JUST DID IT BECAUSE I WAS THE ONLY ONE WHO COULD. THAT'S ALL.
SO I DON'T NEED YOU TO PAY ME BACK!
NEVER FORGET THAT I HATE YOUR GUTS!!
RIN-JOU...
I'VE ALWAYS WONDERED...

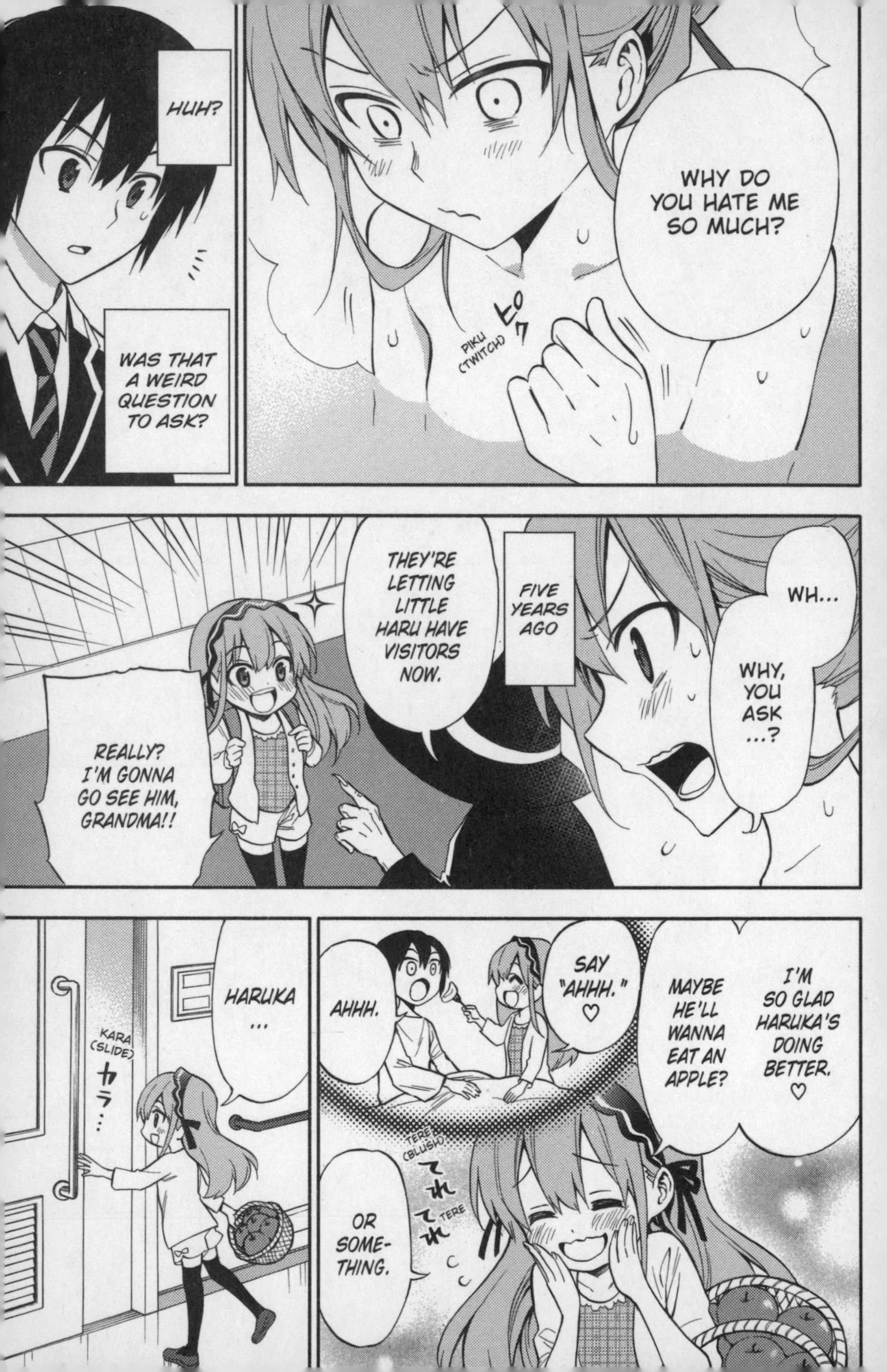
WHY DO YOU HATE ME SO MUCH?
ピク
PIKU (TWITCH)
HUH?
WAS THAT A WEIRD QUESTION TO ASK?
WH...
WHY, YOU ASK ...?
FIVE YEARS AGO
THEY'RE LETTING LITTLE HARU HAVE VISITORS NOW.
REALLY? I'M GONNA GO SEE HIM, GRANDMA!!
I'M SO GLAD HARUKA'S DOING BETTER. ♡
MAYBE HE'LL WANNA EAT AN APPLE?
SAY "AHHH." ♡
AHHH.
てれてれ
TERE (BLUSH) TERE
OR SOME-THING.
HARUKA ...
カラ...
KARA (SLIDE)

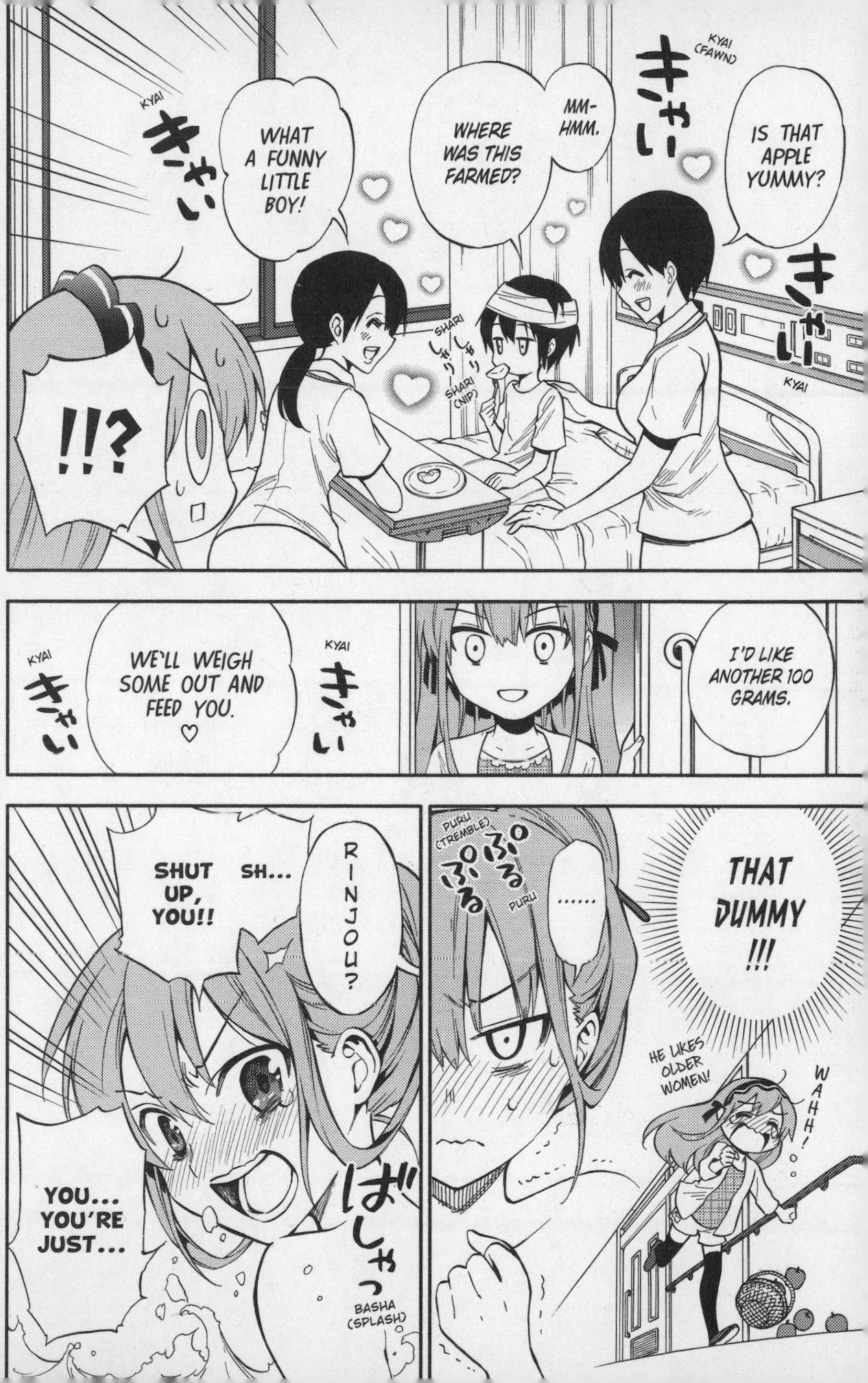
きゃい
KYAI (FAWN)
IS THAT APPLE YUMMY?
きゃい
KYAI
MM-HMM.
WHERE WAS THIS FARMED?
しゃりしゃり
SHARI SHARI (NIP)
WHAT A FUNNY LITTLE BOY!
きゃい
KYAI
!!?
I'D LIKE ANOTHER 100 GRAMS.
きゃい
KYAI
WE'LL WEIGH SOME OUT AND FEED YOU. ♡
きゃい
KYAI
THAT DUMMY !!!
ぷるぷる
PURU (TREMBLE) PURU
......
HE LIKES OLDER WOMEN!
WAHH!
RINJOU?
SH...
SHUT UP, YOU!!
ばしゃっ
BASHA (SPLASH)
YOU... YOU'RE JUST...

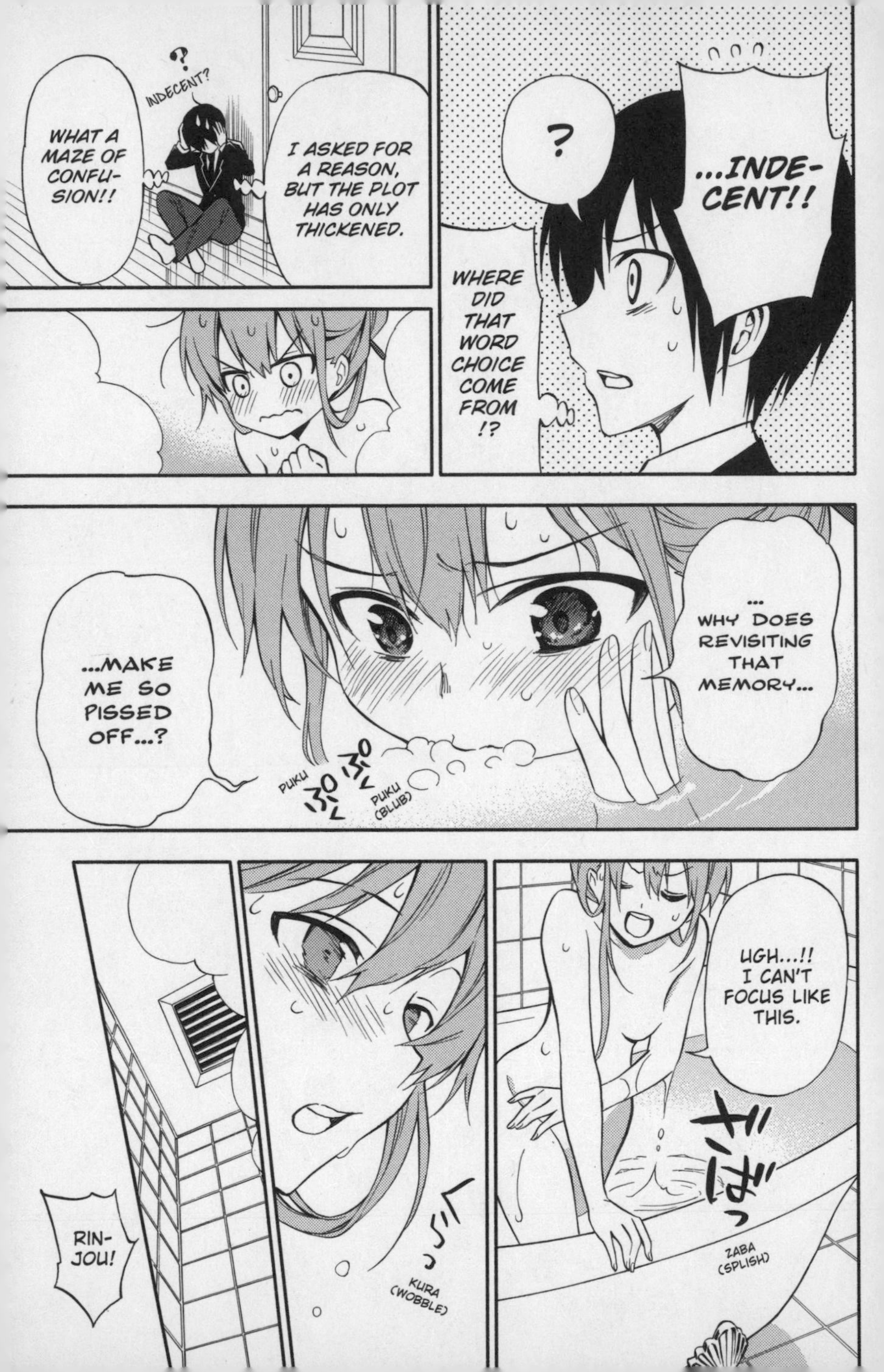
?
...INDE-CENT!!
WHERE DID THAT WORD CHOICE COME FROM!?
I ASKED FOR A REASON, BUT THE PLOT HAS ONLY THICKENED.
?
INDECENT?
WHAT A MAZE OF CONFU-SION!!
... WHY DOES REVISITING THAT MEMORY...
...MAKE ME SO PISSED OFF...?
PUKU
PUKU (BLUB)
UGH...!! I CAN'T FOCUS LIKE THIS.
ZABA (SPLISH)
KURA (WOBBLE)
RIN-JOU!

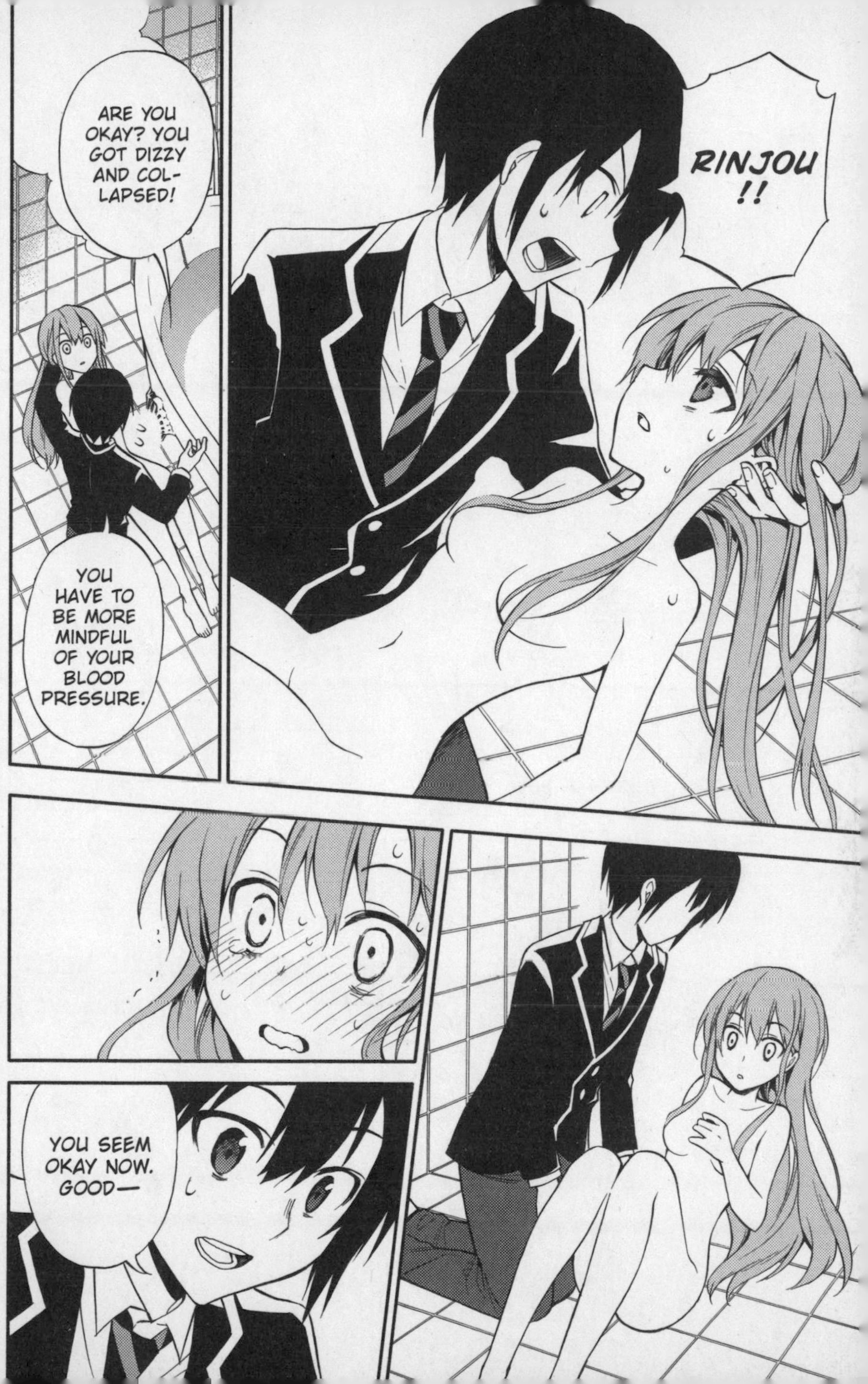
RINJOU!!
ARE YOU OKAY? YOU GOT DIZZY AND COL-LAPSED!
YOU HAVE TO BE MORE MINDFUL OF YOUR BLOOD PRESSURE.
YOU SEEM OKAY NOW. GOOD—

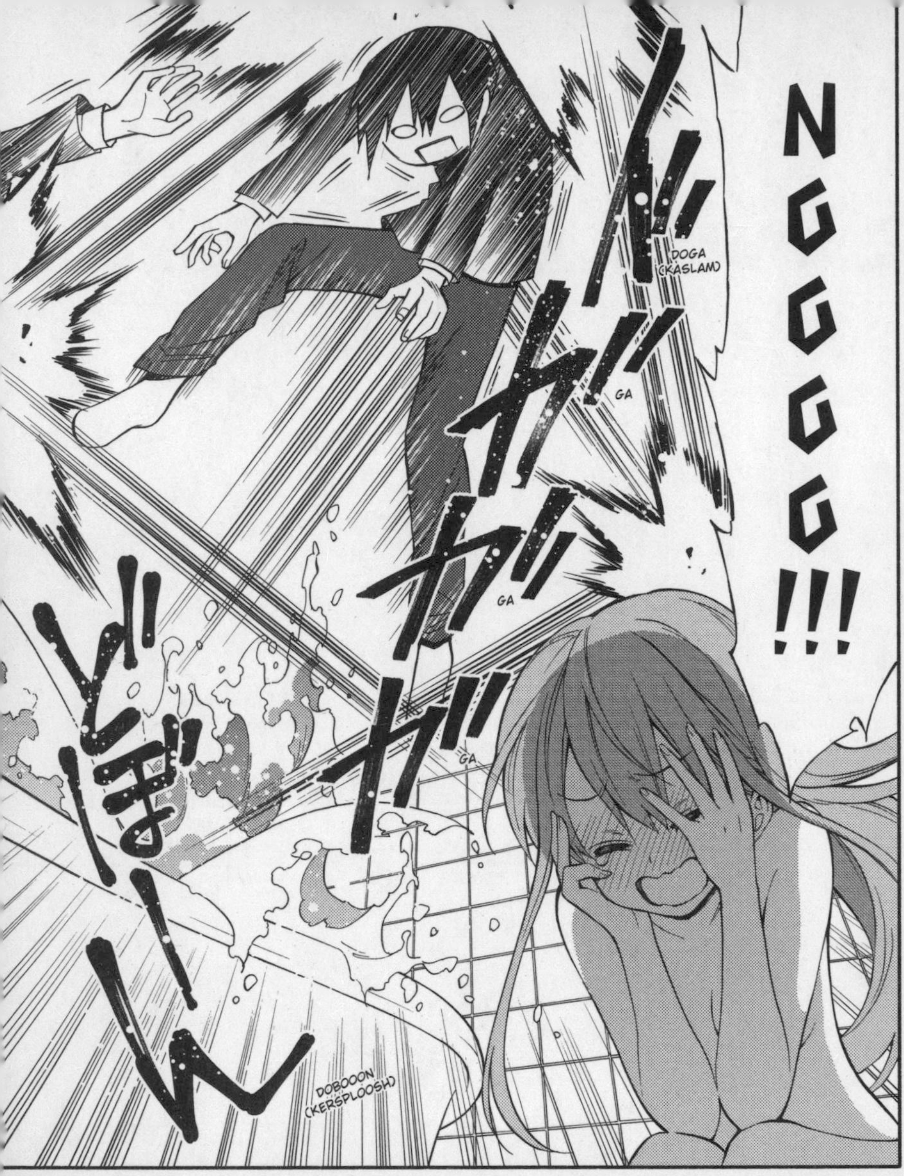
NGGGG!!!
DOGA (KASLAM)
GA
GA
GA
DOBOOON (KERSPLOOSH)

HARUKA KUZE: DECEASED

HARUKA KUZE: ~~DECEASED~~

MIRACULOUSLY REVIVED

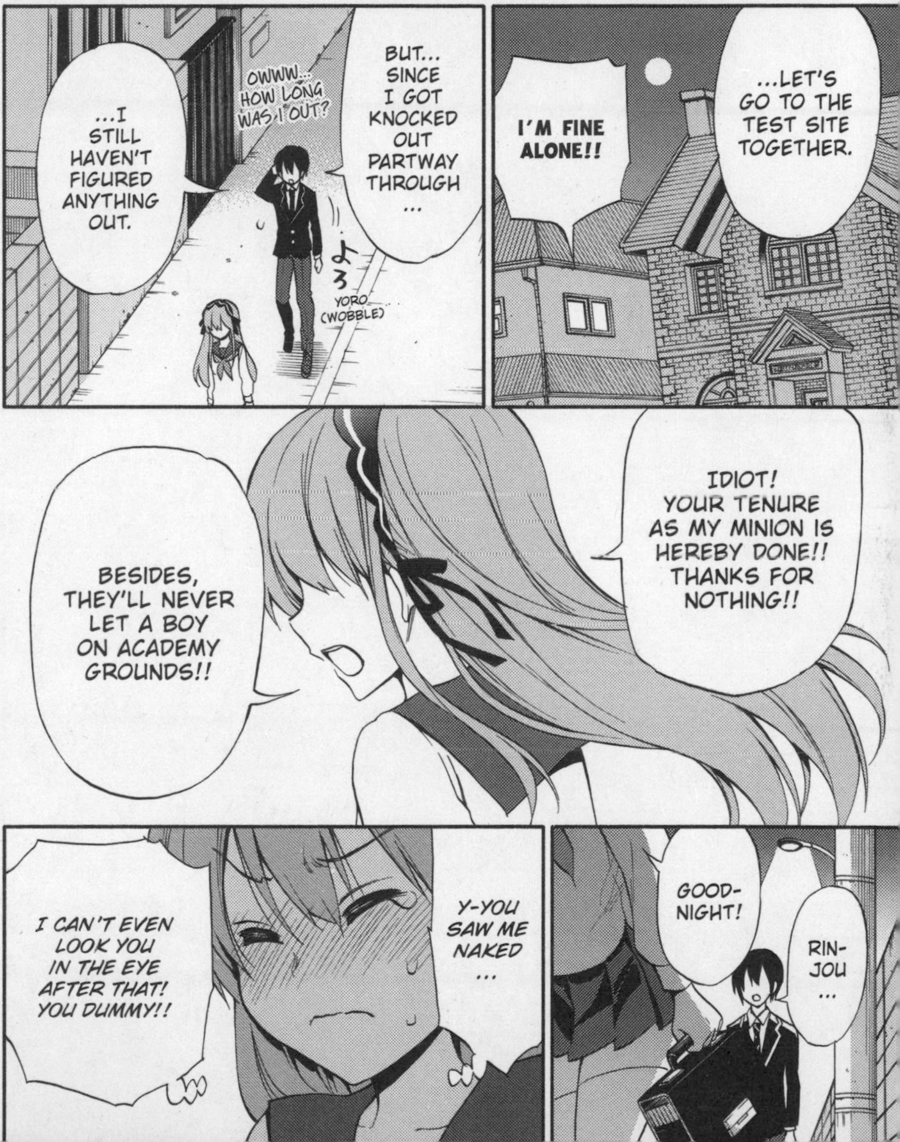
...LET'S GO TO THE TEST SITE TOGETHER.
I'M FINE ALONE!!
BUT... SINCE I GOT KNOCKED OUT PARTWAY THROUGH...
OWWW... HOW LONG WAS I OUT?
よろ
YORO (WOBBLE)
...I STILL HAVEN'T FIGURED ANYTHING OUT.
IDIOT! YOUR TENURE AS MY MINION IS HEREBY DONE!! THANKS FOR NOTHING!!
BESIDES, THEY'LL NEVER LET A BOY ON ACADEMY GROUNDS!!
GOOD-NIGHT!
RIN-JOU...
Y-YOU SAW ME NAKED...
I CAN'T EVEN LOOK YOU IN THE EYE AFTER THAT! YOU DUMMY!!

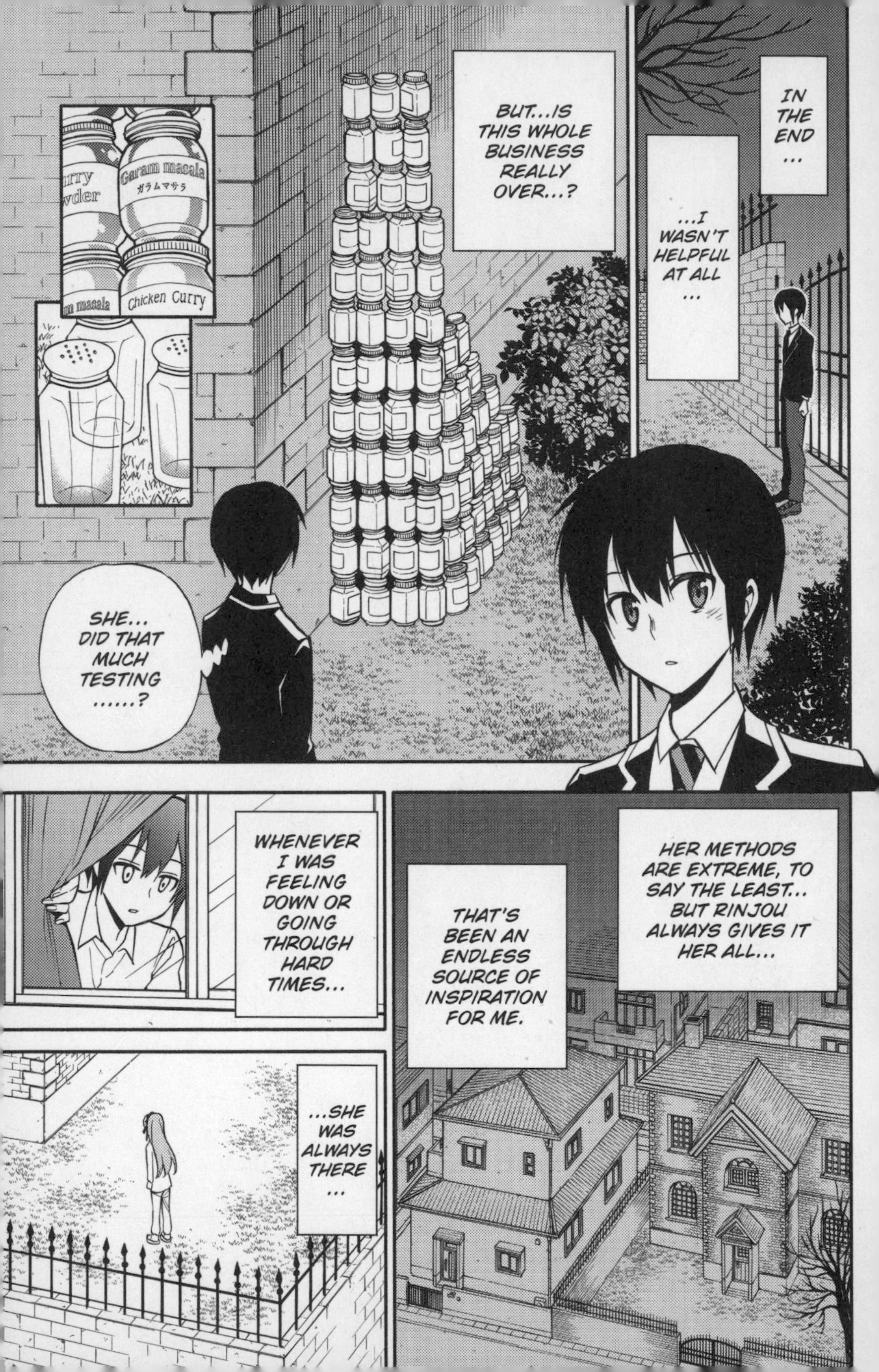
IN THE END...
...I WASN'T HELPFUL AT ALL...
BUT...IS THIS WHOLE BUSINESS REALLY OVER...?
Garam masala
ガラムマサラ
Chicken Curry
SHE... DID THAT MUCH TESTING......?
HER METHODS ARE EXTREME, TO SAY THE LEAST... BUT RINJOU ALWAYS GIVES IT HER ALL...
THAT'S BEEN AN ENDLESS SOURCE OF INSPIRATION FOR ME.
WHENEVER I WAS FEELING DOWN OR GOING THROUGH HARD TIMES...
...SHE WAS ALWAYS THERE...

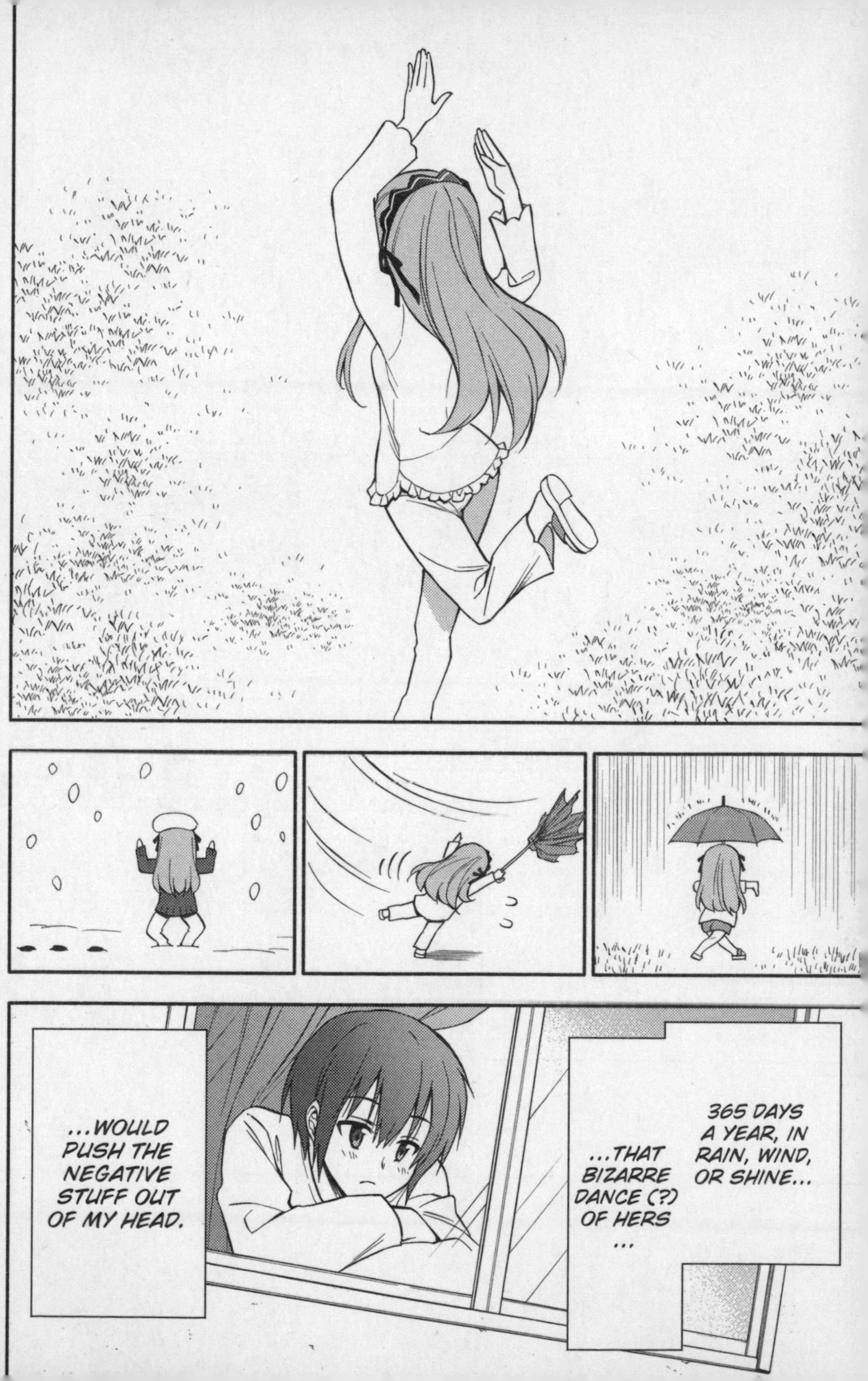
365 DAYS A YEAR, IN RAIN, WIND, OR SHINE...
...THAT BIZARRE DANCE (?) OF HERS ...
...WOULD PUSH THE NEGATIVE STUFF OUT OF MY HEAD.

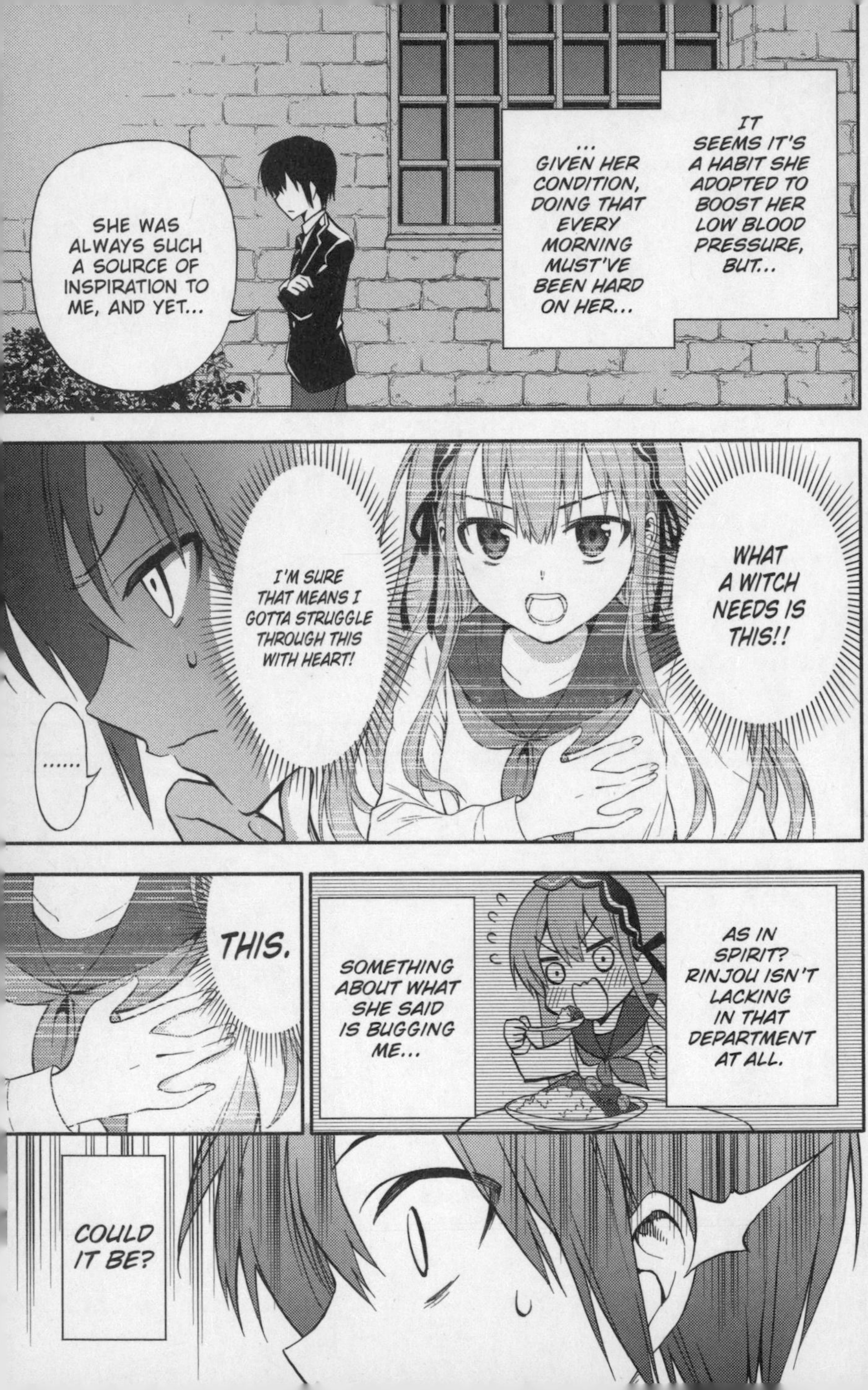
IT SEEMS IT'S A HABIT SHE ADOPTED TO BOOST HER LOW BLOOD PRESSURE, BUT...
... GIVEN HER CONDITION, DOING THAT EVERY MORNING MUST'VE BEEN HARD ON HER...
SHE WAS ALWAYS SUCH A SOURCE OF INSPIRATION TO ME, AND YET...
WHAT A WITCH NEEDS IS THIS!!
I'M SURE THAT MEANS I GOTTA STRUGGLE THROUGH THIS WITH HEART!
......
AS IN SPIRIT? RINJOU ISN'T LACKING IN THAT DEPARTMENT AT ALL.
SOMETHING ABOUT WHAT SHE SAID IS BUGGING ME...
THIS.
COULD IT BE?

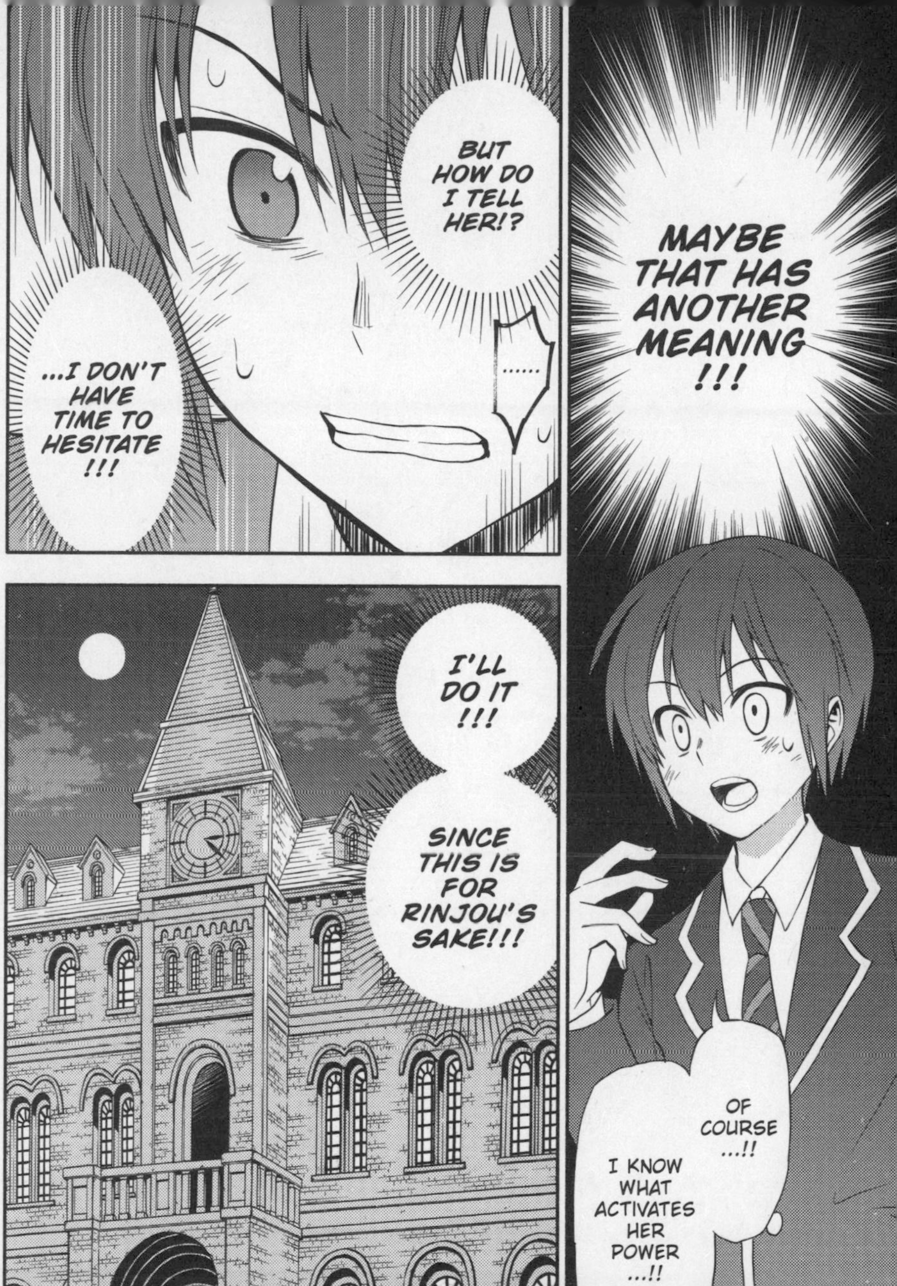
MAYBE THAT HAS ANOTHER MEANING!!!
OF COURSE...!!
I KNOW WHAT ACTIVATES HER POWER...!!
BUT HOW DO I TELL HER!?
......
...I DON'T HAVE TIME TO HESITATE!!!
I'LL DO IT!!!
SINCE THIS IS FOR RINJOU'S SAKE!!!

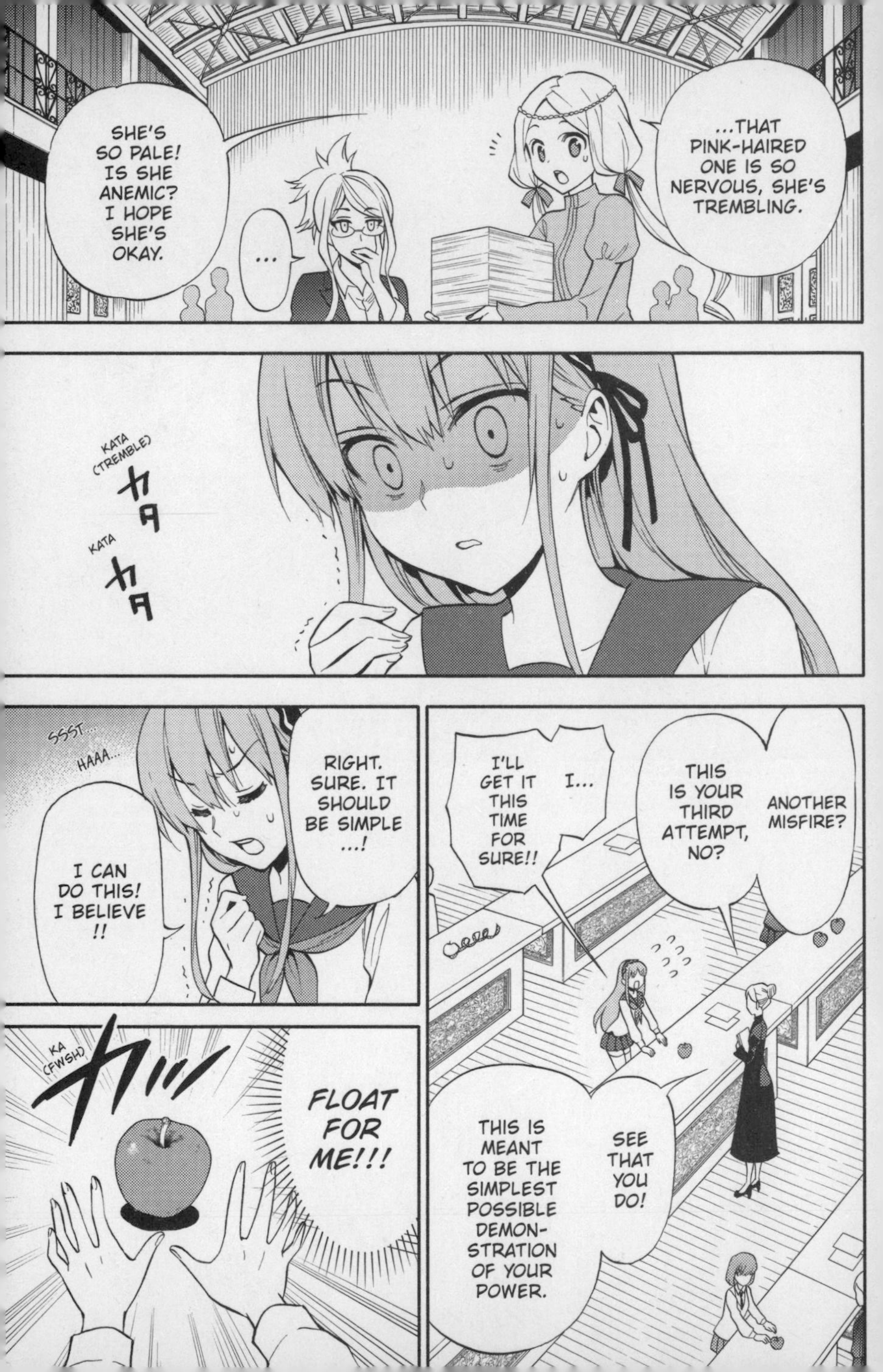
...THAT PINK-HAIRED ONE IS SO NERVOUS, SHE'S TREMBLING.
SHE'S SO PALE! IS SHE ANEMIC? I HOPE SHE'S OKAY.
...
KATA (TREMBLE)
カタ
KATA
カタ
ANOTHER MISFIRE?
THIS IS YOUR THIRD ATTEMPT, NO?
I...
I'LL GET IT THIS TIME FOR SURE!!
SEE THAT YOU DO!
THIS IS MEANT TO BE THE SIMPLEST POSSIBLE DEMONSTRATION OF YOUR POWER.
RIGHT. SURE. IT SHOULD BE SIMPLE ...!
SSST... HAAA...
I CAN DO THIS! I BELIEVE!!
FLOAT FOR ME!!!
KA (FWSH)
カッ

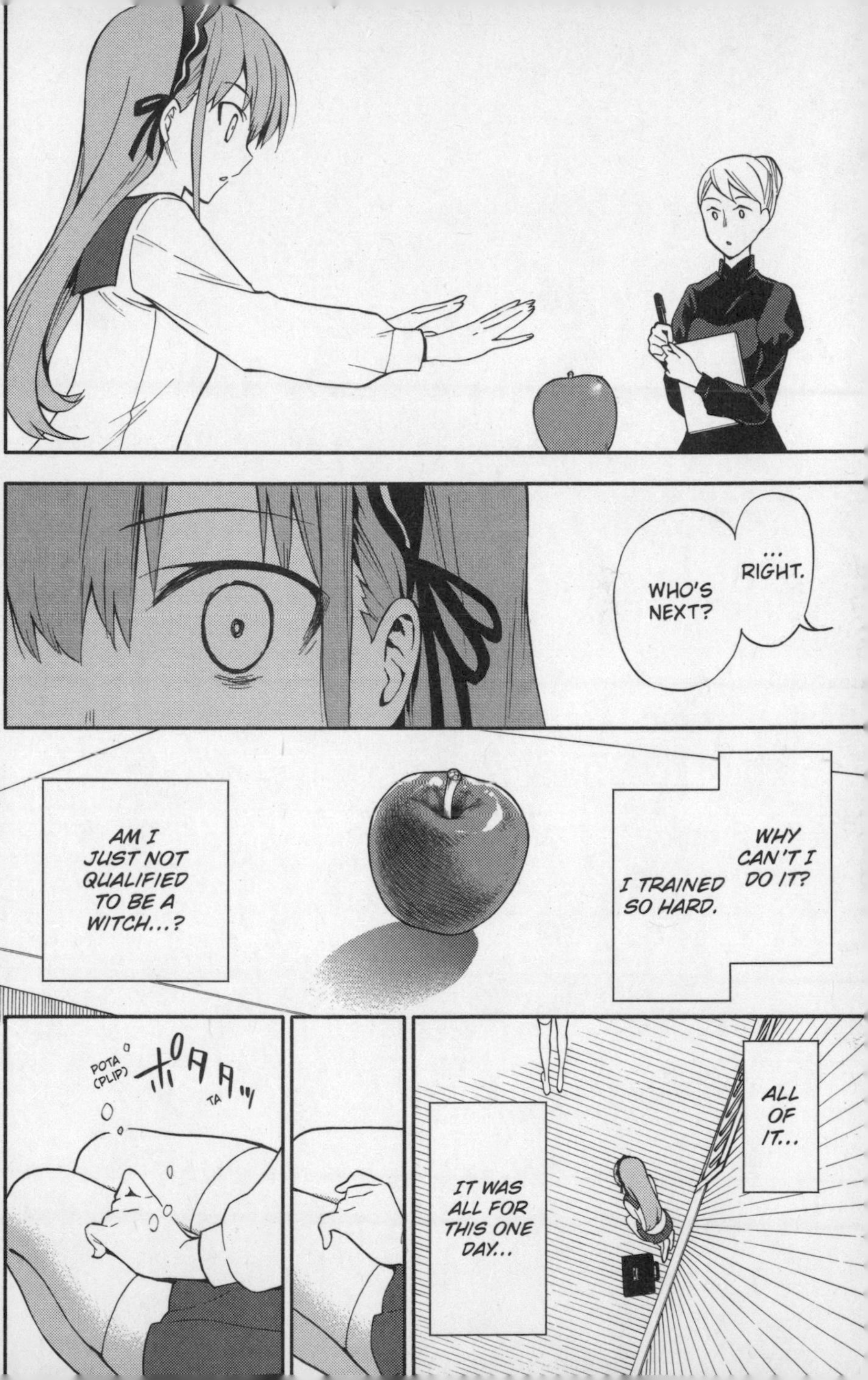
... RIGHT.
WHO'S NEXT?
WHY CAN'T I DO IT?
I TRAINED SO HARD.
AM I JUST NOT QUALIFIED TO BE A WITCH...?
ALL OF IT...
IT WAS ALL FOR THIS ONE DAY...
POTA (PLIP)
TA

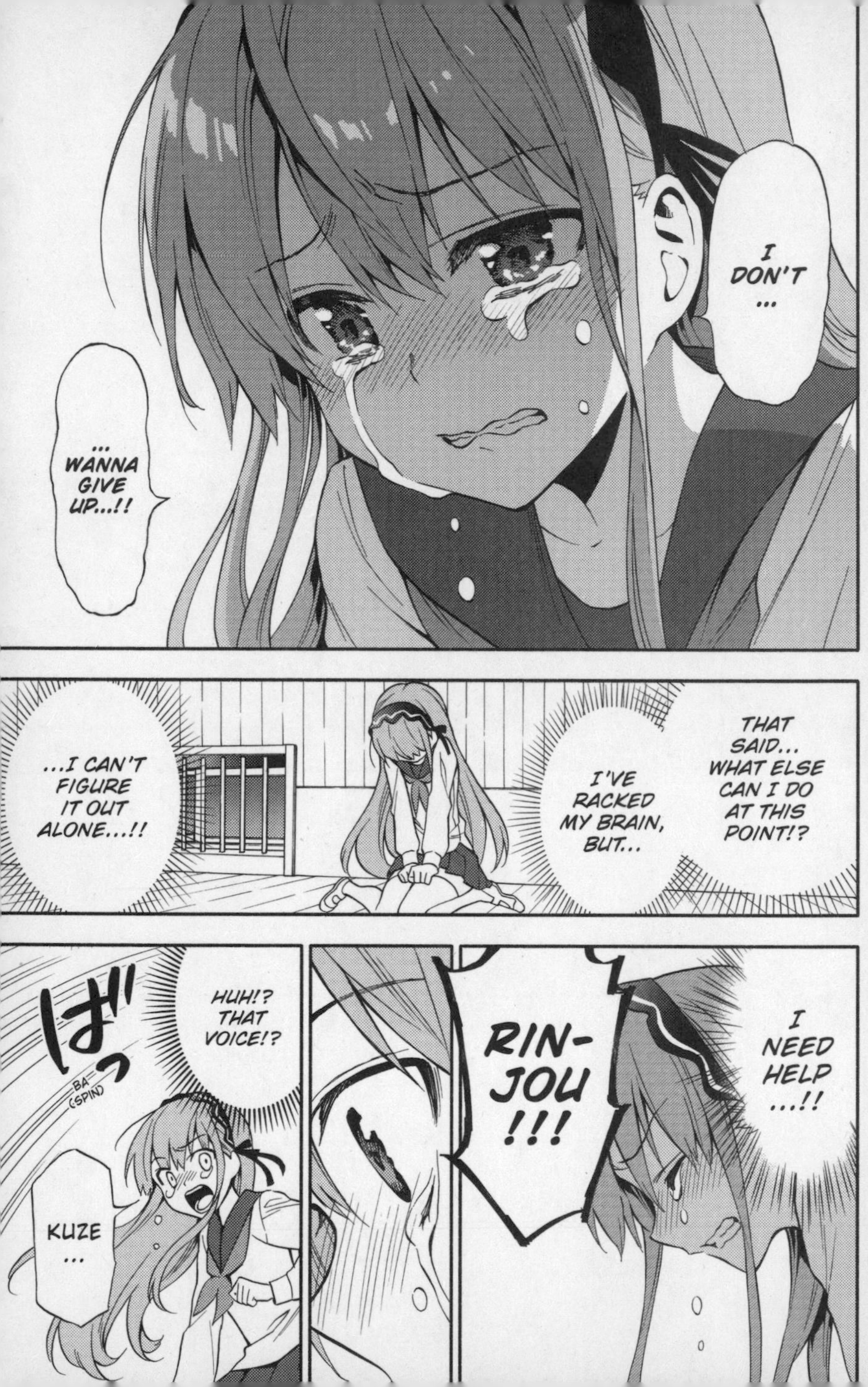
I DON'T ...
... WANNA GIVE UP...!!
THAT SAID... WHAT ELSE CAN I DO AT THIS POINT!?
I'VE RACKED MY BRAIN, BUT...
...I CAN'T FIGURE IT OUT ALONE...!!
I NEED HELP ...!!
RIN-JOU !!!
HUH!? THAT VOICE!?
ばっ
BA (SPIN)
KUZE ...

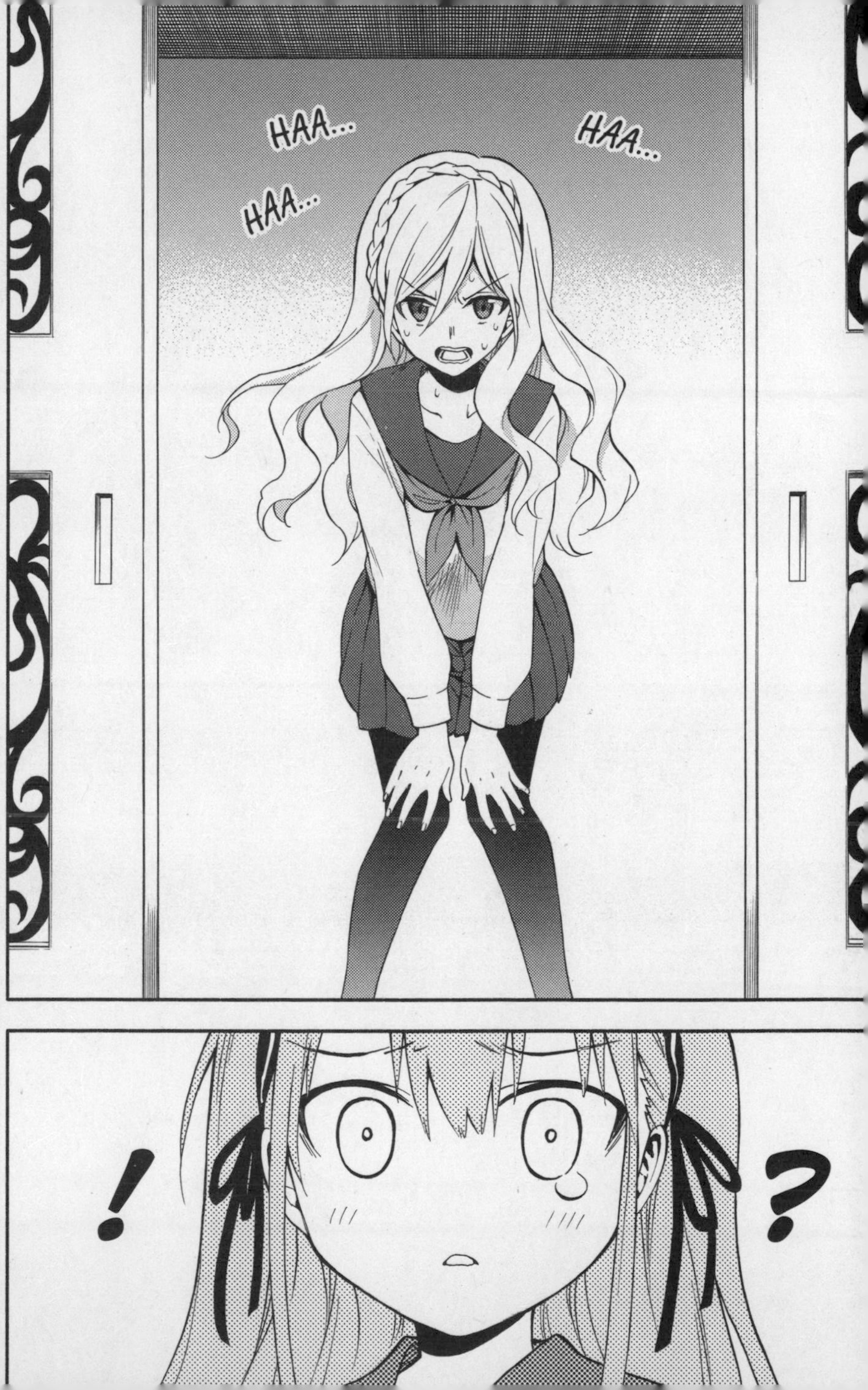
HAA...
HAA...
HAA...
?
!

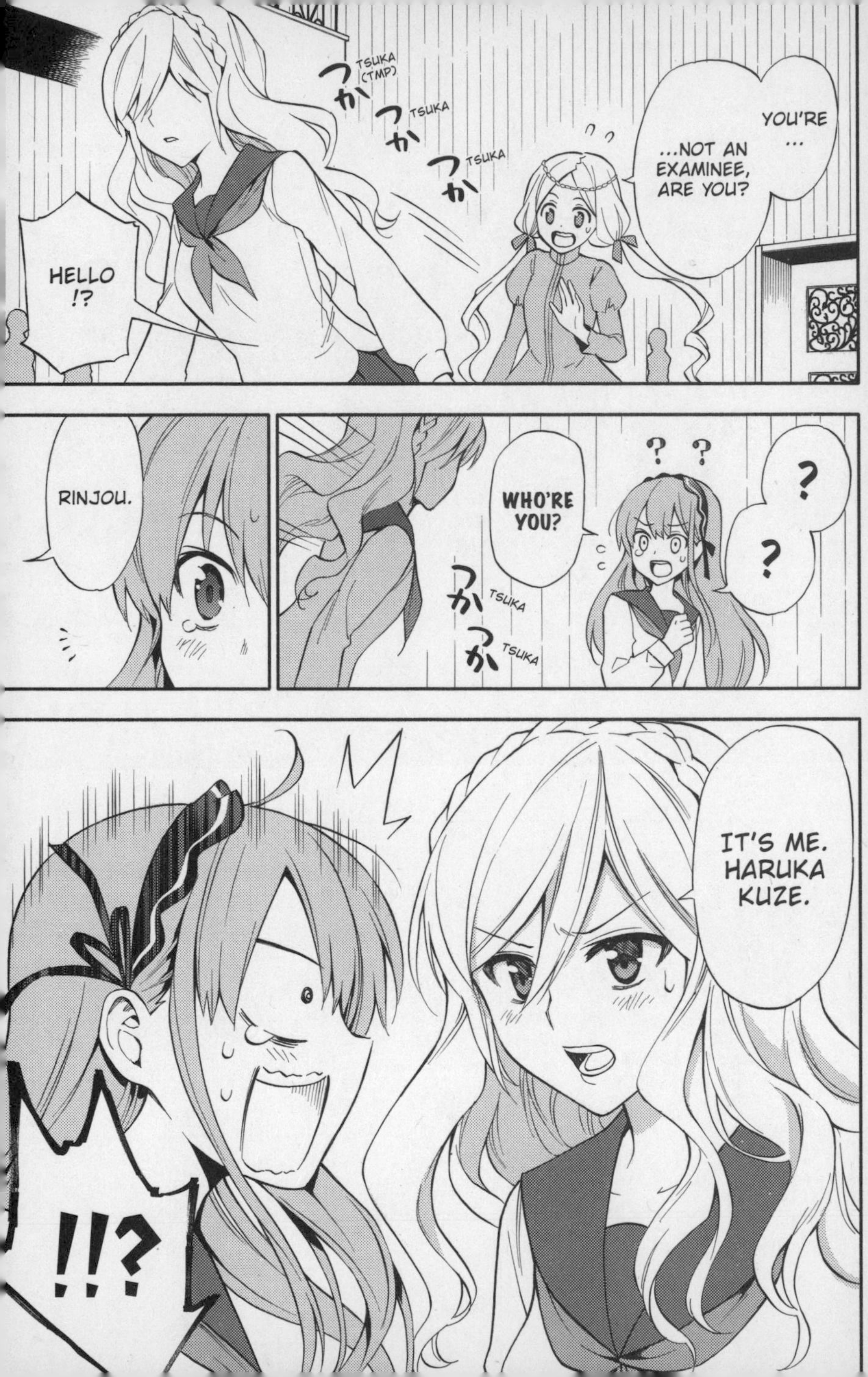
YOU'RE ...
...NOT AN EXAMINEE, ARE YOU?
つか TSUKA (TMP)
つか TSUKA
つか TSUKA
HELLO !?
?
?
WHO'RE YOU?
つか TSUKA
つか TSUKA
RINJOU.
IT'S ME. HARUKA KUZE.
!!?

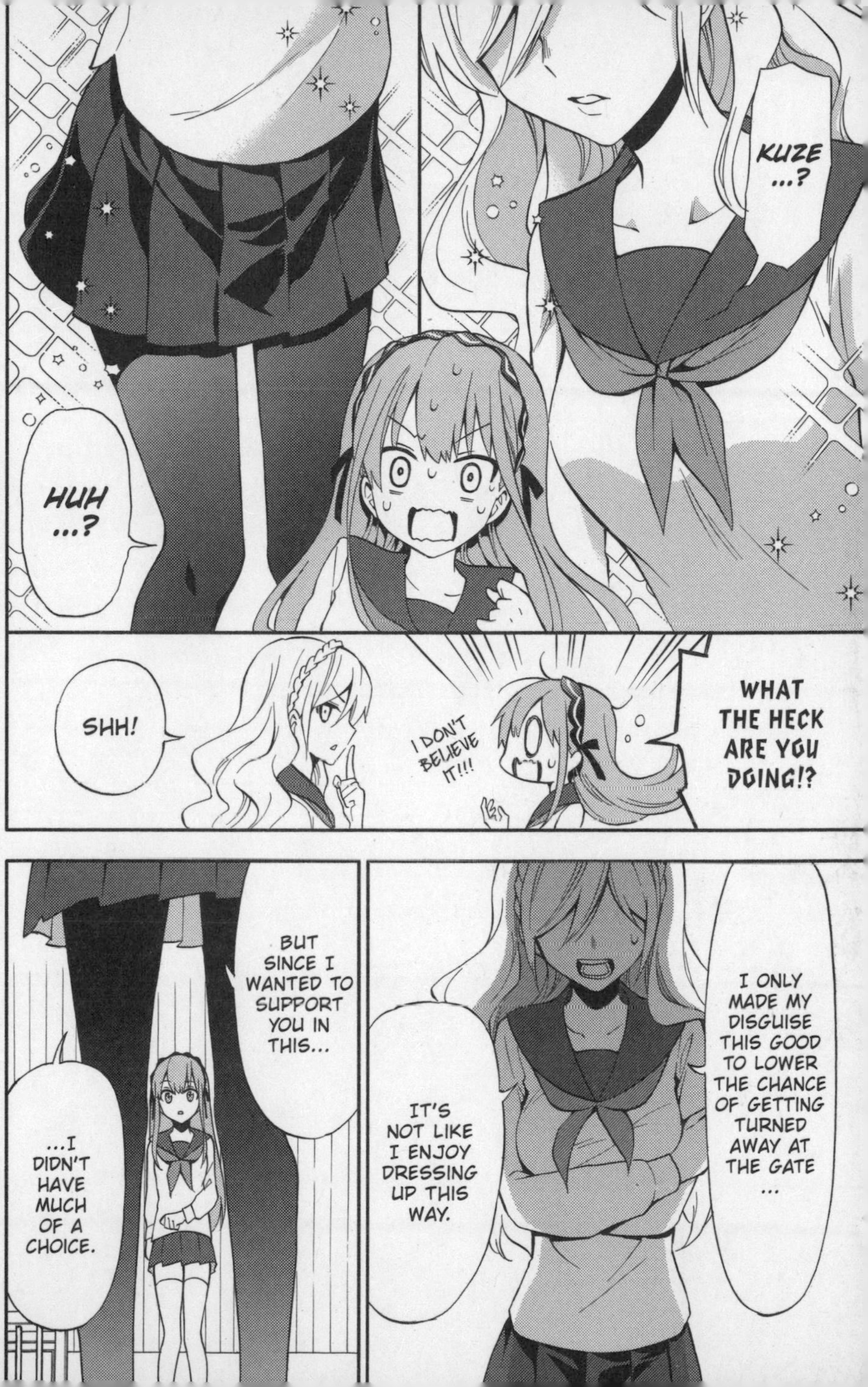
KUZE ...?
HUH ...?
WHAT THE HECK ARE YOU DOING!?
I DON'T BELIEVE IT!!!
SHH!
I ONLY MADE MY DISGUISE THIS GOOD TO LOWER THE CHANCE OF GETTING TURNED AWAY AT THE GATE ...
IT'S NOT LIKE I ENJOY DRESSING UP THIS WAY.
BUT SINCE I WANTED TO SUPPORT YOU IN THIS...
...I DIDN'T HAVE MUCH OF A CHOICE.

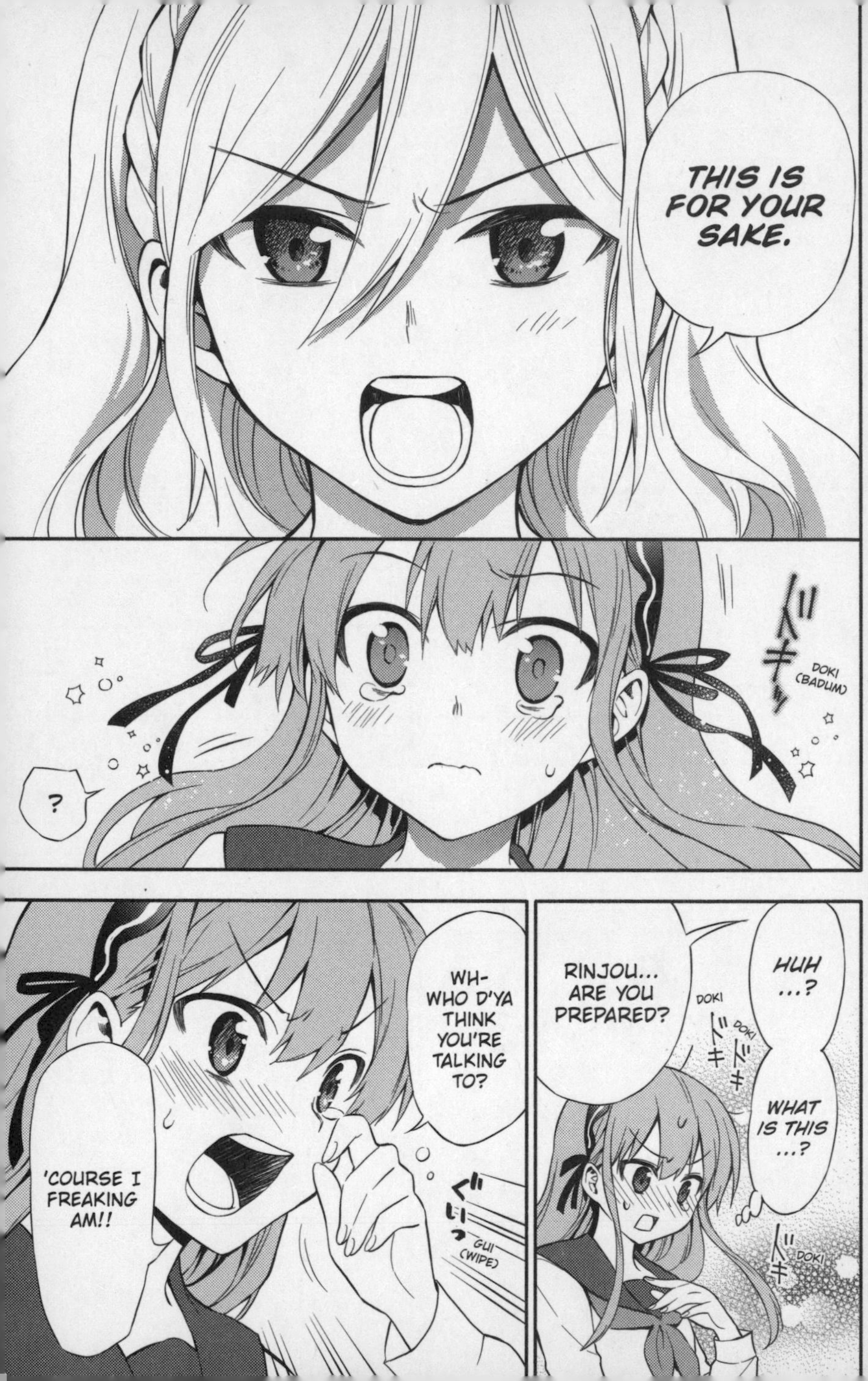
THIS IS FOR YOUR SAKE.
DOKI (BADUM)
?
HUH ...?
DOKI
DOKI
RINJOU... ARE YOU PREPARED?
WHAT IS THIS ...?
DOKI
WH- WHO D'YA THINK YOU'RE TALKING TO?
GUI (WIPE)
'COURSE I FREAKING AM!!

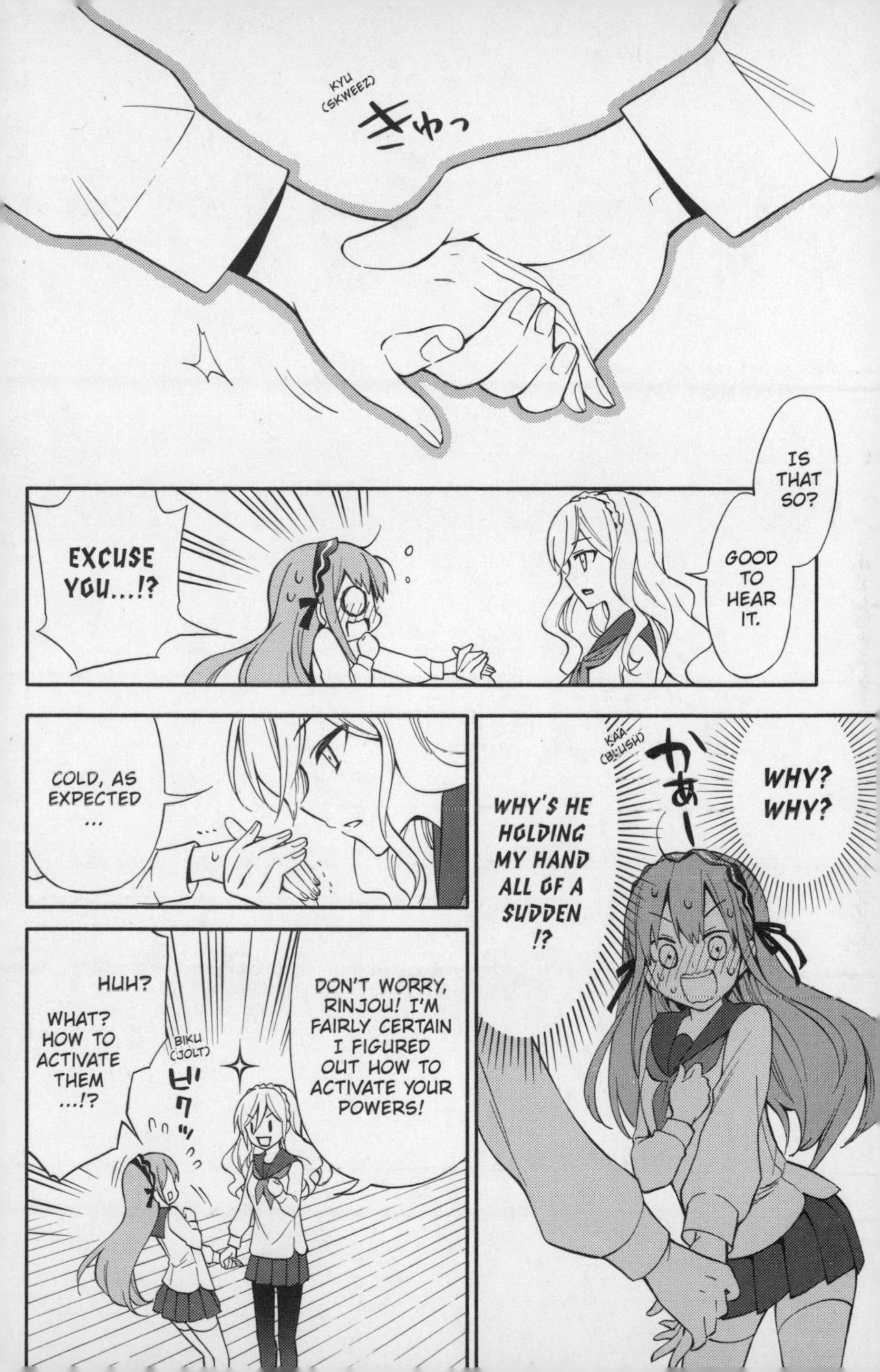
KYU (SKWEEZ)
きゅっ
IS THAT SO?
GOOD TO HEAR IT.
EXCUSE YOU...!?
WHY? WHY?
KA'A (BLUSH)
かぁー
WHY'S HE HOLDING MY HAND ALL OF A SUDDEN!?
COLD, AS EXPECTED...
...
DON'T WORRY, RINJOU! I'M FAIRLY CERTAIN I FIGURED OUT HOW TO ACTIVATE YOUR POWERS!
BIKU (JOLT)
ビクッ
HUH?
WHAT? HOW TO ACTIVATE THEM...!?

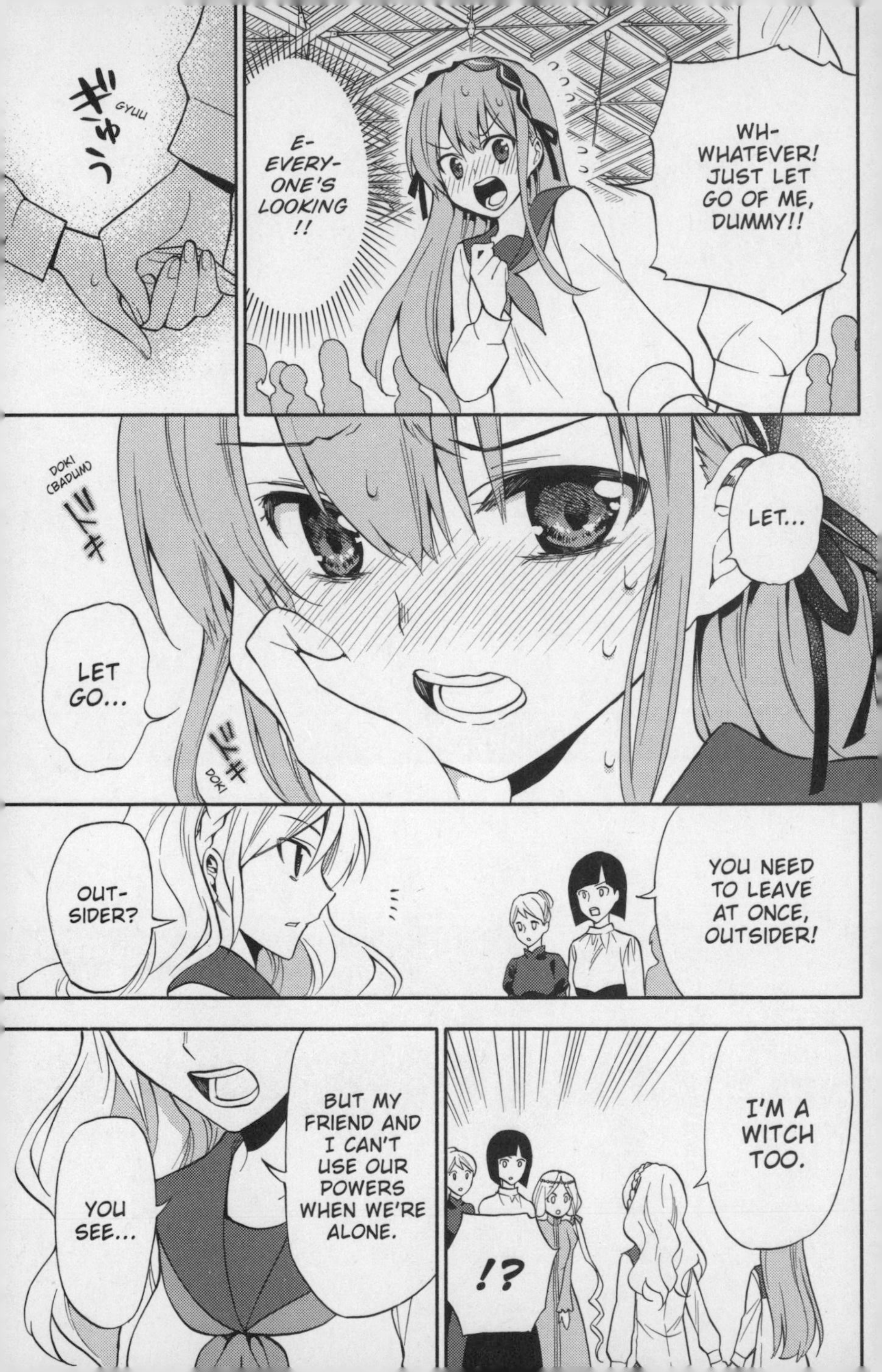
WH-WHATEVER! JUST LET GO OF ME, DUMMY!!
E-EVERYONE'S LOOKING!!
ぎゅう
GYUU
LET...
ドキ
DOKI (BADUM)
LET GO...
ドキ
DOKI
YOU NEED TO LEAVE AT ONCE, OUTSIDER!
OUT-SIDER?
I'M A WITCH TOO.
!?
BUT MY FRIEND AND I CAN'T USE OUR POWERS WHEN WE'RE ALONE.
YOU SEE...

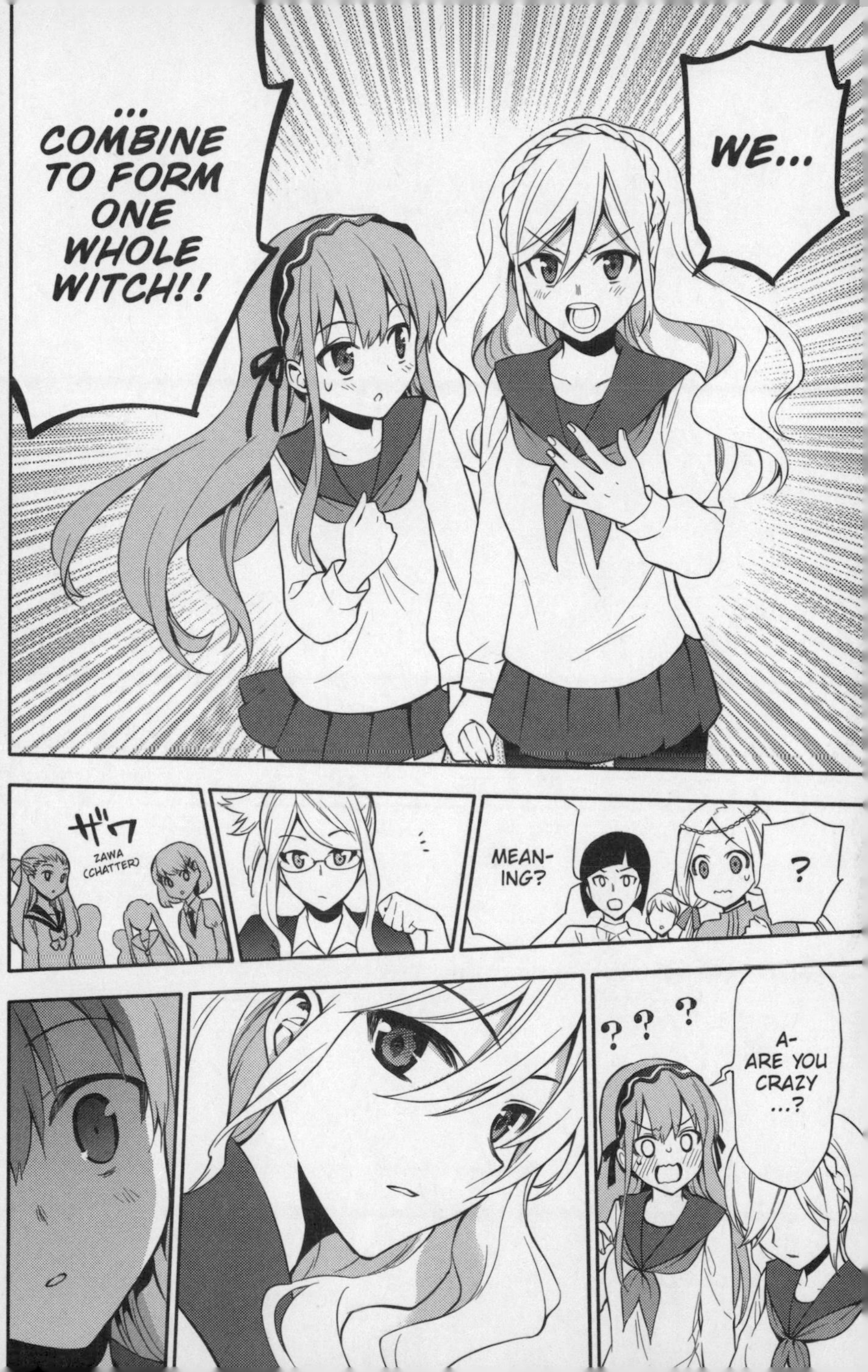
WE...
...COMBINE TO FORM ONE WHOLE WITCH!!
?
MEAN-ING?
ザワ
ZAWA (CHATTER)
? ? ?
A- ARE YOU CRAZY ...?

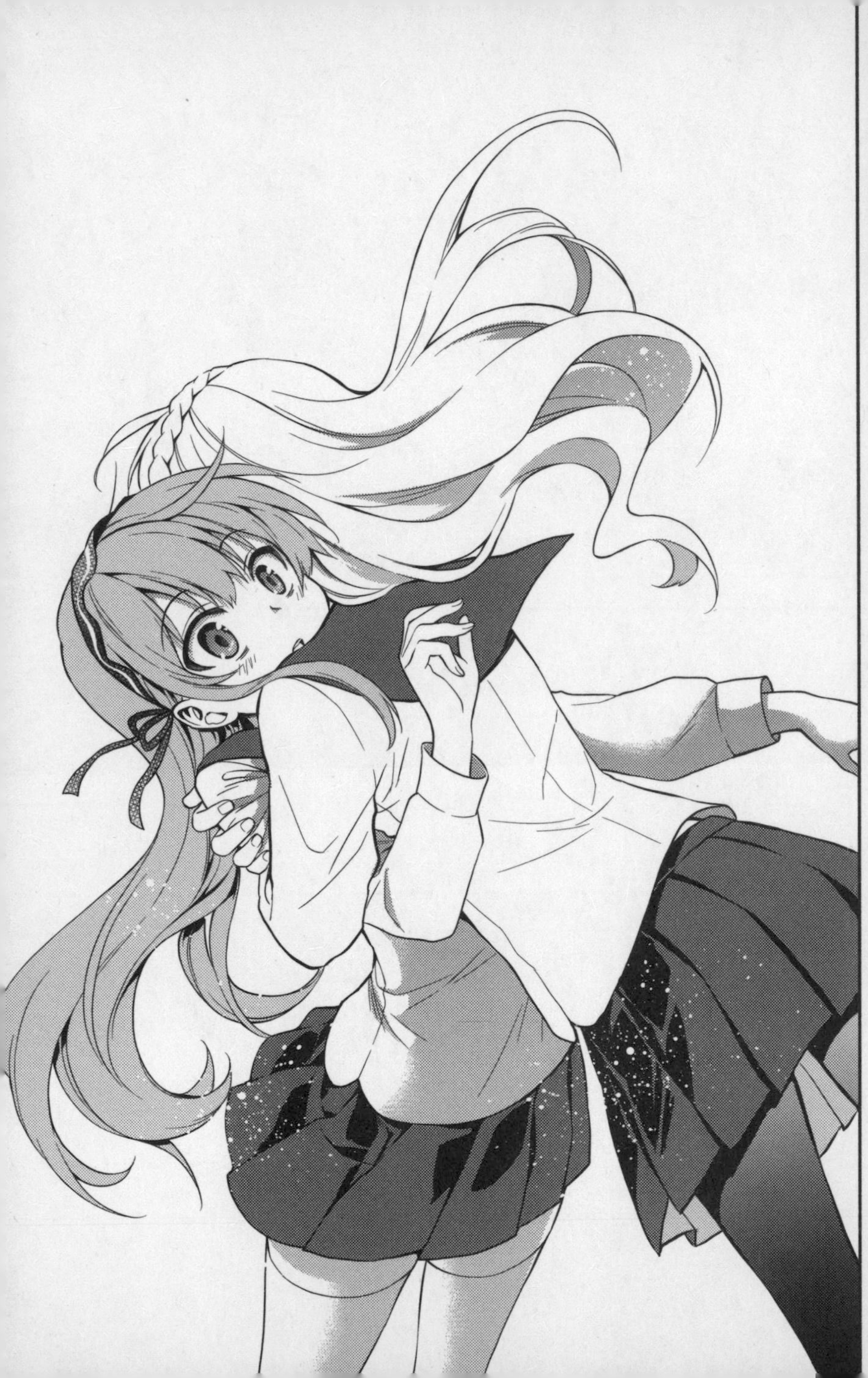

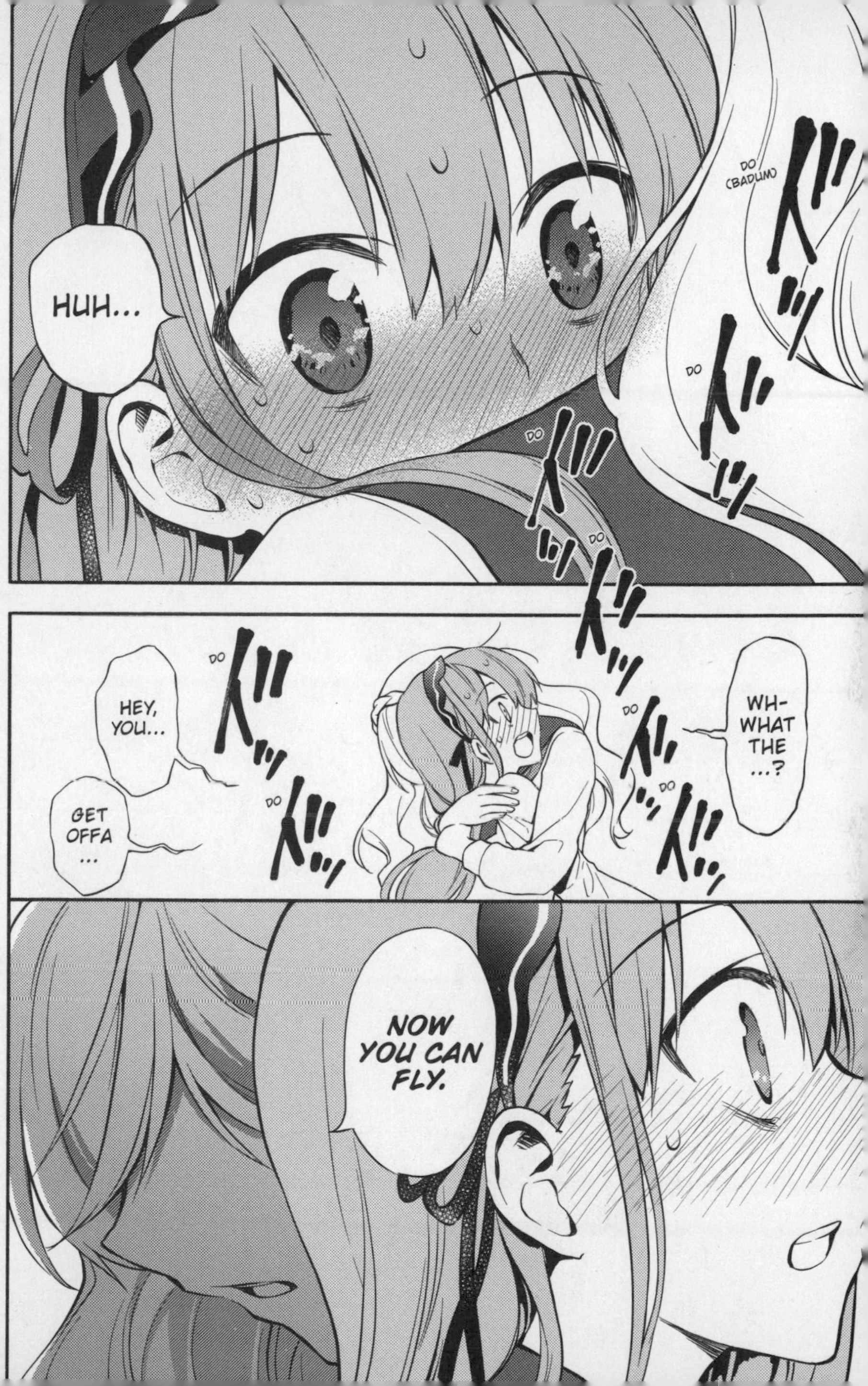
DO (BADUM)
DO
DO
HUH...
DO
WH-WHAT THE...?
DO
DO
DO
DO
HEY, YOU...
GET OFFA...
NOW YOU CAN FLY.

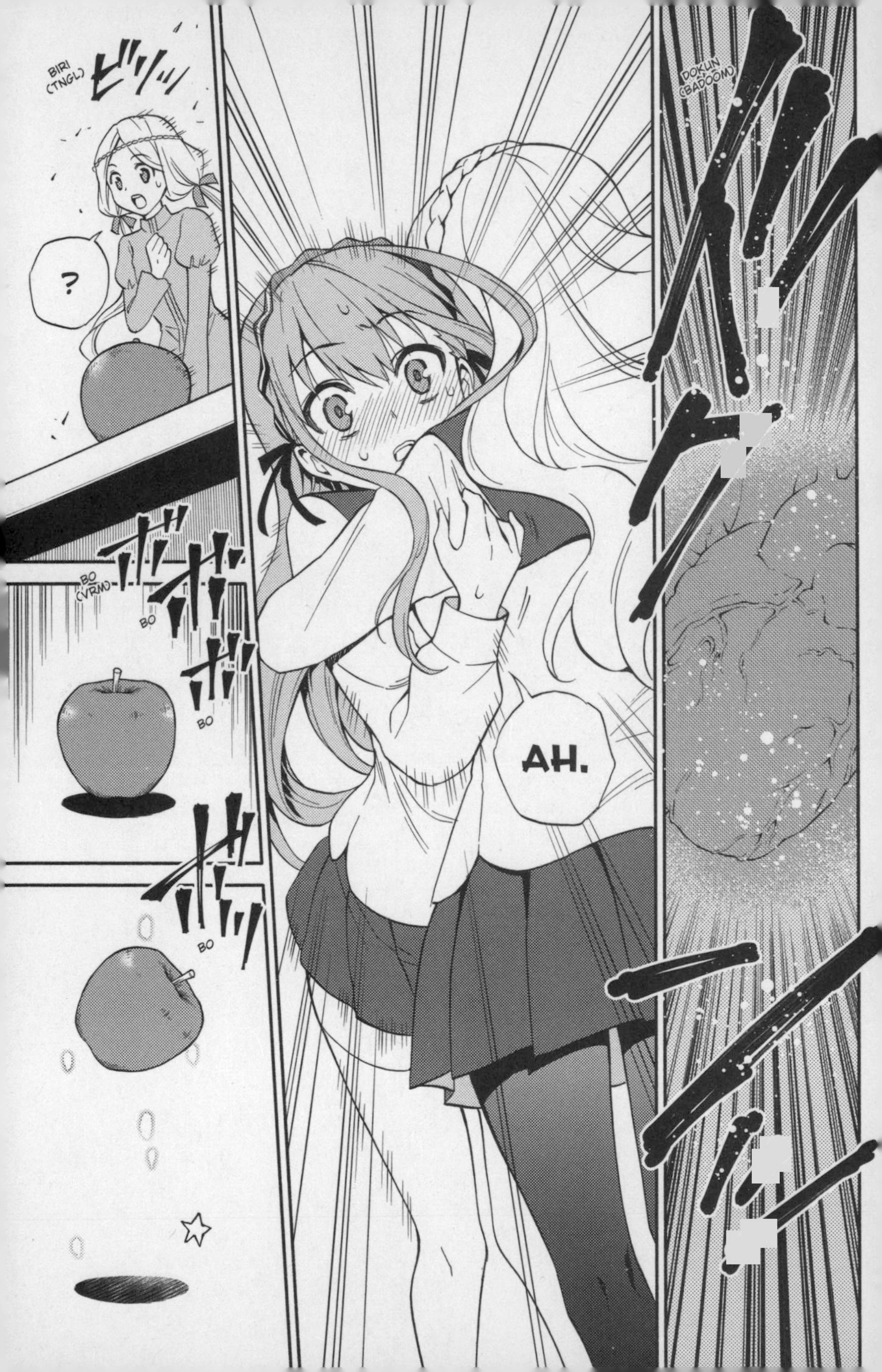

DOKUN (BADOOM)
AH.
BIRI (TNGL)
?
BO (VRM)
BO
BO
BO

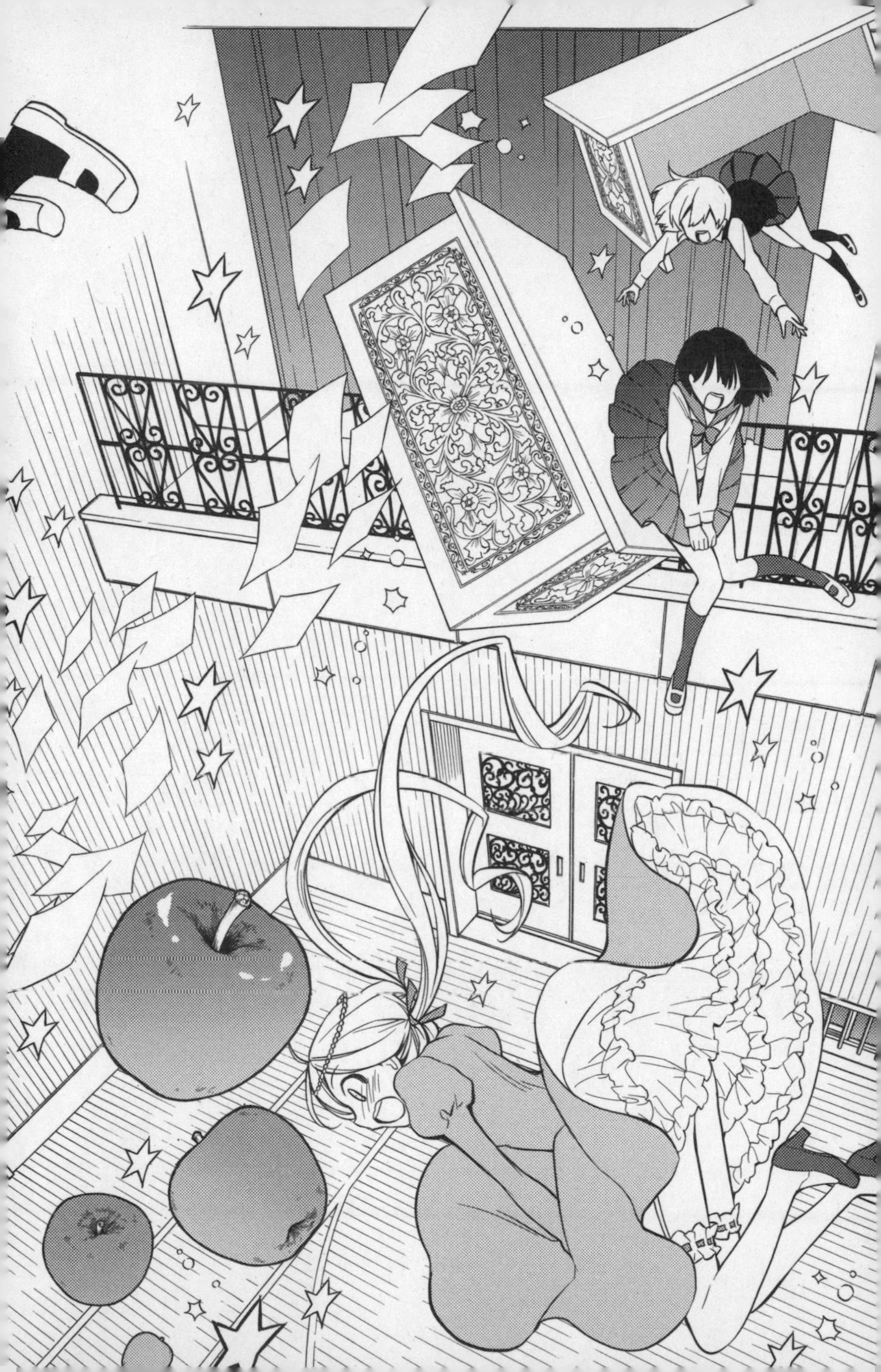

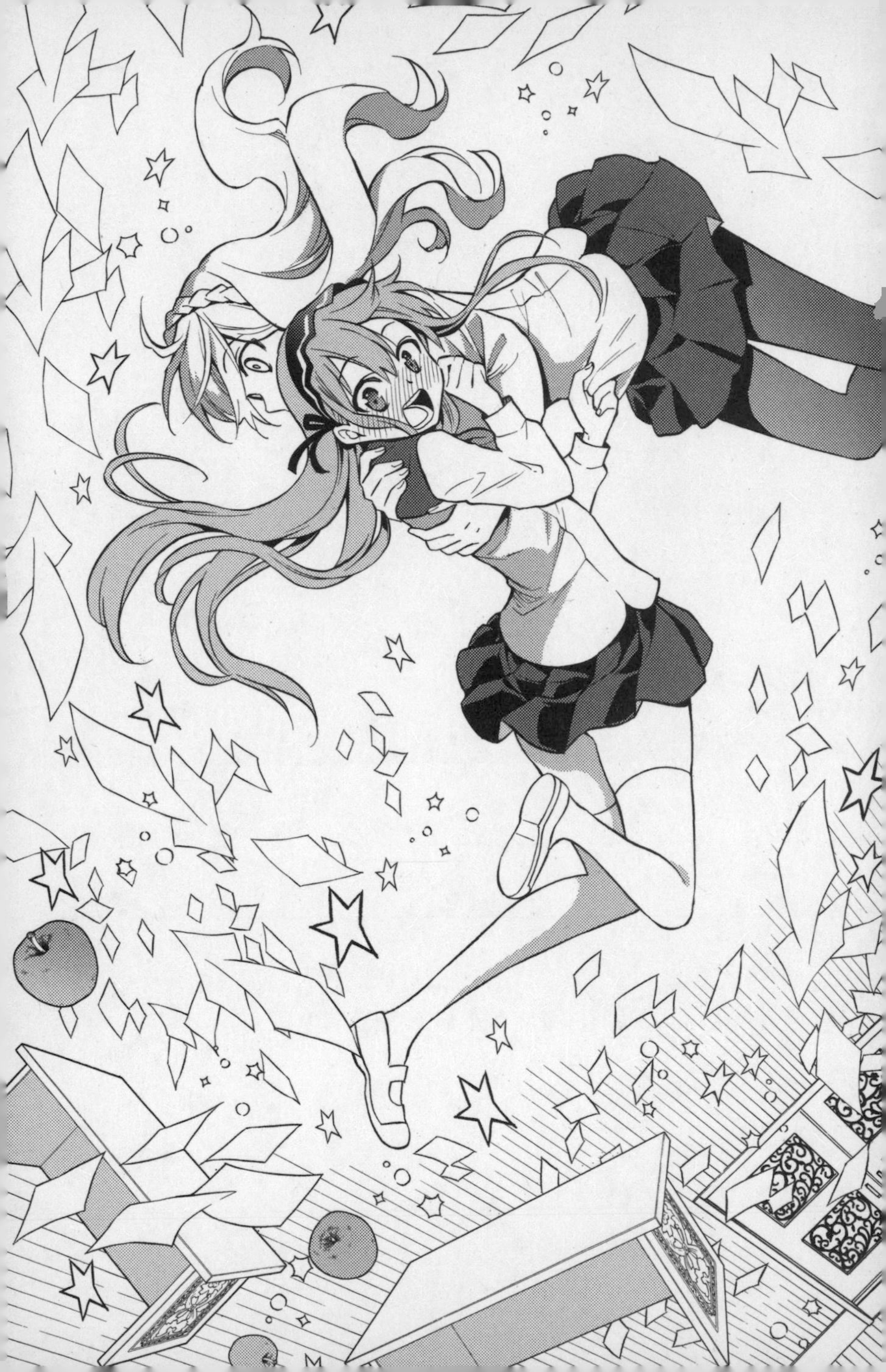

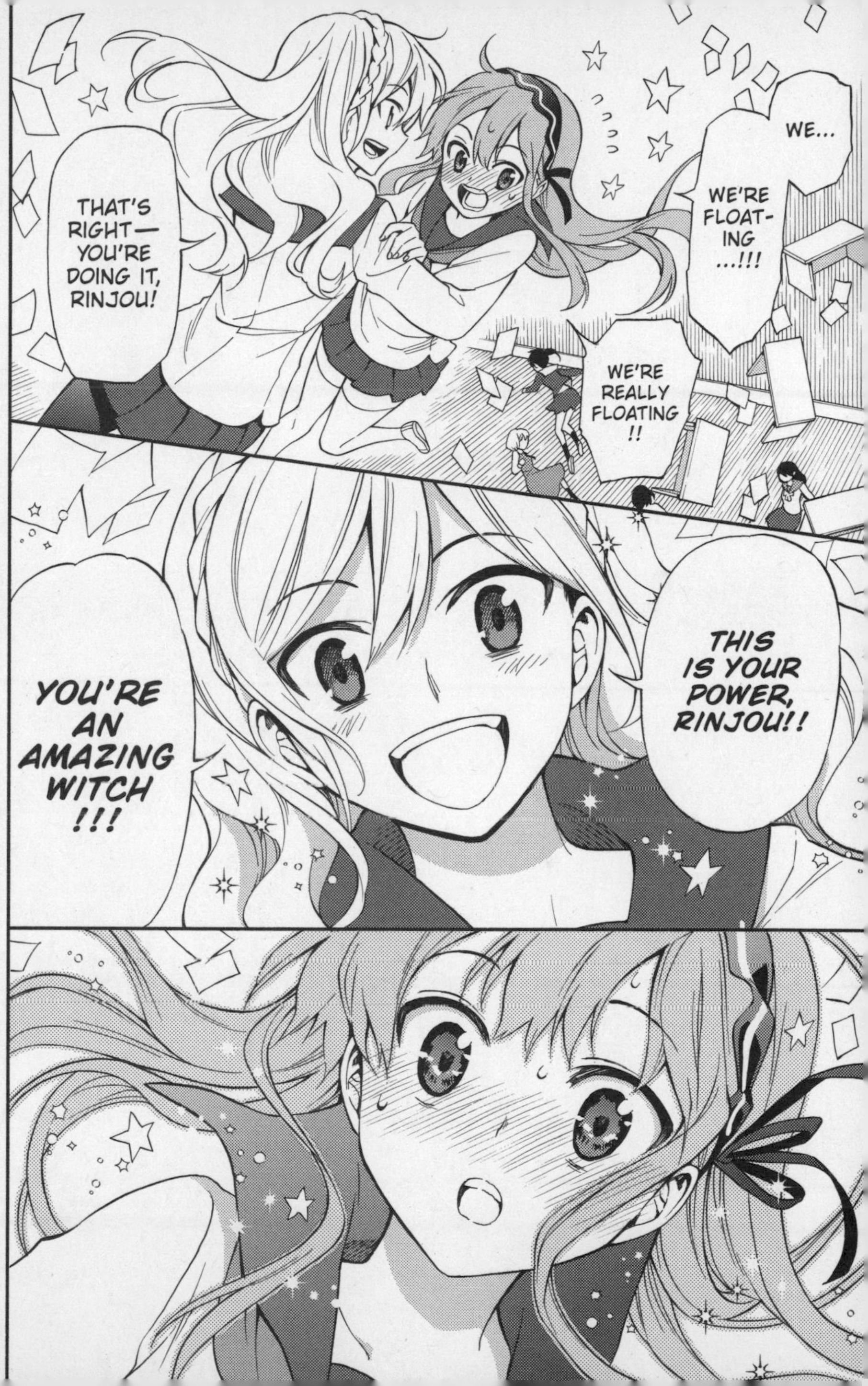
WE...
WE'RE FLOATING...!!!
WE'RE REALLY FLOATING!!
THAT'S RIGHT—YOU'RE DOING IT, RINJOU!
THIS IS YOUR POWER, RINJOU!!
YOU'RE AN AMAZING WITCH!!!

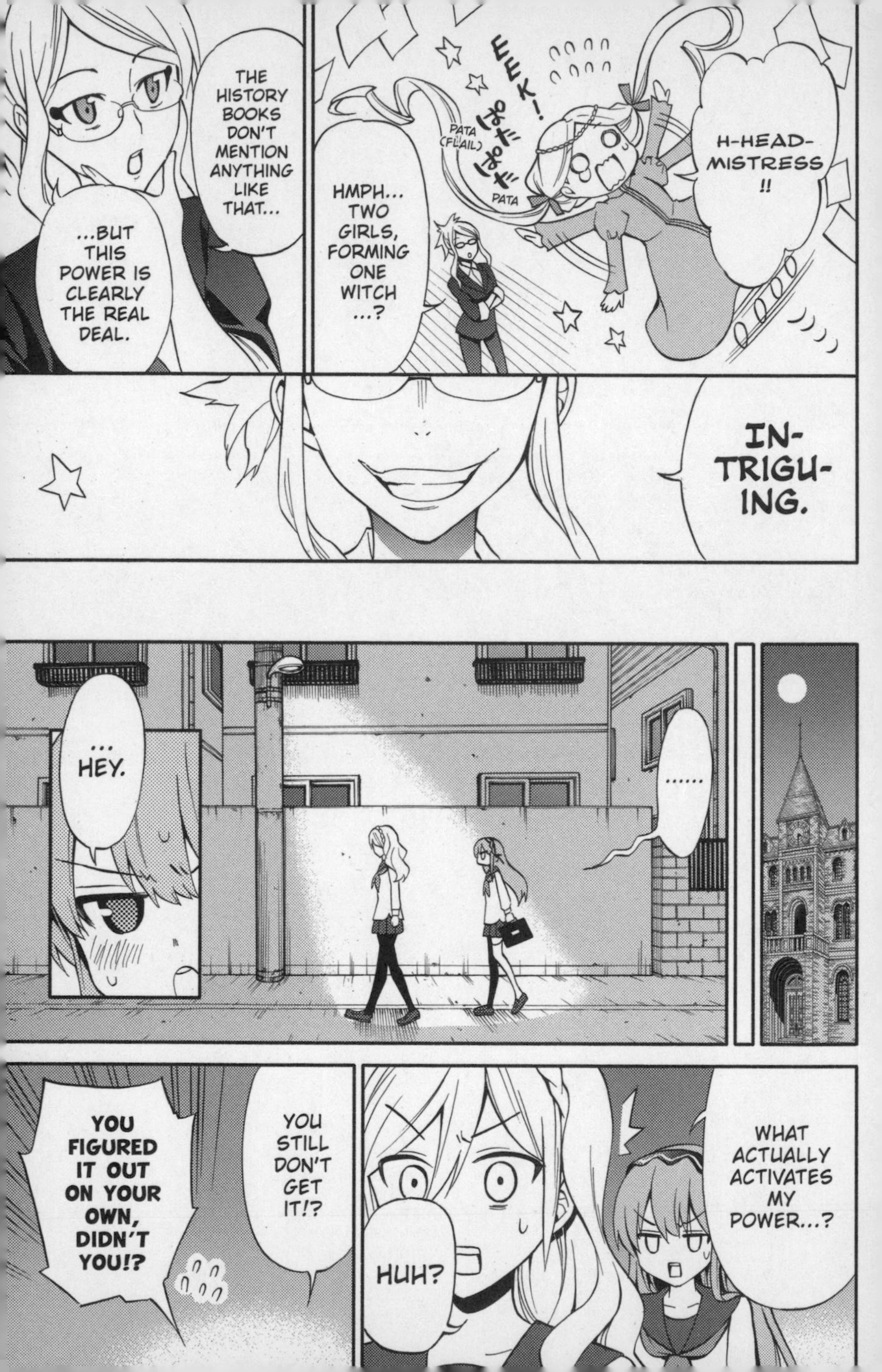
H-HEAD-MISTRESS!!
EEK!
PATA (FLAIL) PATA
ぱたぱた
HMPH... TWO GIRLS, FORMING ONE WITCH...?
THE HISTORY BOOKS DON'T MENTION ANYTHING LIKE THAT...
...BUT THIS POWER IS CLEARLY THE REAL DEAL.
IN-TRIGU-ING.
......
... HEY.
WHAT ACTUALLY ACTIVATES MY POWER...?
HUH?
YOU STILL DON'T GET IT!?
YOU FIGURED IT OUT ON YOUR OWN, DIDN'T YOU!?

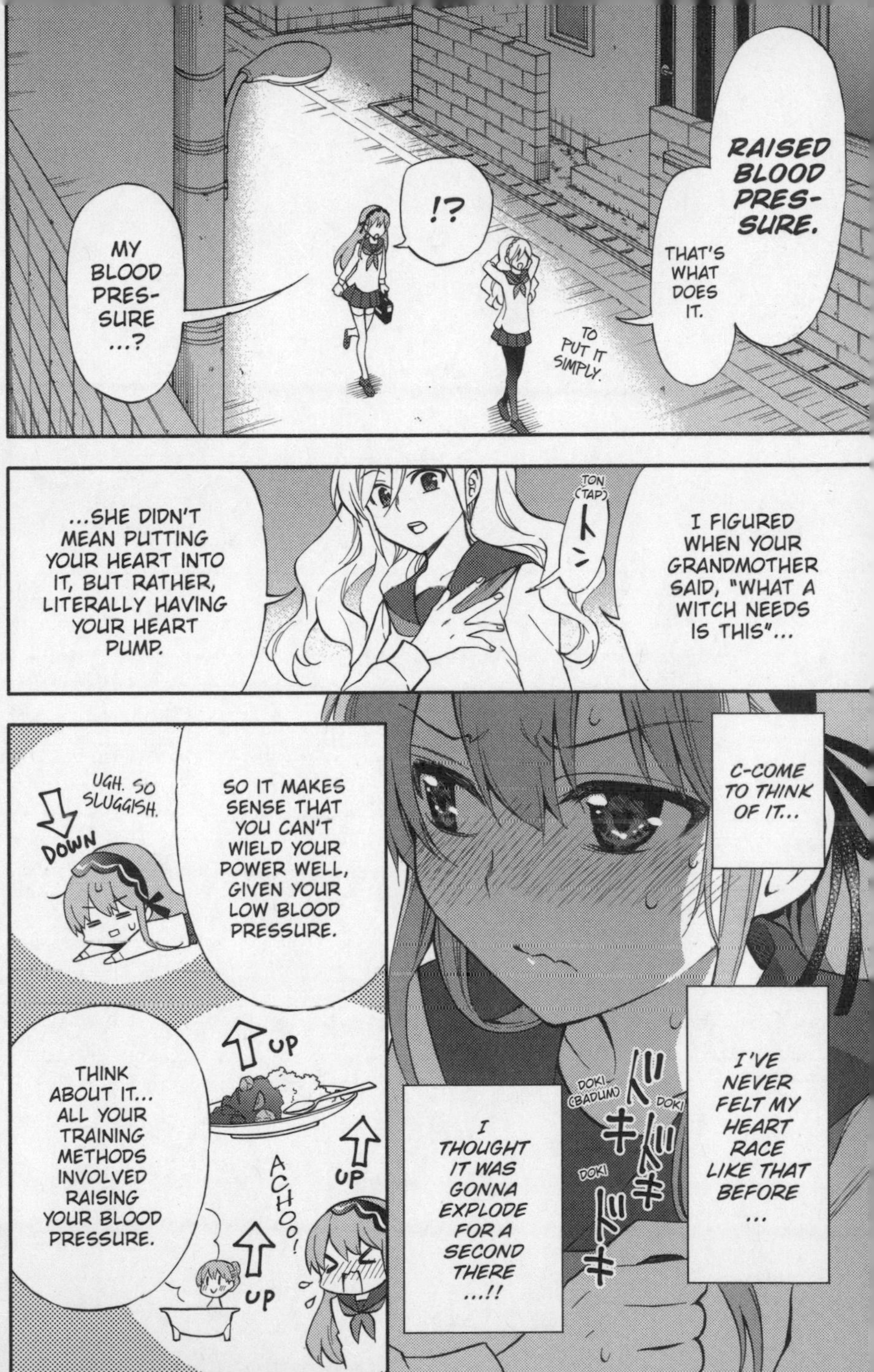
RAISED BLOOD PRES-SURE.
THAT'S WHAT DOES IT.
TO PUT IT SIMPLY.
!?
MY BLOOD PRES-SURE...?
I FIGURED WHEN YOUR GRANDMOTHER SAID, "WHAT A WITCH NEEDS IS THIS"...
TON (TAP)
...SHE DIDN'T MEAN PUTTING YOUR HEART INTO IT, BUT RATHER, LITERALLY HAVING YOUR HEART PUMP.
C-COME TO THINK OF IT...
I'VE NEVER FELT MY HEART RACE LIKE THAT BEFORE...
DOKI (BADUM) DOKI DOKI
I THOUGHT IT WAS GONNA EXPLODE FOR A SECOND THERE...!!
SO IT MAKES SENSE THAT YOU CAN'T WIELD YOUR POWER WELL, GIVEN YOUR LOW BLOOD PRESSURE.
UGH. SO SLUGGISH.
DOWN
THINK ABOUT IT... ALL YOUR TRAINING METHODS INVOLVED RAISING YOUR BLOOD PRESSURE.
UP
UP
ACHOO!
UP

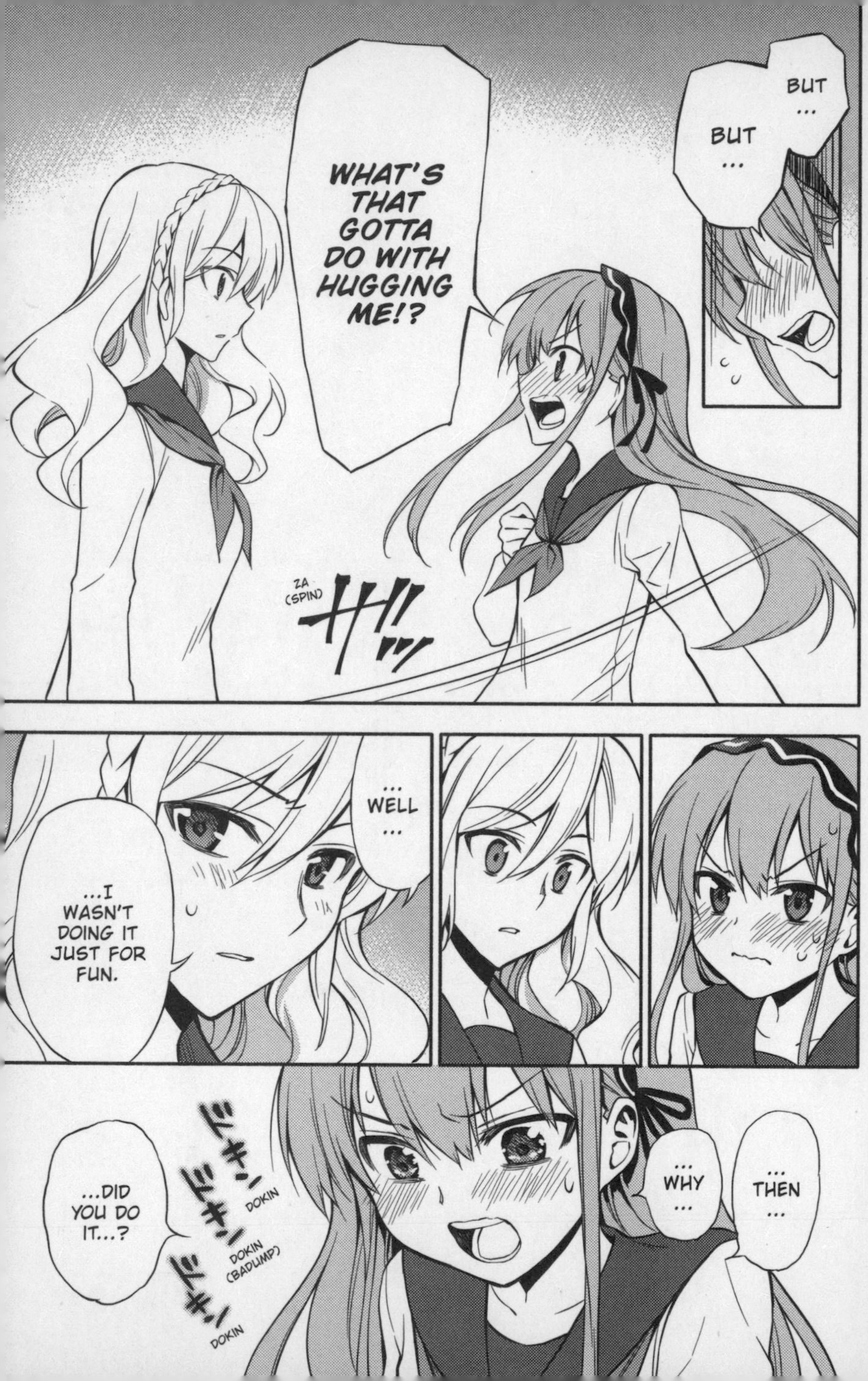

BUT ...
BUT ...
WHAT'S THAT GOTTA DO WITH HUGGING ME!?
ZA (SPIN)
... WELL ...
...I WASN'T DOING IT JUST FOR FUN.
... THEN ...
... WHY ...
...DID YOU DO IT...?
DOKIN
DOKIN (BADUMP)
DOKIN

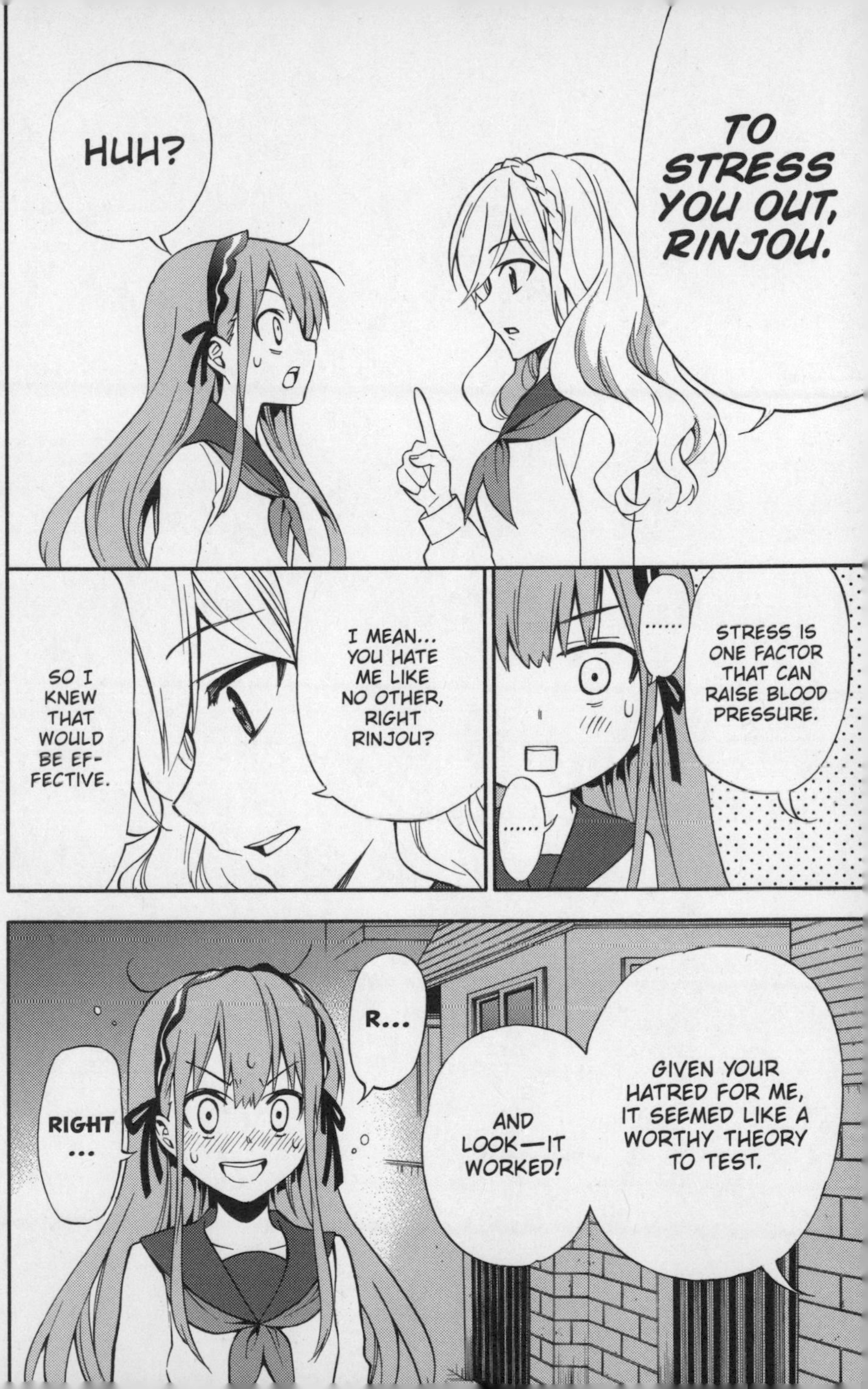
TO STRESS YOU OUT, RINJOU.
HUH?
STRESS IS ONE FACTOR THAT CAN RAISE BLOOD PRESSURE.
......
......
I MEAN... YOU HATE ME LIKE NO OTHER, RIGHT RINJOU?
SO I KNEW THAT WOULD BE EF-FECTIVE.
GIVEN YOUR HATRED FOR ME, IT SEEMED LIKE A WORTHY THEORY TO TEST.
AND LOOK—IT WORKED!
R...
RIGHT...

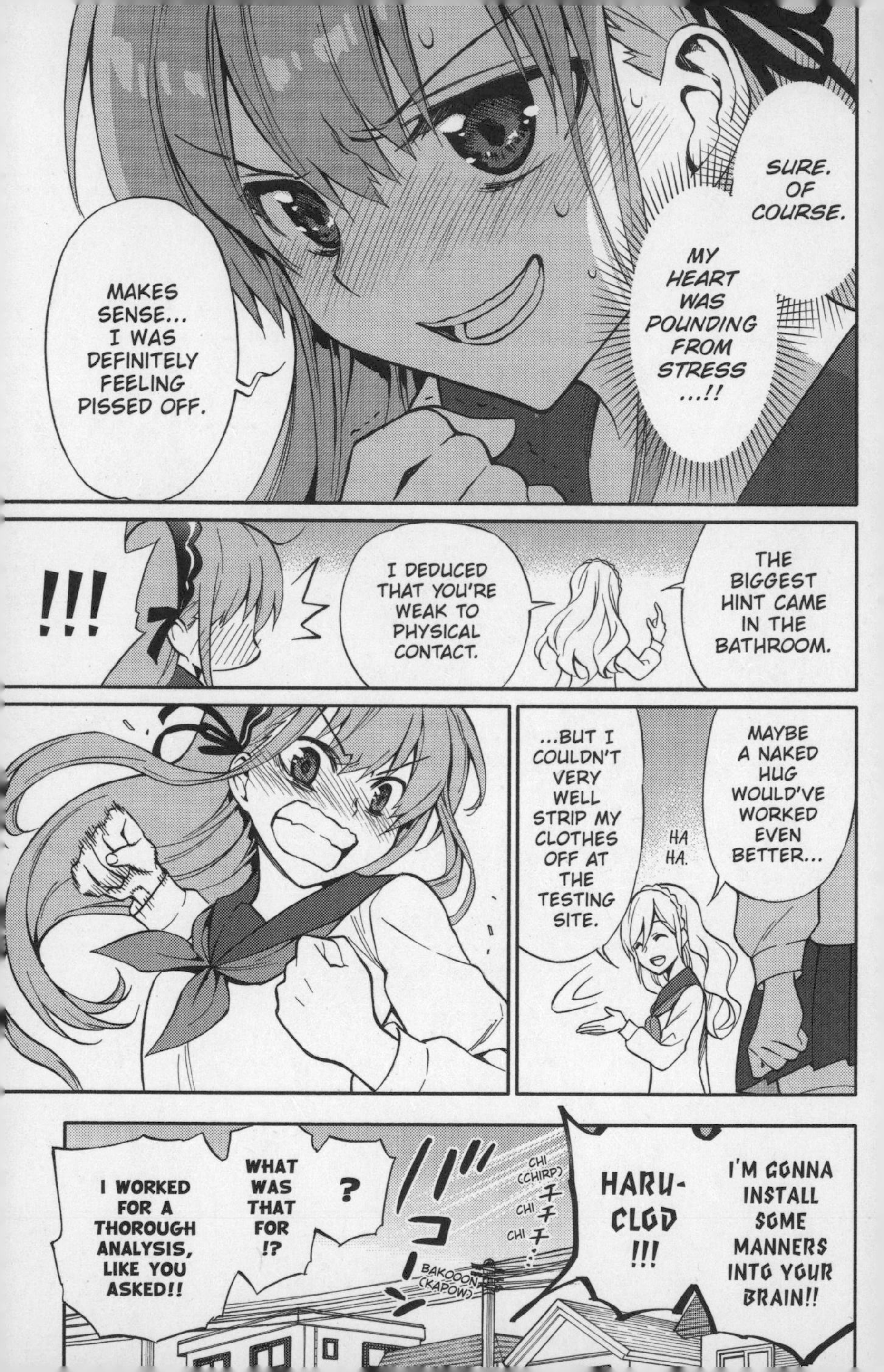
SURE. OF COURSE.
MY HEART WAS POUNDING FROM STRESS ...!!
MAKES SENSE... I WAS DEFINITELY FEELING PISSED OFF.
THE BIGGEST HINT CAME IN THE BATHROOM.
I DEDUCED THAT YOU'RE WEAK TO PHYSICAL CONTACT.
!!!
MAYBE A NAKED HUG WOULD'VE WORKED EVEN BETTER...
HA HA.
...BUT I COULDN'T VERY WELL STRIP MY CLOTHES OFF AT THE TESTING SITE.
I'M GONNA INSTALL SOME MANNERS INTO YOUR BRAIN!!
HARU-CLOD!!!
CHI (CHIRP)
CHI
CHI
BAKOOON (KAPOW)
?
WHAT WAS THAT FOR!?
I WORKED FOR A THOROUGH ANALYSIS, LIKE YOU ASKED!!

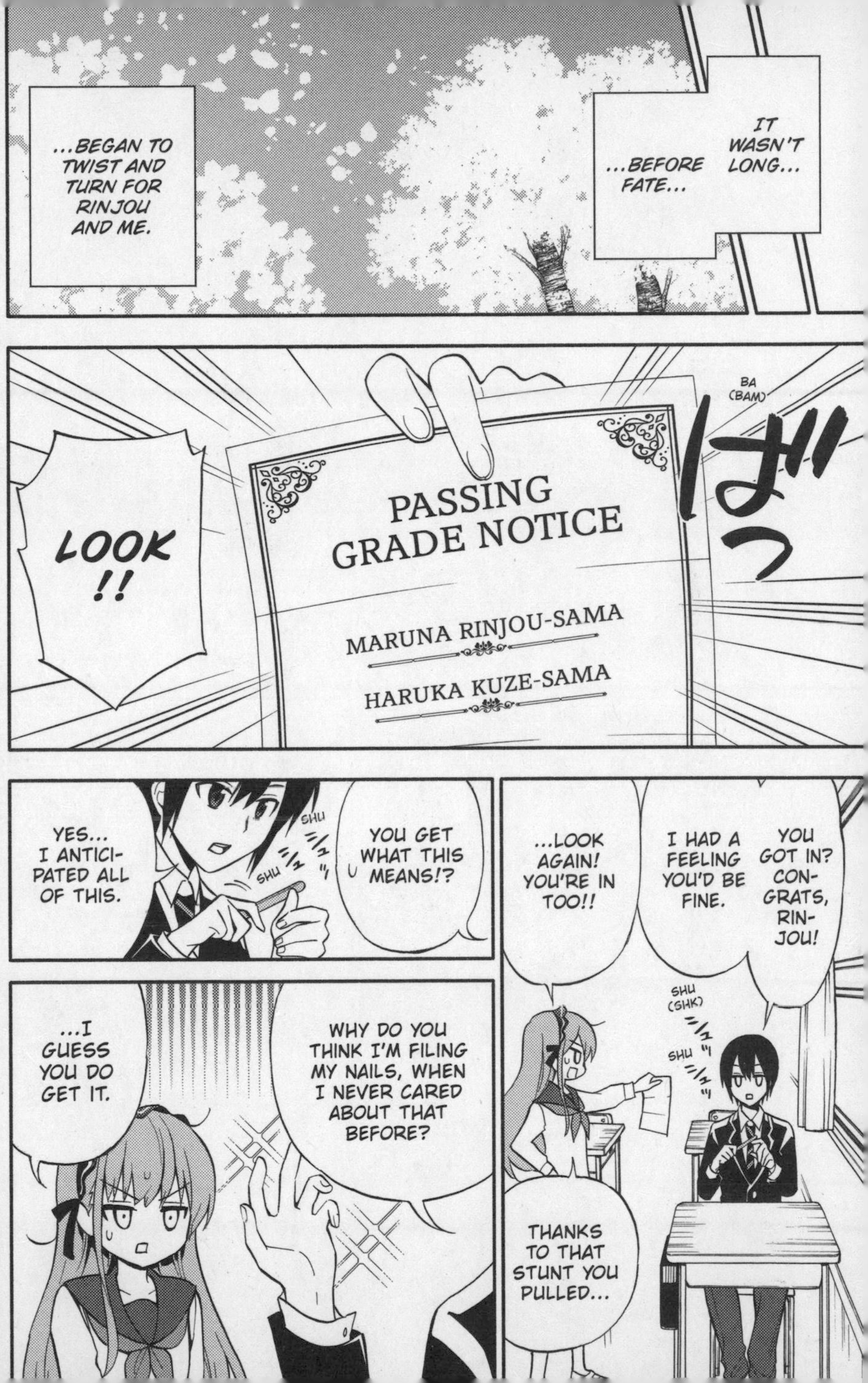
IT WASN'T LONG...
...BEFORE FATE...
...BEGAN TO TWIST AND TURN FOR RINJOU AND ME.
BA (BAM)
ばっ
PASSING GRADE NOTICE
MARUNA RINJOU-SAMA
HARUKA KUZE-SAMA
LOOK!!
YOU GOT IN? CON-GRATS, RIN-JOU!
I HAD A FEELING YOU'D BE FINE.
...LOOK AGAIN! YOU'RE IN TOO!!
SHU (SHK)
SHU
THANKS TO THAT STUNT YOU PULLED...
YOU GET WHAT THIS MEANS!?
SHU
SHU
YES... I ANTICI-PATED ALL OF THIS.
WHY DO YOU THINK I'M FILING MY NAILS, WHEN I NEVER CARED ABOUT THAT BEFORE?
...I GUESS YOU DO GET IT.

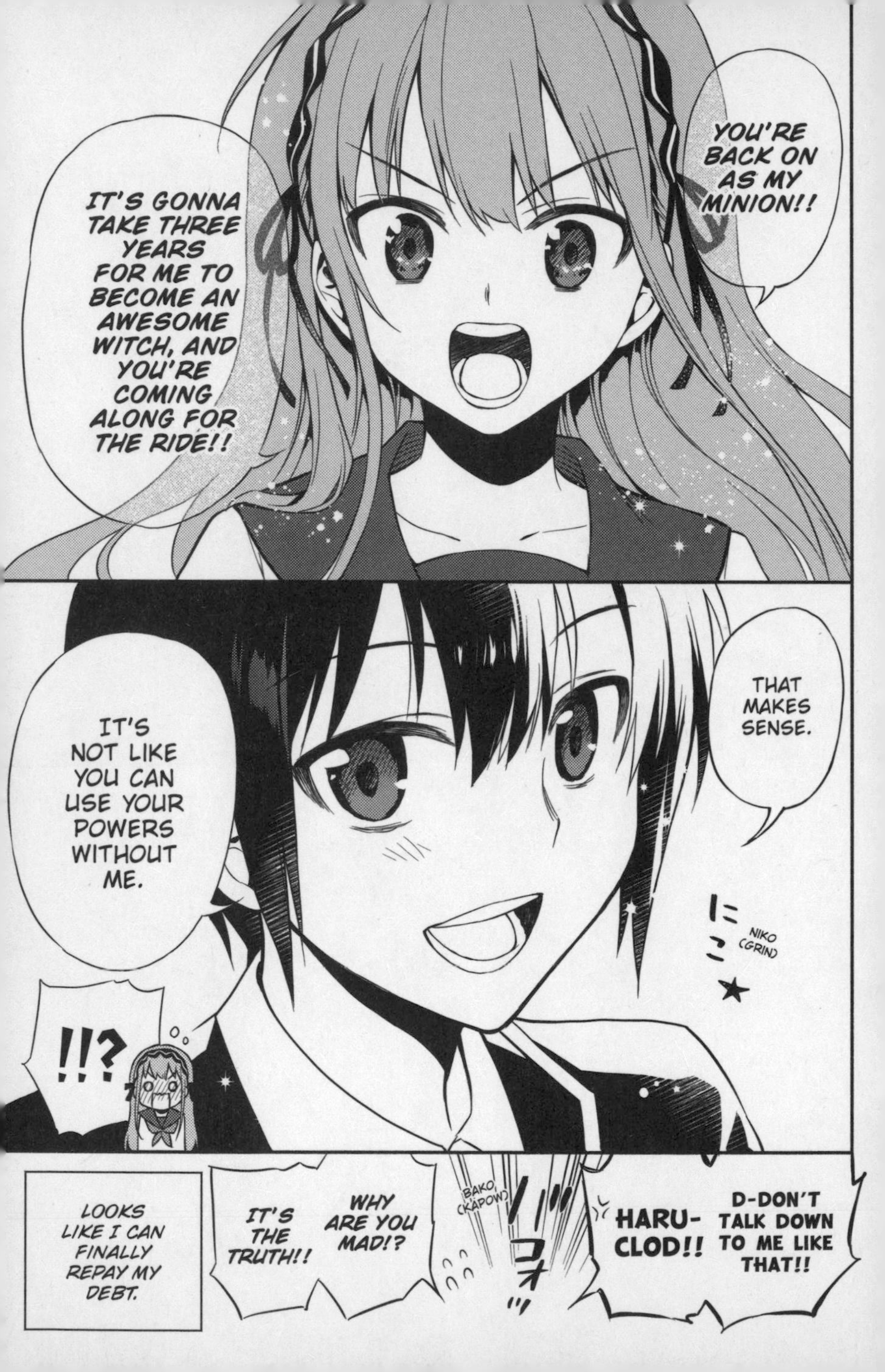
YOU'RE BACK ON AS MY MINION!!
IT'S GONNA TAKE THREE YEARS FOR ME TO BECOME AN AWESOME WITCH, AND YOU'RE COMING ALONG FOR THE RIDE!!
THAT MAKES SENSE.
IT'S NOT LIKE YOU CAN USE YOUR POWERS WITHOUT ME.
にこ
NIKO (GRIN)
!!?
D-DON'T TALK DOWN TO ME LIKE THAT!!
HARU-CLOD!!
BAKO (KAPOW)
WHY ARE YOU MAD!?
IT'S THE TRUTH!!
LOOKS LIKE I CAN FINALLY REPAY MY DEBT.

If Witch, Then Which?

LET'S HEAD TO SCHOOL TOGETHER.
YOU'RE WEIRDLY INTO THIS, AREN'T YOU?
? ?

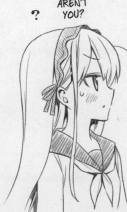

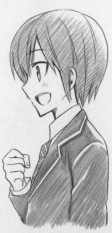

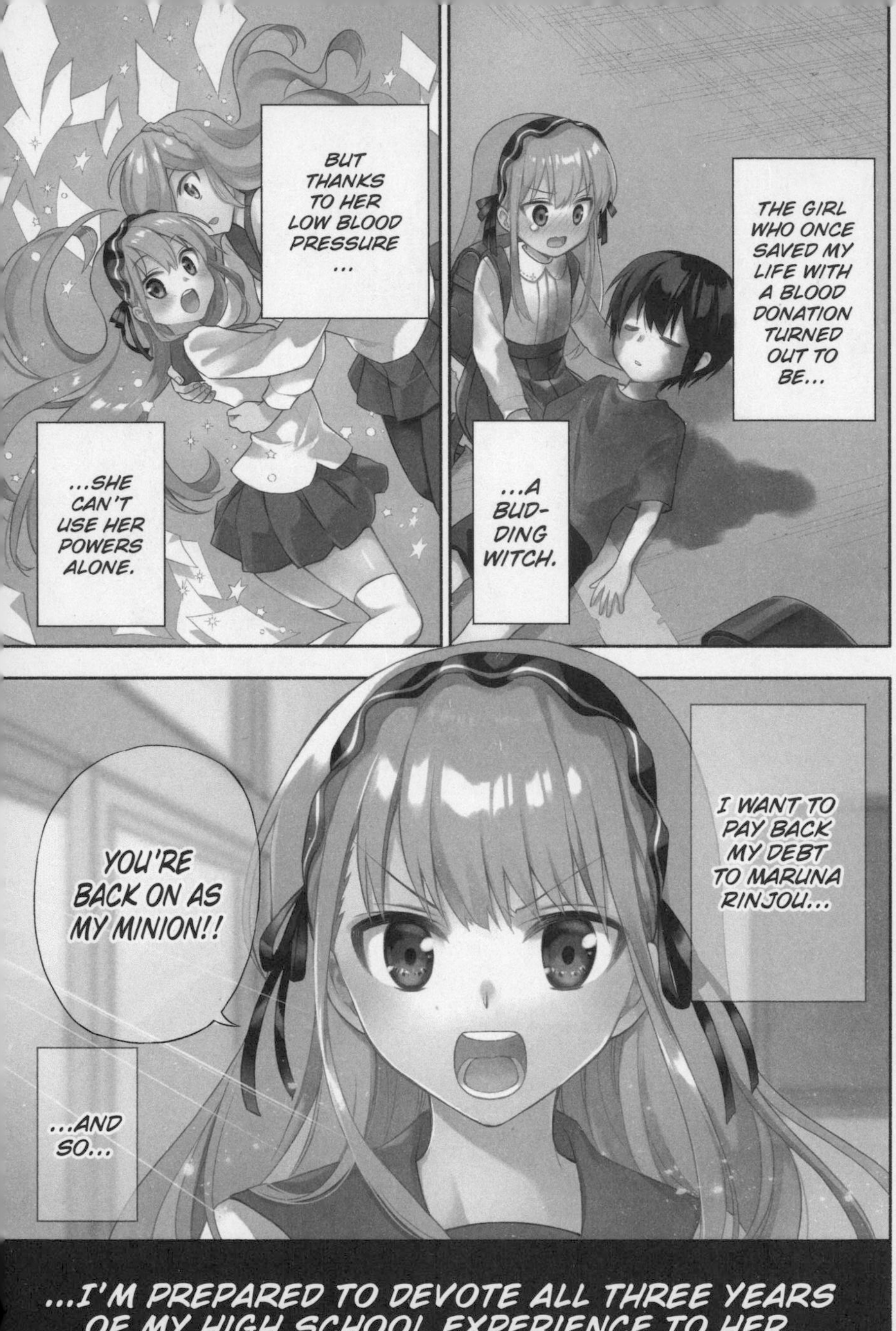
THE GIRL WHO ONCE SAVED MY LIFE WITH A BLOOD DONATION TURNED OUT TO BE...
...A BUD-DING WITCH.
BUT THANKS TO HER LOW BLOOD PRESSURE...
...SHE CAN'T USE HER POWERS ALONE.
I WANT TO PAY BACK MY DEBT TO MARUNA RINJOU...
YOU'RE BACK ON AS MY MINION!!
...AND SO...
...I'M PREPARED TO DEVOTE ALL THREE YEARS OF MY HIGH SCHOOL EXPERIENCE TO HER.

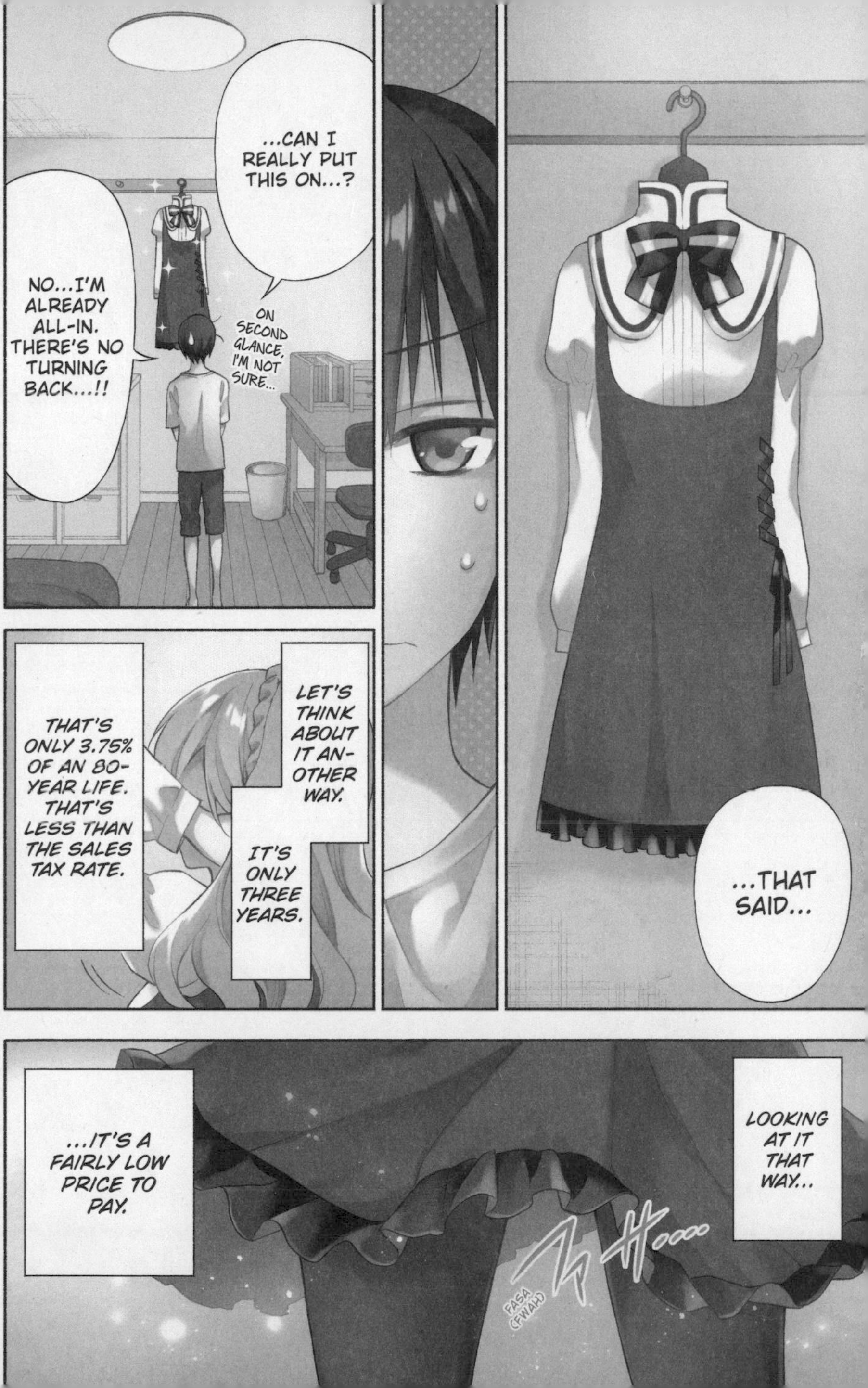
...THAT SAID...
...CAN I REALLY PUT THIS ON...?
ON SECOND GLANCE, I'M NOT SURE...
NO...I'M ALREADY ALL-IN. THERE'S NO TURNING BACK...!!
LET'S THINK ABOUT IT AN-OTHER WAY.
IT'S ONLY THREE YEARS.
THAT'S ONLY 3.75% OF AN 80-YEAR LIFE. THAT'S LESS THAN THE SALES TAX RATE.
LOOKING AT IT THAT WAY...
FASA (FWAH)
...IT'S A FAIRLY LOW PRICE TO PAY.

MAGIC.2

A Witch's Power Is Love

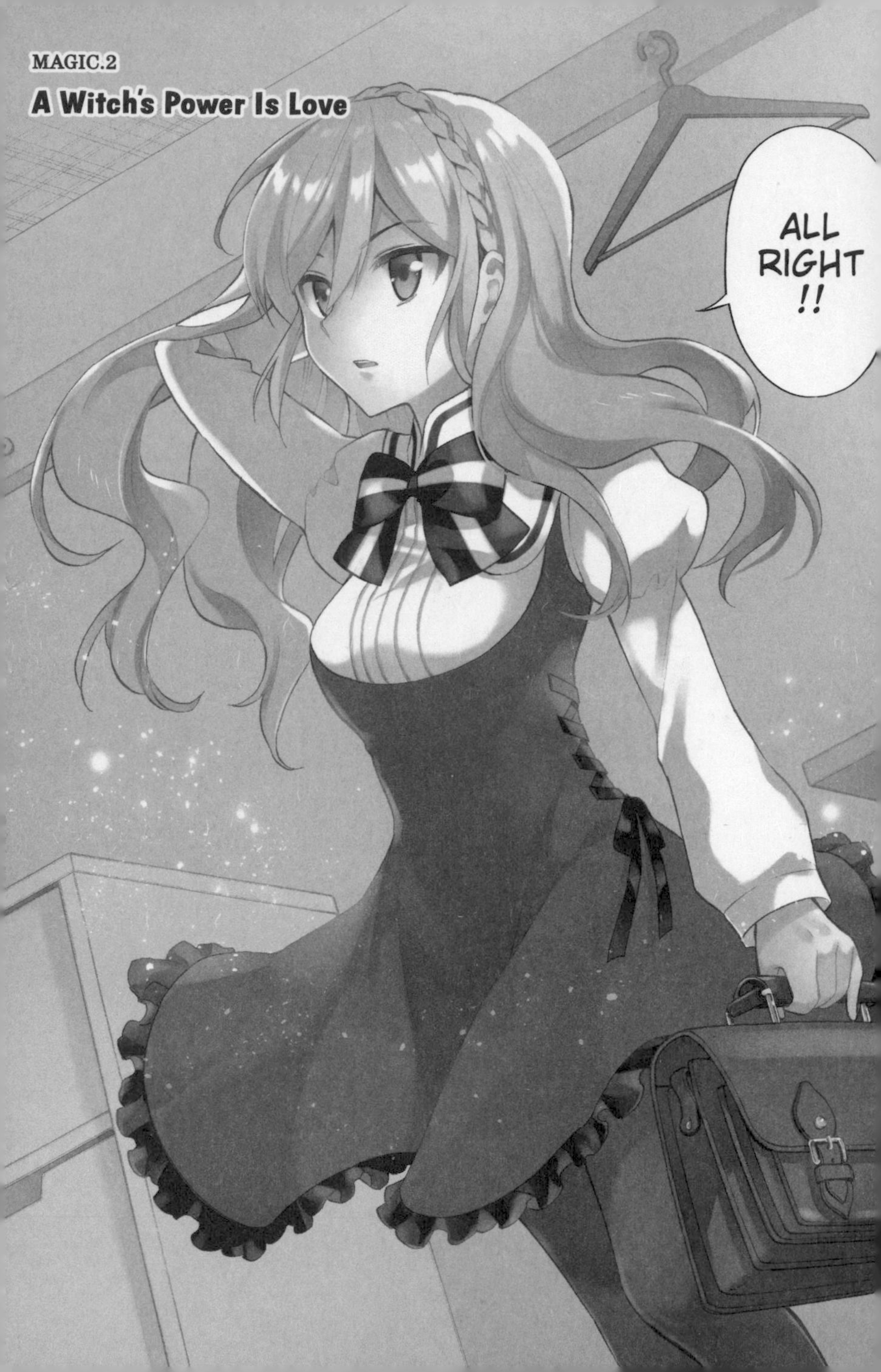
ALL RIGHT !!

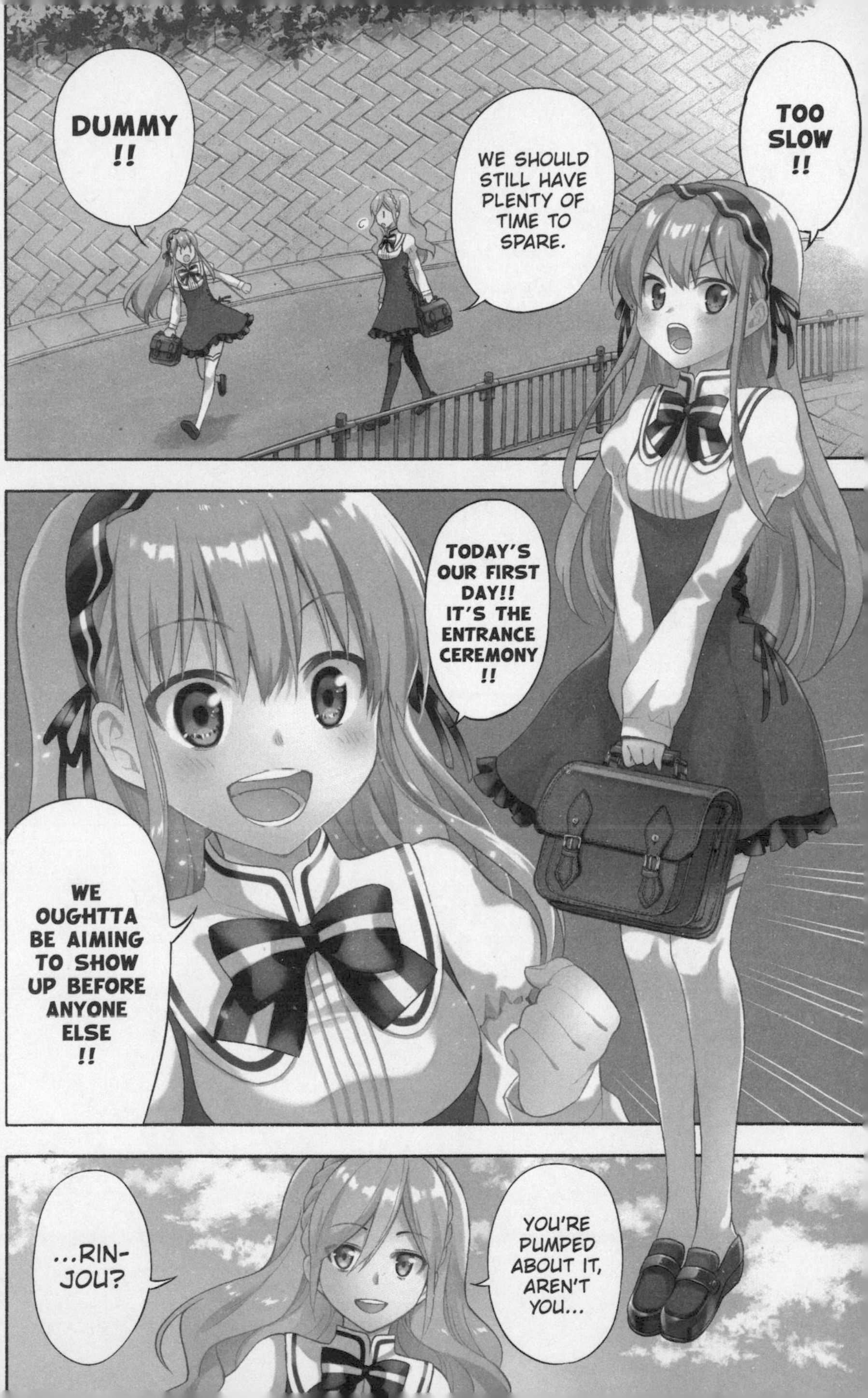
TOO SLOW!!
WE SHOULD STILL HAVE PLENTY OF TIME TO SPARE.
DUMMY!!
TODAY'S OUR FIRST DAY!! IT'S THE ENTRANCE CEREMONY!!
WE OUGHTTA BE AIMING TO SHOW UP BEFORE ANYONE ELSE!!
YOU'RE PUMPED ABOUT IT, AREN'T YOU...
...RIN-JOU?

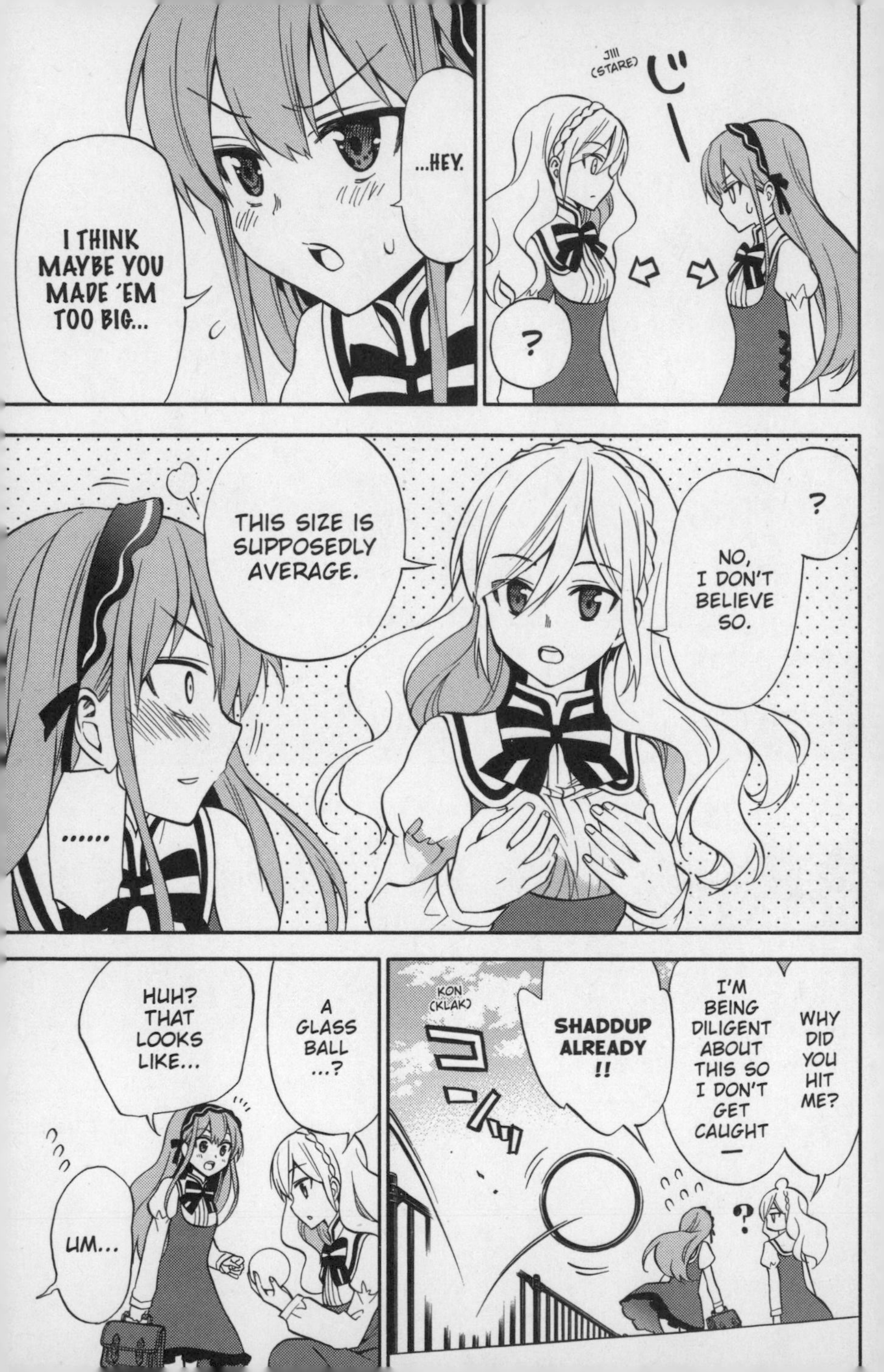
JIII (STARE)
?
...HEY.
I THINK MAYBE YOU MADE 'EM TOO BIG...
?
NO, I DON'T BELIEVE SO.
THIS SIZE IS SUPPOSEDLY AVERAGE.
......
I'M BEING DILIGENT ABOUT THIS SO I DON'T GET CAUGHT—
WHY DID YOU HIT ME?
SHADDUP ALREADY!!
KON (KLAK)
A GLASS BALL ...?
HUH? THAT LOOKS LIKE...
UM...

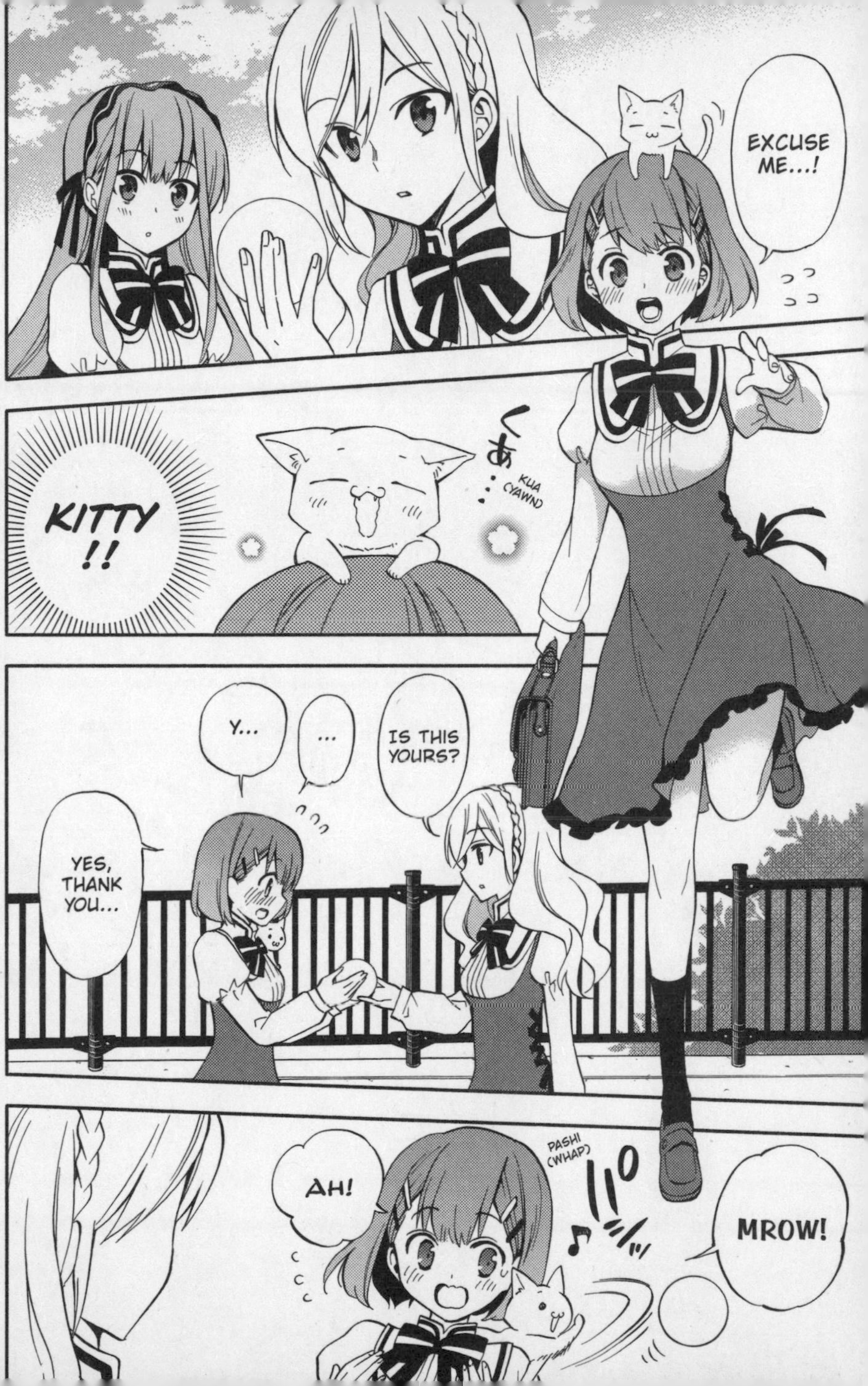
EXCUSE ME...!
くあ…
KUA (YAWN)
KITTY!!
IS THIS YOURS?
...
Y...
YES, THANK YOU...
MROW!
PASHI (WHAP)
AH!

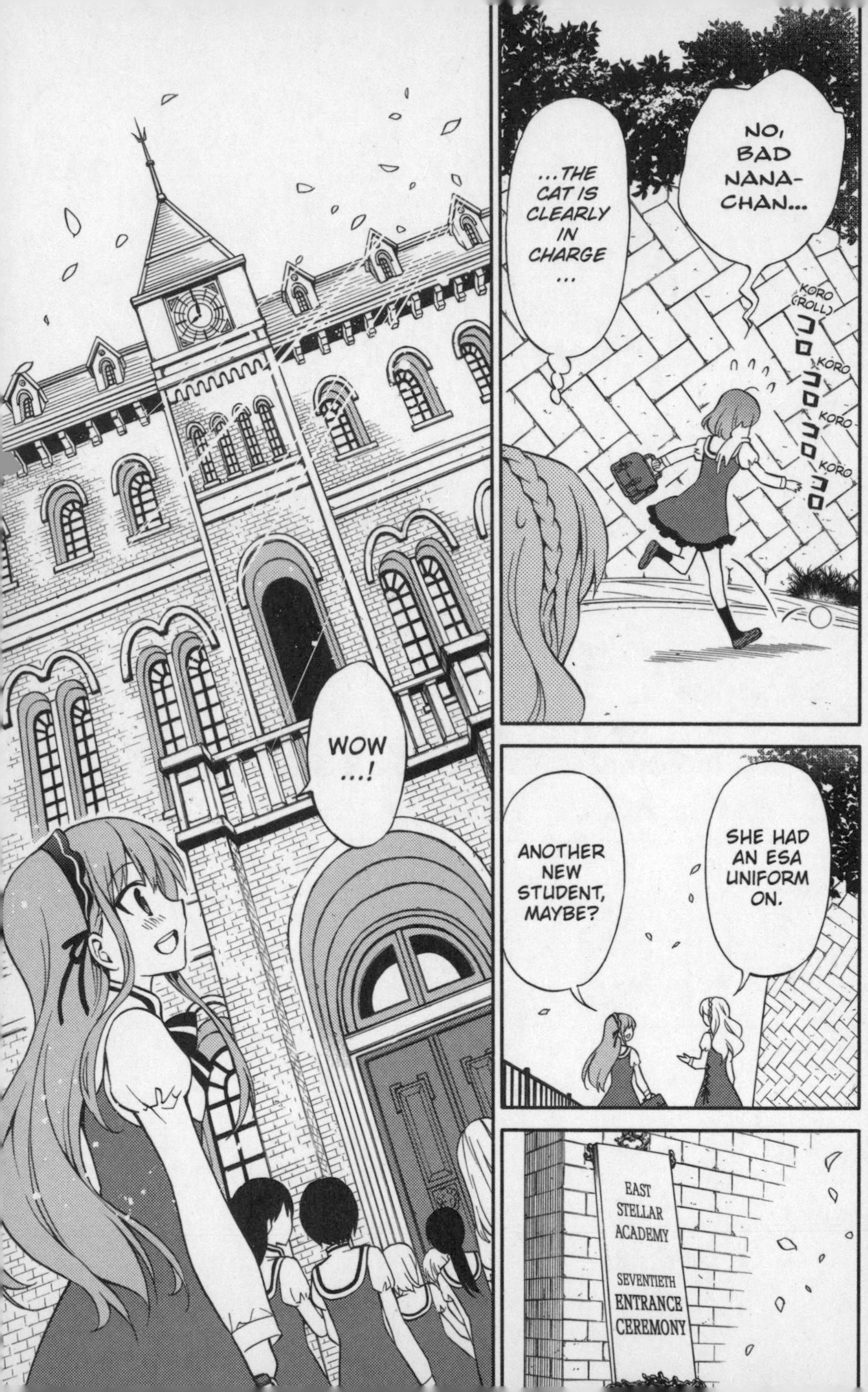
NO, BAD NANA-CHAN...
...THE CAT IS CLEARLY IN CHARGE...
KORO (ROLL)
コロ
KORO
コロ
KORO
コロ
KORO
コロ
SHE HAD AN ESA UNIFORM ON.
ANOTHER NEW STUDENT, MAYBE?
EAST STELLAR ACADEMY
SEVENTIETH ENTRANCE CEREMONY
WOW ...!

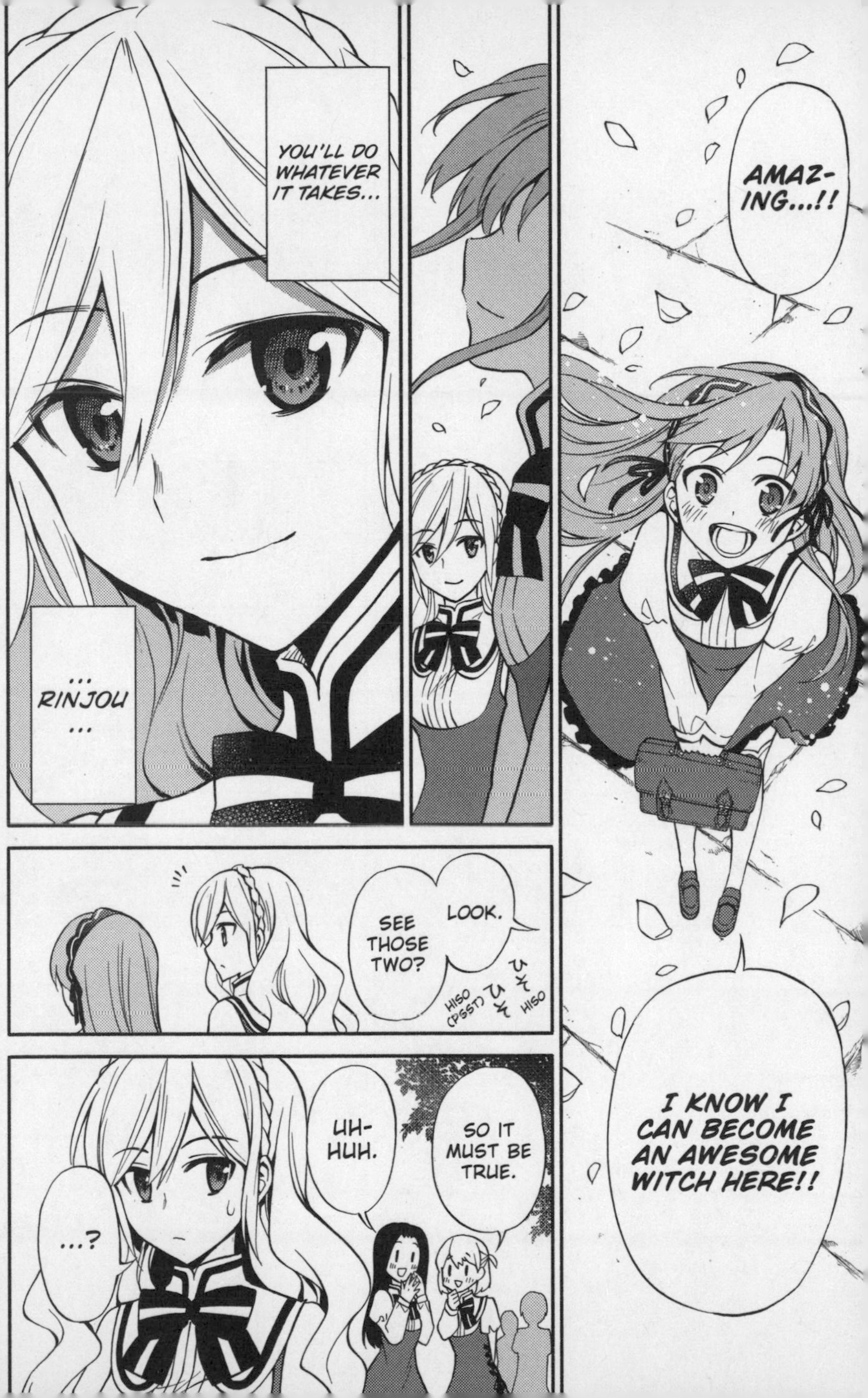
AMAZ-ING...!!
I KNOW I CAN BECOME AN AWESOME WITCH HERE!!
YOU'LL DO WHATEVER IT TAKES...
... RINJOU ...
LOOK.
SEE THOSE TWO?
ひそ ひそ
HISO (PSST) HISO
SO IT MUST BE TRUE.
UH-HUH.
...?

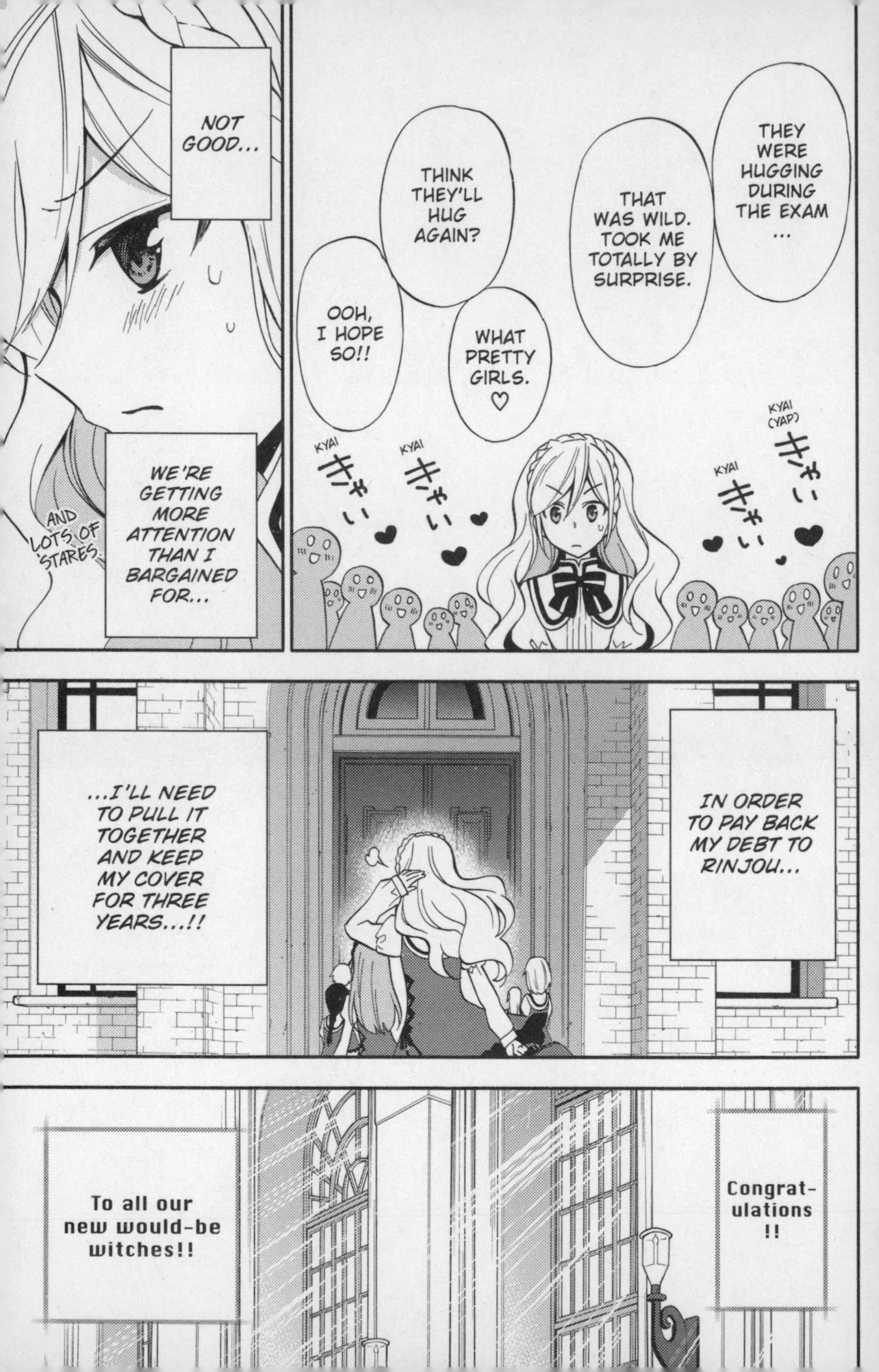
THEY WERE HUGGING DURING THE EXAM ...
THAT WAS WILD. TOOK ME TOTALLY BY SURPRISE.
THINK THEY'LL HUG AGAIN?
WHAT PRETTY GIRLS. ♡
OOH, I HOPE SO!!
KYAI (YAP)
KYAI
KYAI
KYAI
NOT GOOD...
WE'RE GETTING MORE ATTENTION THAN I BARGAINED FOR...
AND LOTS OF STARES.
IN ORDER TO PAY BACK MY DEBT TO RINJOU...
...I'LL NEED TO PULL IT TOGETHER AND KEEP MY COVER FOR THREE YEARS...!!
Congrat-ulations!!
To all our new would-be witches!!

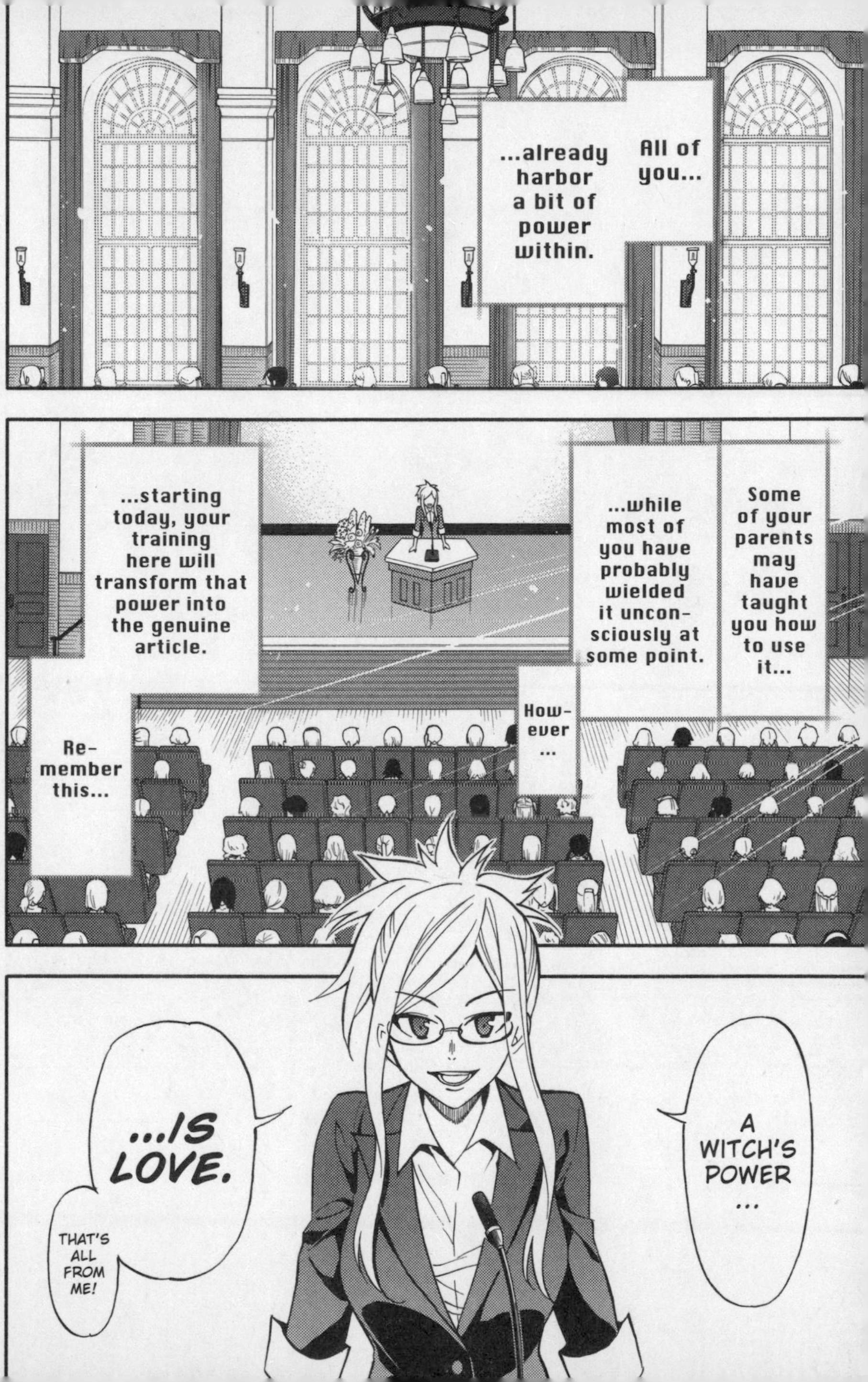
All of you...
...already harbor a bit of power within.
Some of your parents may have taught you how to use it...
...while most of you have probably wielded it unconsciously at some point.
However...
...starting today, your training here will transform that power into the genuine article.
Remember this...
A WITCH'S POWER ...
...IS LOVE.
THAT'S ALL FROM ME!

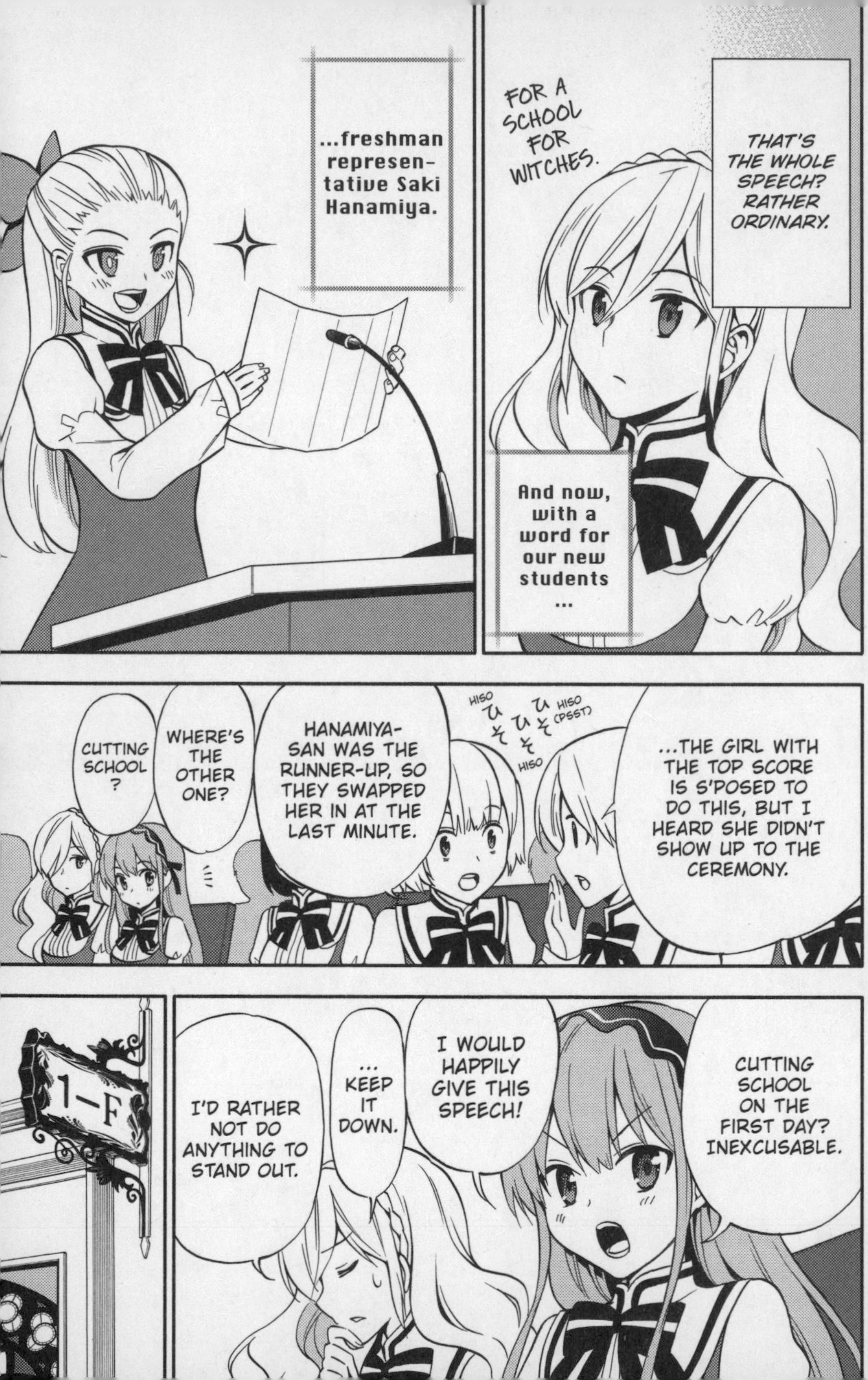

THAT'S THE WHOLE SPEECH? RATHER ORDINARY.
FOR A SCHOOL FOR WITCHES.
And now, with a word for our new students ...
...freshman representative Saki Hanamiya.
...THE GIRL WITH THE TOP SCORE IS S'POSED TO DO THIS, BUT I HEARD SHE DIDN'T SHOW UP TO THE CEREMONY.
ひそ HISO ひそ HISO ひそ HISO (PSST)
HANAMIYA-SAN WAS THE RUNNER-UP, SO THEY SWAPPED HER IN AT THE LAST MINUTE.
WHERE'S THE OTHER ONE?
CUTTING SCHOOL?
CUTTING SCHOOL ON THE FIRST DAY? INEXCUSABLE.
I WOULD HAPPILY GIVE THIS SPEECH!
... KEEP IT DOWN.
I'D RATHER NOT DO ANYTHING TO STAND OUT.
1-F

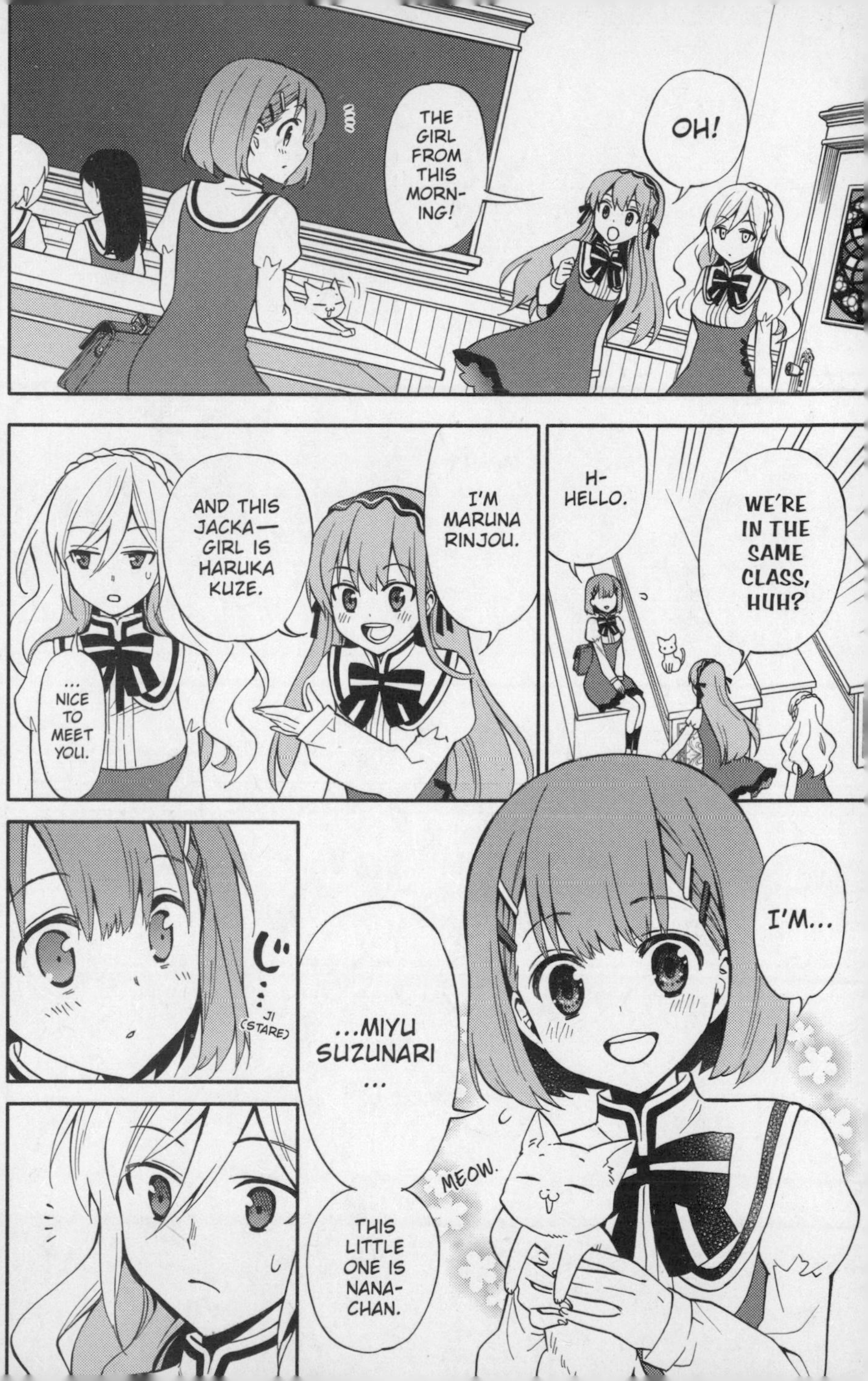
OH!
THE GIRL FROM THIS MORNING!
WE'RE IN THE SAME CLASS, HUH?
H-HELLO.
I'M MARUNA RINJOU.
AND THIS JACKA— GIRL IS HARUKA KUZE.
...NICE TO MEET YOU.
I'M...
...MIYU SUZUNARI ...
MEOW.
THIS LITTLE ONE IS NANA-CHAN.
JI (STARE)

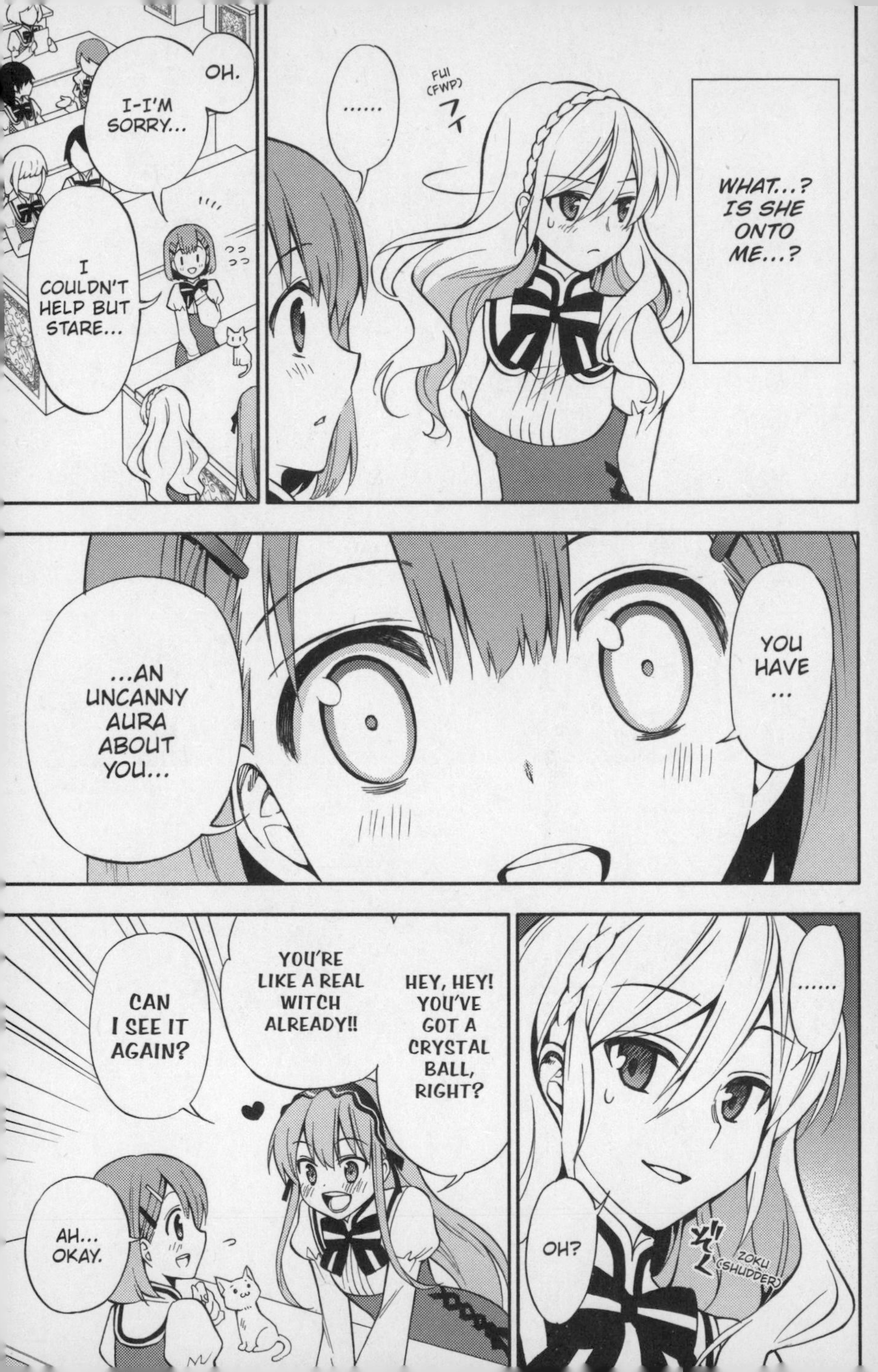
WHAT...? IS SHE ONTO ME...?
FUI (FWP)
......
OH.
I-I'M SORRY...
I COULDN'T HELP BUT STARE...
YOU HAVE ...
...AN UNCANNY AURA ABOUT YOU...
......
OH?
ZOKU (SHUDDER)
HEY, HEY! YOU'VE GOT A CRYSTAL BALL, RIGHT?
YOU'RE LIKE A REAL WITCH ALREADY!!
CAN I SEE IT AGAIN?
AH... OKAY.

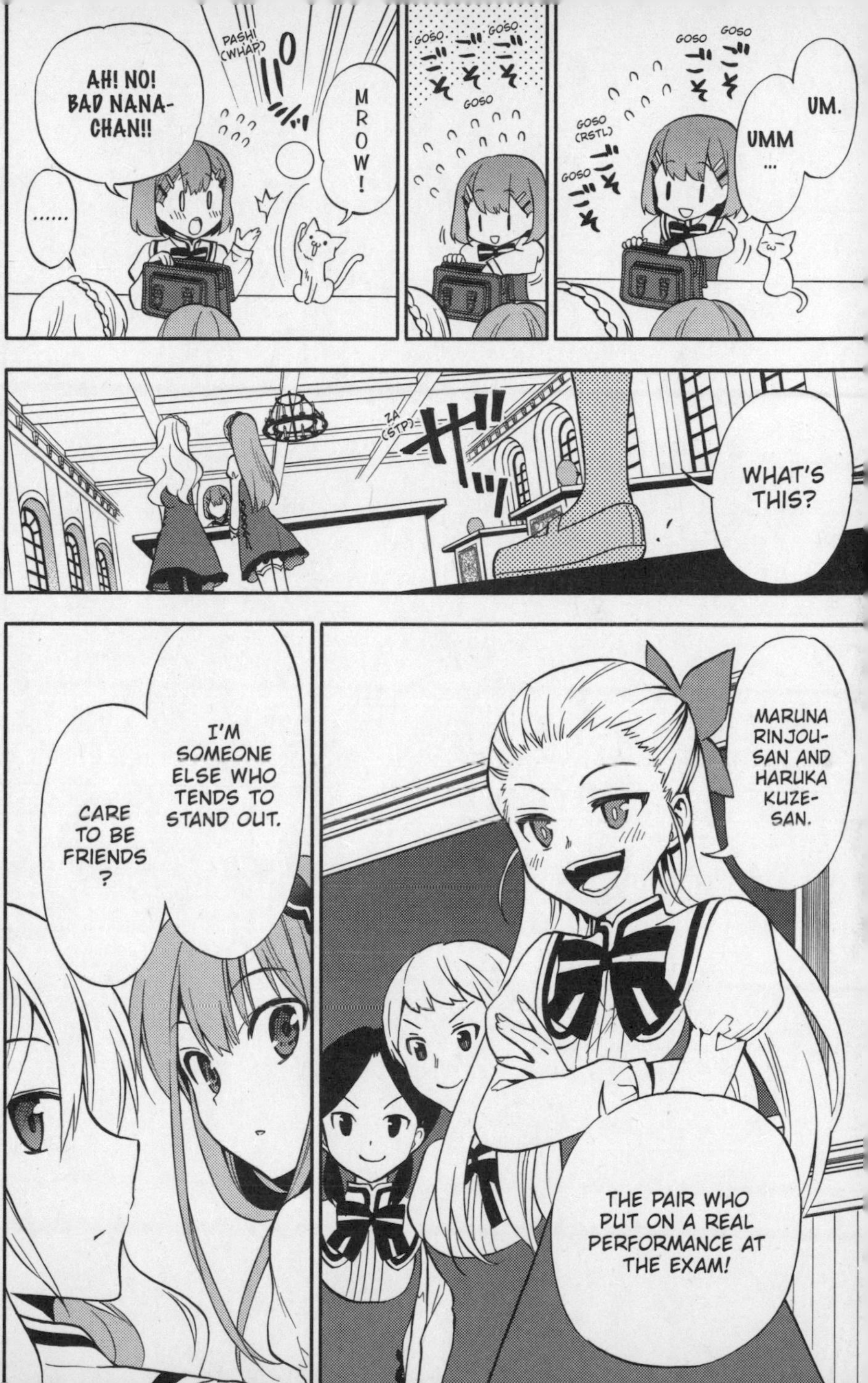
UM.
UMM ...
GOSO GOSO
GOSO (RSTL)
GOSO
GOSO GOSO
GOSO
MROW!
PASH! (WHAP)
AH! NO! BAD NANA-CHAN!!
......
WHAT'S THIS?
ZA (STP)
MARUNA RINJOU-SAN AND HARUKA KUZE-SAN.
THE PAIR WHO PUT ON A REAL PERFORMANCE AT THE EXAM!
I'M SOMEONE ELSE WHO TENDS TO STAND OUT.
CARE TO BE FRIENDS ?

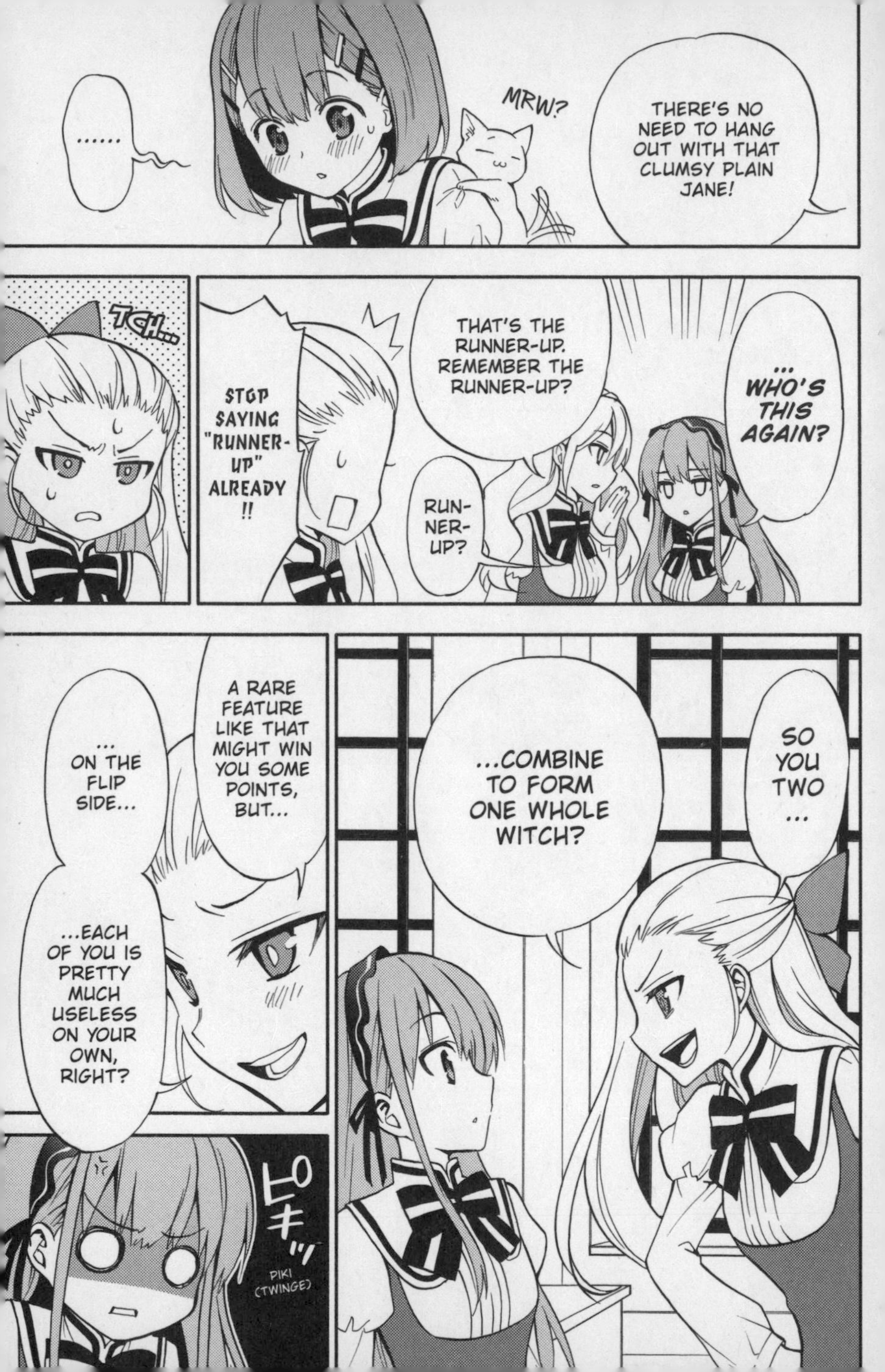
THERE'S NO NEED TO HANG OUT WITH THAT CLUMSY PLAIN JANE!
MRW?
......
... WHO'S THIS AGAIN?
THAT'S THE RUNNER-UP. REMEMBER THE RUNNER-UP?
RUN-NER-UP?
STOP SAYING "RUNNER-UP" ALREADY!!
TCH...
SO YOU TWO ...
...COMBINE TO FORM ONE WHOLE WITCH?
A RARE FEATURE LIKE THAT MIGHT WIN YOU SOME POINTS, BUT...
... ON THE FLIP SIDE...
...EACH OF YOU IS PRETTY MUCH USELESS ON YOUR OWN, RIGHT?
ピキッ
PIKI (TWINGE)

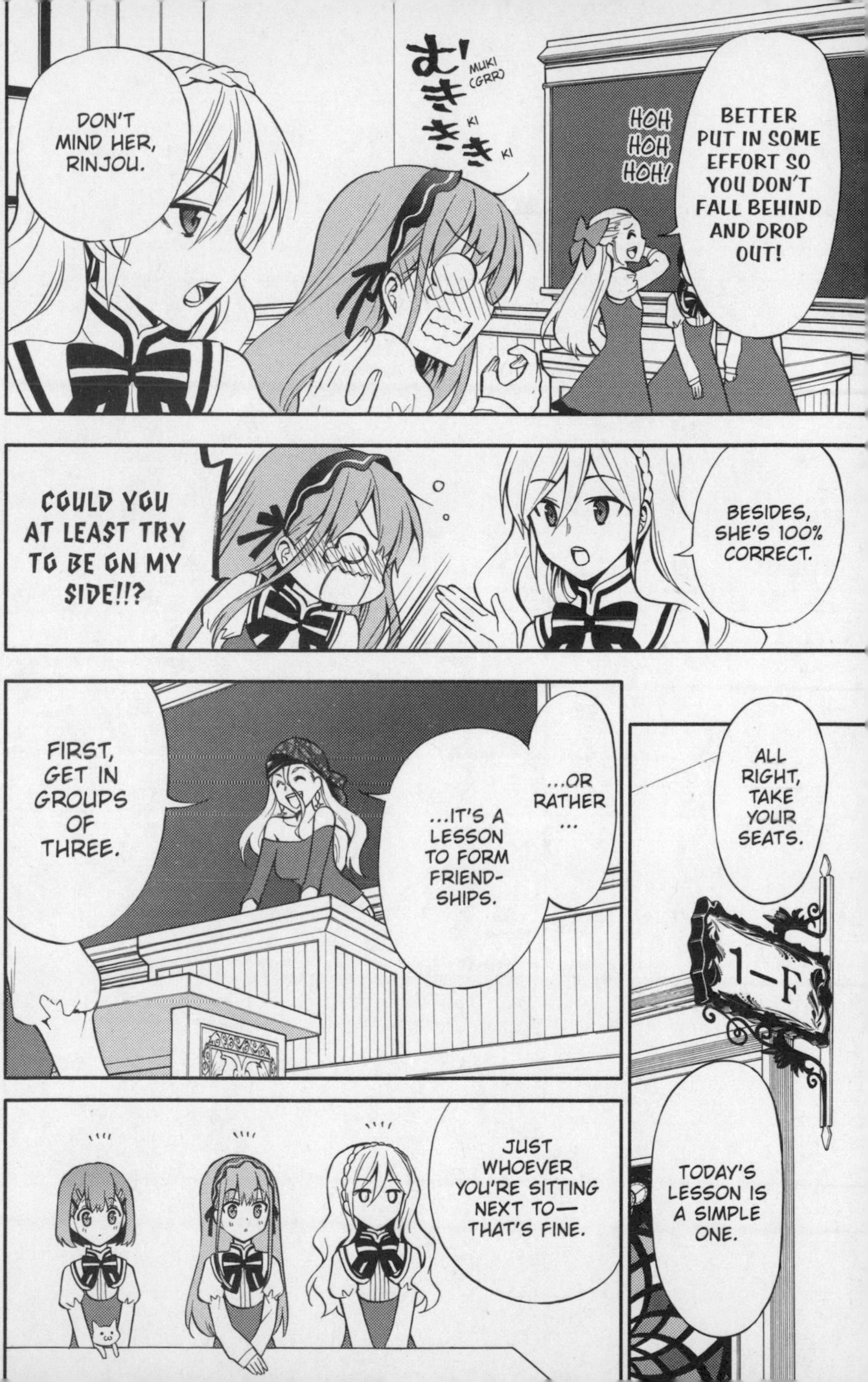
BETTER PUT IN SOME EFFORT SO YOU DON'T FALL BEHIND AND DROP OUT!
HOH HOH HOH!
むききき
MUKI (GRR) KI KI
DON'T MIND HER, RINJOU.
BESIDES, SHE'S 100% CORRECT.
COULD YOU AT LEAST TRY TO BE ON MY SIDE!!?
ALL RIGHT, TAKE YOUR SEATS.
1—F
TODAY'S LESSON IS A SIMPLE ONE.
...OR RATHER...
...IT'S A LESSON TO FORM FRIEND-SHIPS.
FIRST, GET IN GROUPS OF THREE.
JUST WHOEVER YOU'RE SITTING NEXT TO— THAT'S FINE.

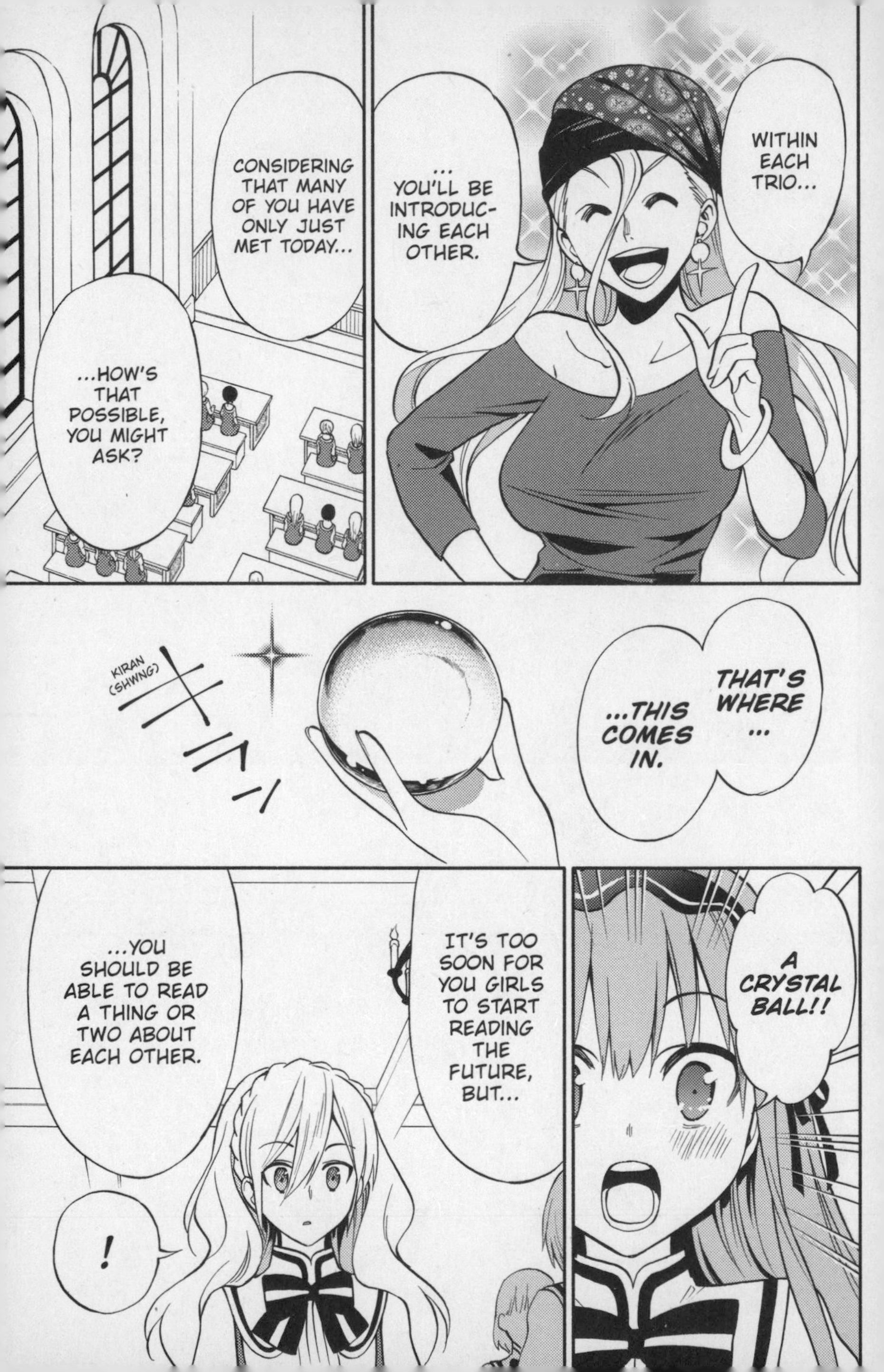
WITHIN EACH TRIO...
... YOU'LL BE INTRODUCING EACH OTHER.
CONSIDERING THAT MANY OF YOU HAVE ONLY JUST MET TODAY...
...HOW'S THAT POSSIBLE, YOU MIGHT ASK?
THAT'S WHERE ...
...THIS COMES IN.
KIRAN (SHWNG)
A CRYSTAL BALL!!
IT'S TOO SOON FOR YOU GIRLS TO START READING THE FUTURE, BUT...
...YOU SHOULD BE ABLE TO READ A THING OR TWO ABOUT EACH OTHER.
!

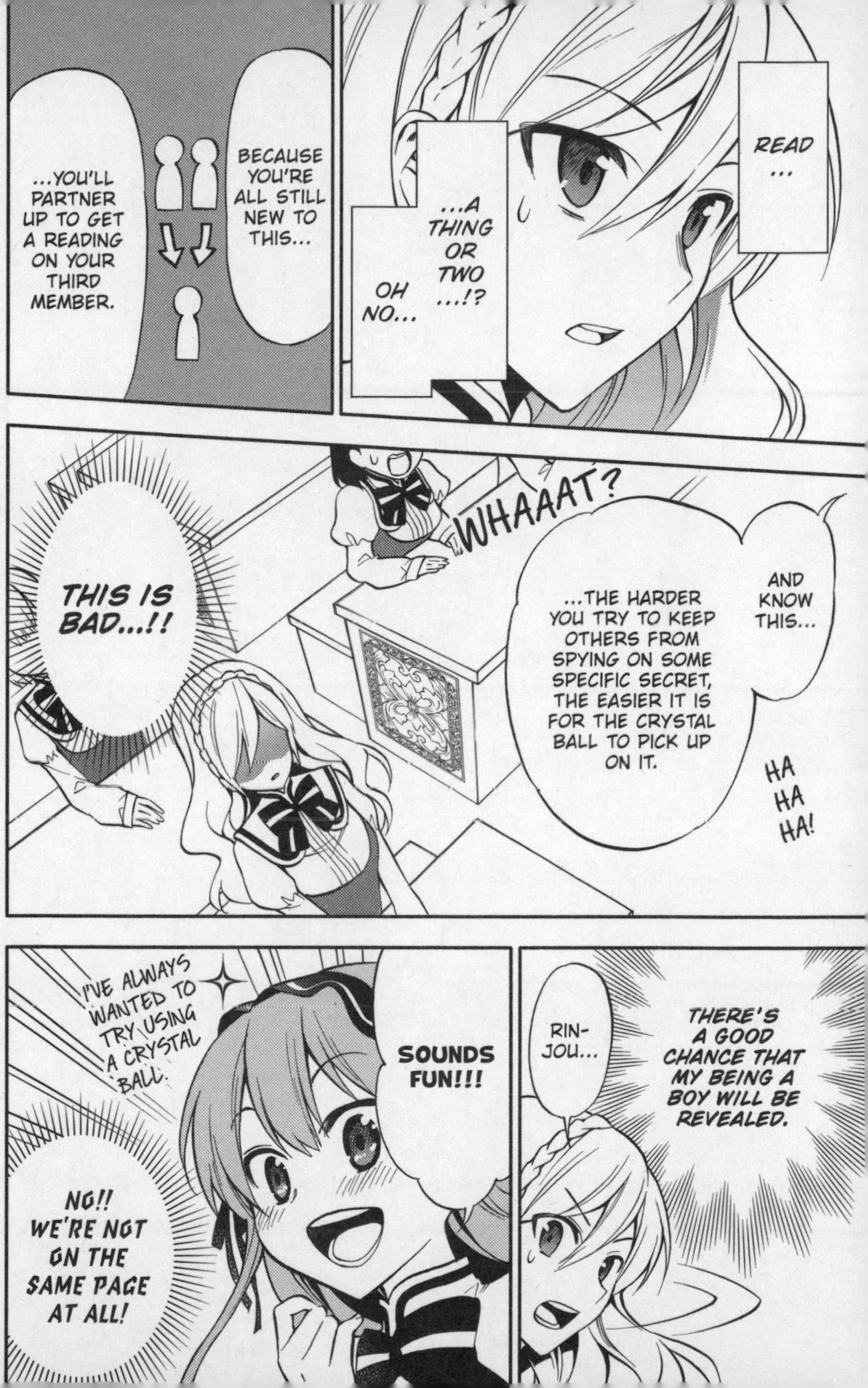
READ...
...A THING OR TWO ...!?
OH NO...
BECAUSE YOU'RE ALL STILL NEW TO THIS...
...YOU'LL PARTNER UP TO GET A READING ON YOUR THIRD MEMBER.
AND KNOW THIS...
...THE HARDER YOU TRY TO KEEP OTHERS FROM SPYING ON SOME SPECIFIC SECRET, THE EASIER IT IS FOR THE CRYSTAL BALL TO PICK UP ON IT.
HA HA HA!
WHAAAT?
THIS IS BAD...!!
THERE'S A GOOD CHANCE THAT MY BEING A BOY WILL BE REVEALED.
RIN-JOU...
SOUNDS FUN!!!
I'VE ALWAYS WANTED TO TRY USING A CRYSTAL BALL.
NO!! WE'RE NOT ON THE SAME PAGE AT ALL!

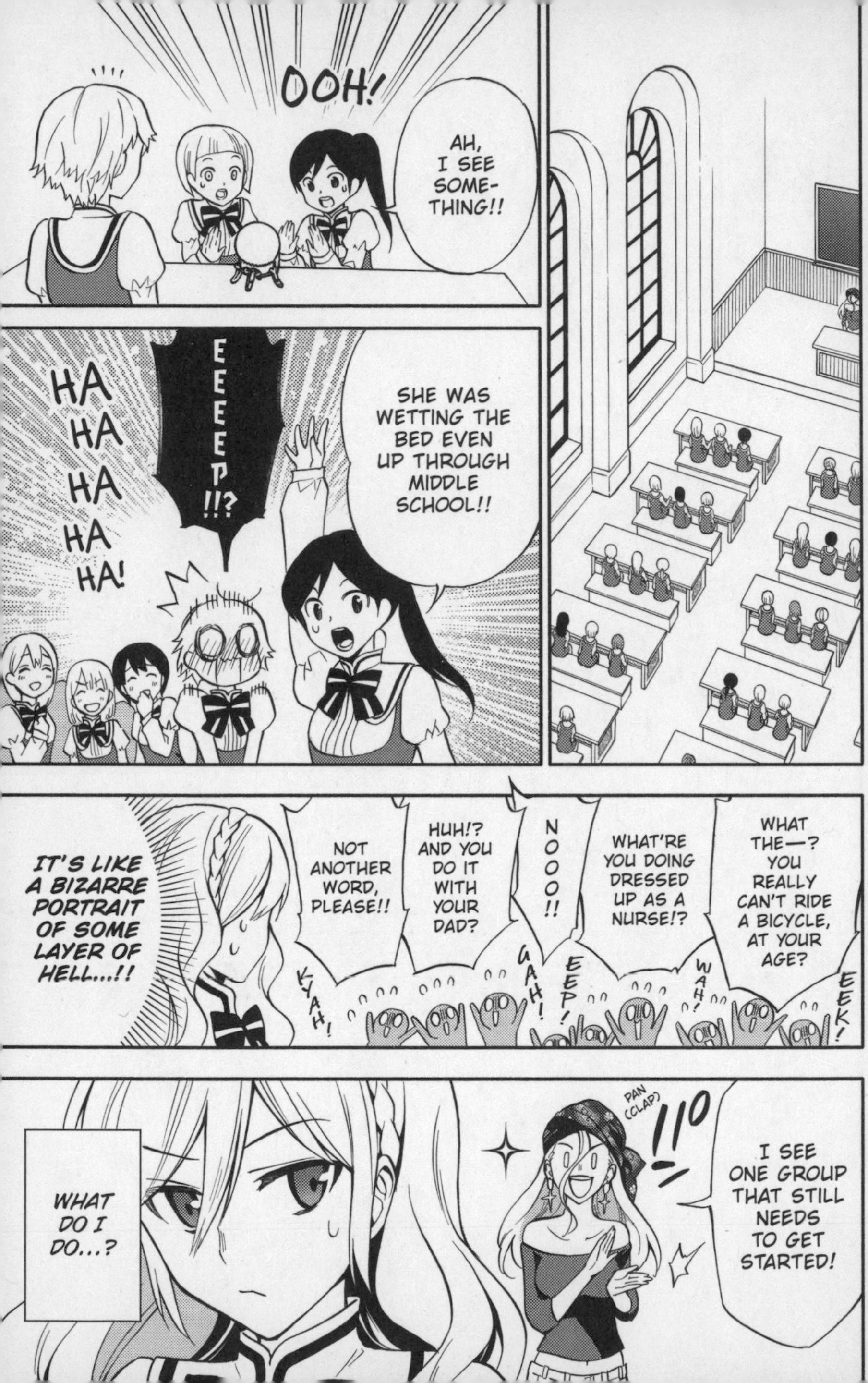
OOH!
AH, I SEE SOMETHING!!
SHE WAS WETTING THE BED EVEN UP THROUGH MIDDLE SCHOOL!!
EEEEEP!!?
HA HA HA HA HA!
WHAT THE—? YOU REALLY CAN'T RIDE A BICYCLE, AT YOUR AGE?
EEK!
WHAT'RE YOU DOING DRESSED UP AS A NURSE!?
WAH!
NOOOO!!
EEP!
GAH!
HUH!? AND YOU DO IT WITH YOUR DAD?
NOT ANOTHER WORD, PLEASE!!
KYAH!
IT'S LIKE A BIZARRE PORTRAIT OF SOME LAYER OF HELL...!!
PAN (CLAP)
I SEE ONE GROUP THAT STILL NEEDS TO GET STARTED!
WHAT DO I DO...?

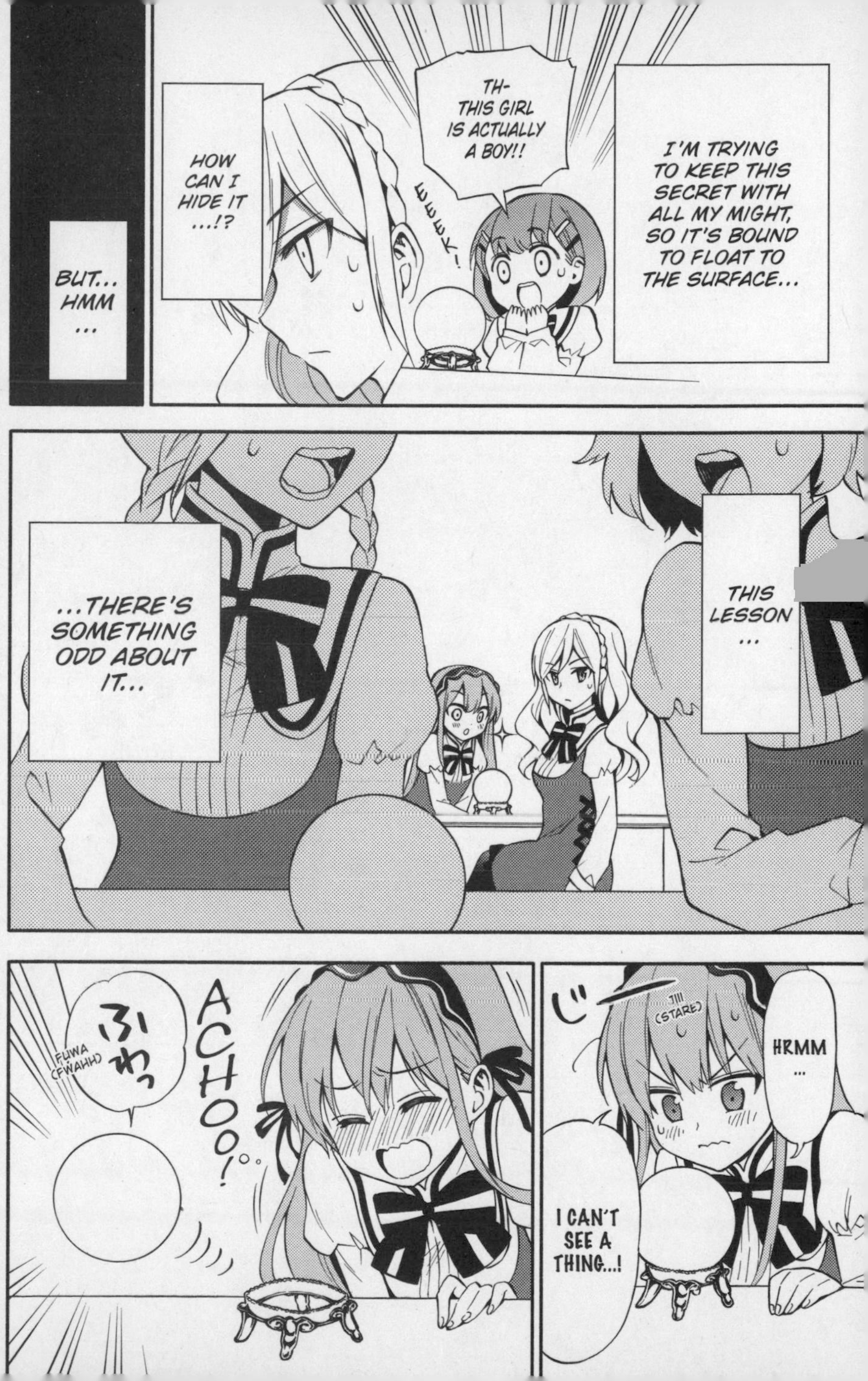
I'M TRYING TO KEEP THIS SECRET WITH ALL MY MIGHT, SO IT'S BOUND TO FLOAT TO THE SURFACE...
TH- THIS GIRL IS ACTUALLY A BOY!!
EEEK!
HOW CAN I HIDE IT ...!?
BUT... HMM ...
THIS LESSON ...
...THERE'S SOMETHING ODD ABOUT IT...
じー
JIII (STARE)
HRMM ...
I CAN'T SEE A THING...!
ACHOO!
ふわっ
FUWA (FWAHH)

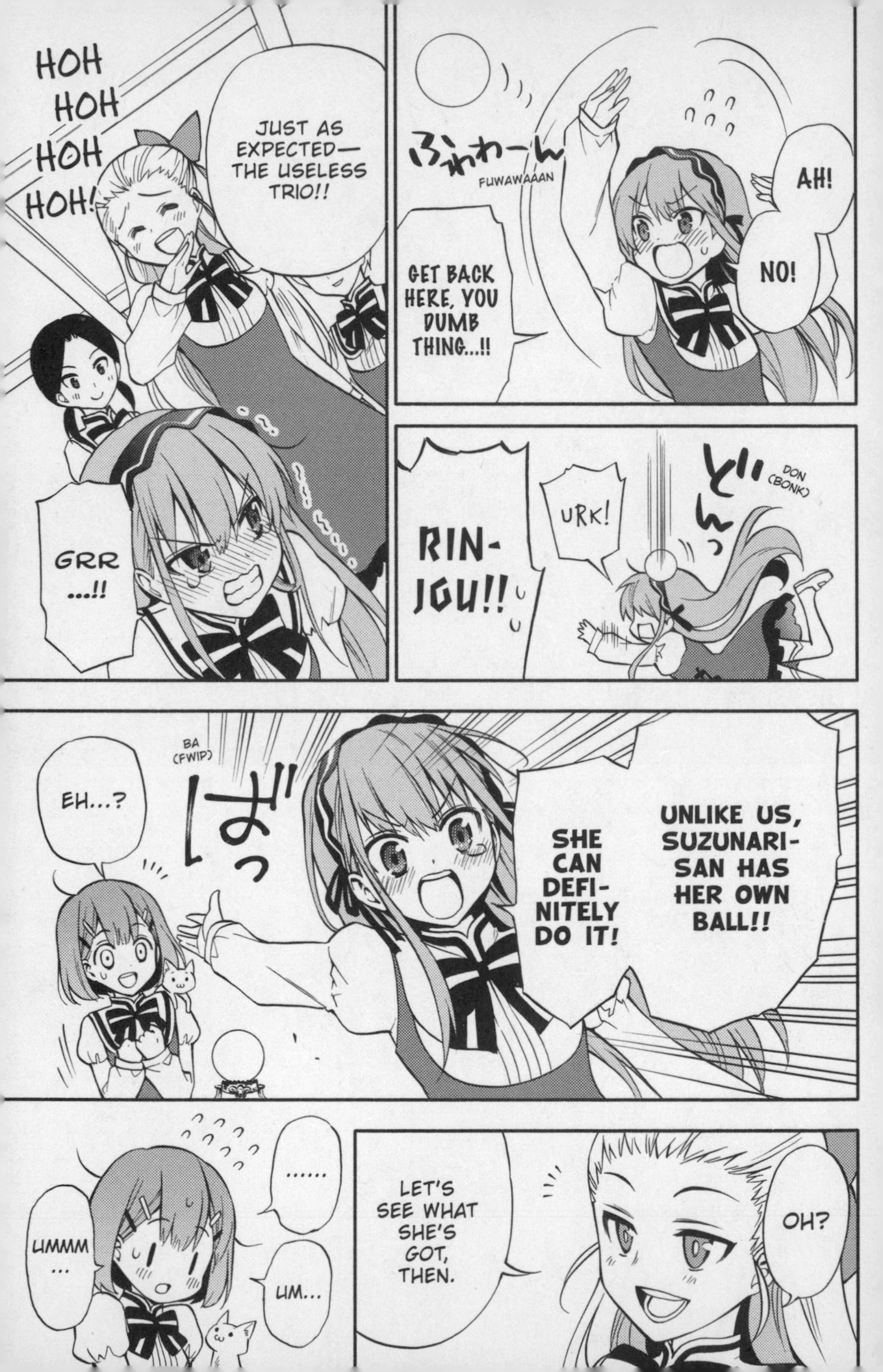
AH!
NO!
ふわわーん
FUWAWAAAN
GET BACK HERE, YOU DUMB THING...!!
どんっ
DON (BONK)
URK!
RIN-JOU!!
HOH HOH HOH HOH!
JUST AS EXPECTED— THE USELESS TRIO!!
GRR ...!!
UNLIKE US, SUZUNARI-SAN HAS HER OWN BALL!!
SHE CAN DEFINITELY DO IT!
ばっ
BA (FWIP)
EH...?
OH?
LET'S SEE WHAT SHE'S GOT, THEN.
......
UMMM ...
UM...

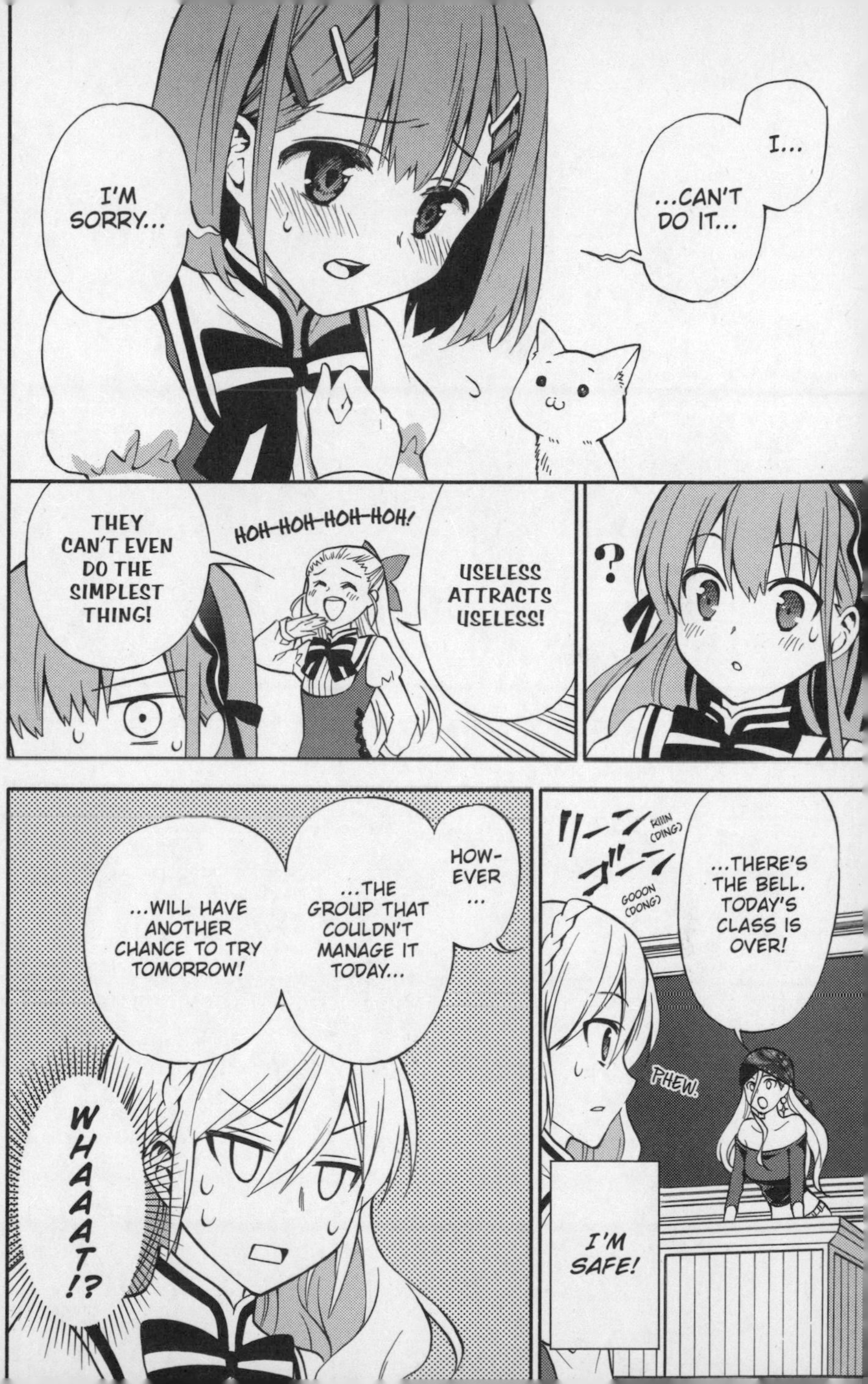
I...
...CAN'T DO IT...
I'M SORRY...
?
USELESS ATTRACTS USELESS!
HOH-HOH-HOH-HOH!
THEY CAN'T EVEN DO THE SIMPLEST THING!
KIIIN (DING)
GOOON (DONG)
...THERE'S THE BELL. TODAY'S CLASS IS OVER!
PHEW.
I'M SAFE!
HOW-EVER...
...THE GROUP THAT COULDN'T MANAGE IT TODAY...
...WILL HAVE ANOTHER CHANCE TO TRY TOMORROW!
WHAAAT!?

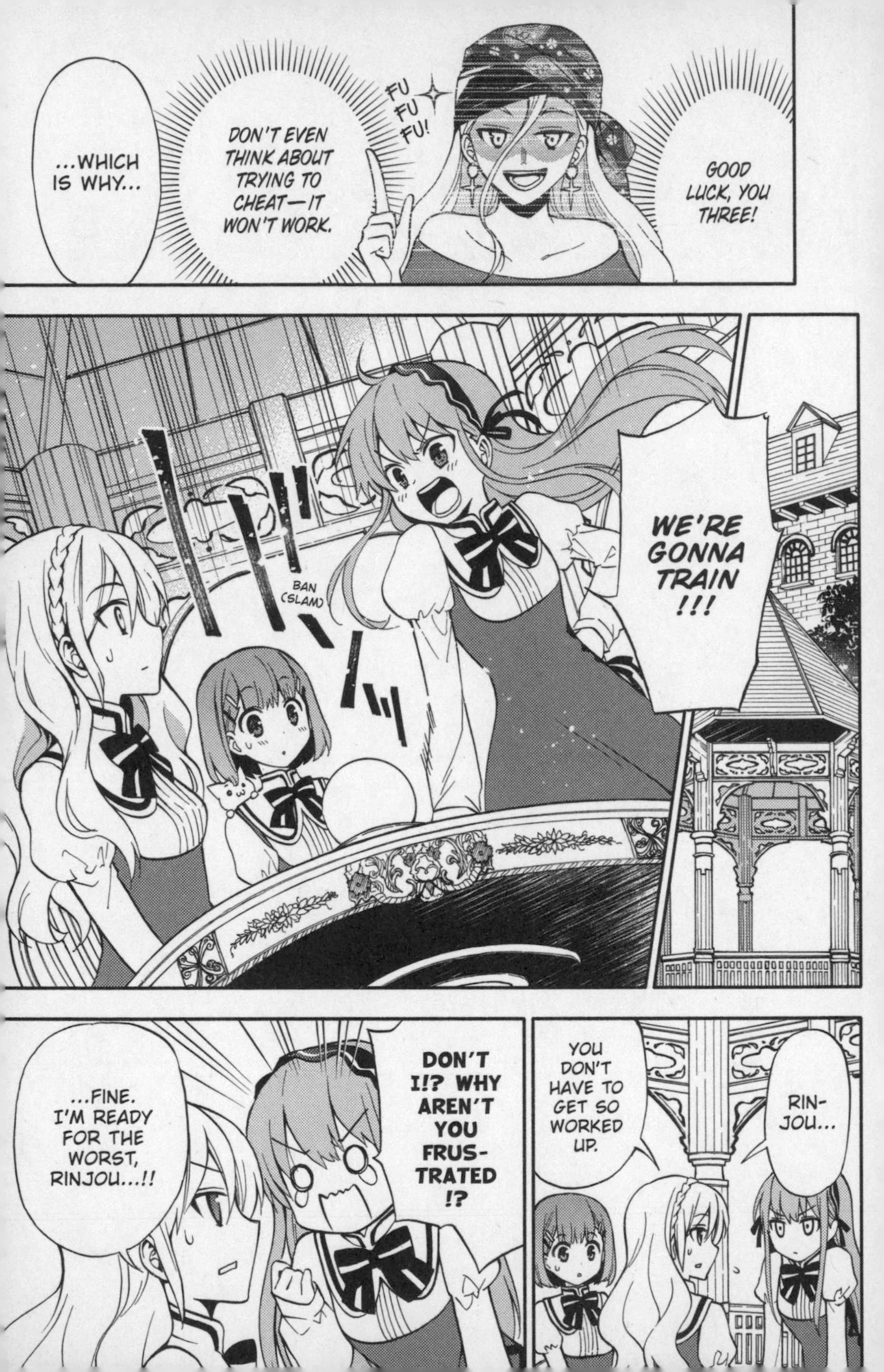
GOOD LUCK, YOU THREE!
FU FU FU!
DON'T EVEN THINK ABOUT TRYING TO CHEAT—IT WON'T WORK.
...WHICH IS WHY...
WE'RE GONNA TRAIN!!!
BAN (SLAM)
RIN-JOU...
YOU DON'T HAVE TO GET SO WORKED UP.
DON'T I!? WHY AREN'T YOU FRUS-TRATED!?
...FINE. I'M READY FOR THE WORST, RINJOU...!!

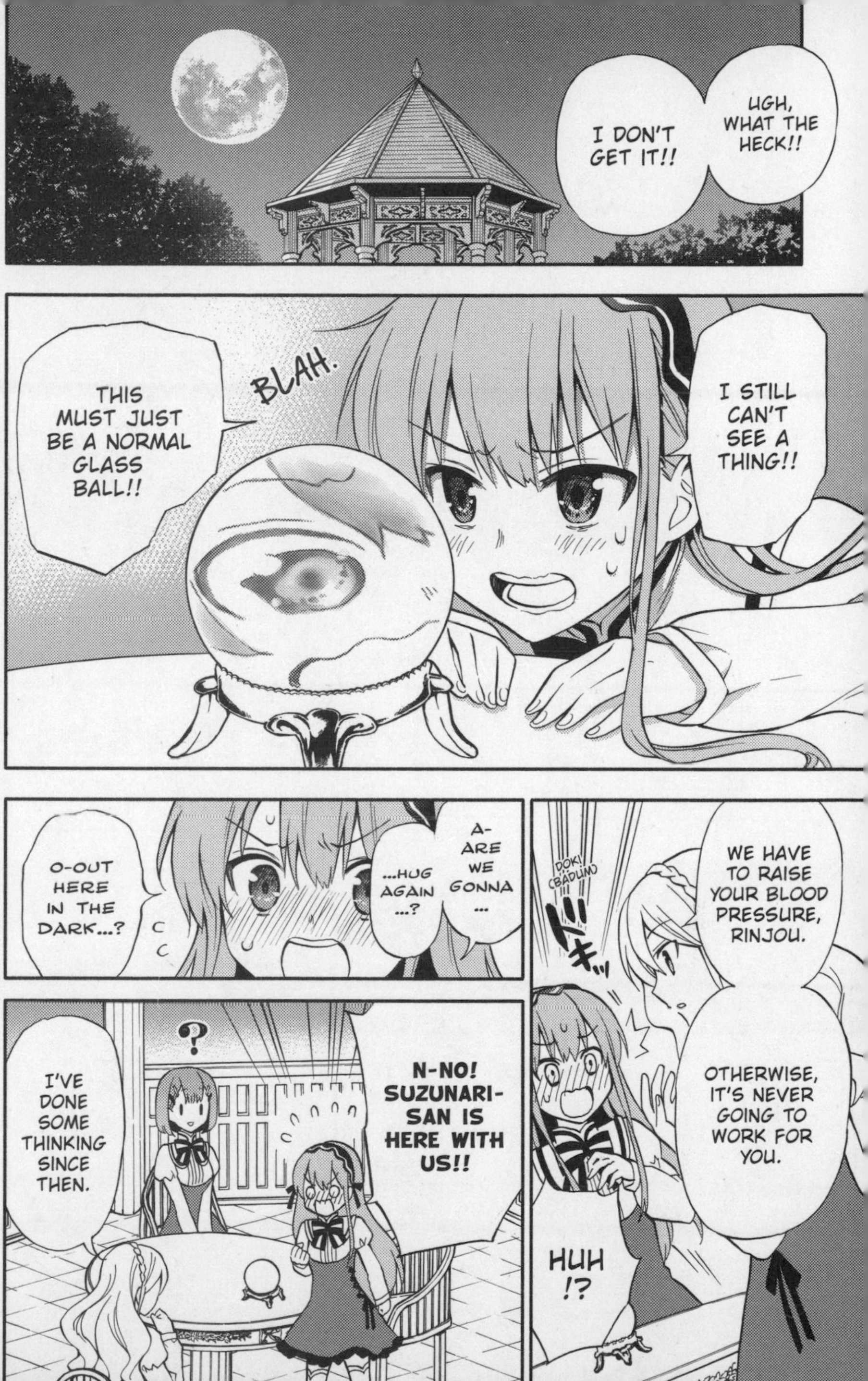
UGH, WHAT THE HECK!!
I DON'T GET IT!!
I STILL CAN'T SEE A THING!!
BLAH.
THIS MUST JUST BE A NORMAL GLASS BALL!!
WE HAVE TO RAISE YOUR BLOOD PRESSURE, RINJOU.
DOKI (BADUMP)
ドキッ
OTHERWISE, IT'S NEVER GOING TO WORK FOR YOU.
HUH!?
A-ARE WE GONNA...
...HUG AGAIN...?
O-OUT HERE IN THE DARK...?
N-NO! SUZUNARI-SAN IS HERE WITH US!!
I'VE DONE SOME THINKING SINCE THEN.

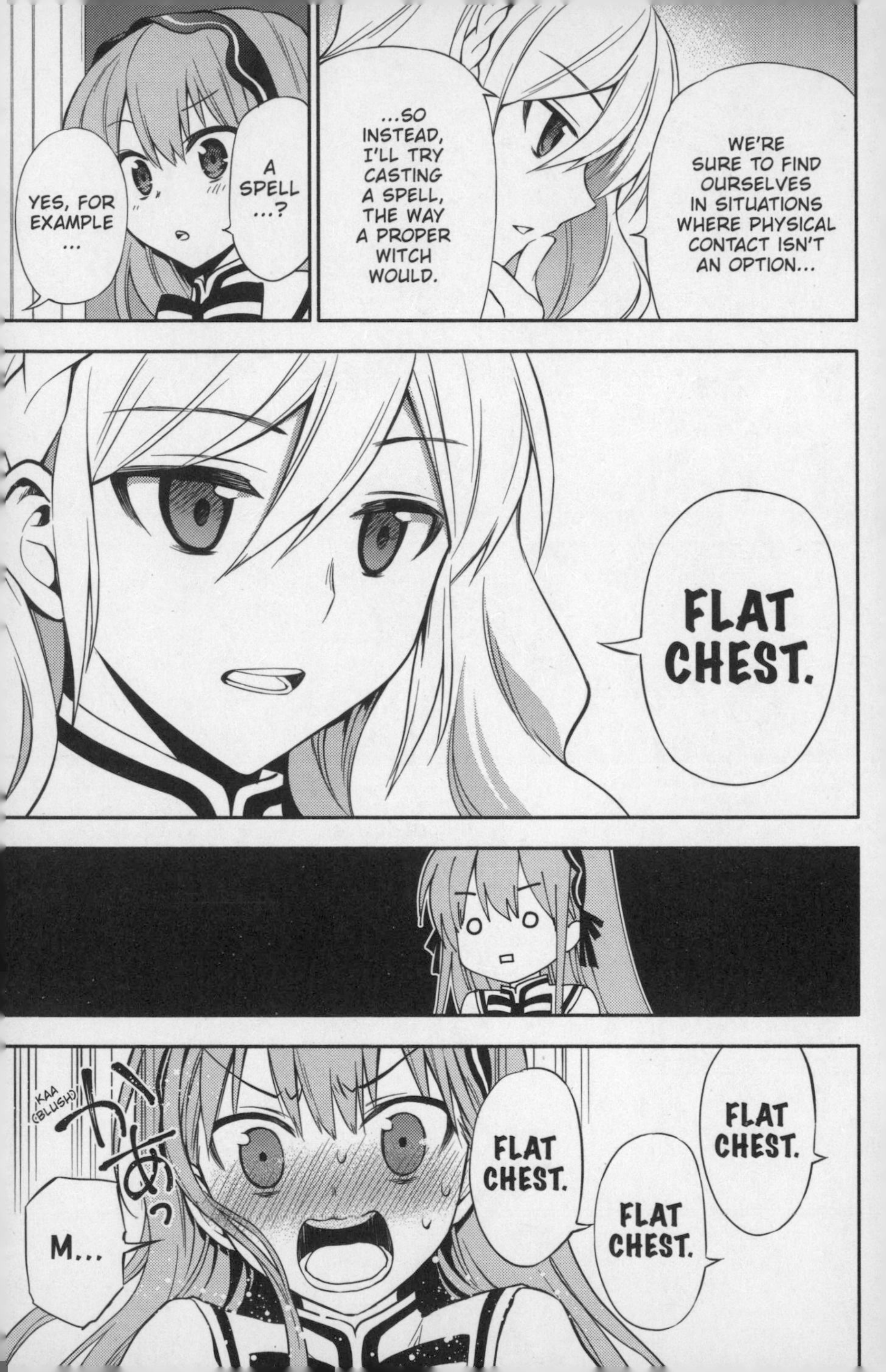
WE'RE SURE TO FIND OURSELVES IN SITUATIONS WHERE PHYSICAL CONTACT ISN'T AN OPTION...
...SO INSTEAD, I'LL TRY CASTING A SPELL, THE WAY A PROPER WITCH WOULD.
A SPELL ...?
YES, FOR EXAMPLE ...
FLAT CHEST.
FLAT CHEST.
FLAT CHEST.
FLAT CHEST.
KAA (BLUSH)
M...

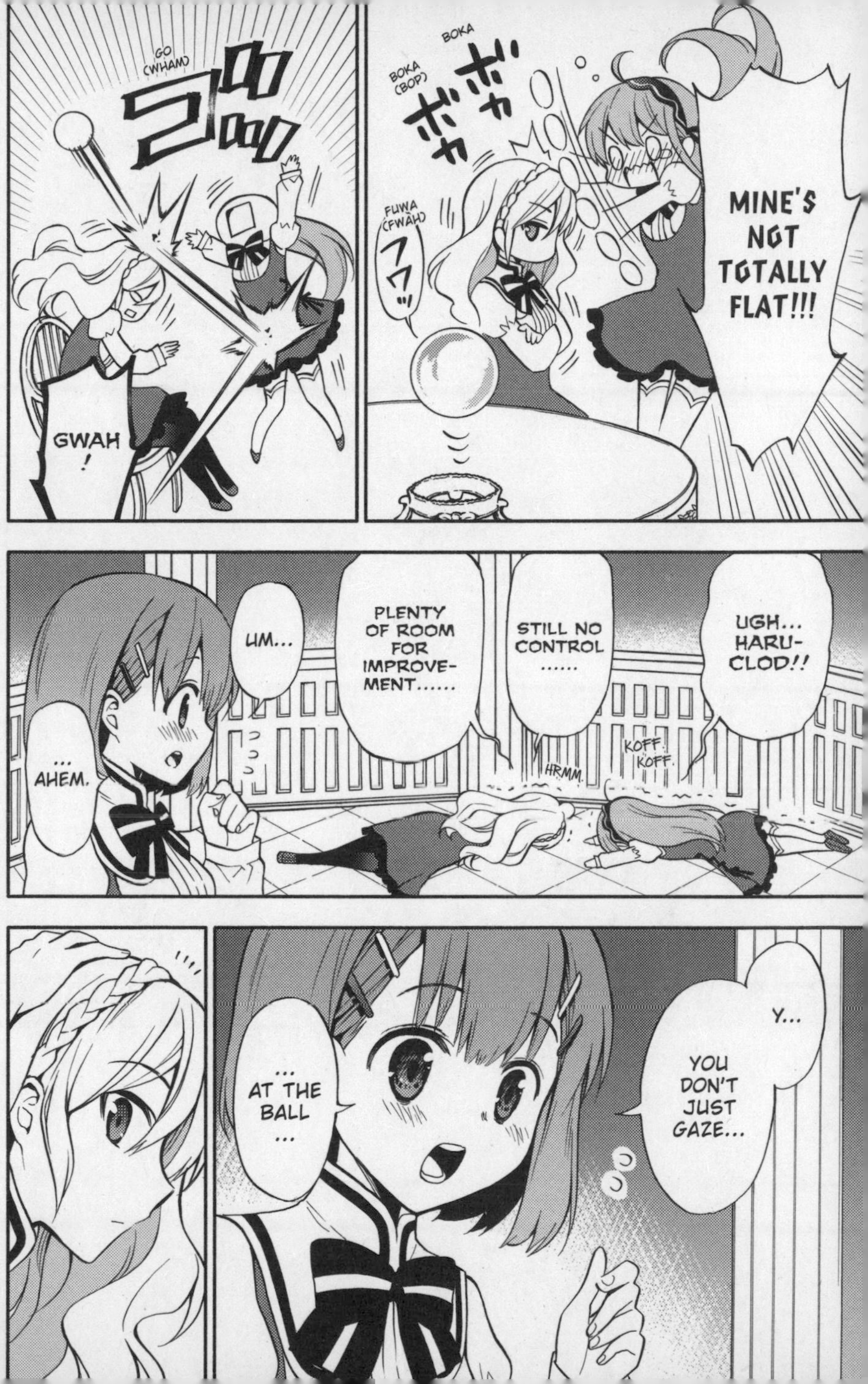
BOKA
BOKA (BOP)
MINE'S NOT TOTALLY FLAT!!!
FUWA (FWAH)
GO (WHAM)
GWAH!
UGH... HARU-CLOD!!
KOFF. KOFF.
STILL NO CONTROL ......
HRMM.
PLENTY OF ROOM FOR IMPROVE-MENT......
UM...
... AHEM.
Y...
YOU DON'T JUST GAZE...
... AT THE BALL ...

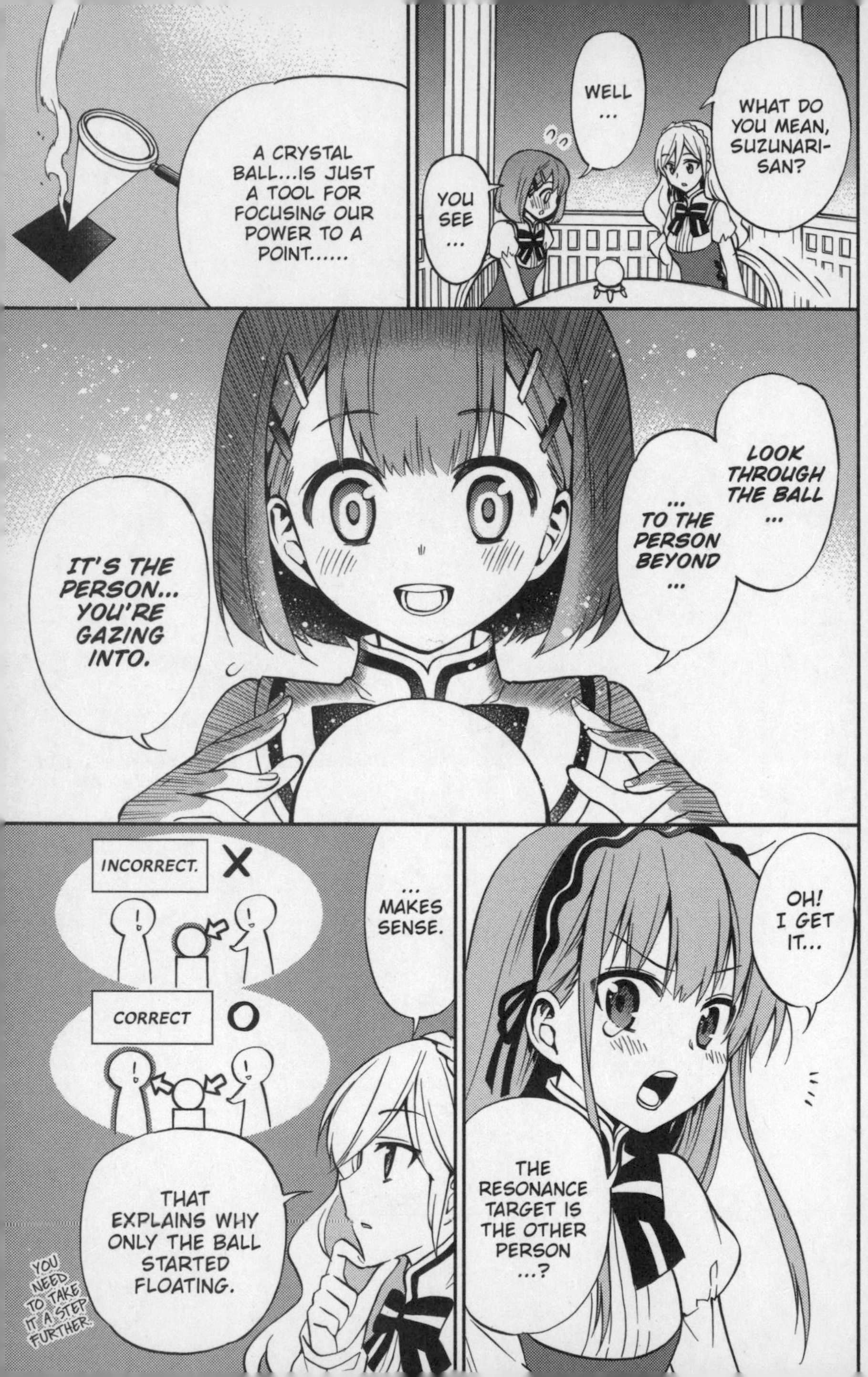
WHAT DO YOU MEAN, SUZUNARI-SAN?
WELL...
YOU SEE...
A CRYSTAL BALL...IS JUST A TOOL FOR FOCUSING OUR POWER TO A POINT......
LOOK THROUGH THE BALL...
...TO THE PERSON BEYOND...
IT'S THE PERSON... YOU'RE GAZING INTO.
OH! I GET IT...
THE RESONANCE TARGET IS THE OTHER PERSON...?
...MAKES SENSE.
INCORRECT.
X
CORRECT
O
THAT EXPLAINS WHY ONLY THE BALL STARTED FLOATING.
YOU NEED TO TAKE IT A STEP FURTHER.

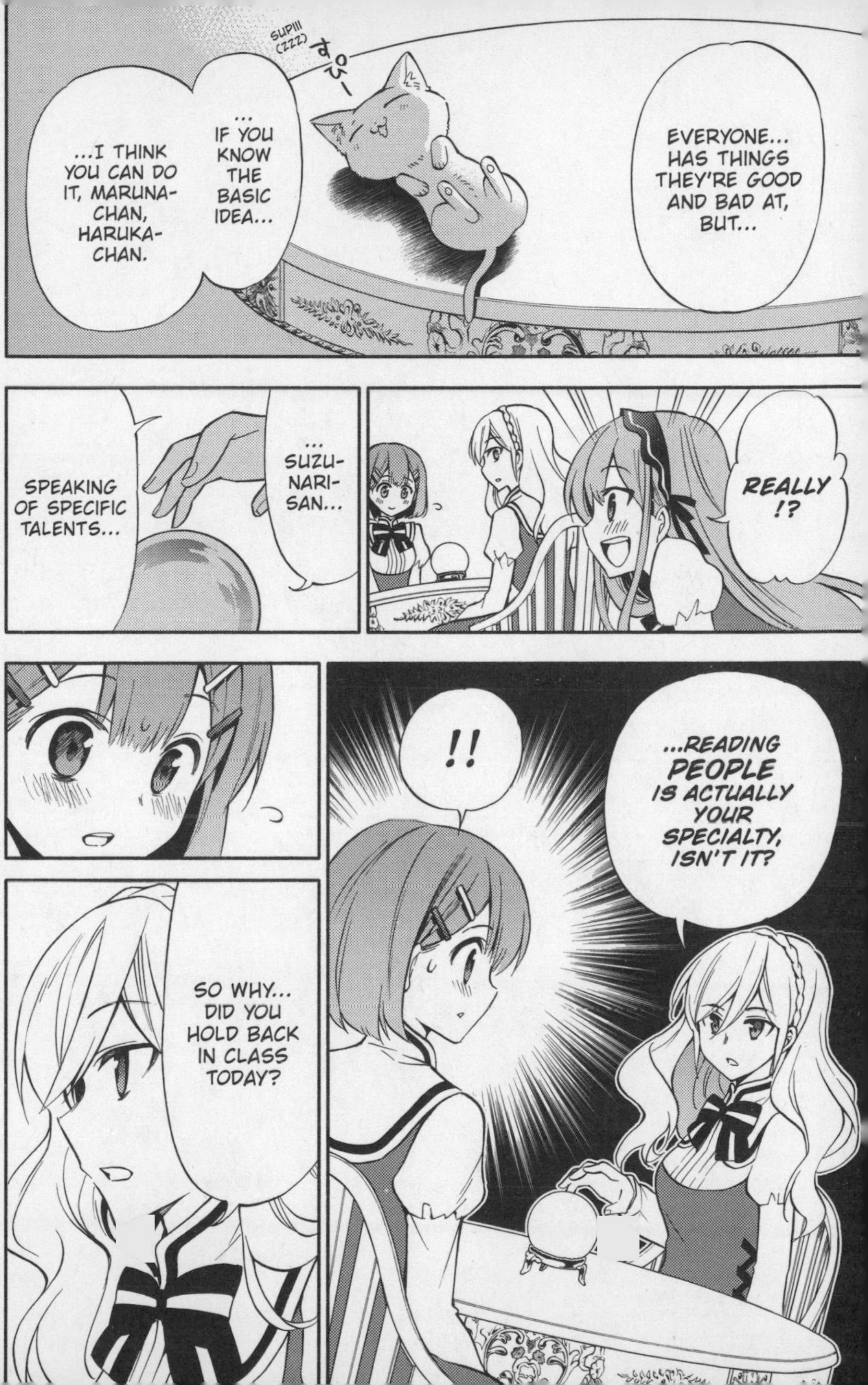
EVERYONE... HAS THINGS THEY'RE GOOD AND BAD AT, BUT...
SUPIII (ZZZ)
すぴー
...IF YOU KNOW THE BASIC IDEA...
...I THINK YOU CAN DO IT, MARUNA-CHAN, HARUKA-CHAN.
REALLY!?
...SUZU-NARI-SAN...
SPEAKING OF SPECIFIC TALENTS...
...READING PEOPLE IS ACTUALLY YOUR SPECIALTY, ISN'T IT?
!!
SO WHY... DID YOU HOLD BACK IN CLASS TODAY?

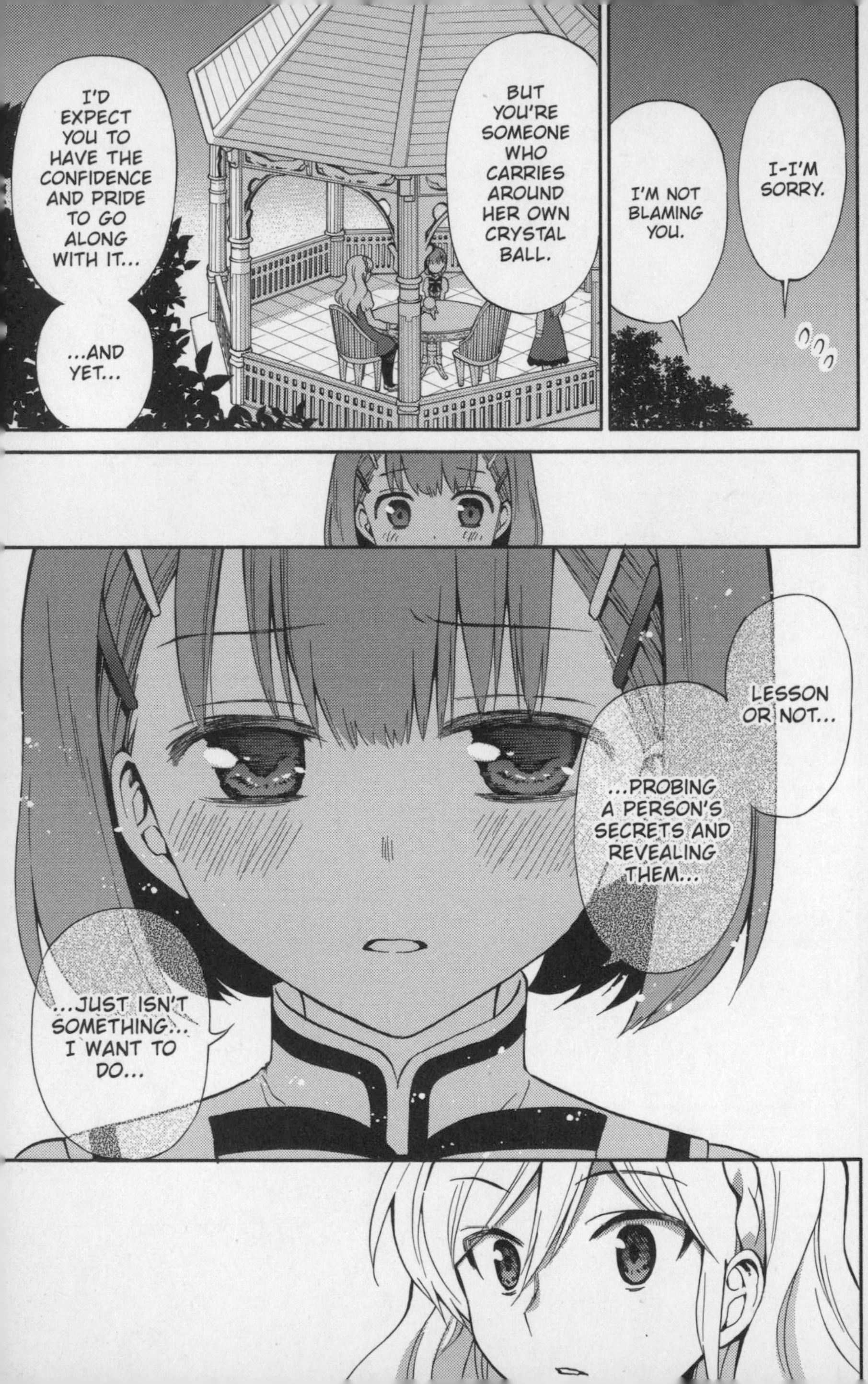
I-I'M SORRY.
I'M NOT BLAMING YOU.
BUT YOU'RE SOMEONE WHO CARRIES AROUND HER OWN CRYSTAL BALL.
I'D EXPECT YOU TO HAVE THE CONFIDENCE AND PRIDE TO GO ALONG WITH IT...
...AND YET...
LESSON OR NOT...
...PROBING A PERSON'S SECRETS AND REVEALING THEM...
...JUST ISN'T SOMETHING... I WANT TO DO...

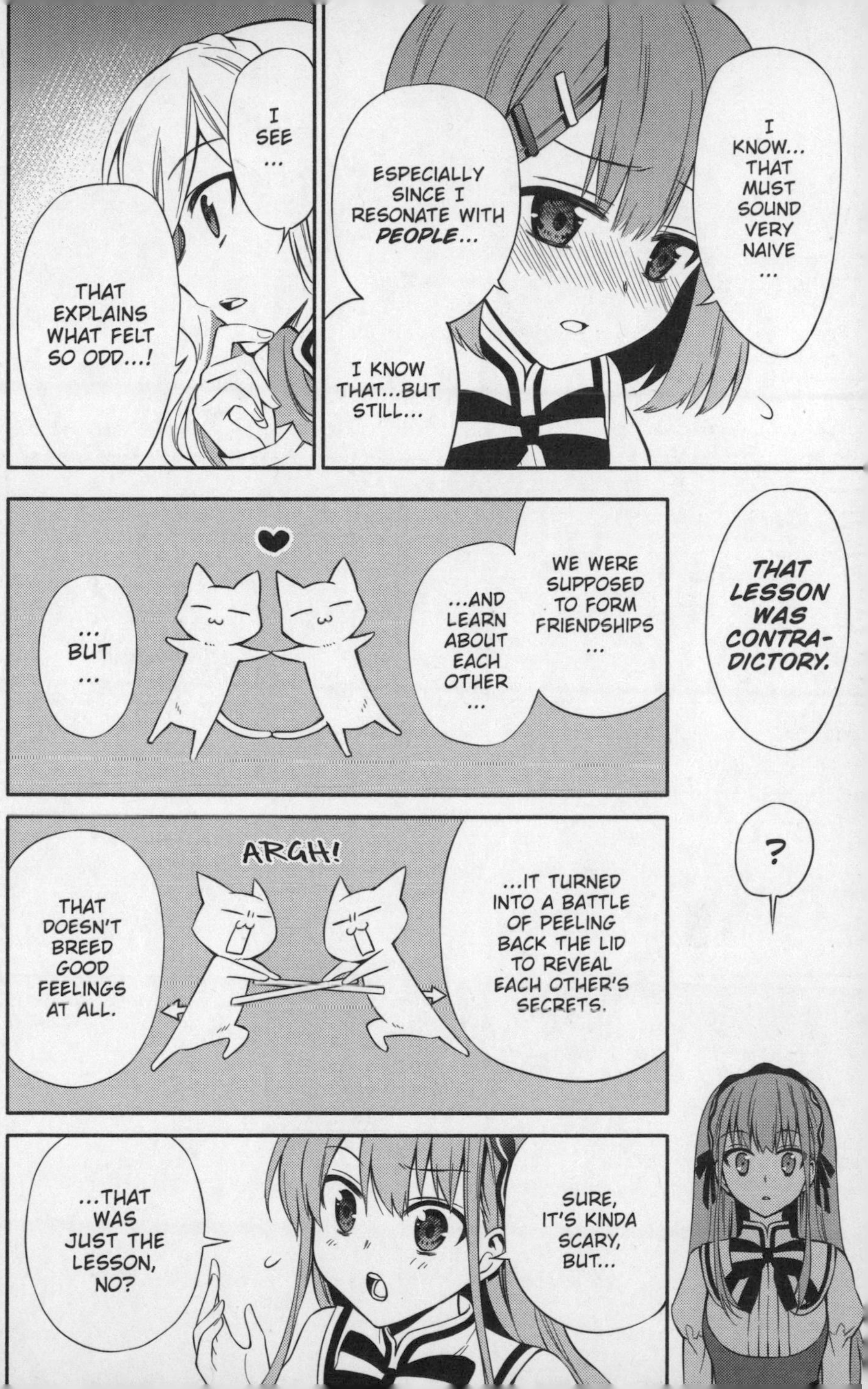
I KNOW... THAT MUST SOUND VERY NAIVE...
ESPECIALLY SINCE I RESONATE WITH *PEOPLE*...
I KNOW THAT...BUT STILL...
I SEE...
THAT EXPLAINS WHAT FELT SO ODD...!
THAT LESSON WAS CONTRA-DICTORY.
WE WERE SUPPOSED TO FORM FRIENDSHIPS...
...AND LEARN ABOUT EACH OTHER...
...BUT...
?
...IT TURNED INTO A BATTLE OF PEELING BACK THE LID TO REVEAL EACH OTHER'S SECRETS.
ARGH!
THAT DOESN'T BREED GOOD FEELINGS AT ALL.
SURE, IT'S KINDA SCARY, BUT...
...THAT WAS JUST THE LESSON, NO?

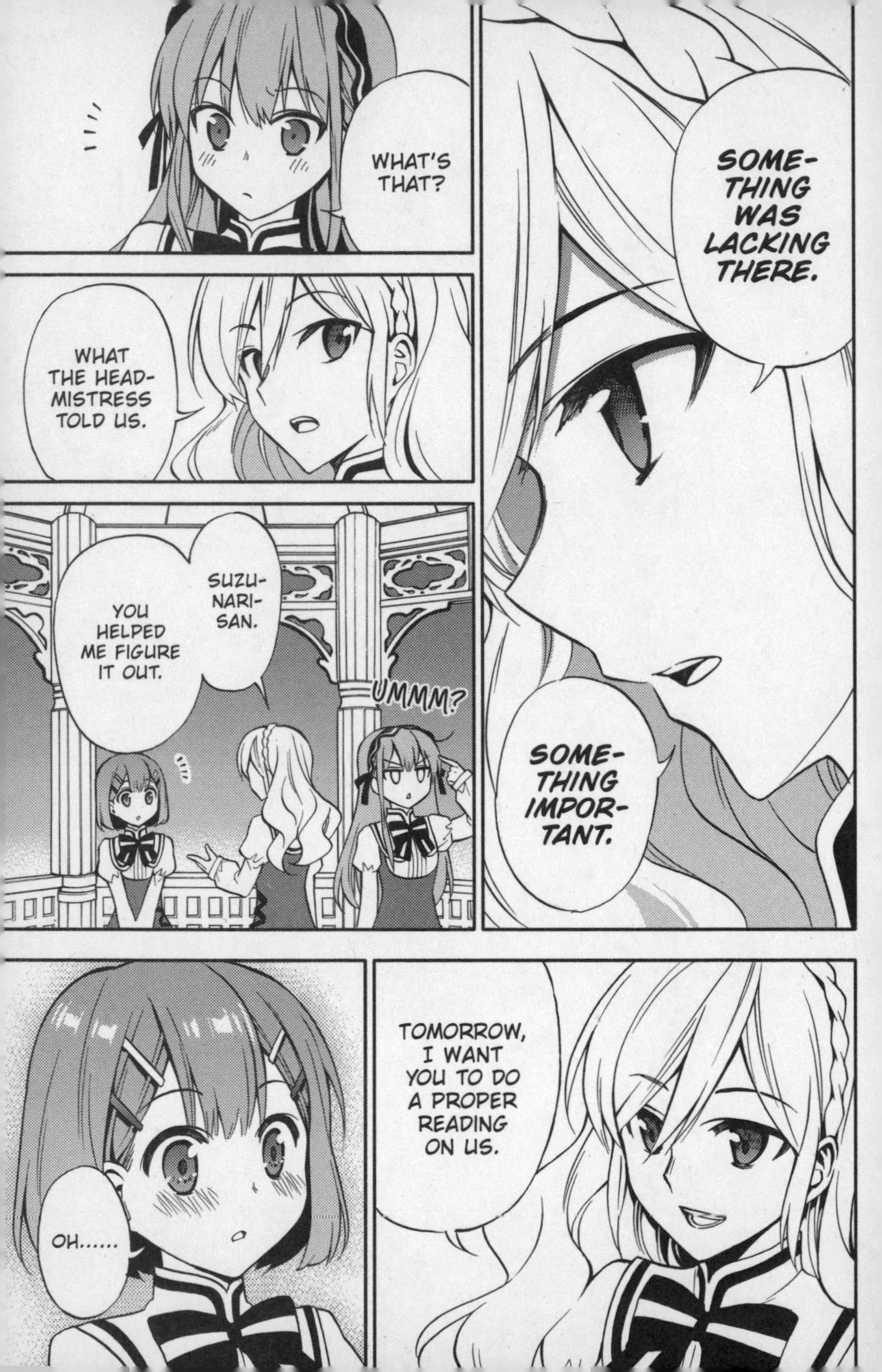
SOMETHING WAS LACKING THERE.
SOMETHING IMPORTANT.
WHAT'S THAT?
WHAT THE HEADMISTRESS TOLD US.
SUZUNARI-SAN.
YOU HELPED ME FIGURE IT OUT.
UMMM?
TOMORROW, I WANT YOU TO DO A PROPER READING ON US.
OH......

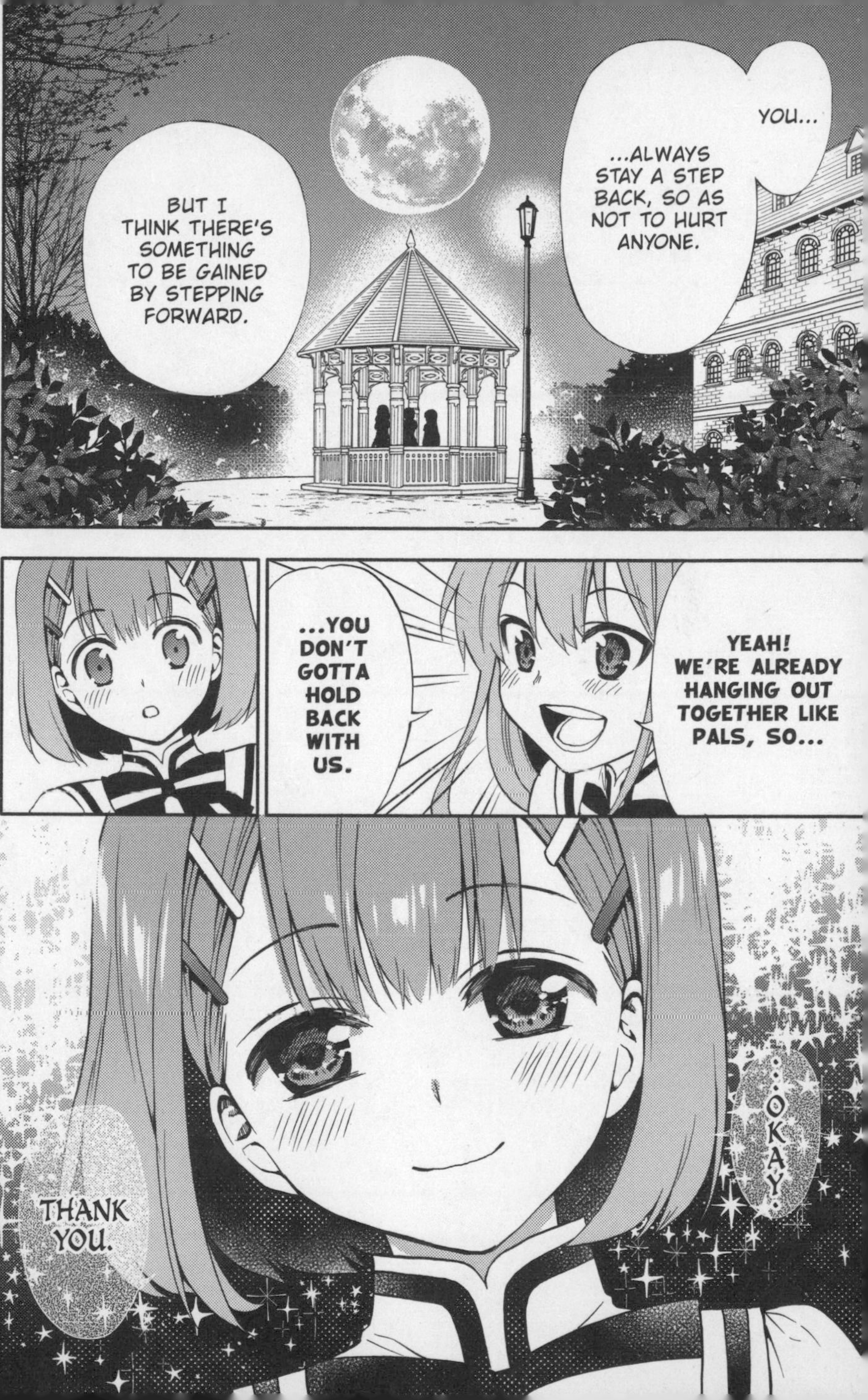
YOU...
...ALWAYS STAY A STEP BACK, SO AS NOT TO HURT ANYONE.
BUT I THINK THERE'S SOMETHING TO BE GAINED BY STEPPING FORWARD.
YEAH! WE'RE ALREADY HANGING OUT TOGETHER LIKE PALS, SO...
...YOU DON'T GOTTA HOLD BACK WITH US.
...OKAY.
THANK YOU.

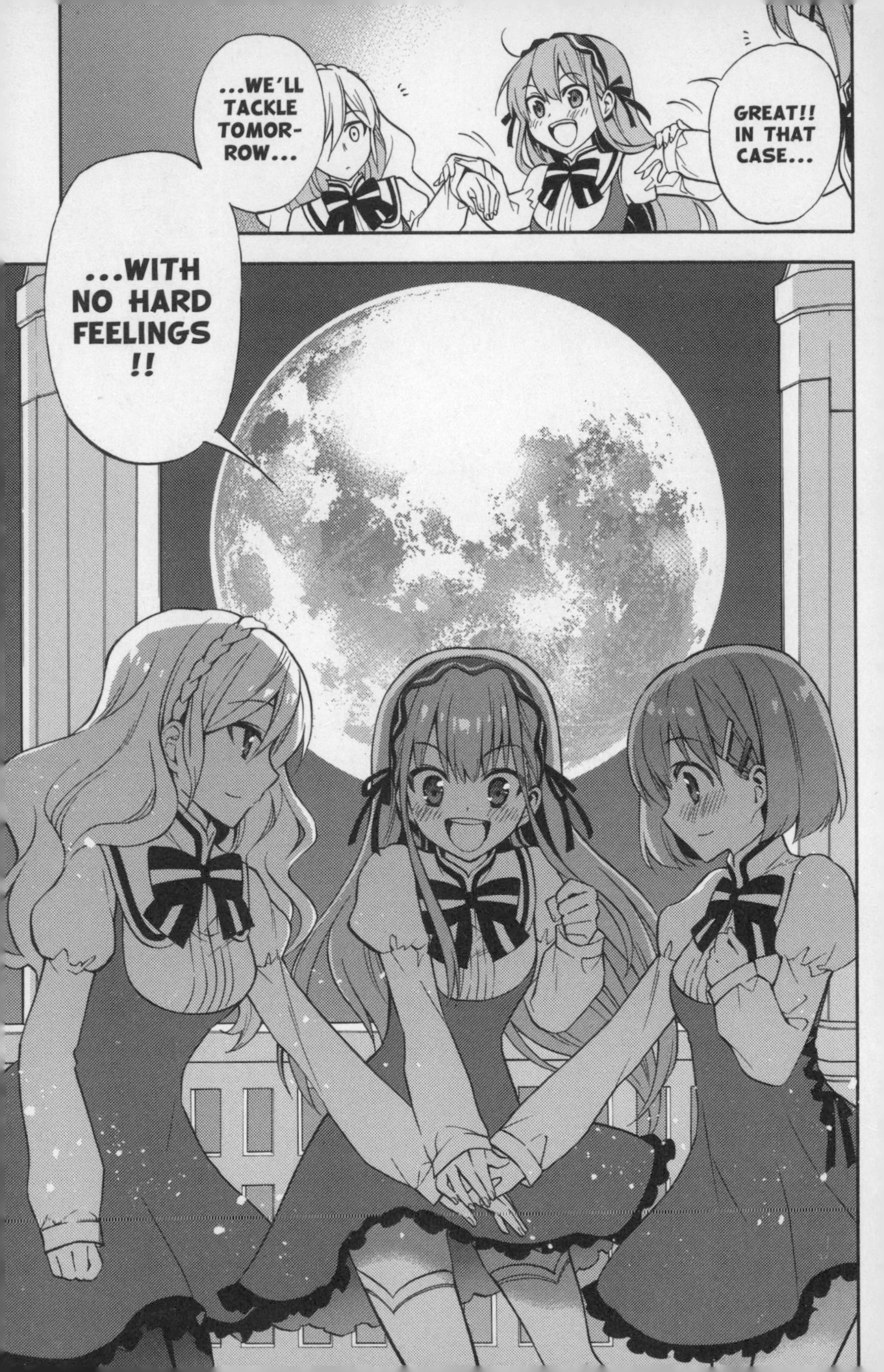
GREAT!! IN THAT CASE...
...WE'LL TACKLE TOMOR-ROW...
...WITH NO HARD FEELINGS!!

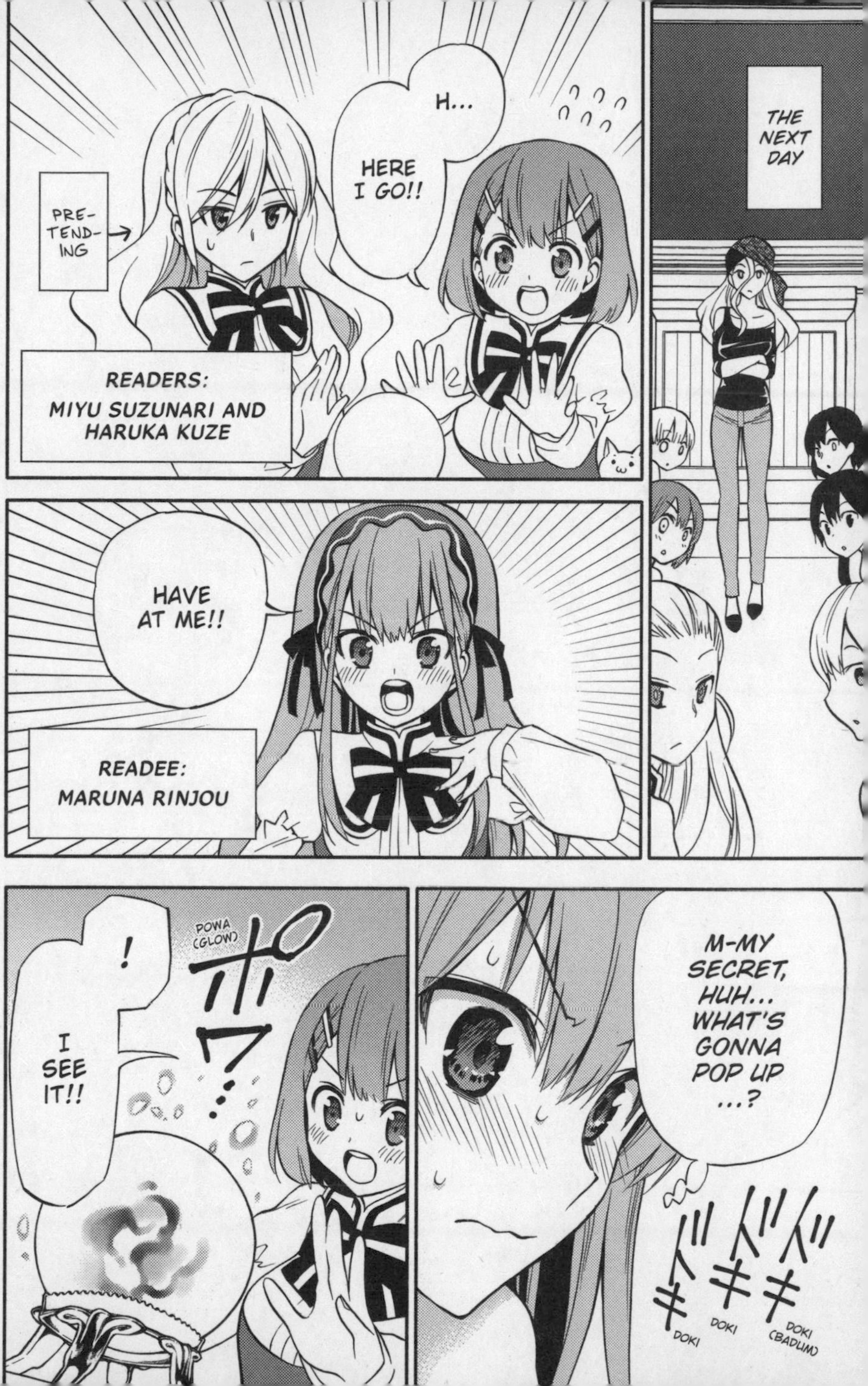
THE NEXT DAY
H...
HERE I GO!!
PRE-TEND-ING
READERS:
MIYU SUZUNARI AND HARUKA KUZE
HAVE AT ME!!
READEE:
MARUNA RINJOU
M-MY SECRET, HUH... WHAT'S GONNA POP UP ...?
DOKI
DOKI
DOKI (BADUM)
POWA (GLOW)
!
I SEE IT!!

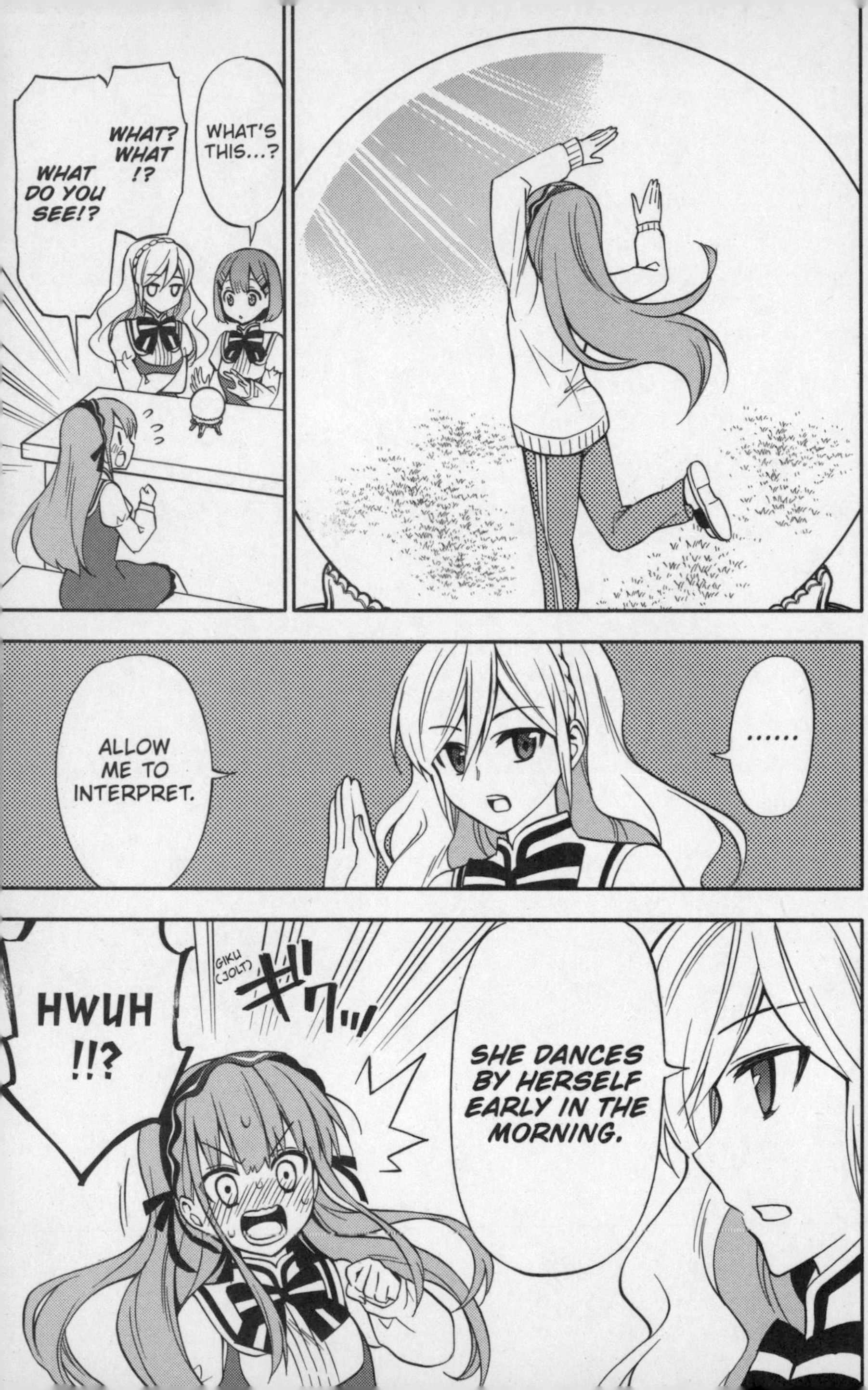
WHAT'S THIS...?
WHAT? WHAT!?
WHAT DO YOU SEE!?
......
ALLOW ME TO INTERPRET.
SHE DANCES BY HERSELF EARLY IN THE MORNING.
GIKU (JOLT)
HWUH!!?

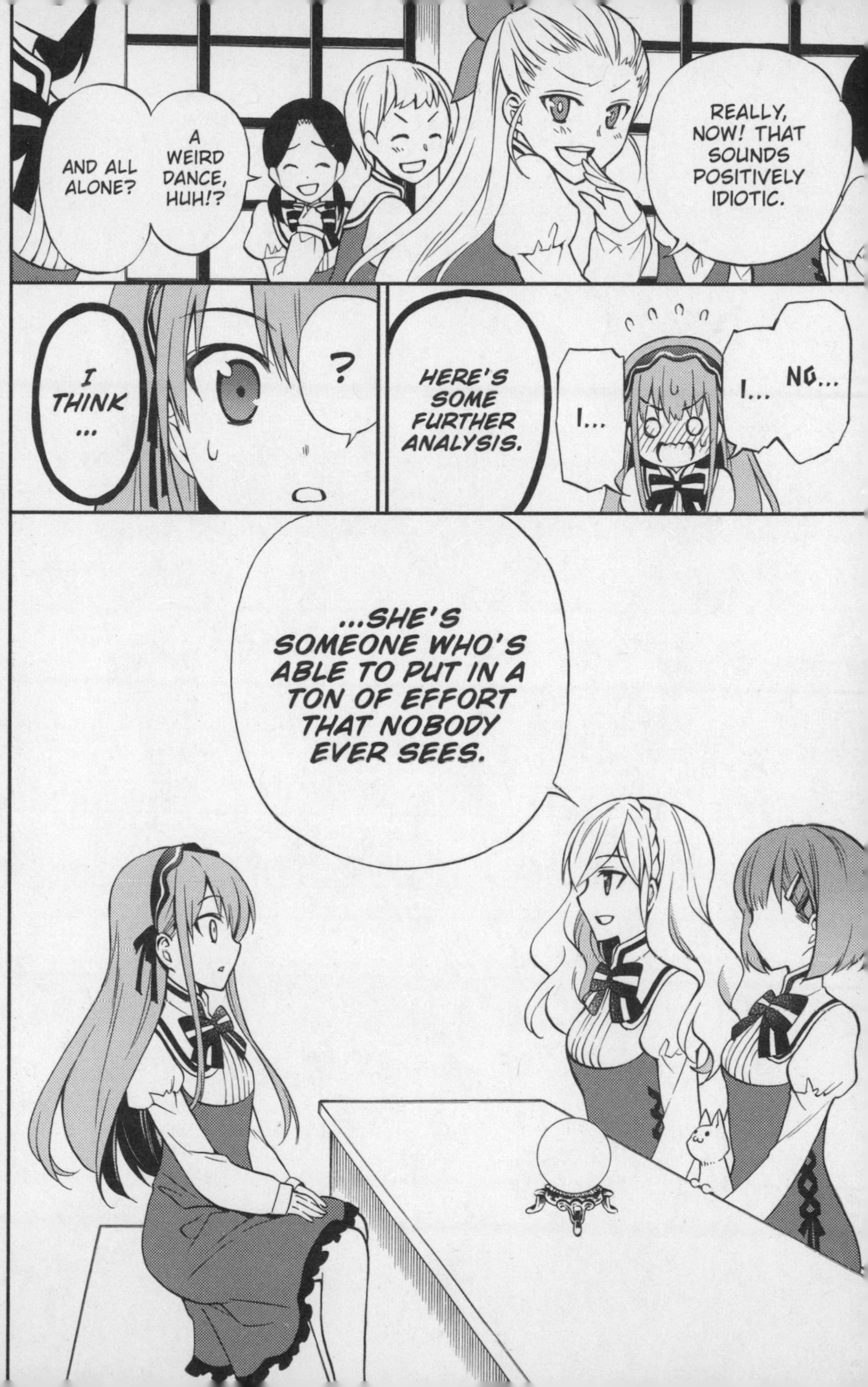
REALLY, NOW! THAT SOUNDS POSITIVELY IDIOTIC.
A WEIRD DANCE, HUH!?
AND ALL ALONE?
I... NO...
I...
HERE'S SOME FURTHER ANALYSIS.
?
I THINK ...
...SHE'S SOMEONE WHO'S ABLE TO PUT IN A TON OF EFFORT THAT NOBODY EVER SEES.

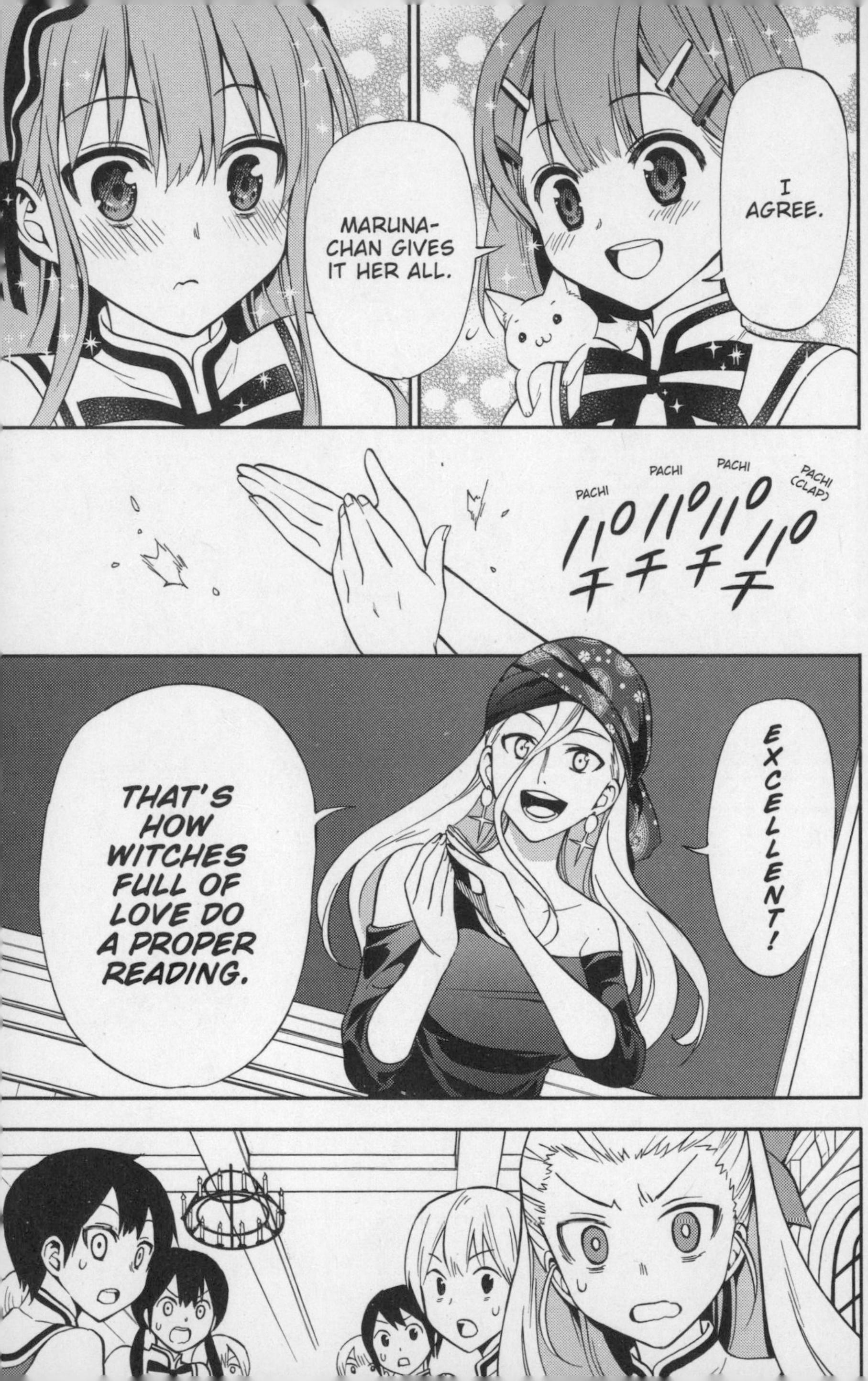
I AGREE.
MARUNA-CHAN GIVES IT HER ALL.
PACHI (CLAP)
PACHI
PACHI
PACHI
パチパチパチパチ
EXCELLENT!
THAT'S HOW WITCHES FULL OF LOVE DO A PROPER READING.

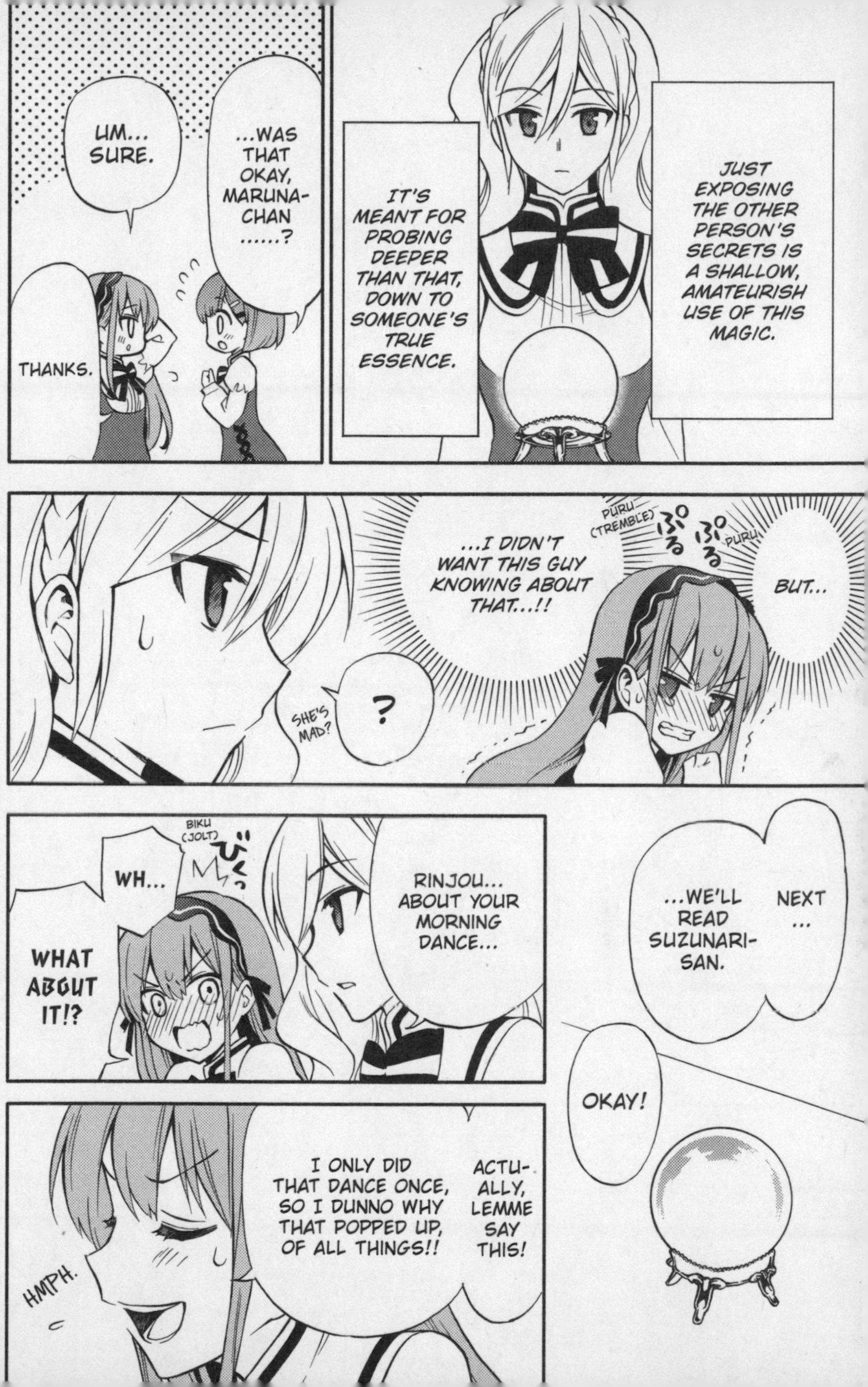
JUST EXPOSING THE OTHER PERSON'S SECRETS IS A SHALLOW, AMATEURISH USE OF THIS MAGIC.
IT'S MEANT FOR PROBING DEEPER THAN THAT, DOWN TO SOMEONE'S TRUE ESSENCE.
...WAS THAT OKAY, MARUNA-CHAN ......?
UM... SURE.
THANKS.
BUT...
PURU (TREMBLE)
PURU
...I DIDN'T WANT THIS GUY KNOWING ABOUT THAT...!!
?
SHE'S MAD?
NEXT ...
...WE'LL READ SUZUNARI-SAN.
OKAY!
RINJOU... ABOUT YOUR MORNING DANCE...
BIKU (JOLT)
WH...
WHAT ABOUT IT!?
ACTU-ALLY, LEMME SAY THIS!
I ONLY DID THAT DANCE ONCE, SO I DUNNO WHY THAT POPPED UP, OF ALL THINGS!!
HMPH.

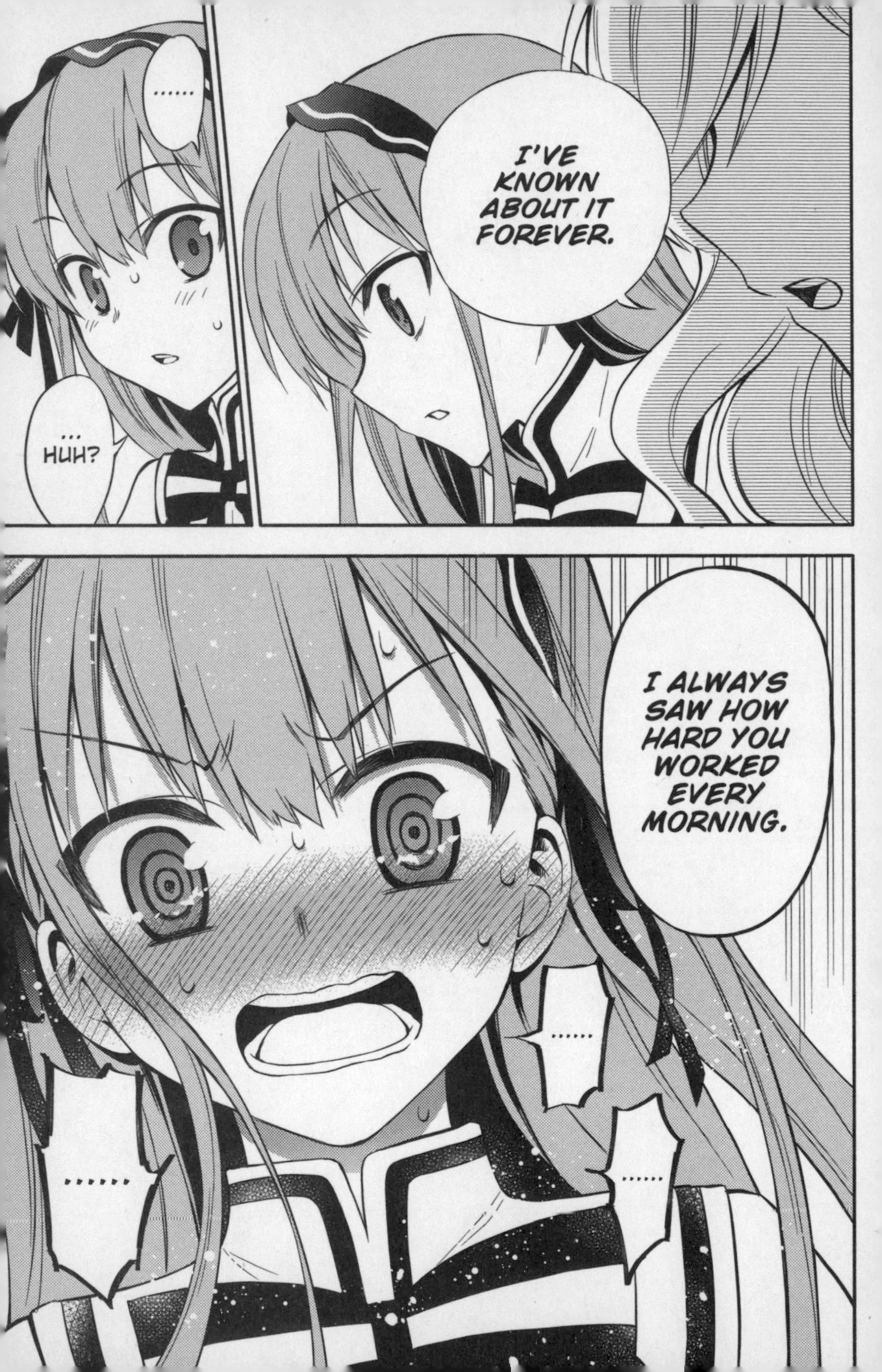
I'VE KNOWN ABOUT IT FOREVER.
......
... HUH?
I ALWAYS SAW HOW HARD YOU WORKED EVERY MORNING.
......
......
......

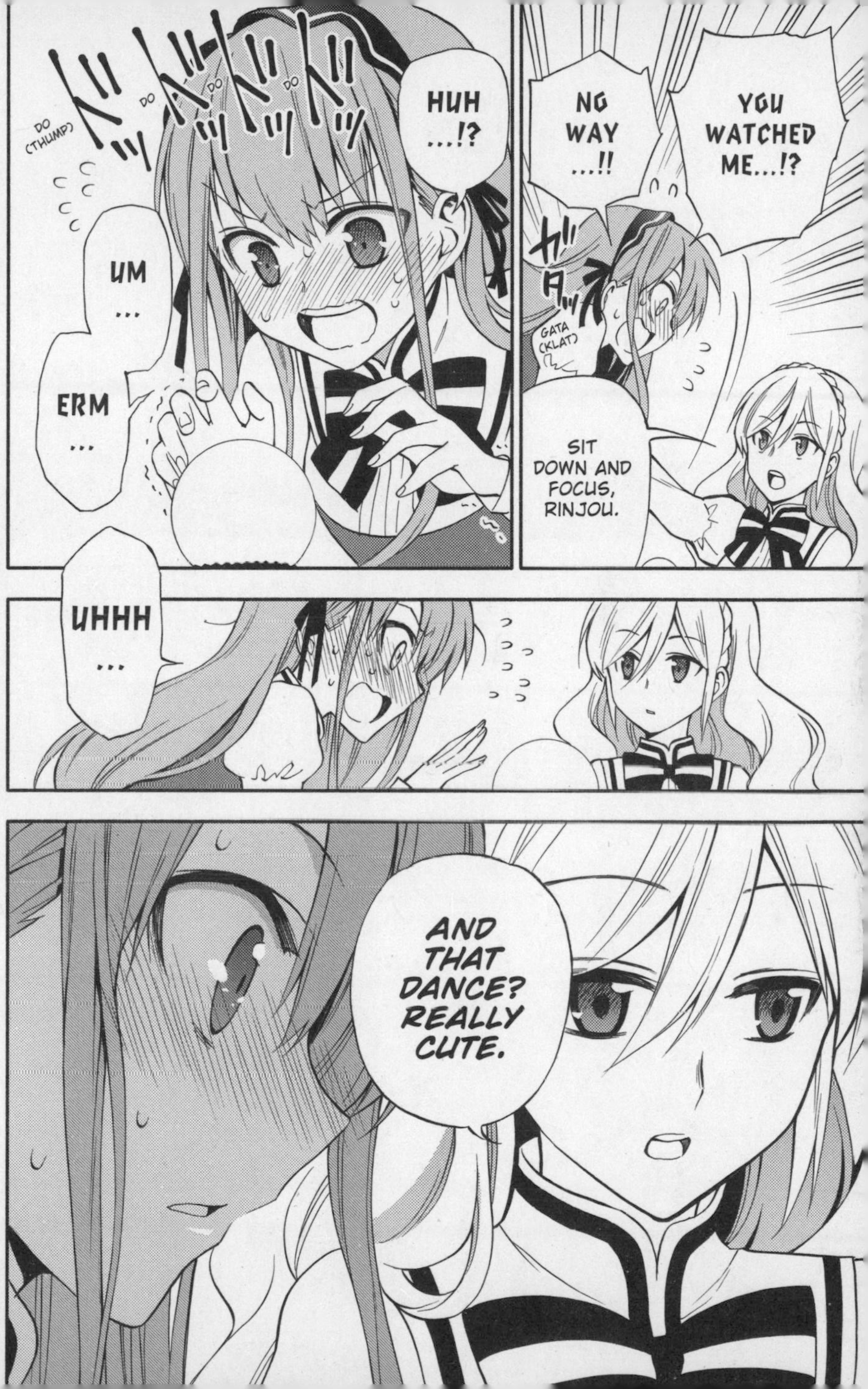
YOU WATCHED ME...!?
NO WAY ...!!
GATA (KLAT)
SIT DOWN AND FOCUS, RINJOU.
HUH ...!?
DO DO DO
DO (THUMP)
UM ...
ERM ...
UHHH ...
AND THAT DANCE? REALLY CUTE.

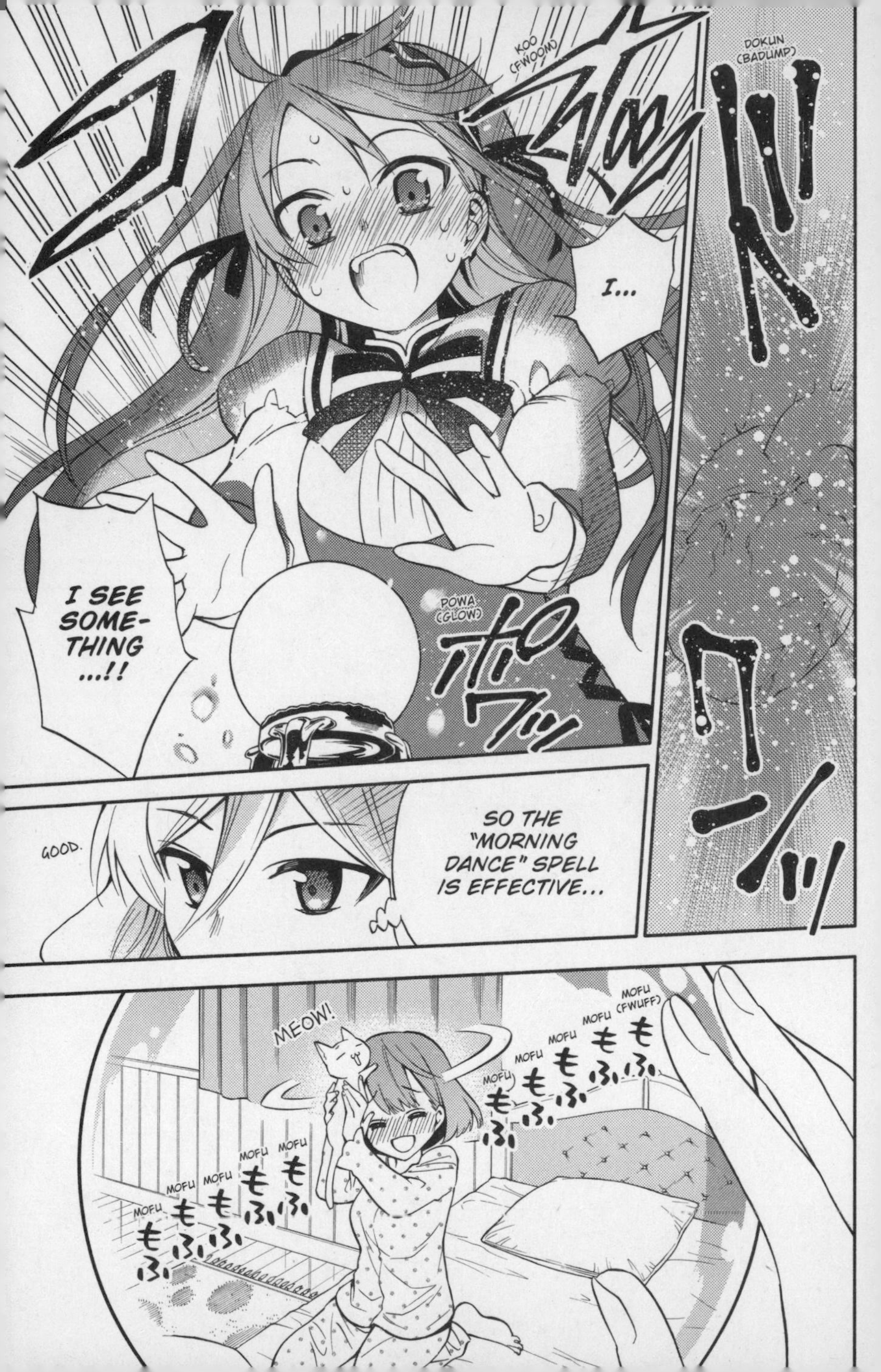
DOKUN (BADUMP)
KOO (FWOOM)
I...
POWA (GLOW)
I SEE SOME-THING...!!
SO THE "MORNING DANCE" SPELL IS EFFECTIVE...
GOOD.
MOFU (FWUFF) MOFU MOFU MOFU MOFU
MEOW!
MOFU MOFU MOFU MOFU

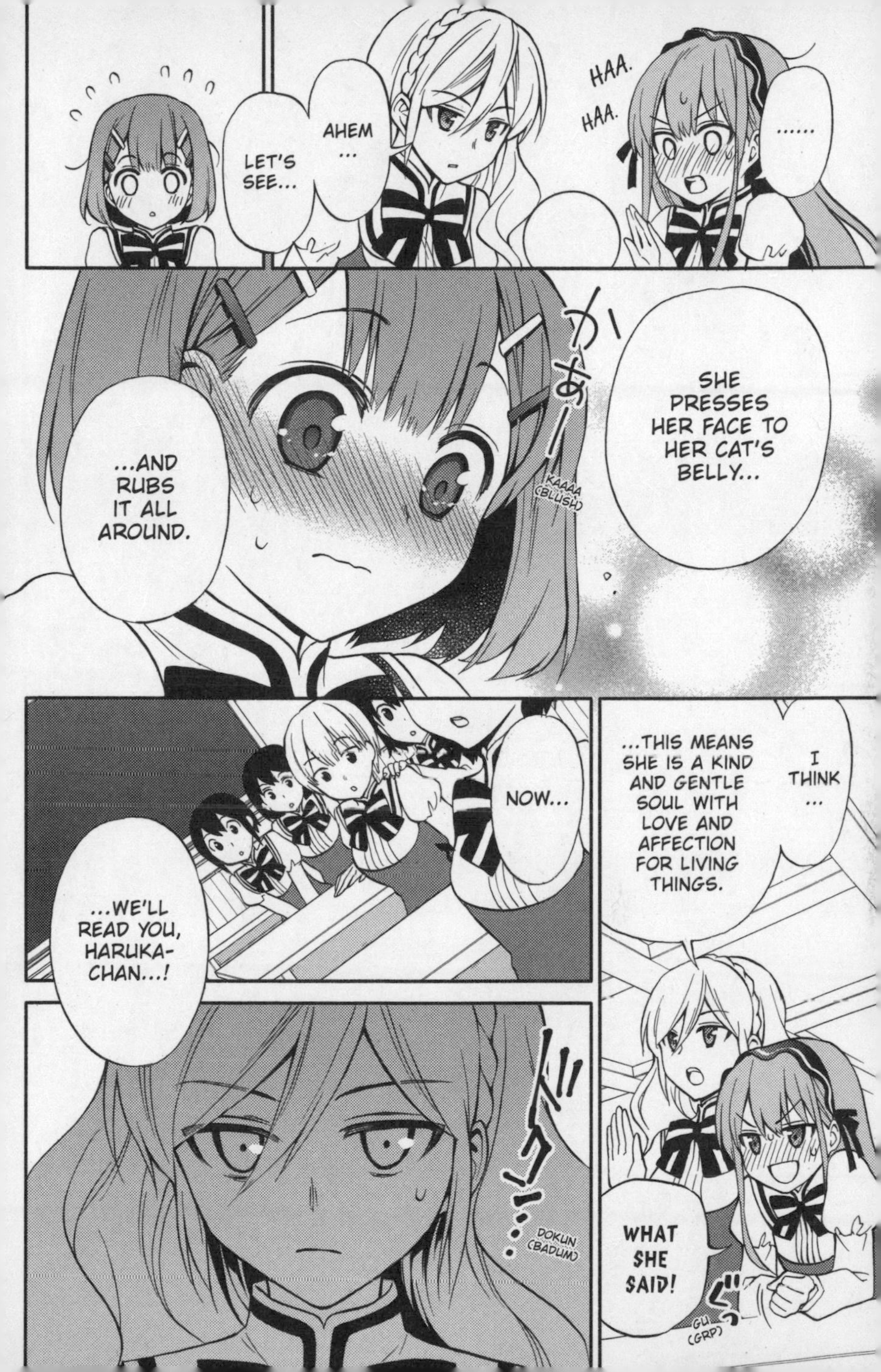
HAA.
HAA.
......
AHEM ...
LET'S SEE...
SHE PRESSES HER FACE TO HER CAT'S BELLY...
KAAAA (BLUSH)
...AND RUBS IT ALL AROUND.
I THINK ...
...THIS MEANS SHE IS A KIND AND GENTLE SOUL WITH LOVE AND AFFECTION FOR LIVING THINGS.
WHAT SHE SAID!
GU (GRP)
NOW...
...WE'LL READ YOU, HARUKA-CHAN...!
DOKUN (BADUM)

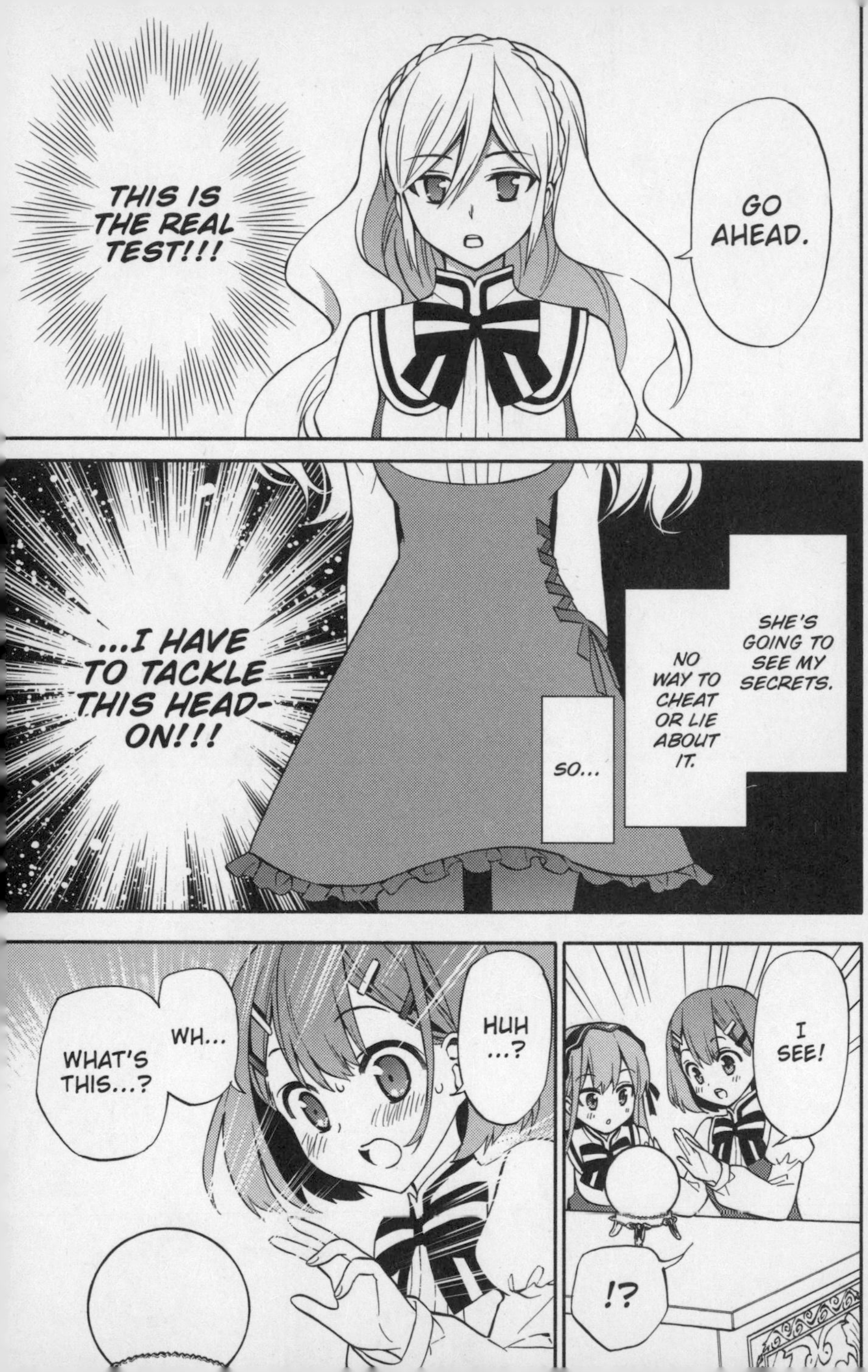
GO AHEAD.
THIS IS THE REAL TEST!!!
SHE'S GOING TO SEE MY SECRETS.
NO WAY TO CHEAT OR LIE ABOUT IT.
SO...
...I HAVE TO TACKLE THIS HEAD-ON!!!
I SEE!
!?
HUH...?
WH...
WHAT'S THIS...?

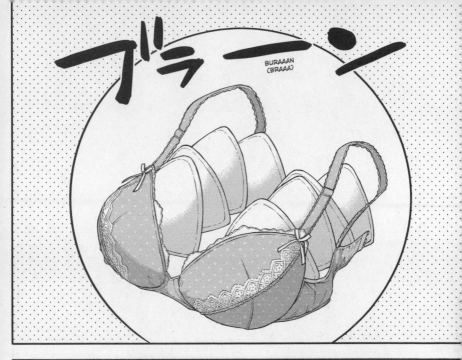

BURAAAN
(BRAAA)

P-PILES OF PADDING!?

......

ERM...

SHE...

ZAWA
(CHATTER)

?

WHAT DO YOU SEE?

WHAT'S UP?

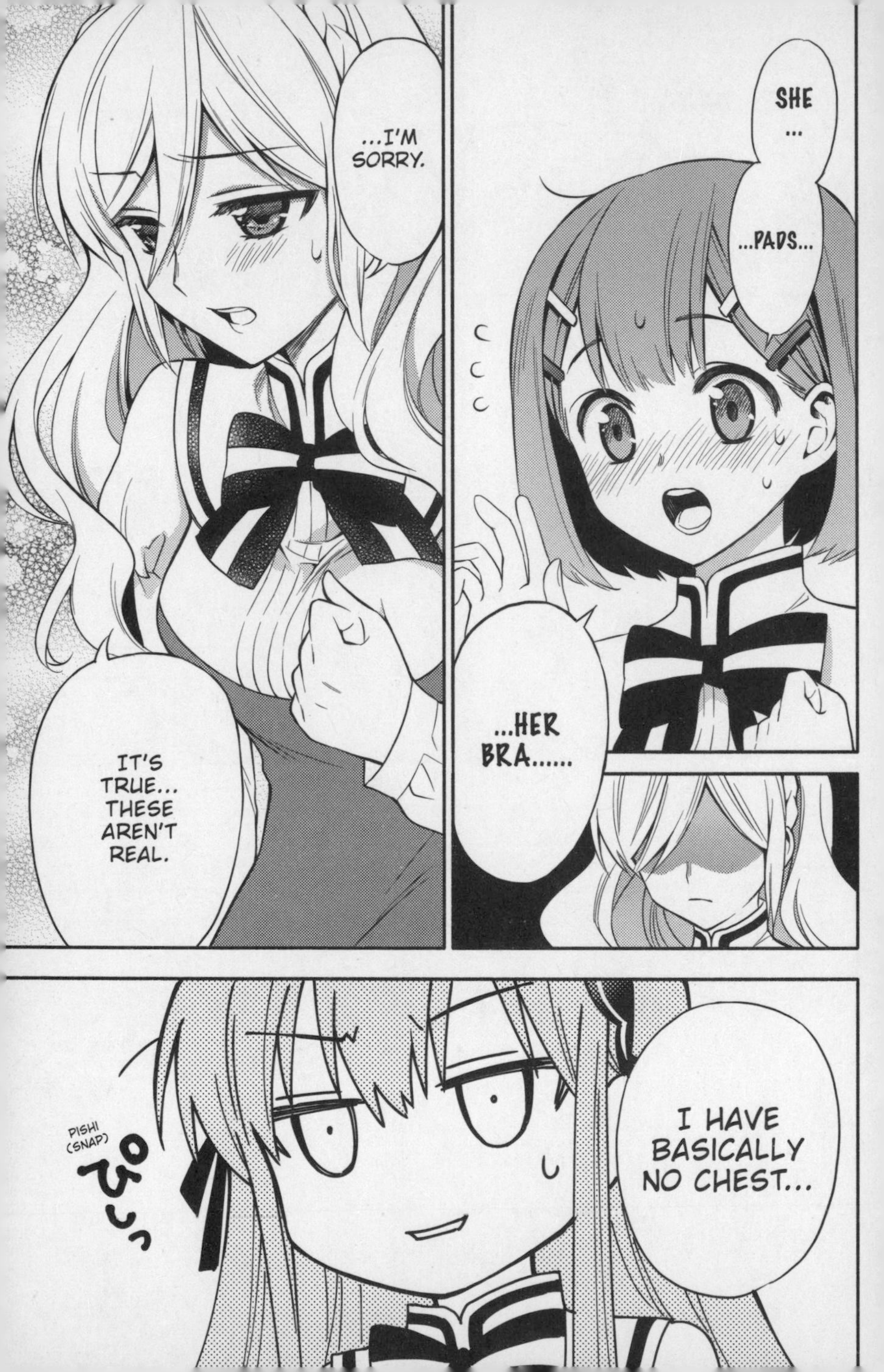
SHE ...
...PADS...
...HER BRA......
...I'M SORRY.
IT'S TRUE... THESE AREN'T REAL.
I HAVE BASICALLY NO CHEST...
ぴしっ
PISHI (SNAP)

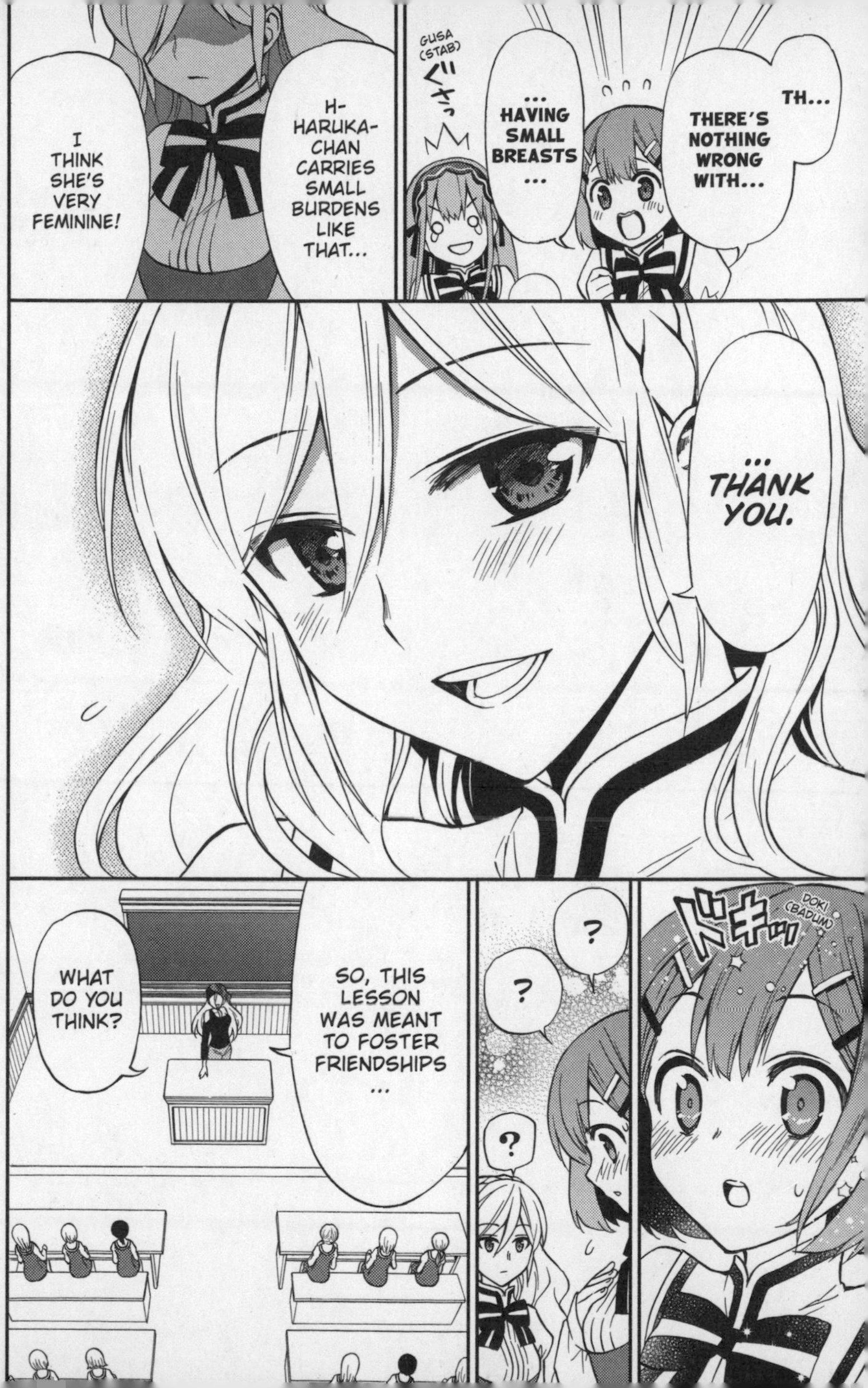
TH... THERE'S NOTHING WRONG WITH...
... HAVING SMALL BREASTS ...
GUSA (STAB)
H-HARUKA-CHAN CARRIES SMALL BURDENS LIKE THAT...
I THINK SHE'S VERY FEMININE!
... THANK YOU.
DOKI (BADUM)
?
?
?
SO, THIS LESSON WAS MEANT TO FOSTER FRIENDSHIPS ...
WHAT DO YOU THINK?

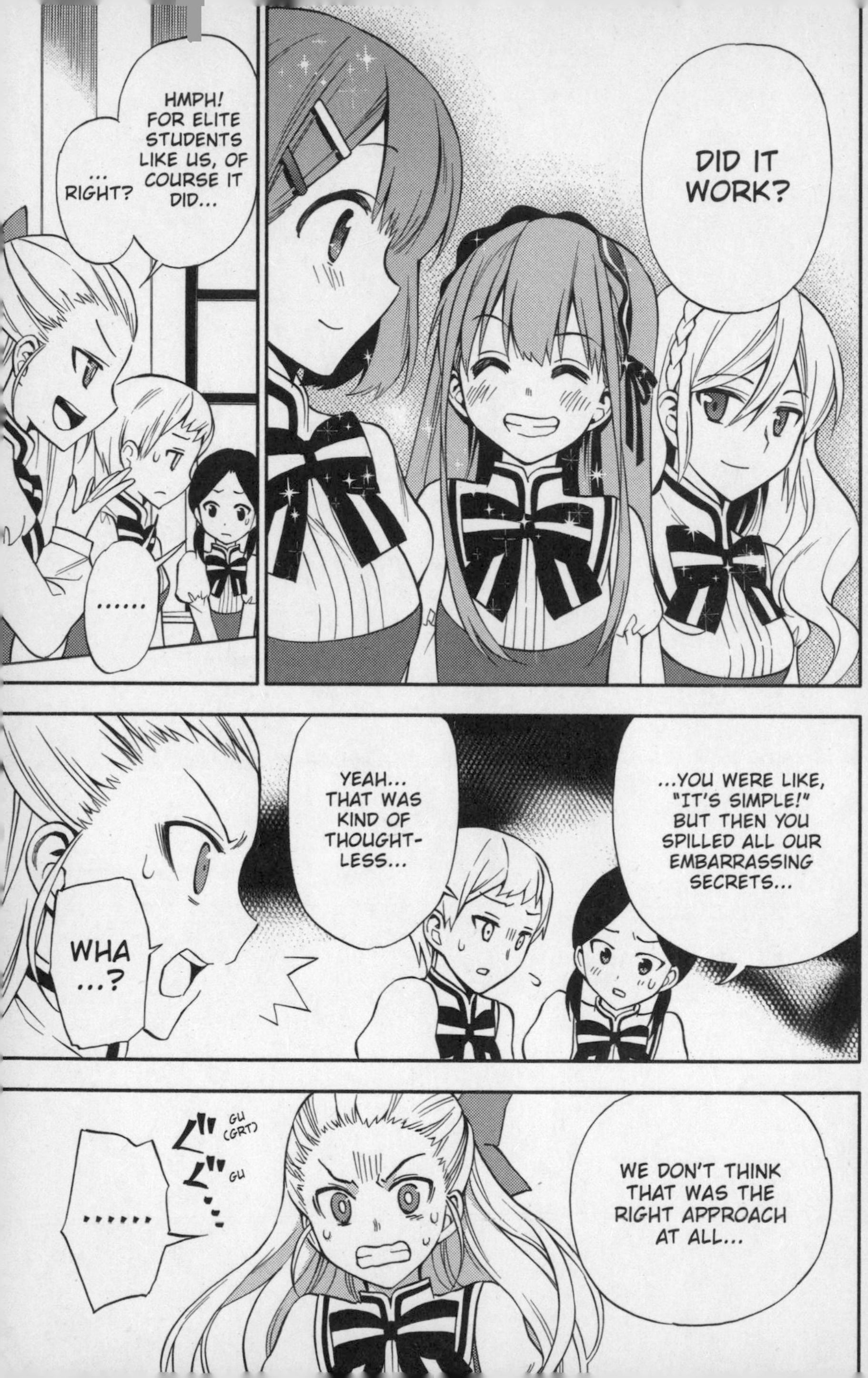
DID IT WORK?
HMPH! FOR ELITE STUDENTS LIKE US, OF COURSE IT DID...
...RIGHT?
......
...YOU WERE LIKE, "IT'S SIMPLE!" BUT THEN YOU SPILLED ALL OUR EMBARRASSING SECRETS...
YEAH... THAT WAS KIND OF THOUGHT-LESS...
WHA ...?
WE DON'T THINK THAT WAS THE RIGHT APPROACH AT ALL...
ぐ GU (GRT)
ぐ GU
......

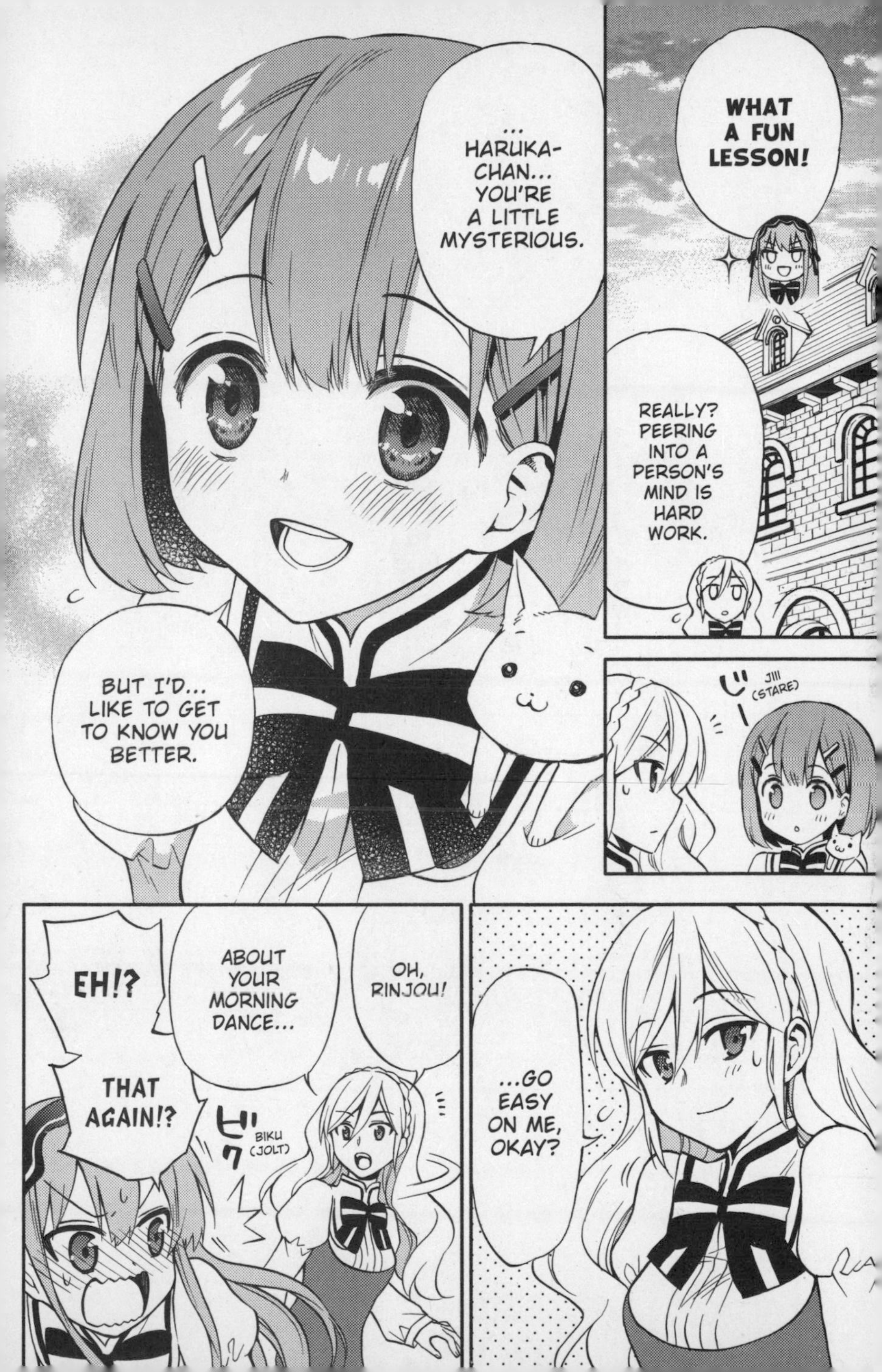
WHAT A FUN LESSON!
REALLY? PEERING INTO A PERSON'S MIND IS HARD WORK.
JIII (STARE)
... HARUKA-CHAN... YOU'RE A LITTLE MYSTERIOUS.
BUT I'D... LIKE TO GET TO KNOW YOU BETTER.
...GO EASY ON ME, OKAY?
OH, RINJOU!
ABOUT YOUR MORNING DANCE...
BIKU (JOLT)
EH!?
THAT AGAIN!?

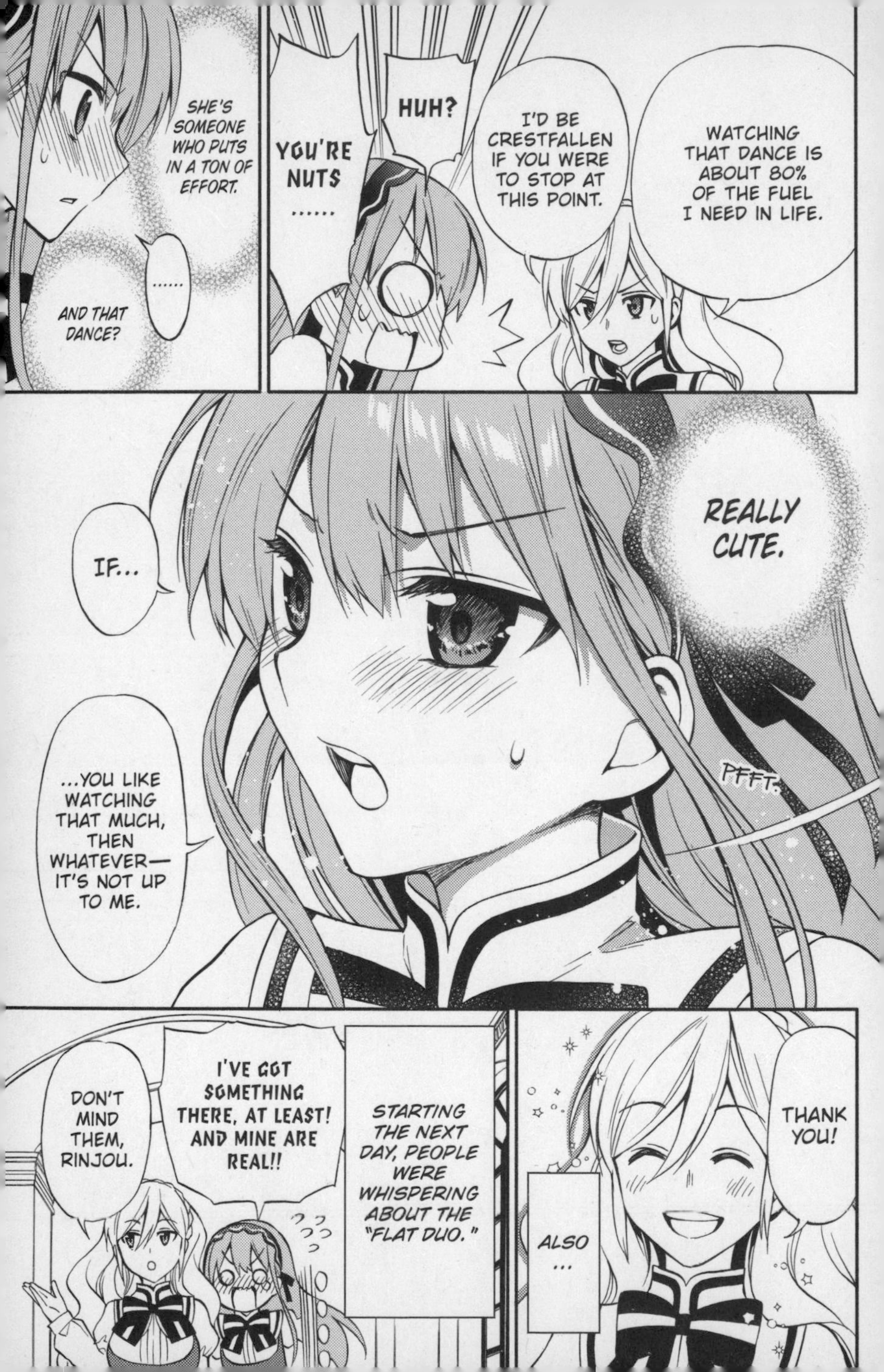
WATCHING THAT DANCE IS ABOUT 80% OF THE FUEL I NEED IN LIFE.
I'D BE CRESTFALLEN IF YOU WERE TO STOP AT THIS POINT.
HUH?
YOU'RE NUTS ......
SHE'S SOMEONE WHO PUTS IN A TON OF EFFORT.
......
AND THAT DANCE?
REALLY CUTE.
PFFT.
IF...
...YOU LIKE WATCHING THAT MUCH, THEN WHATEVER—IT'S NOT UP TO ME.
THANK YOU!
ALSO ...
STARTING THE NEXT DAY, PEOPLE WERE WHISPERING ABOUT THE "FLAT DUO."
I'VE GOT SOMETHING THERE, AT LEAST! AND MINE ARE REAL!!
DON'T MIND THEM, RINJOU.

If Witch, then Which?

PEOPLE CALL HER MA○FOY BEHIND HER BACK

THE NAME IS HANAMIYA!!

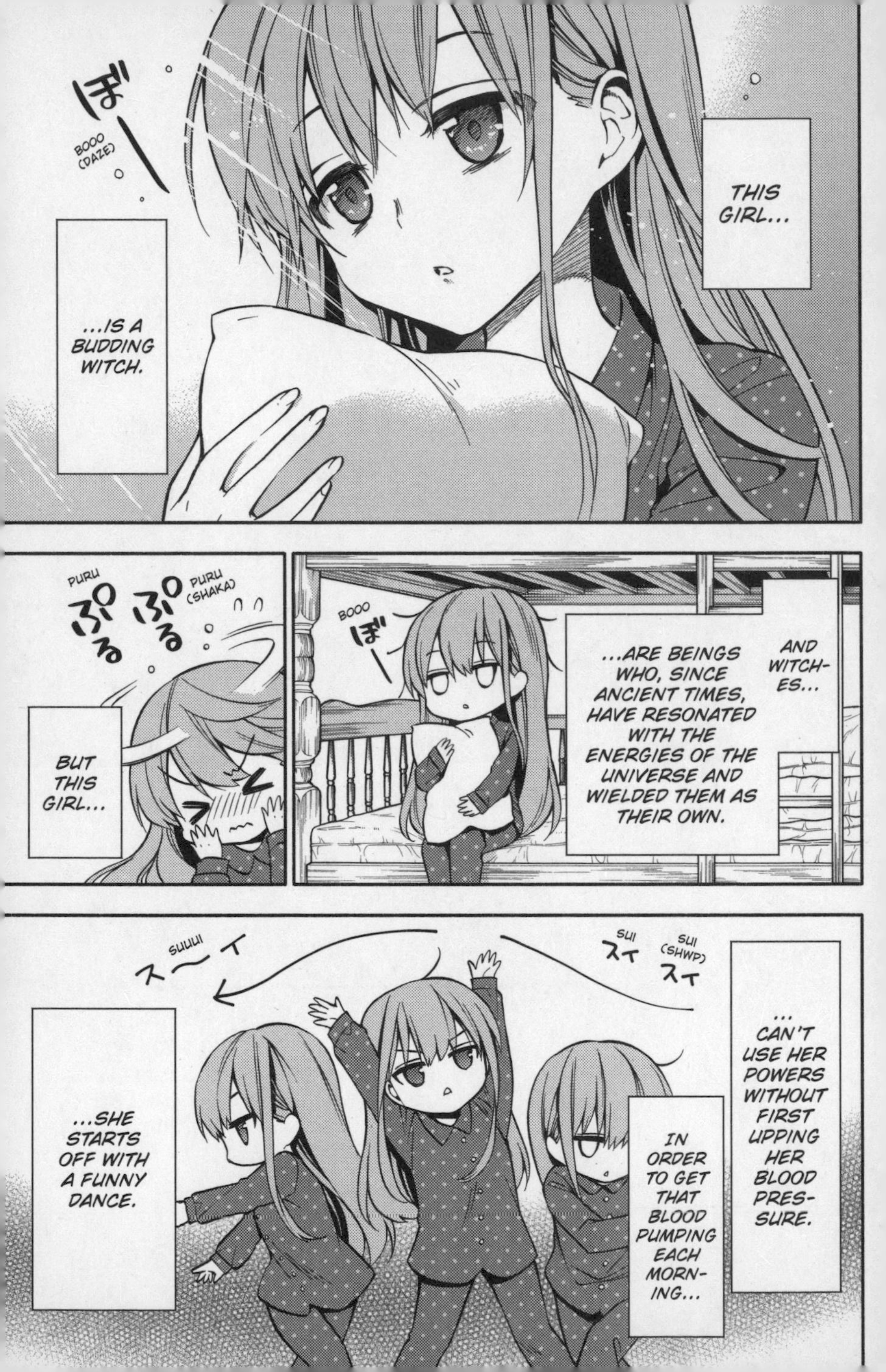
THIS GIRL...
ぼー
BOOO (DAZE)
...IS A BUDDING WITCH.
AND WITCHES...
...ARE BEINGS WHO, SINCE ANCIENT TIMES, HAVE RESONATED WITH THE ENERGIES OF THE UNIVERSE AND WIELDED THEM AS THEIR OWN.
ぼー
BOOO
ぷる ぷる
PURU PURU (SHAKA)
BUT THIS GIRL...
...CAN'T USE HER POWERS WITHOUT FIRST UPPING HER BLOOD PRESSURE.
スィ スィ
SUI SUI (SHWP)
IN ORDER TO GET THAT BLOOD PUMPING EACH MORNING...
スーイ
SUUUI
...SHE STARTS OFF WITH A FUNNY DANCE.

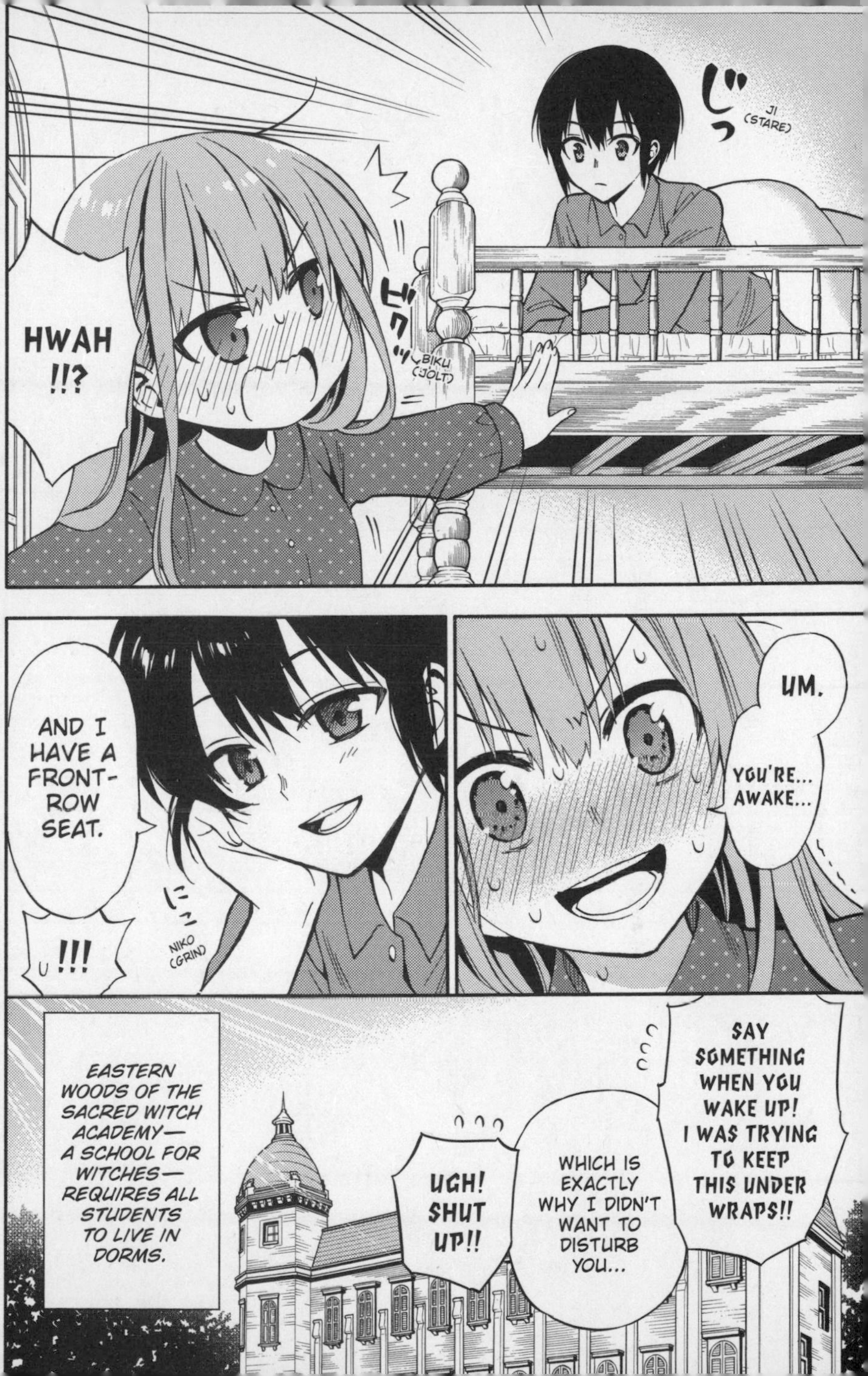
じっ
JI (STARE)
ビクッ
BIKU (JOLT)
HWAH !!?
UM.
YOU'RE... AWAKE...
AND I HAVE A FRONT-ROW SEAT.
にこ
NIKO (GRIN)
!!!
SAY SOMETHING WHEN YOU WAKE UP! I WAS TRYING TO KEEP THIS UNDER WRAPS!!
WHICH IS EXACTLY WHY I DIDN'T WANT TO DISTURB YOU...
UGH! SHUT UP!!
EASTERN WOODS OF THE SACRED WITCH ACADEMY—A SCHOOL FOR WITCHES—REQUIRES ALL STUDENTS TO LIVE IN DORMS.

MAGIC.3

Weight-Wary Witch

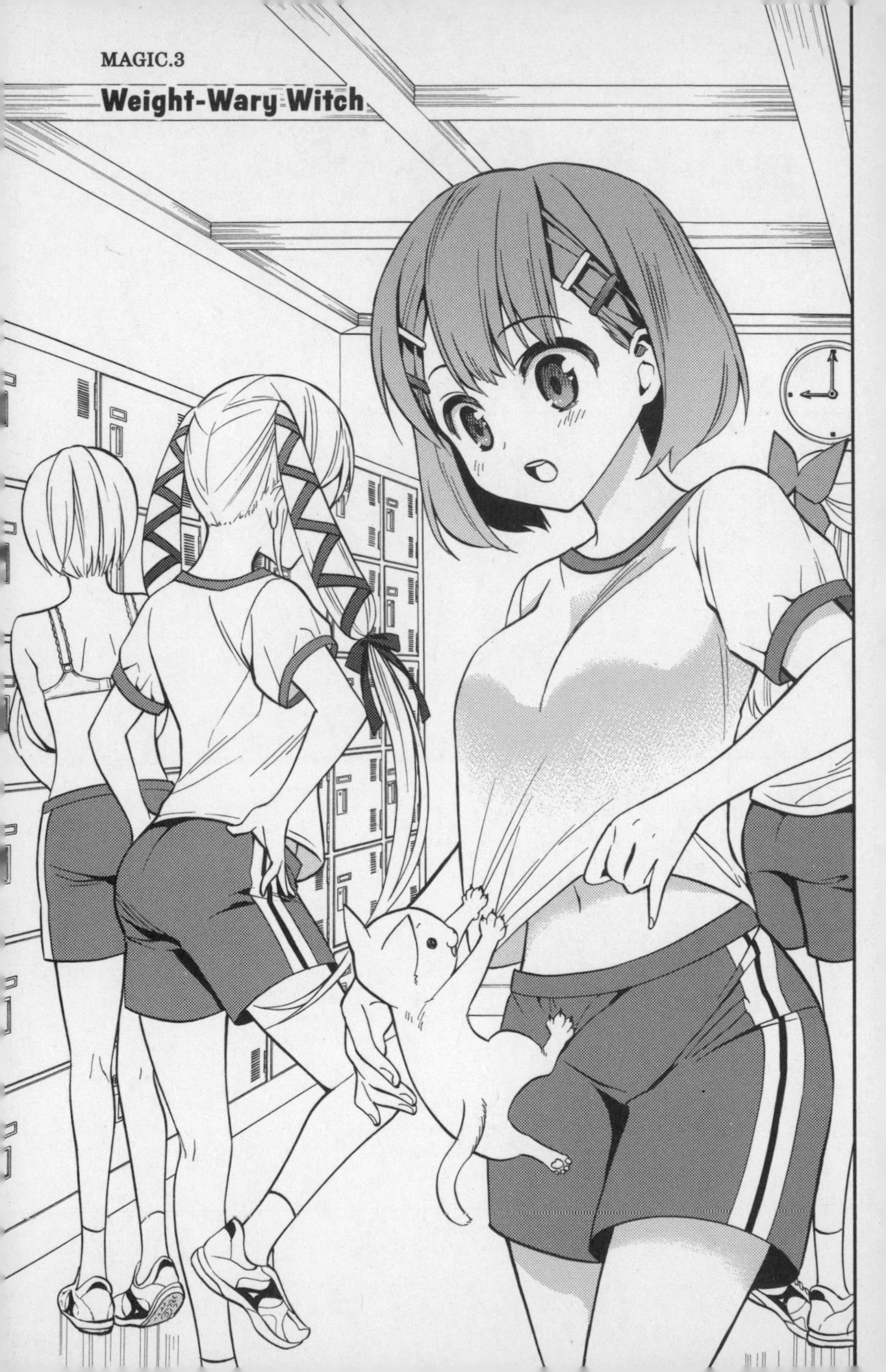

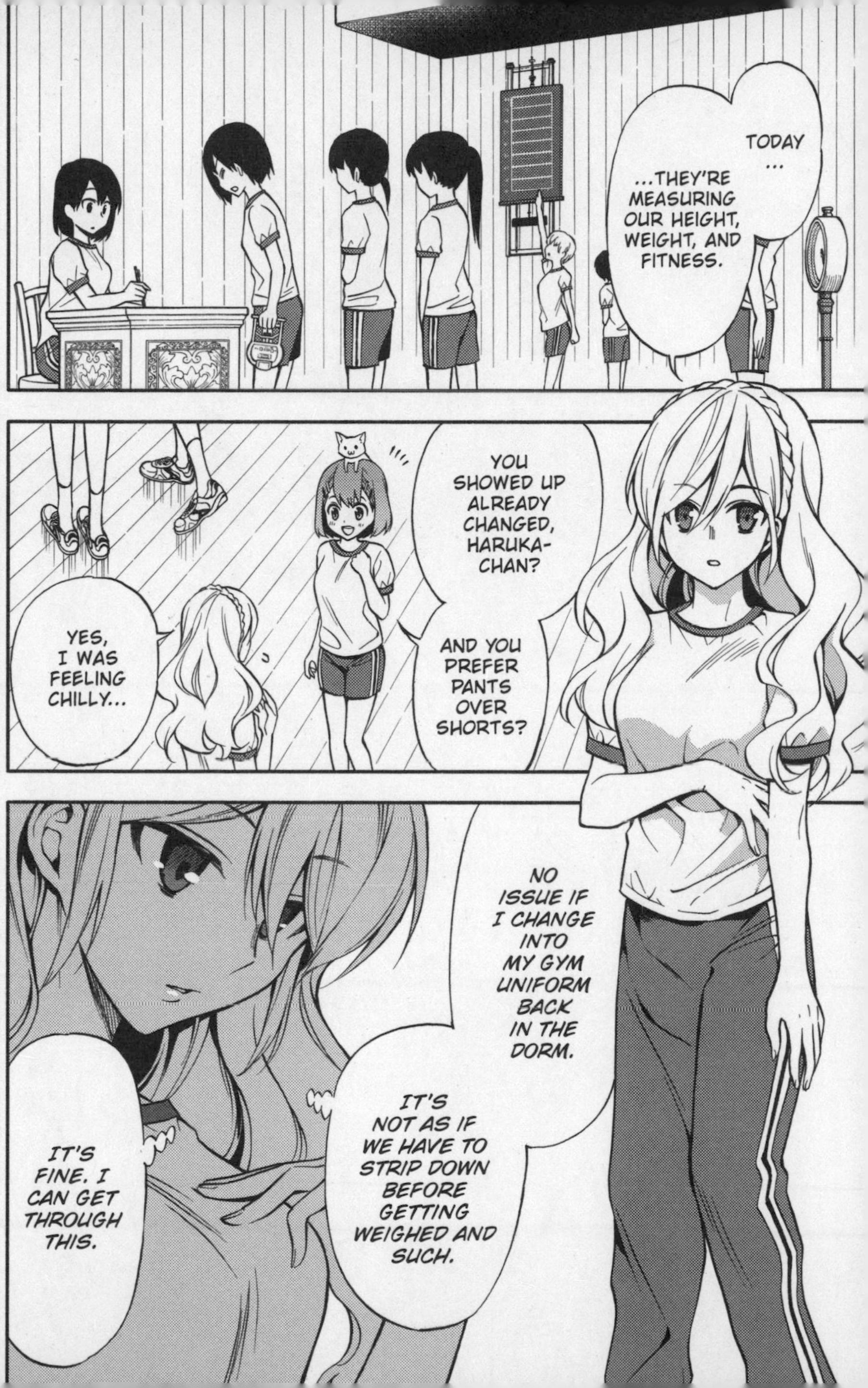
TODAY ... ...THEY'RE MEASURING OUR HEIGHT, WEIGHT, AND FITNESS.
YOU SHOWED UP ALREADY CHANGED, HARUKA-CHAN?
AND YOU PREFER PANTS OVER SHORTS?
YES, I WAS FEELING CHILLY...
NO ISSUE IF I CHANGE INTO MY GYM UNIFORM BACK IN THE DORM.
IT'S NOT AS IF WE HAVE TO STRIP DOWN BEFORE GETTING WEIGHED AND SUCH.
IT'S FINE. I CAN GET THROUGH THIS.

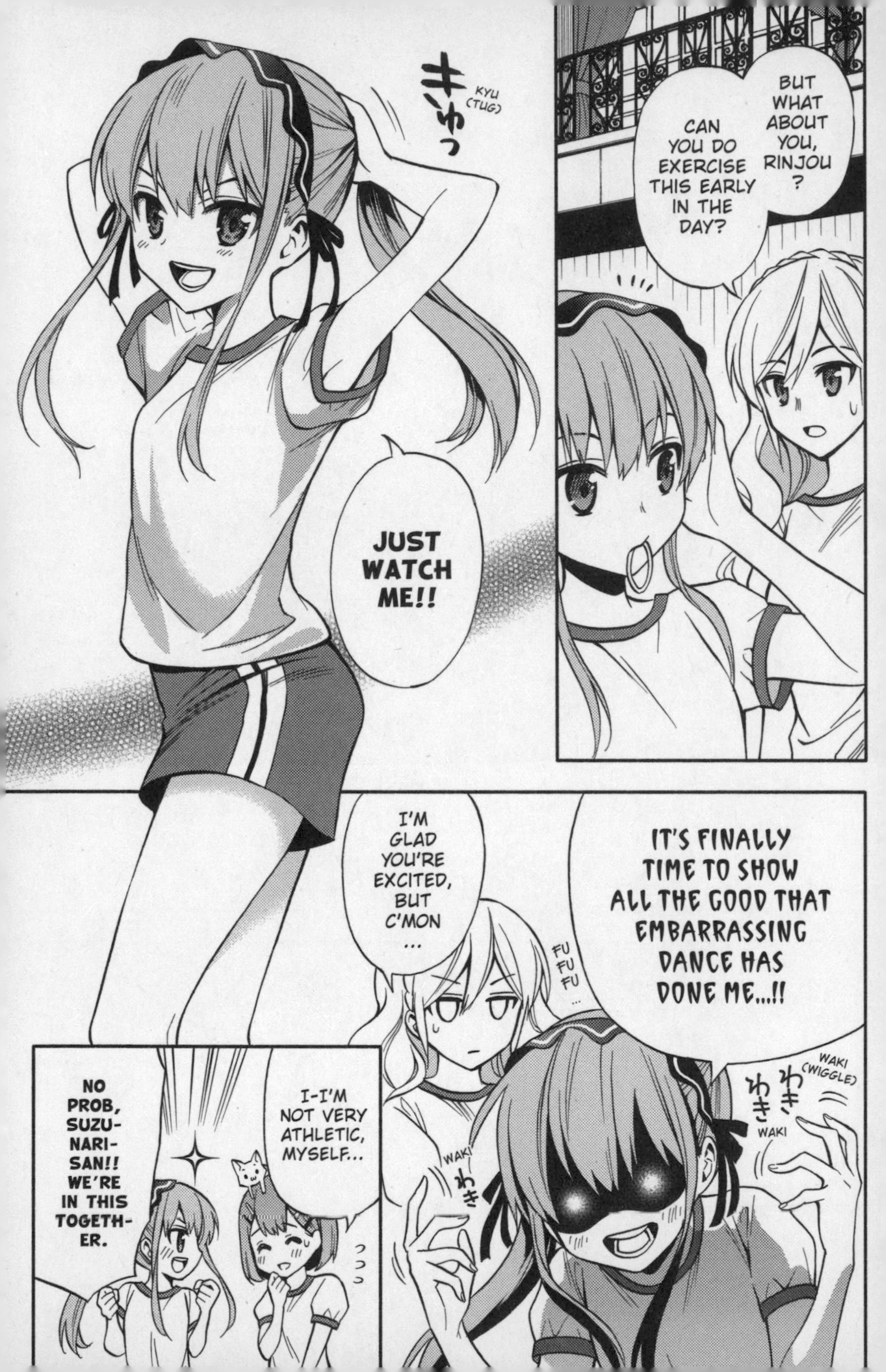
BUT WHAT ABOUT YOU, RINJOU?
CAN YOU DO EXERCISE THIS EARLY IN THE DAY?
KYU (TUG)
JUST WATCH ME!!
IT'S FINALLY TIME TO SHOW ALL THE GOOD THAT EMBARRASSING DANCE HAS DONE ME...!!
I'M GLAD YOU'RE EXCITED, BUT C'MON...
FU FU FU...
WAKI (WIGGLE)
WAKI
WAKI
I-I'M NOT VERY ATHLETIC, MYSELF...
NO PROB, SUZUNARI-SAN!! WE'RE IN THIS TOGETHER.

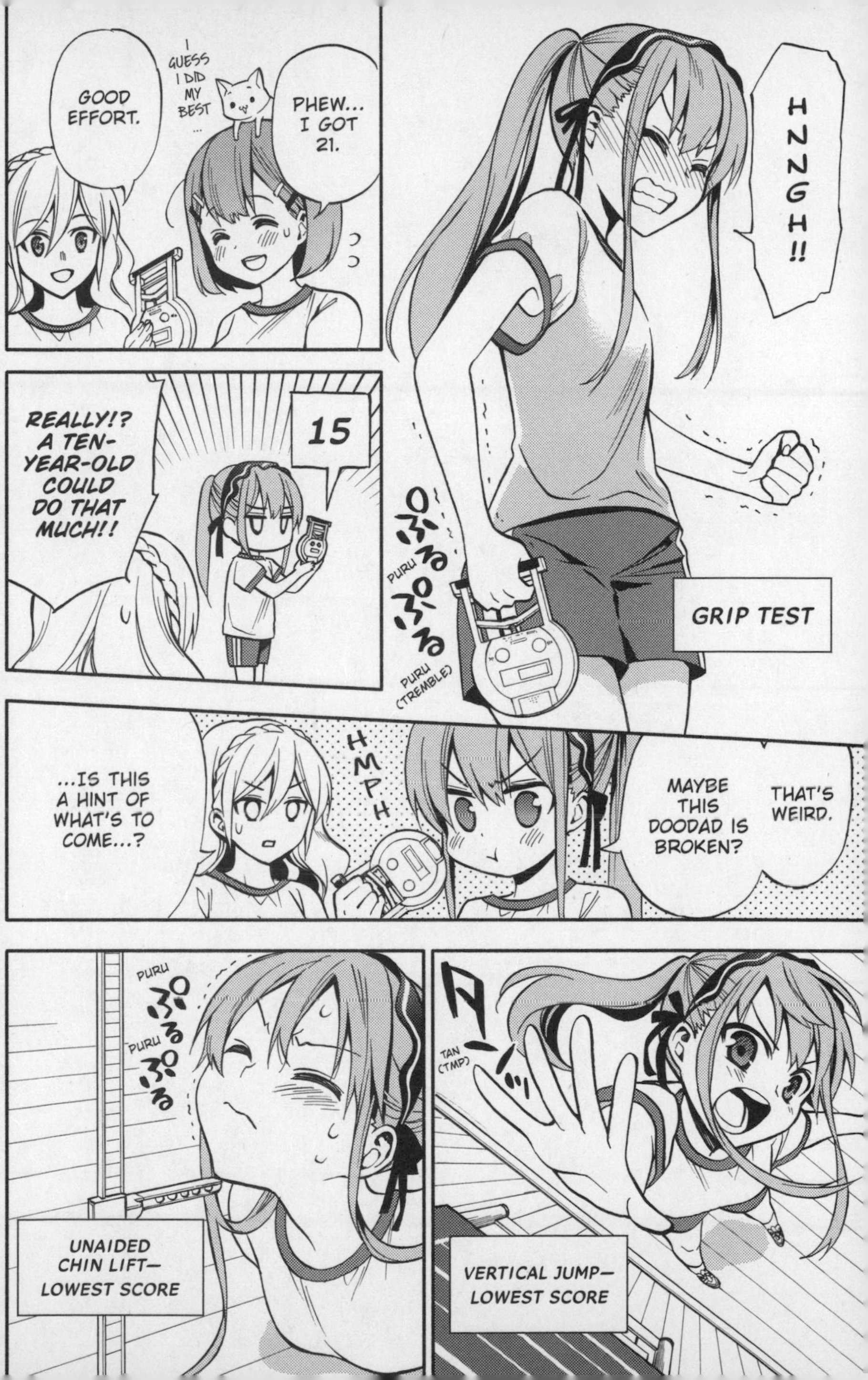
HNNGH!!
GRIP TEST
ぷるぷる
PURU PURU (TREMBLE)
PHEW... I GOT 21.
I GUESS I DID MY BEST ...
GOOD EFFORT.
15
REALLY!? A TEN-YEAR-OLD COULD DO THAT MUCH!!
THAT'S WEIRD.
MAYBE THIS DOODAD IS BROKEN?
HMPH
...IS THIS A HINT OF WHAT'S TO COME...?
TAN (TMP)
VERTICAL JUMP—LOWEST SCORE
ぷるぷる
PURU PURU
UNAIDED CHIN LIFT—LOWEST SCORE

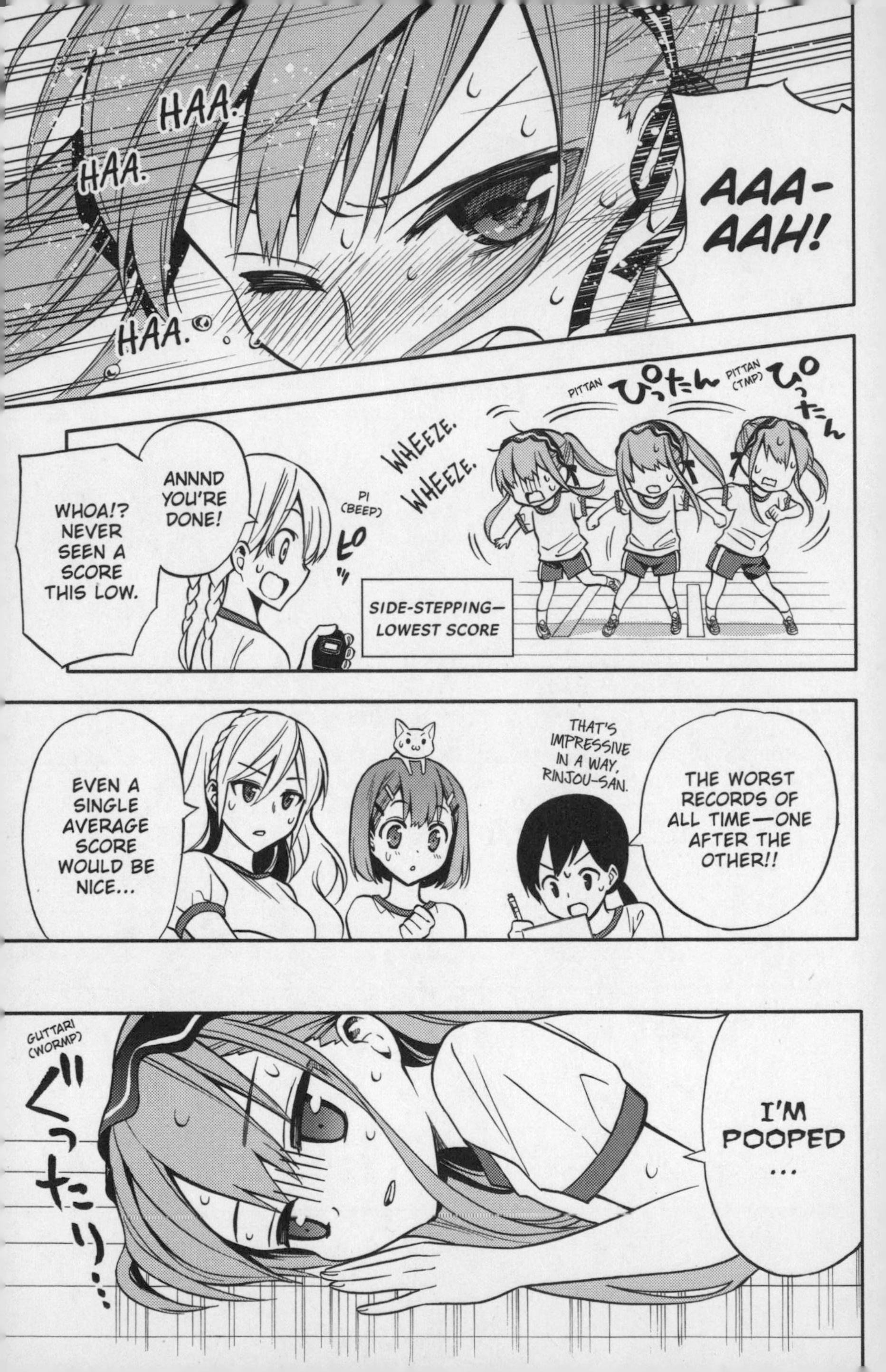
AAA-AAH!
HAA.
HAA.
HAA.
ぴったん
PITTAN (TMP)
ぴったん
PITTAN
WHEEZE. WHEEZE.
PI (BEEP)
ピ
ANNND YOU'RE DONE!
WHOA!? NEVER SEEN A SCORE THIS LOW.
SIDE-STEPPING—LOWEST SCORE
THE WORST RECORDS OF ALL TIME—ONE AFTER THE OTHER!!
THAT'S IMPRESSIVE IN A WAY, RINJOU-SAN.
EVEN A SINGLE AVERAGE SCORE WOULD BE NICE...
I'M POOPED ...
GUTTARI (WORMP)
ぐったり…

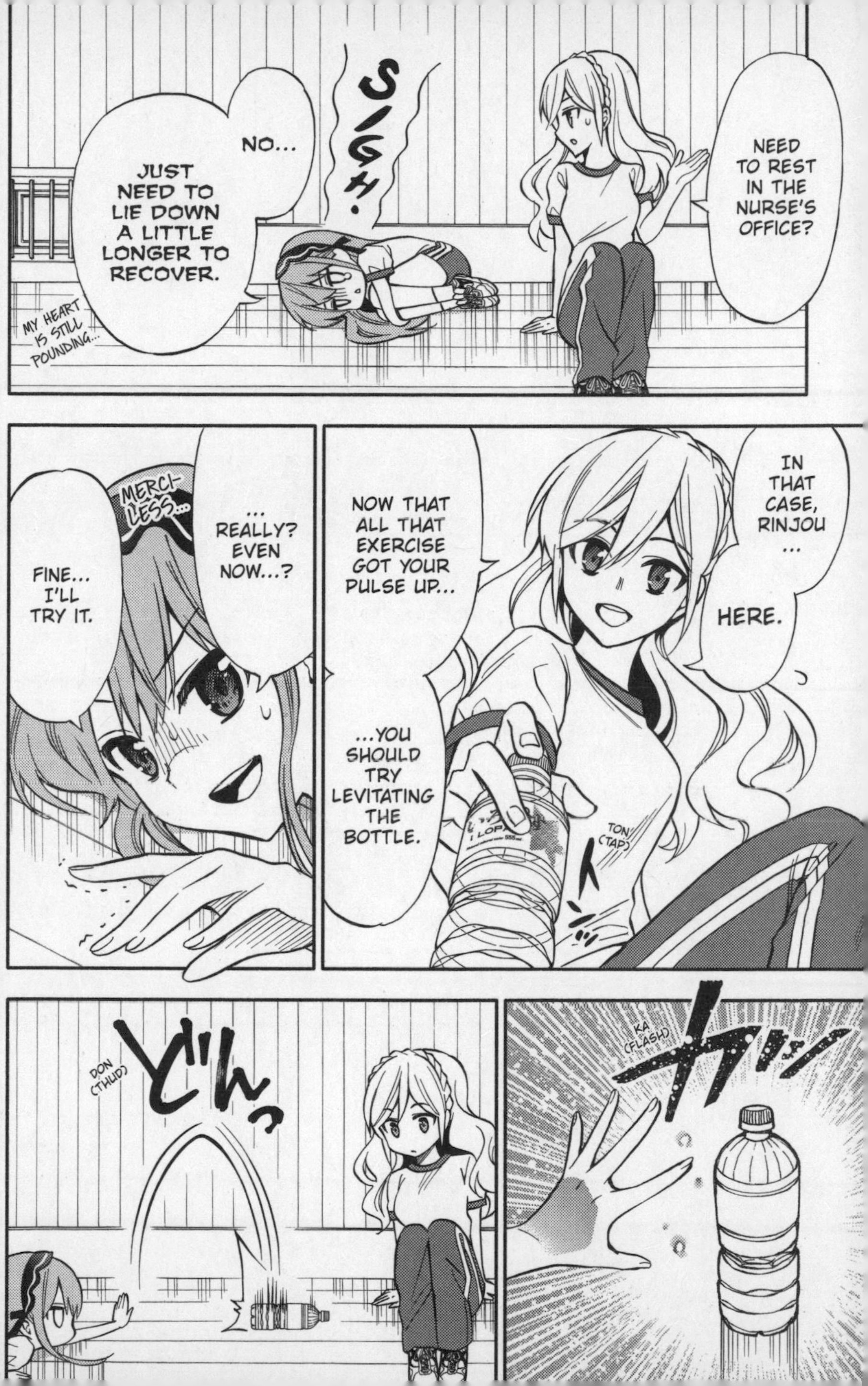
NEED TO REST IN THE NURSE'S OFFICE?
SIGH.
NO...
JUST NEED TO LIE DOWN A LITTLE LONGER TO RECOVER.
MY HEART IS STILL POUNDING...
IN THAT CASE, RINJOU...
HERE.
NOW THAT ALL THAT EXERCISE GOT YOUR PULSE UP...
...YOU SHOULD TRY LEVITATING THE BOTTLE.
TON (TAP)
...REALLY? EVEN NOW...?
MERCI-LESS...
FINE... I'LL TRY IT.
カッ
KA (FLASH)
どんっ
DON (THUD)

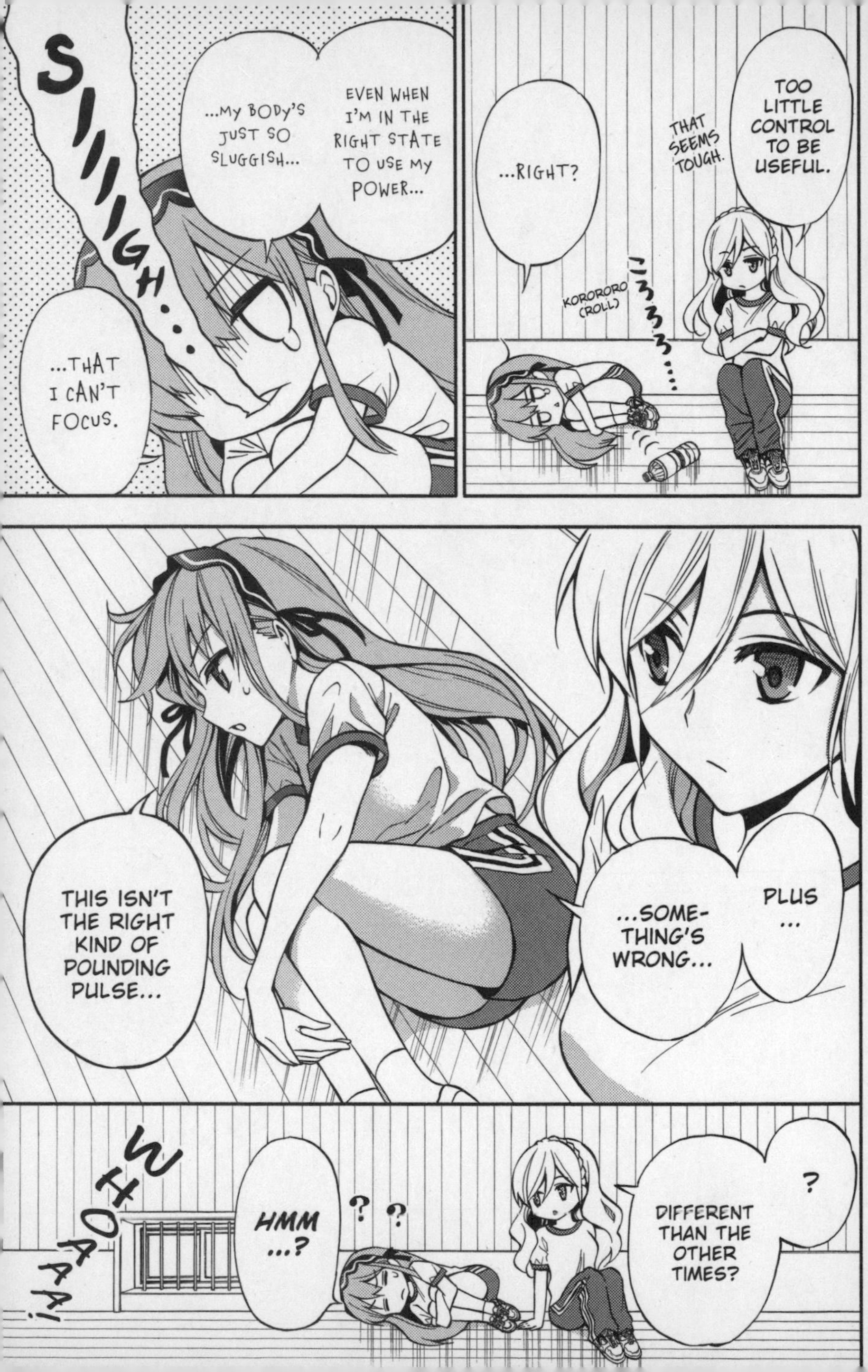
TOO LITTLE CONTROL TO BE USEFUL.
THAT SEEMS TOUGH.
...RIGHT?
ころろろ...
KORORORO (ROLL)
EVEN WHEN I'M IN THE RIGHT STATE TO USE MY POWER...
...MY BODY'S JUST SO SLUGGISH...
SIIIIGH...
...THAT I CAN'T FOCUS.
PLUS ...
...SOME-THING'S WRONG...
THIS ISN'T THE RIGHT KIND OF POUNDING PULSE...
? DIFFERENT THAN THE OTHER TIMES?
HMM ...?
? ?
WHOAAA!

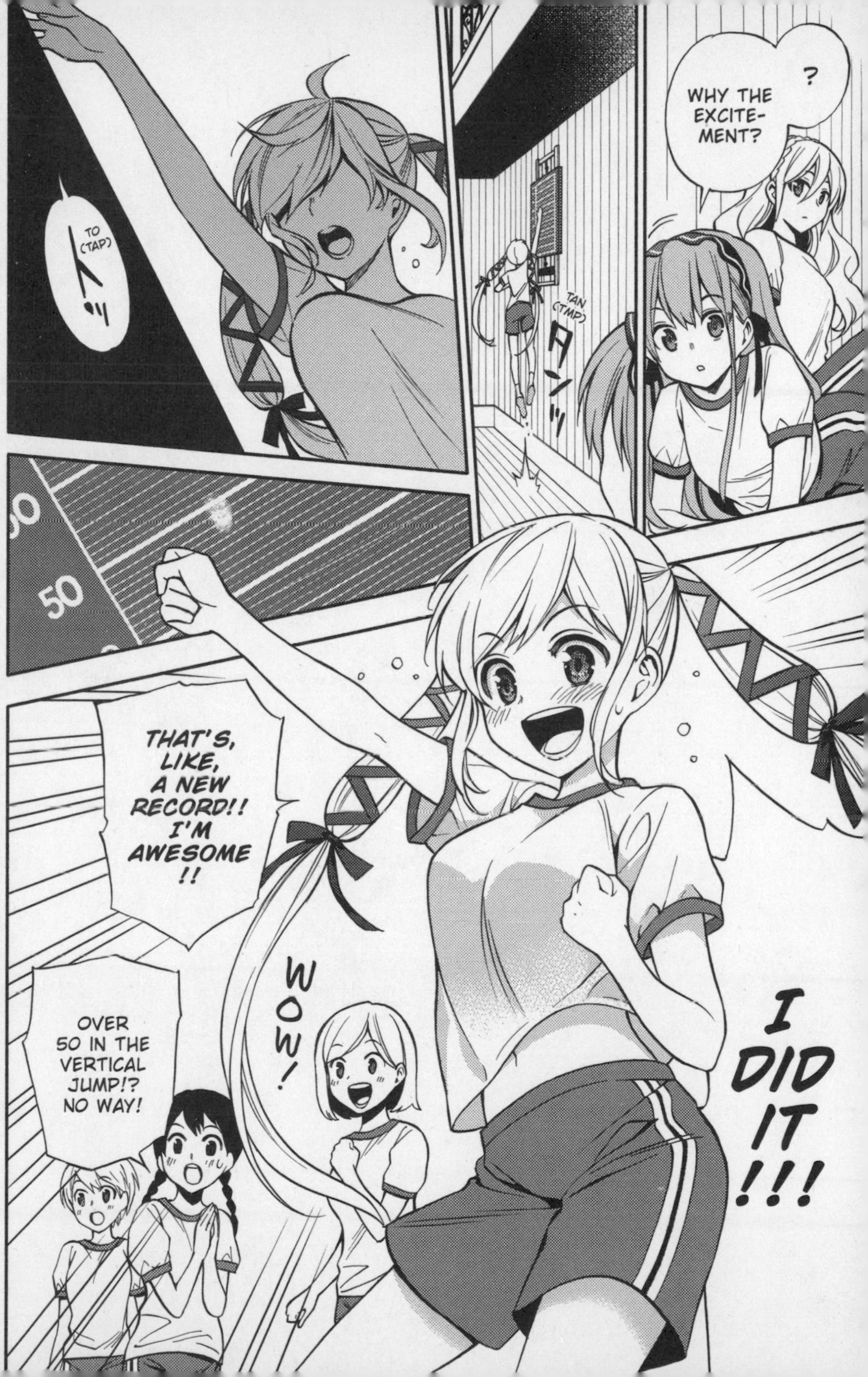
?
WHY THE EXCITE-MENT?
TAN (TMP)
TO (TAP)
50
50
I DID IT!!!
THAT'S, LIKE, A NEW RECORD!! I'M AWESOME!!
WOW!
OVER 50 IN THE VERTICAL JUMP!? NO WAY!

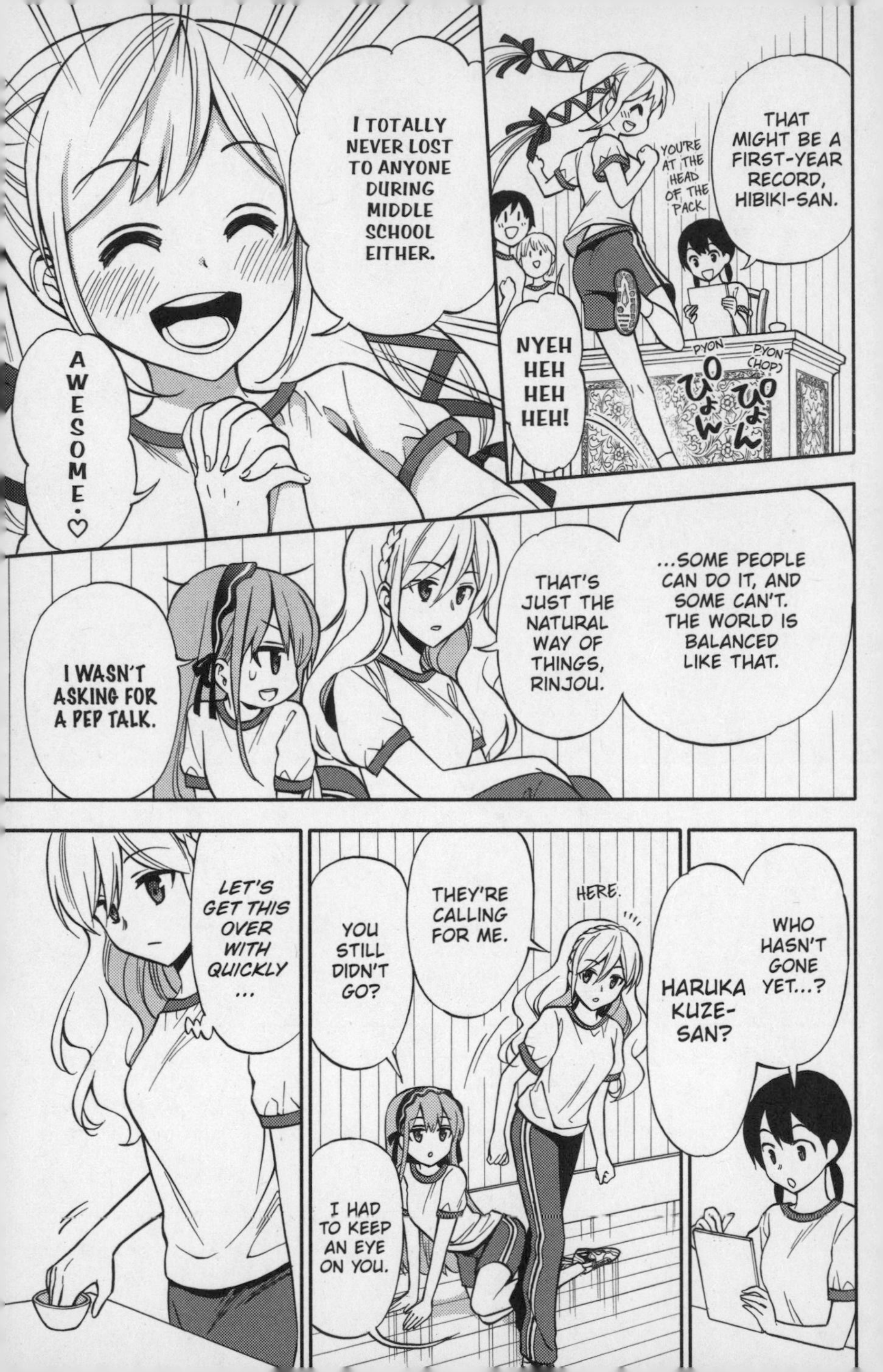
THAT MIGHT BE A FIRST-YEAR RECORD, HIBIKI-SAN.
YOU'RE AT THE HEAD OF THE PACK.
NYEH HEH HEH HEH!
PYON PYON (HOP)
ぴょん ぴょん
I TOTALLY NEVER LOST TO ANYONE DURING MIDDLE SCHOOL EITHER.
AWESOME.♡
...SOME PEOPLE CAN DO IT, AND SOME CAN'T. THE WORLD IS BALANCED LIKE THAT.
THAT'S JUST THE NATURAL WAY OF THINGS, RINJOU.
I WASN'T ASKING FOR A PEP TALK.
WHO HASN'T GONE YET...?
HARUKA KUZE-SAN?
HERE.
THEY'RE CALLING FOR ME.
YOU STILL DIDN'T GO?
I HAD TO KEEP AN EYE ON YOU.
LET'S GET THIS OVER WITH QUICKLY...

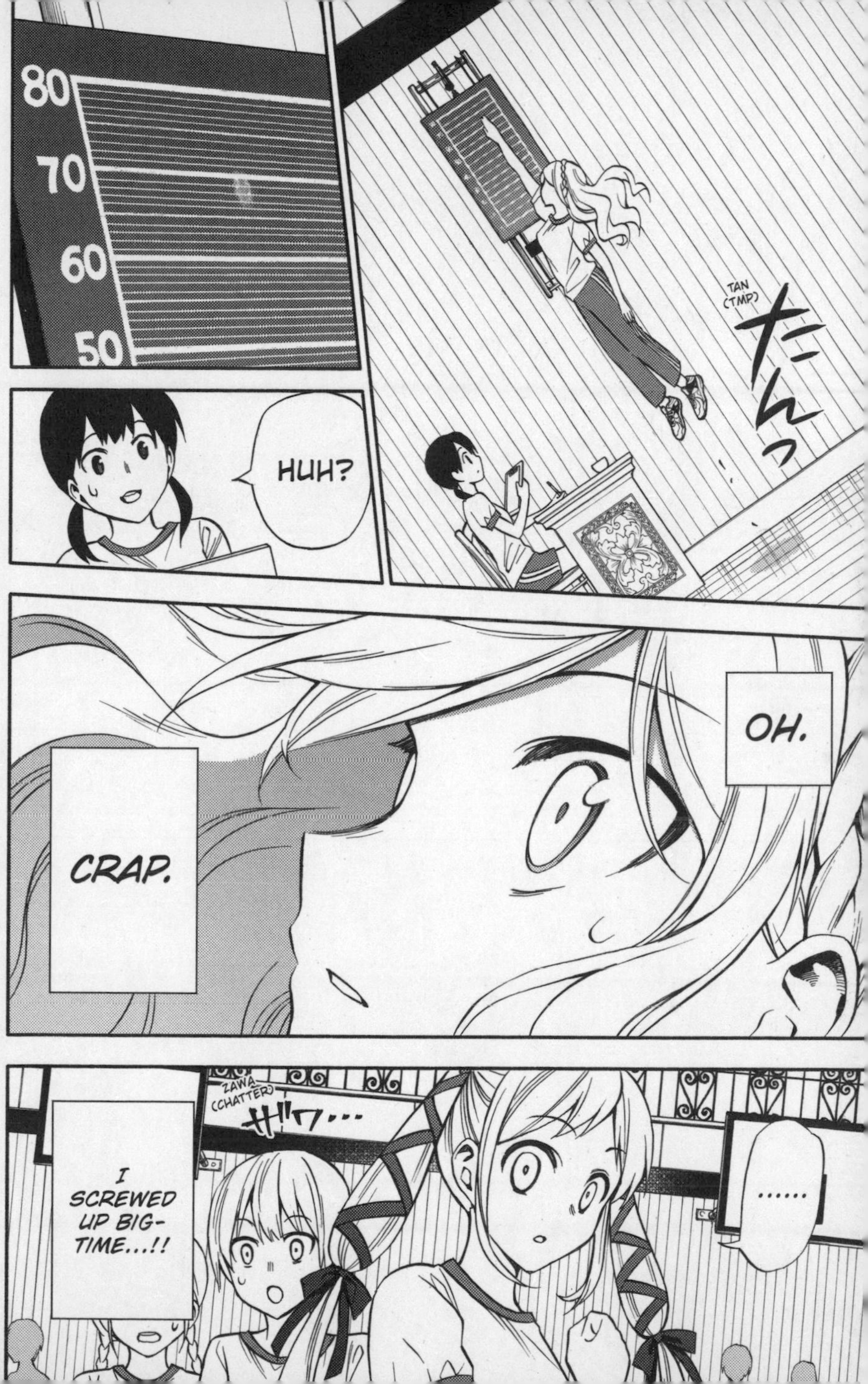
TAN (TMP)
たんっ
80
70
60
50
HUH?
OH.
CRAP.
......
ZAWA (CHATTER)
ザワ...
I SCREWED UP BIG-TIME...!!

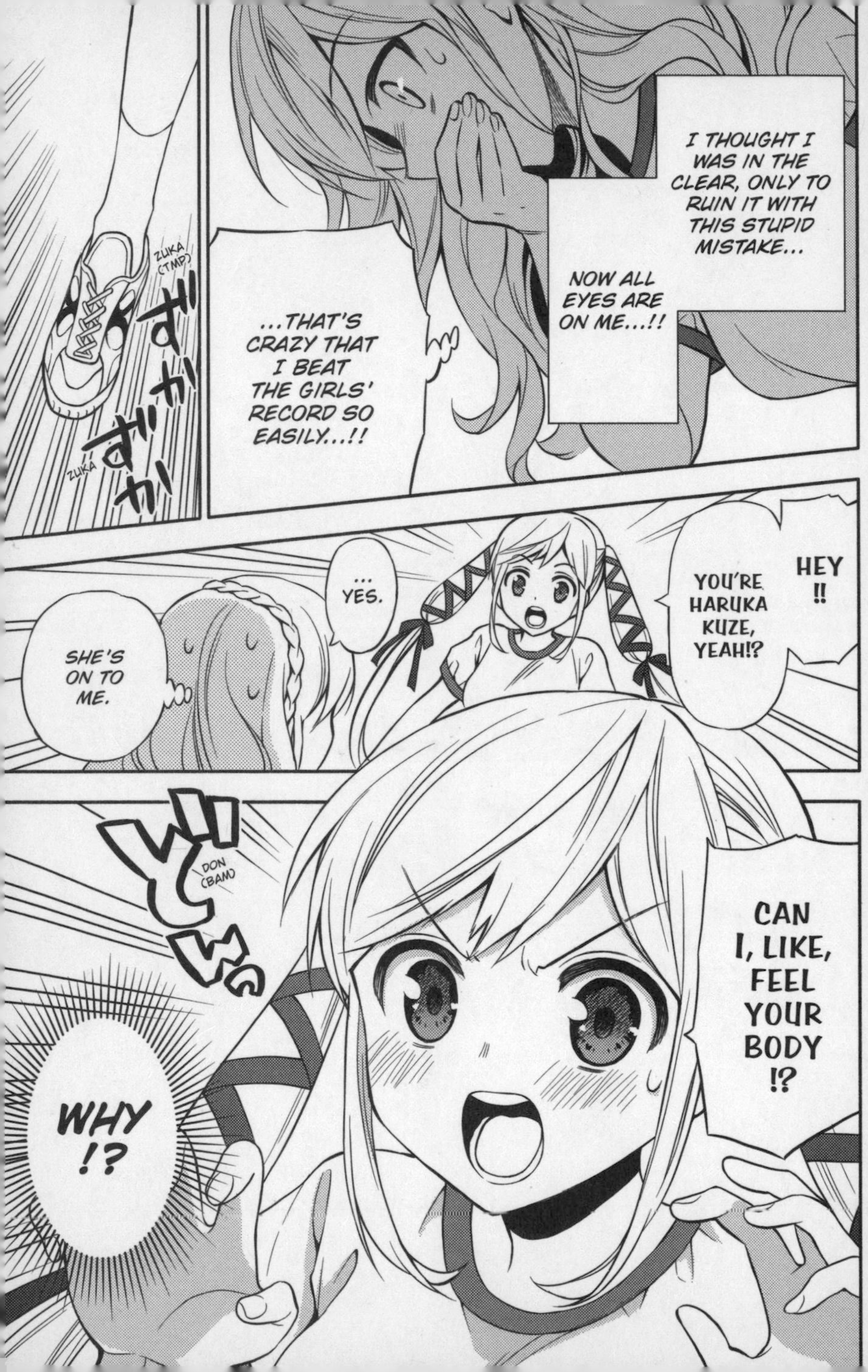
I THOUGHT I WAS IN THE CLEAR, ONLY TO RUIN IT WITH THIS STUPID MISTAKE...
NOW ALL EYES ARE ON ME...!!
...THAT'S CRAZY THAT I BEAT THE GIRLS' RECORD SO EASILY...!!
ZUKA (TMP)
ずかずか
ZUKA
HEY!!
YOU'RE HARUKA KUZE, YEAH!?
... YES.
SHE'S ON TO ME.
CAN I, LIKE, FEEL YOUR BODY!?
どーん
DON (BAM)
WHY!?

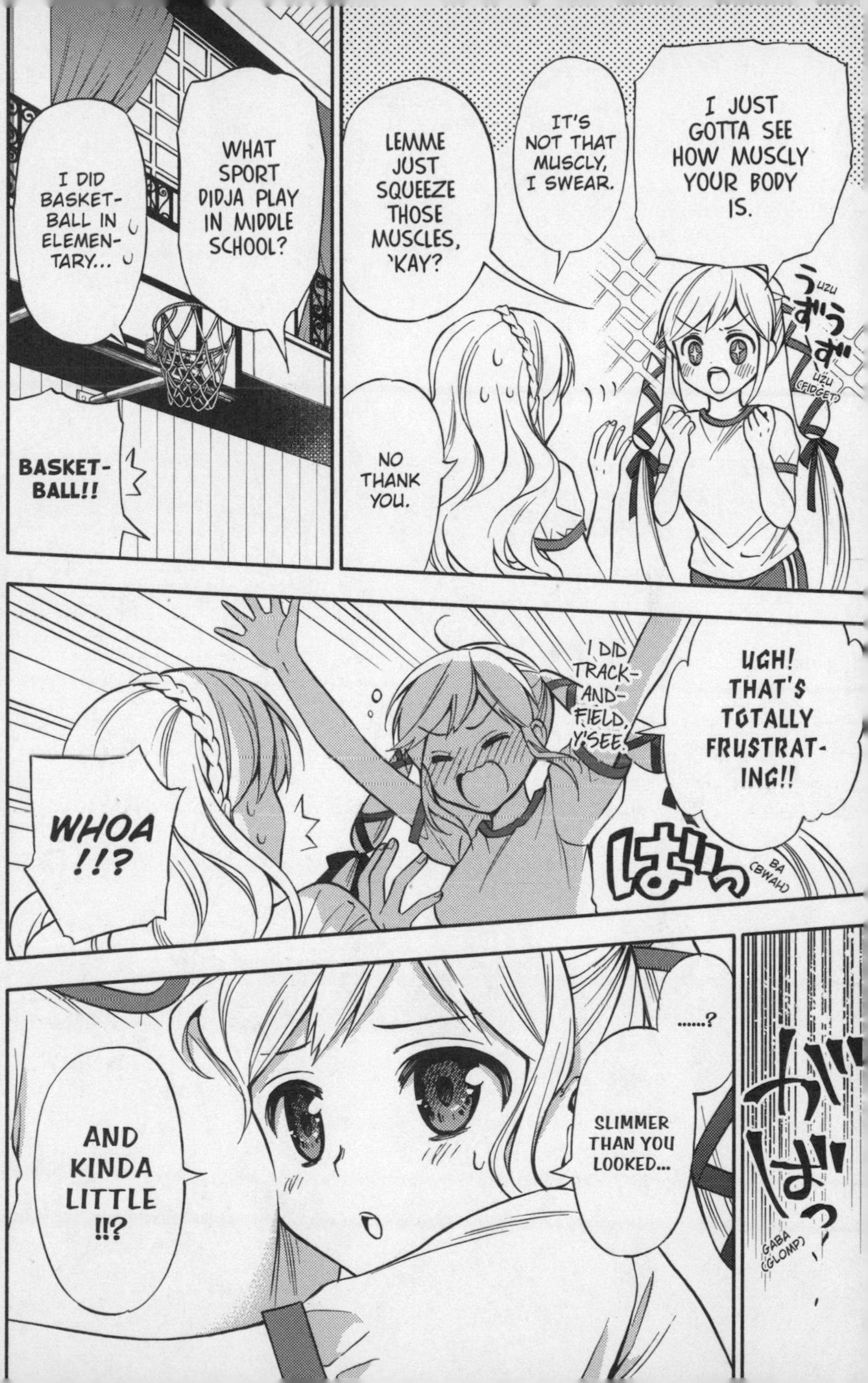
I JUST GOTTA SEE HOW MUSCLY YOUR BODY IS.
うずうず
UZU UZU (FIDGET)
IT'S NOT THAT MUSCLY, I SWEAR.
LEMME JUST SQUEEZE THOSE MUSCLES, 'KAY?
NO THANK YOU.
WHAT SPORT DIDJA PLAY IN MIDDLE SCHOOL?
I DID BASKET-BALL IN ELEMEN-TARY...
BASKET-BALL!!
UGH! THAT'S TOTALLY FRUSTRAT-ING!!
I DID TRACK-AND-FIELD, Y'SEE.
ばっ
BA (BWAH)
WHOA!!?
がばっ
GABA (GLOMP)
......?
SLIMMER THAN YOU LOOKED...
AND KINDA LITTLE!!?

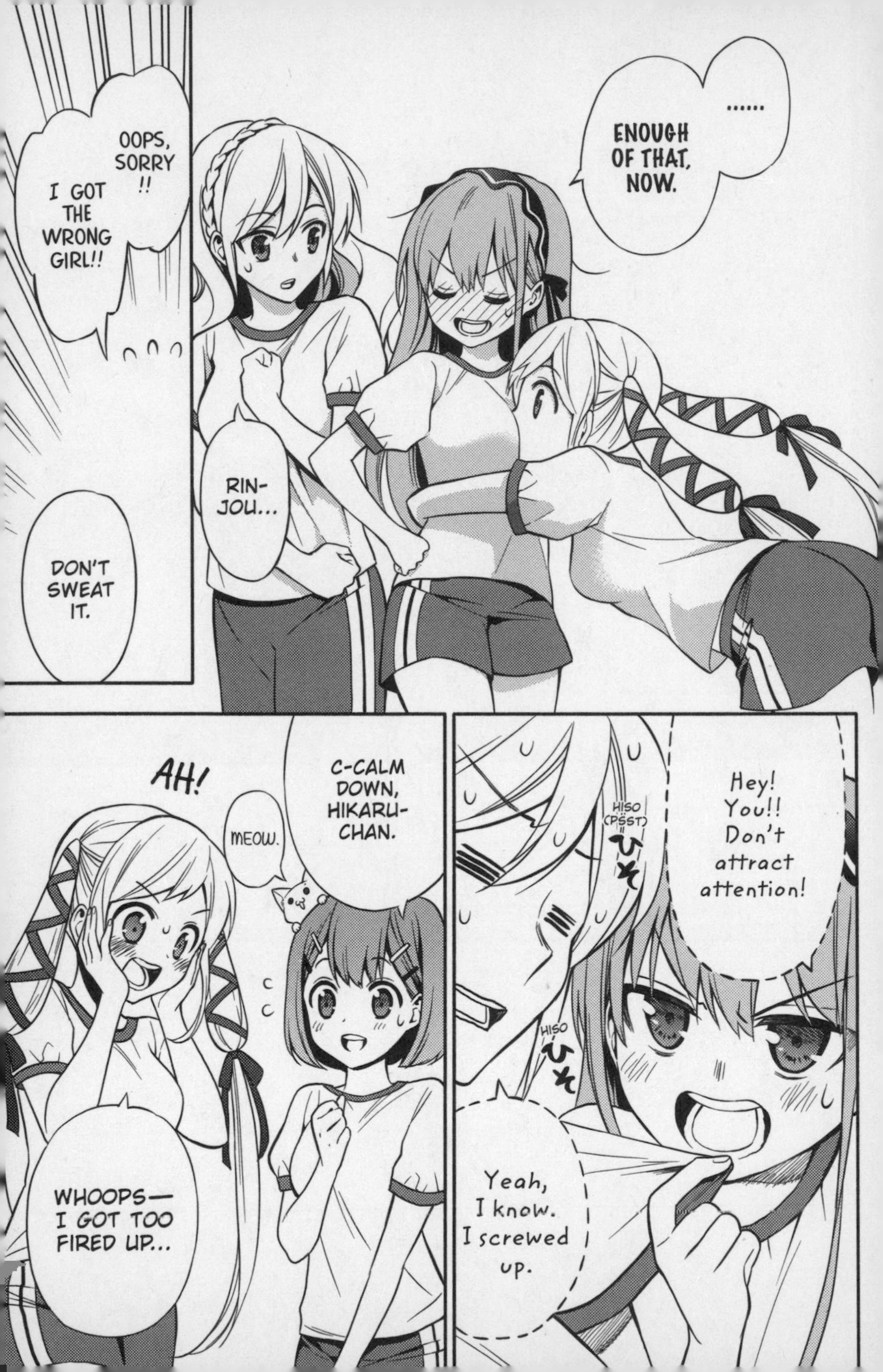

......
ENOUGH OF THAT, NOW.
RIN-JOU...
OOPS, SORRY!!
I GOT THE WRONG GIRL!!
DON'T SWEAT IT.
Hey! You!! Don't attract attention!
HISO (PSST)
HISO
Yeah, I know. I screwed up.
C-CALM DOWN, HIKARU-CHAN.
AH!
MEOW.
WHOOPS— I GOT TOO FIRED UP...

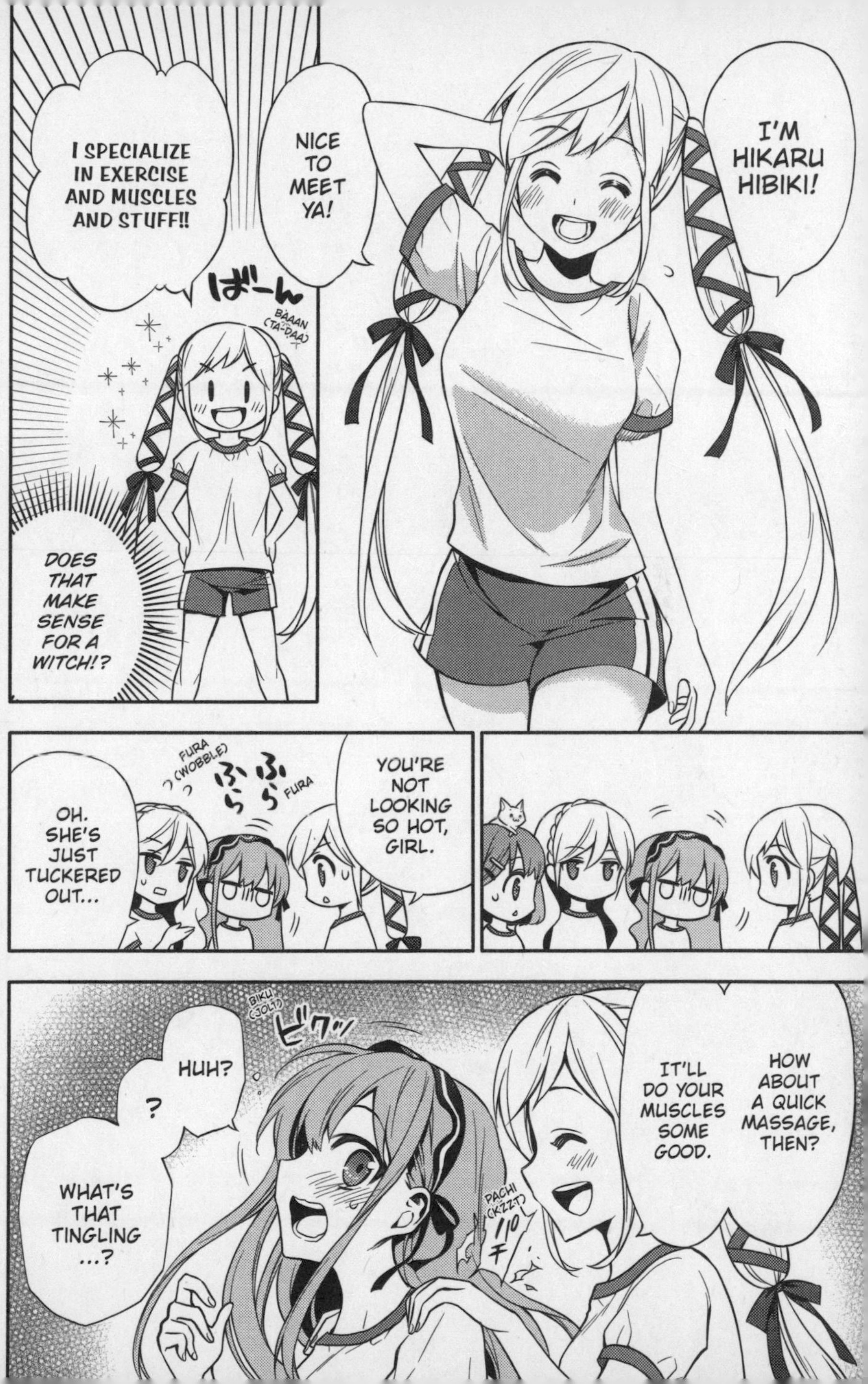
I'M HIKARU HIBIKI!
NICE TO MEET YA!
I SPECIALIZE IN EXERCISE AND MUSCLES AND STUFF!!
ばーん
BAAAN (TA-DAA)
DOES THAT MAKE SENSE FOR A WITCH!?
YOU'RE NOT LOOKING SO HOT, GIRL.
ふらふら
FURA (WOBBLE) FURA
OH. SHE'S JUST TUCKERED OUT...
HOW ABOUT A QUICK MASSAGE, THEN?
IT'LL DO YOUR MUSCLES SOME GOOD.
ビクッ
BIKU (JOLT)
HUH?
?
PACHI (KZZT)
WHAT'S THAT TINGLING ...?

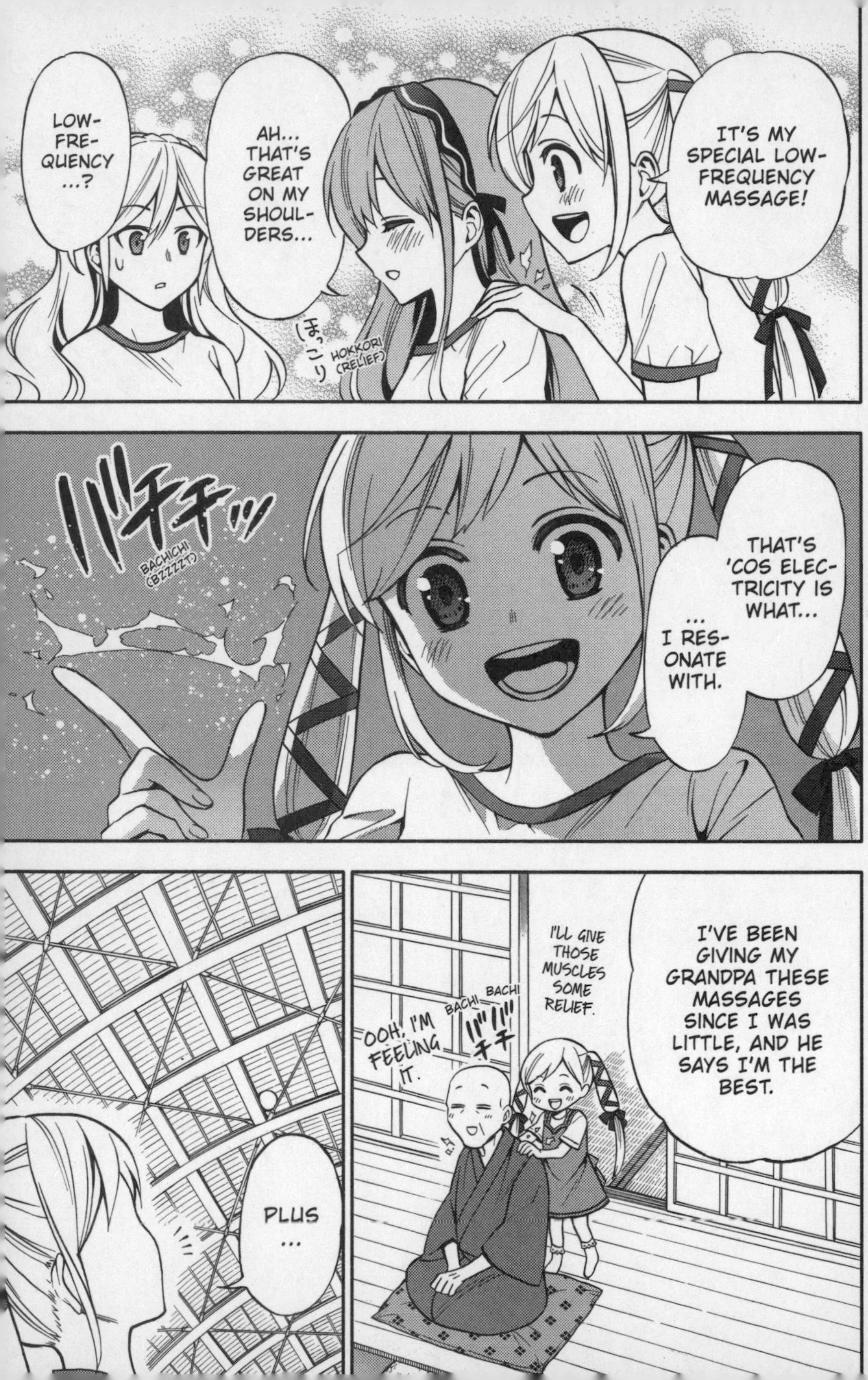
IT'S MY SPECIAL LOW-FREQUENCY MASSAGE!
AH... THAT'S GREAT ON MY SHOULDERS...
ほっこり
HOKKORI (RELIEF)
LOW-FREQUENCY ...?
THAT'S 'COS ELECTRICITY IS WHAT...
... I RESONATE WITH.
バチチッ
BACHICHI (BZZZZT)
I'VE BEEN GIVING MY GRANDPA THESE MASSAGES SINCE I WAS LITTLE, AND HE SAYS I'M THE BEST.
I'LL GIVE THOSE MUSCLES SOME RELIEF.
バチバチ
BACHI BACHI
OOH, I'M FEELING IT.
PLUS ...

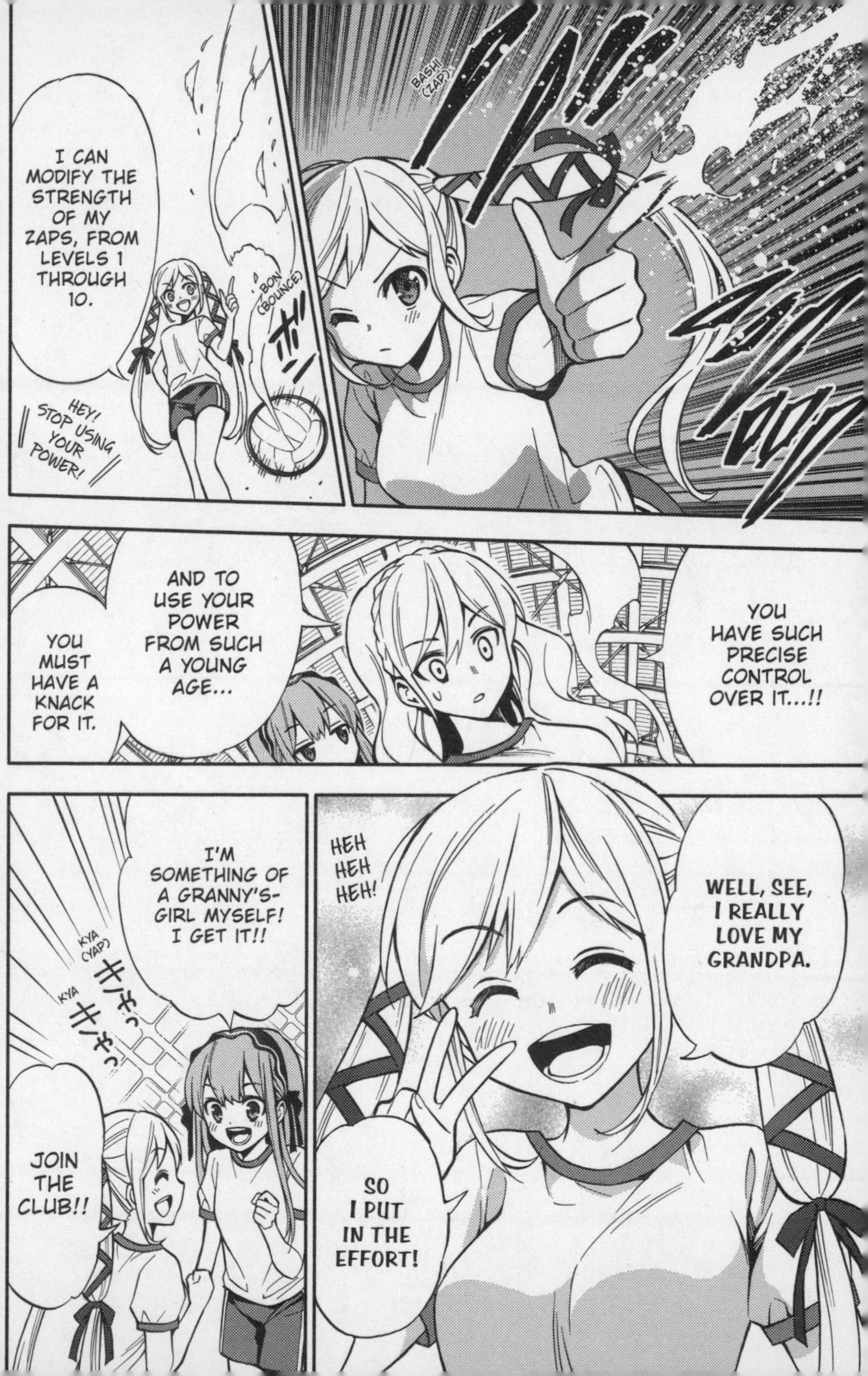
BASHI (ZAP)
I CAN MODIFY THE STRENGTH OF MY ZAPS, FROM LEVELS 1 THROUGH 10.
BON (BOUNCE)
HEY! STOP USING YOUR POWER!
YOU HAVE SUCH PRECISE CONTROL OVER IT...!!
AND TO USE YOUR POWER FROM SUCH A YOUNG AGE...
YOU MUST HAVE A KNACK FOR IT.
WELL, SEE, I REALLY LOVE MY GRANDPA.
HEH HEH HEH!
SO I PUT IN THE EFFORT!
I'M SOMETHING OF A GRANNY'S-GIRL MYSELF! I GET IT!!
KYA (YAP)
KYA
JOIN THE CLUB!!

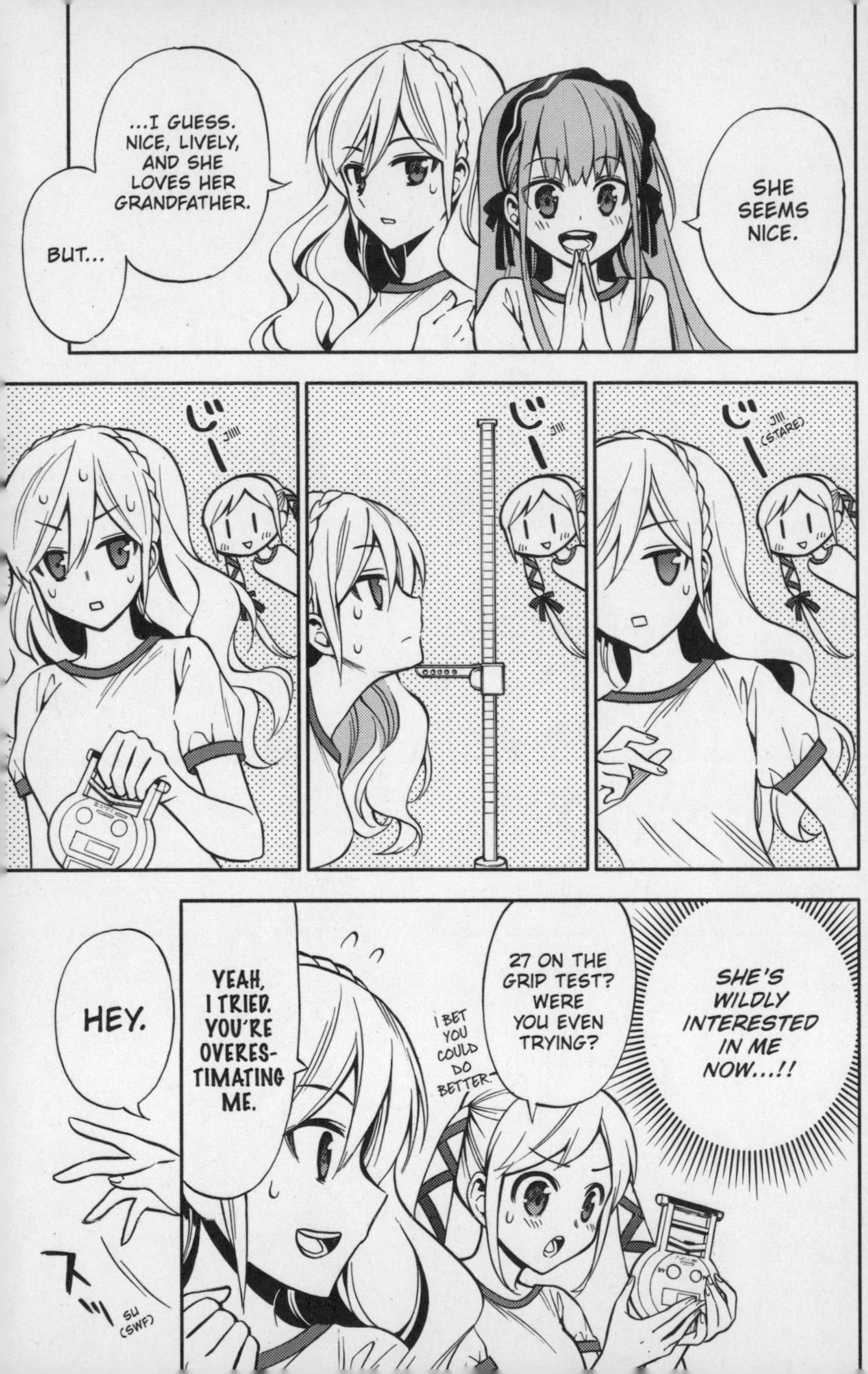
SHE SEEMS NICE.
...I GUESS. NICE, LIVELY, AND SHE LOVES HER GRANDFATHER.
BUT...
じー
JIIII (STARE)
じー
JIIII
じー
JIIII
SHE'S WILDLY INTERESTED IN ME NOW...!!
27 ON THE GRIP TEST? WERE YOU EVEN TRYING?
I BET YOU COULD DO BETTER.
YEAH, I TRIED. YOU'RE OVERES-TIMATING ME.
HEY.
スッ
SU (SWF)

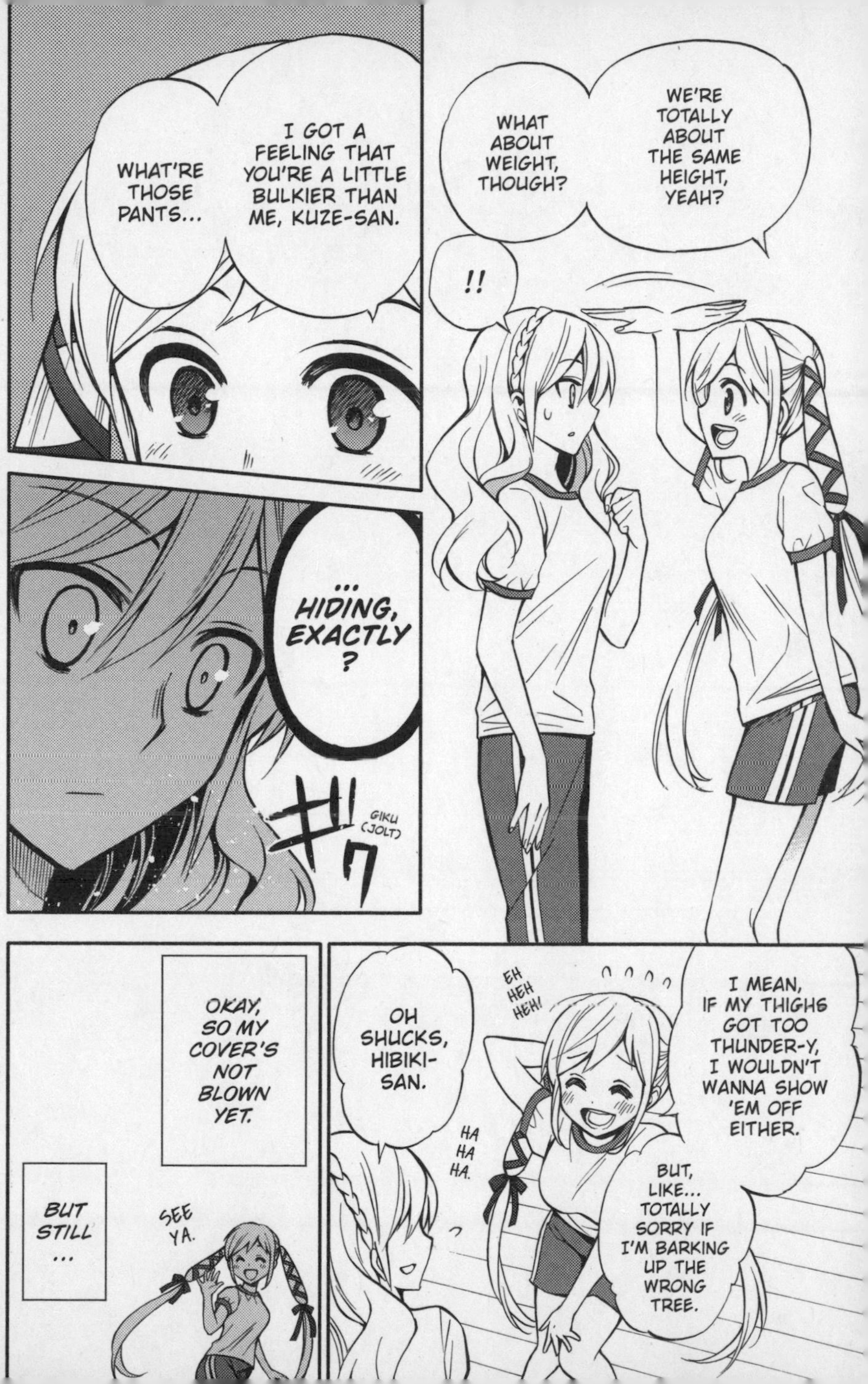
WE'RE TOTALLY ABOUT THE SAME HEIGHT, YEAH?
WHAT ABOUT WEIGHT, THOUGH?
!!
I GOT A FEELING THAT YOU'RE A LITTLE BULKIER THAN ME, KUZE-SAN.
WHAT'RE THOSE PANTS...
...HIDING, EXACTLY?
GIKU (JOLT)
I MEAN, IF MY THIGHS GOT TOO THUNDER-Y, I WOULDN'T WANNA SHOW 'EM OFF EITHER.
EH HEH HEH!
BUT, LIKE... TOTALLY SORRY IF I'M BARKING UP THE WRONG TREE.
OH SHUCKS, HIBIKI-SAN.
HA HA HA.
OKAY, SO MY COVER'S NOT BLOWN YET.
SEE YA.
BUT STILL ...

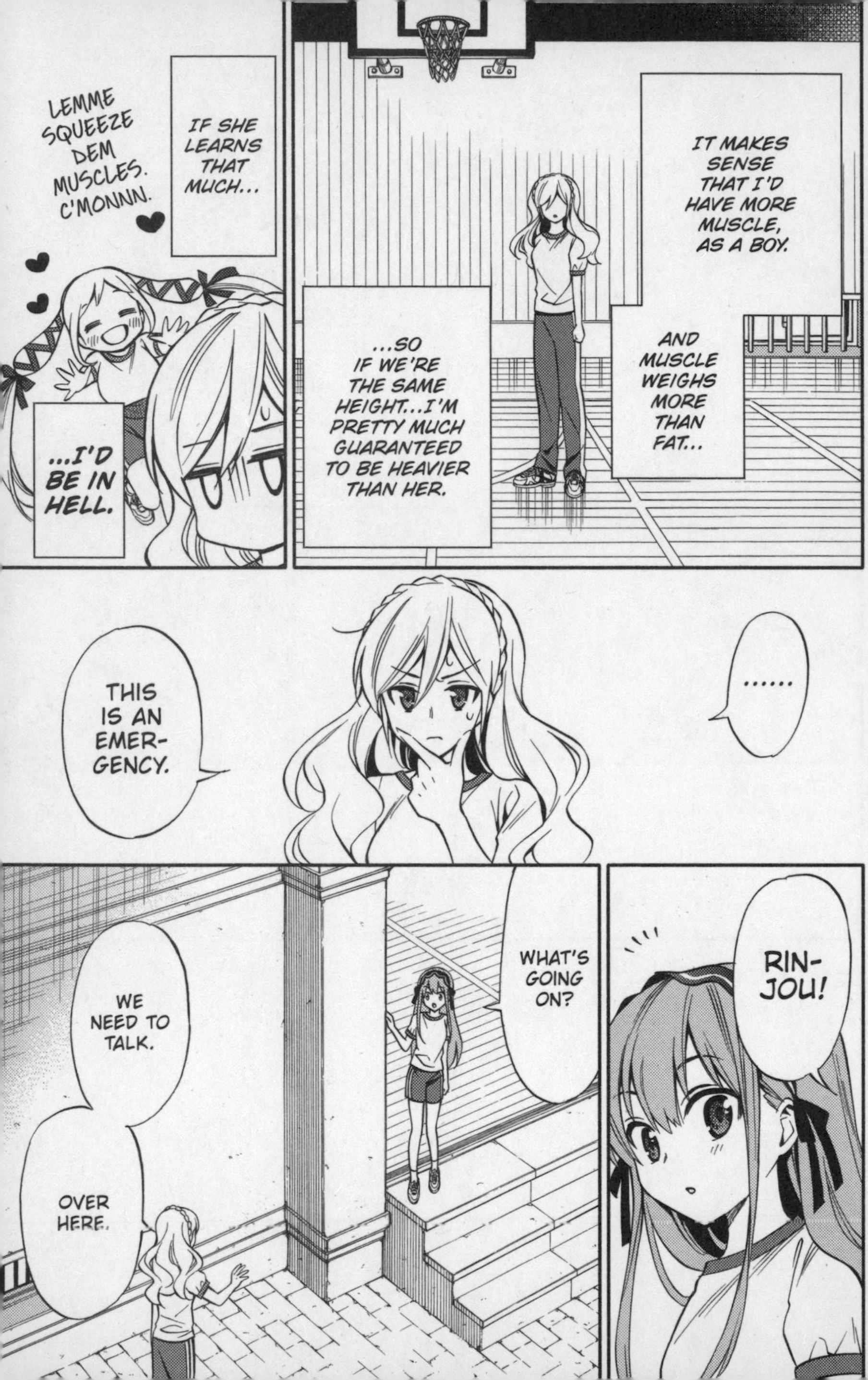
IT MAKES SENSE THAT I'D HAVE MORE MUSCLE, AS A BOY.
AND MUSCLE WEIGHS MORE THAN FAT...
...SO IF WE'RE THE SAME HEIGHT...I'M PRETTY MUCH GUARANTEED TO BE HEAVIER THAN HER.
IF SHE LEARNS THAT MUCH...
LEMME SQUEEZE DEM MUSCLES. C'MONNN.
...I'D BE IN HELL.
......
THIS IS AN EMERGENCY.
RIN-JOU!
WHAT'S GOING ON?
WE NEED TO TALK.
OVER HERE.

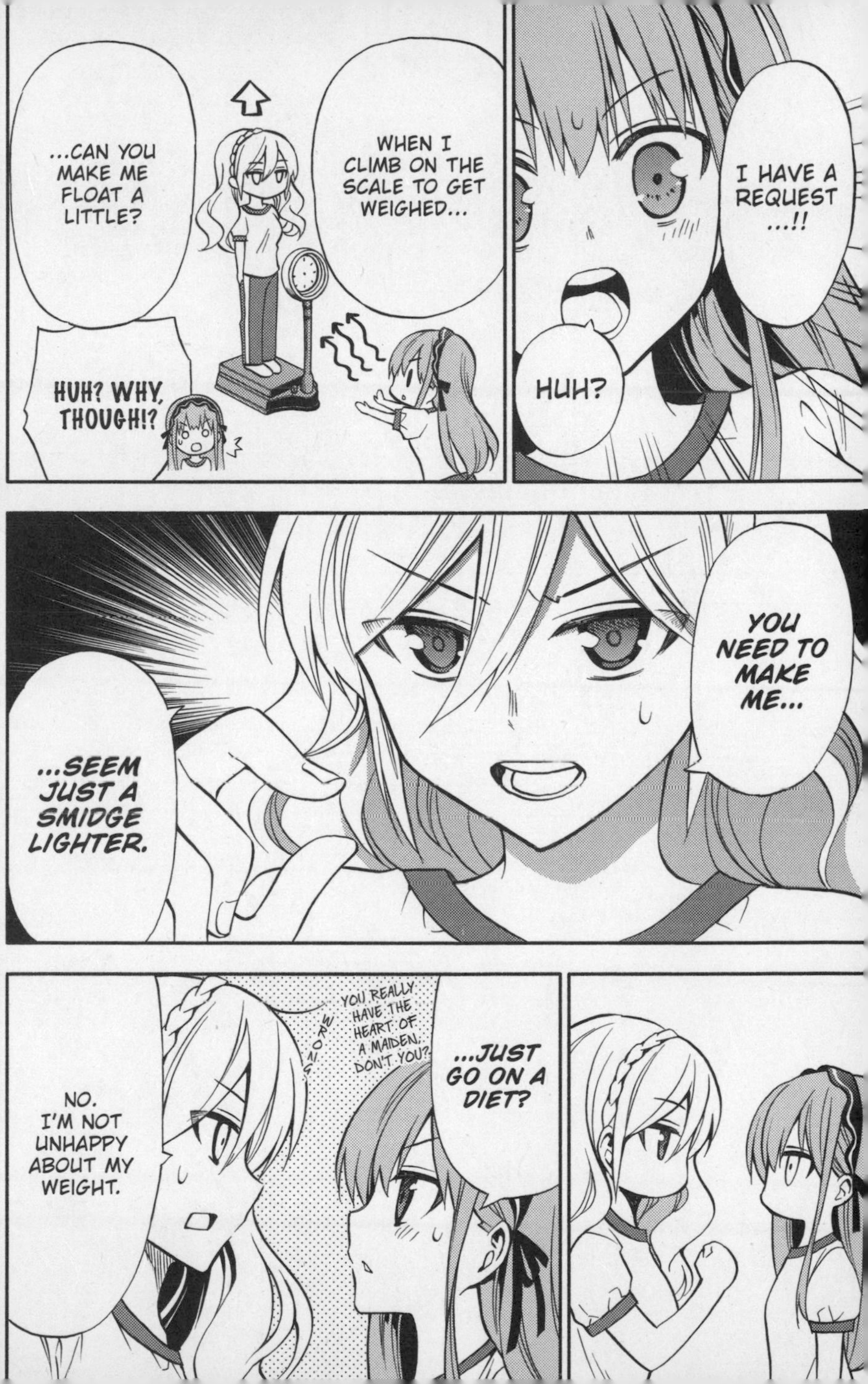
I HAVE A REQUEST ...!!
HUH?
WHEN I CLIMB ON THE SCALE TO GET WEIGHED...
...CAN YOU MAKE ME FLOAT A LITTLE?
HUH? WHY, THOUGH!?
YOU NEED TO MAKE ME...
...SEEM JUST A SMIDGE LIGHTER.
...JUST GO ON A DIET?
YOU REALLY HAVE THE HEART OF A MAIDEN, DON'T YOU?
WRONG
NO. I'M NOT UNHAPPY ABOUT MY WEIGHT.

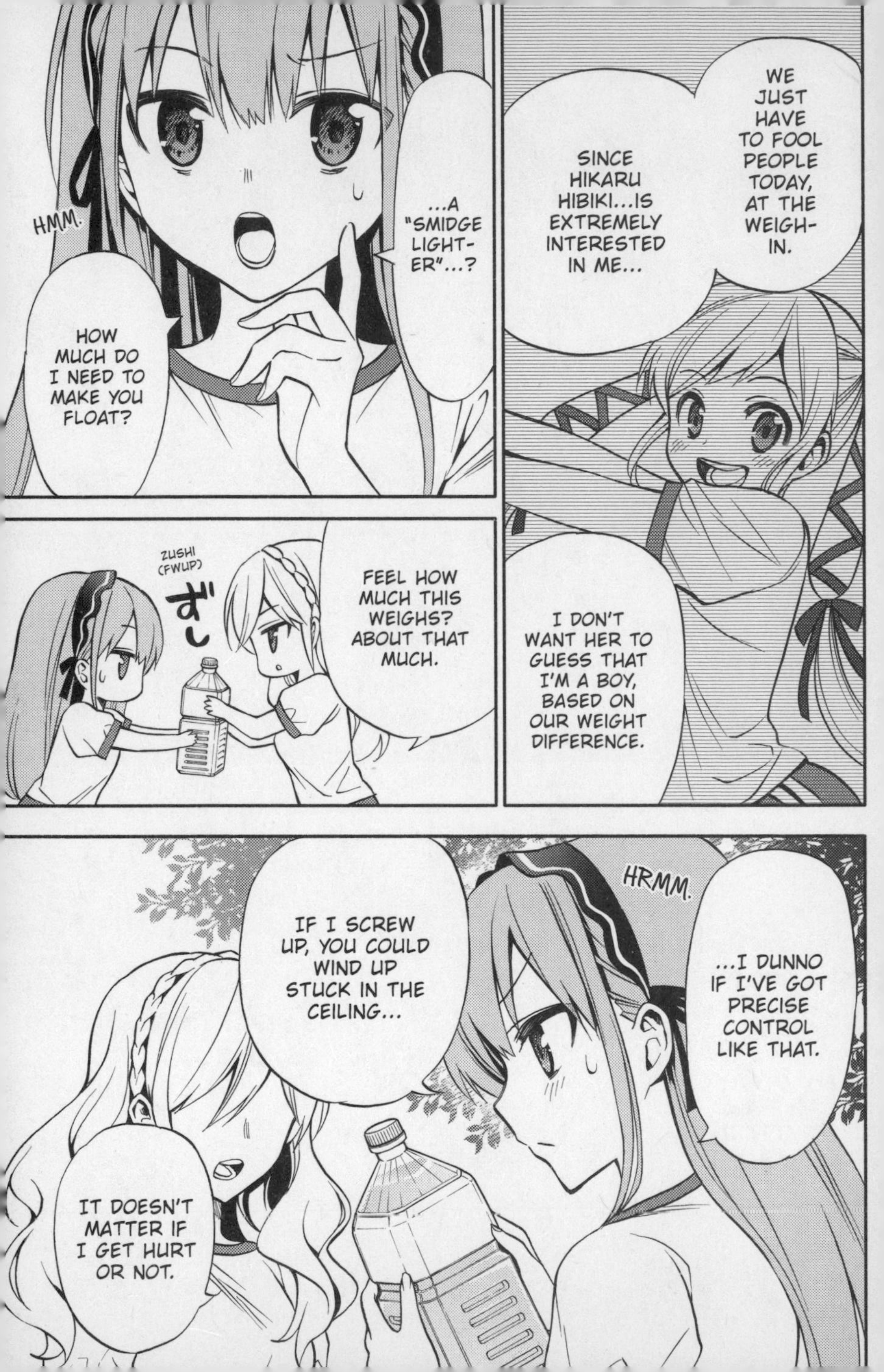
WE JUST HAVE TO FOOL PEOPLE TODAY, AT THE WEIGH-IN.
SINCE HIKARU HIBIKI...IS EXTREMELY INTERESTED IN ME...
I DON'T WANT HER TO GUESS THAT I'M A BOY, BASED ON OUR WEIGHT DIFFERENCE.
...A "SMIDGE LIGHT-ER"...?
HMM.
HOW MUCH DO I NEED TO MAKE YOU FLOAT?
FEEL HOW MUCH THIS WEIGHS? ABOUT THAT MUCH.
ZUSHI (FWUP)
ずし
HRMM.
...I DUNNO IF I'VE GOT PRECISE CONTROL LIKE THAT.
IF I SCREW UP, YOU COULD WIND UP STUCK IN THE CEILING...
IT DOESN'T MATTER IF I GET HURT OR NOT.

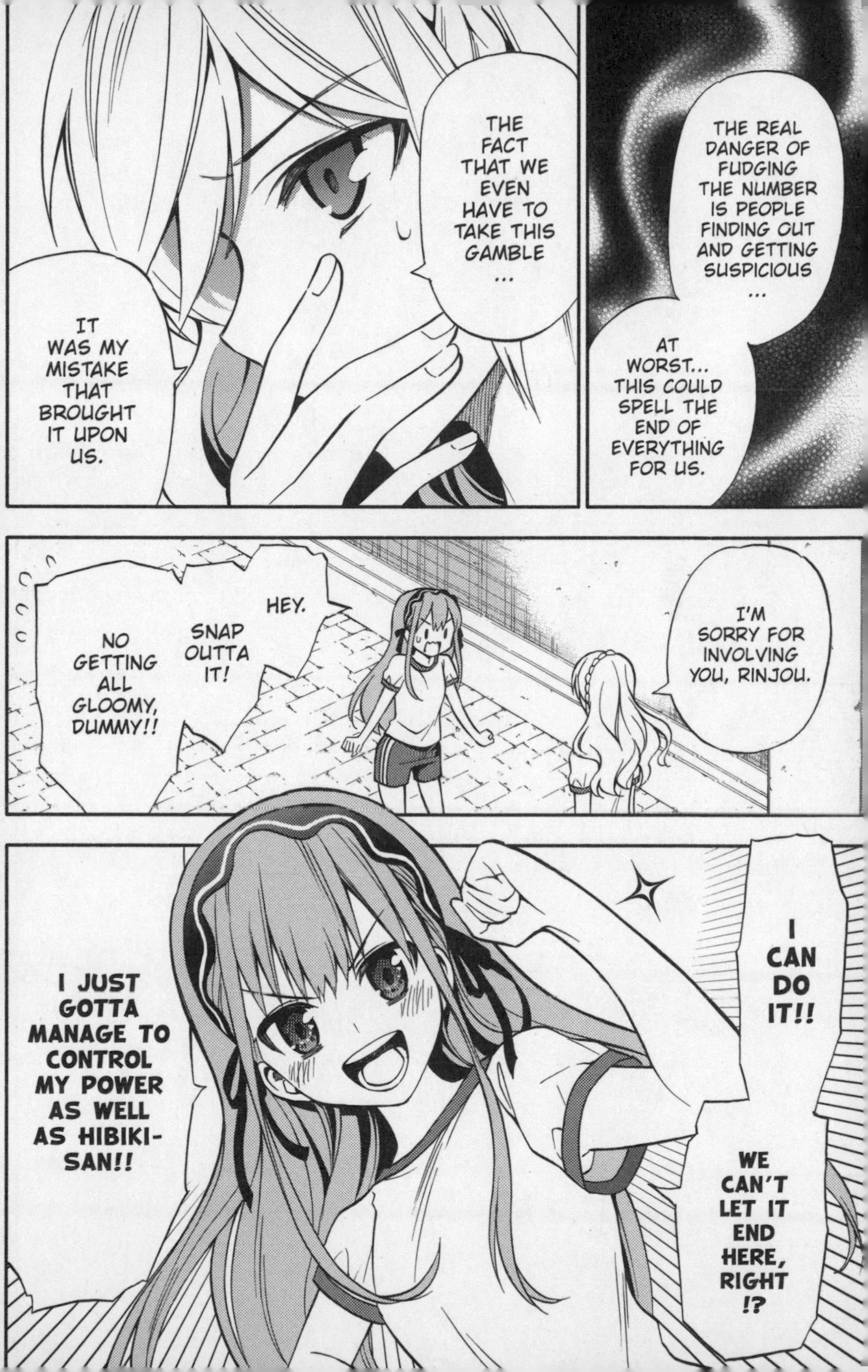
THE REAL DANGER OF FUDGING THE NUMBER IS PEOPLE FINDING OUT AND GETTING SUSPICIOUS ...
AT WORST... THIS COULD SPELL THE END OF EVERYTHING FOR US.
THE FACT THAT WE EVEN HAVE TO TAKE THIS GAMBLE ...
IT WAS MY MISTAKE THAT BROUGHT IT UPON US.
I'M SORRY FOR INVOLVING YOU, RINJOU.
HEY.
SNAP OUTTA IT!
NO GETTING ALL GLOOMY, DUMMY!!
I CAN DO IT!!
WE CAN'T LET IT END HERE, RIGHT!?
I JUST GOTTA MANAGE TO CONTROL MY POWER AS WELL AS HIBIKI-SAN!!

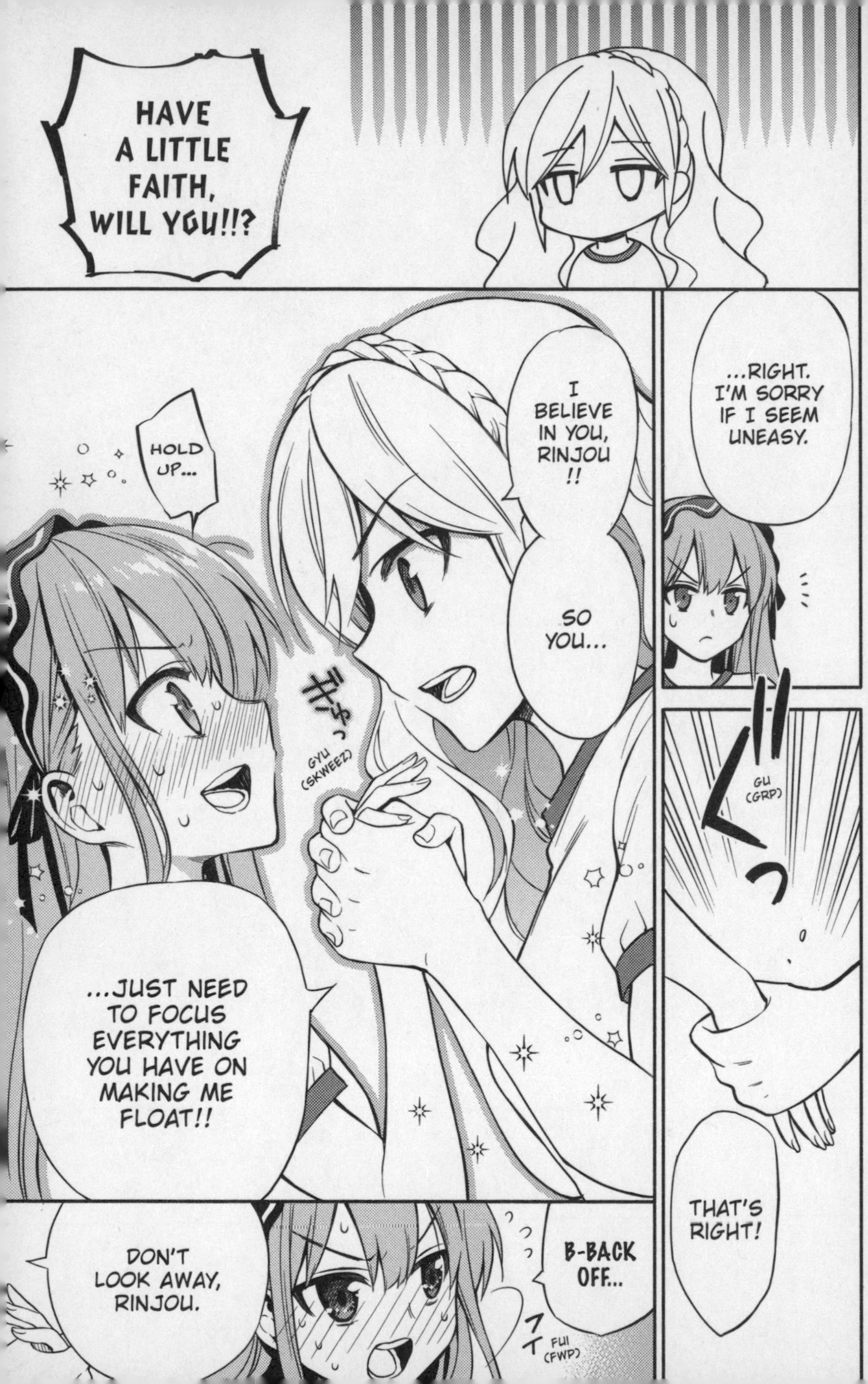
HAVE A LITTLE FAITH, WILL YOU!!?
...RIGHT. I'M SORRY IF I SEEM UNEASY.
GU (GRP)
THAT'S RIGHT!
I BELIEVE IN YOU, RINJOU!!
SO YOU...
HOLD UP...
GYU (SKWEEZ)
...JUST NEED TO FOCUS EVERYTHING YOU HAVE ON MAKING ME FLOAT!!
B-BACK OFF...
FUI (FWP)
DON'T LOOK AWAY, RINJOU.

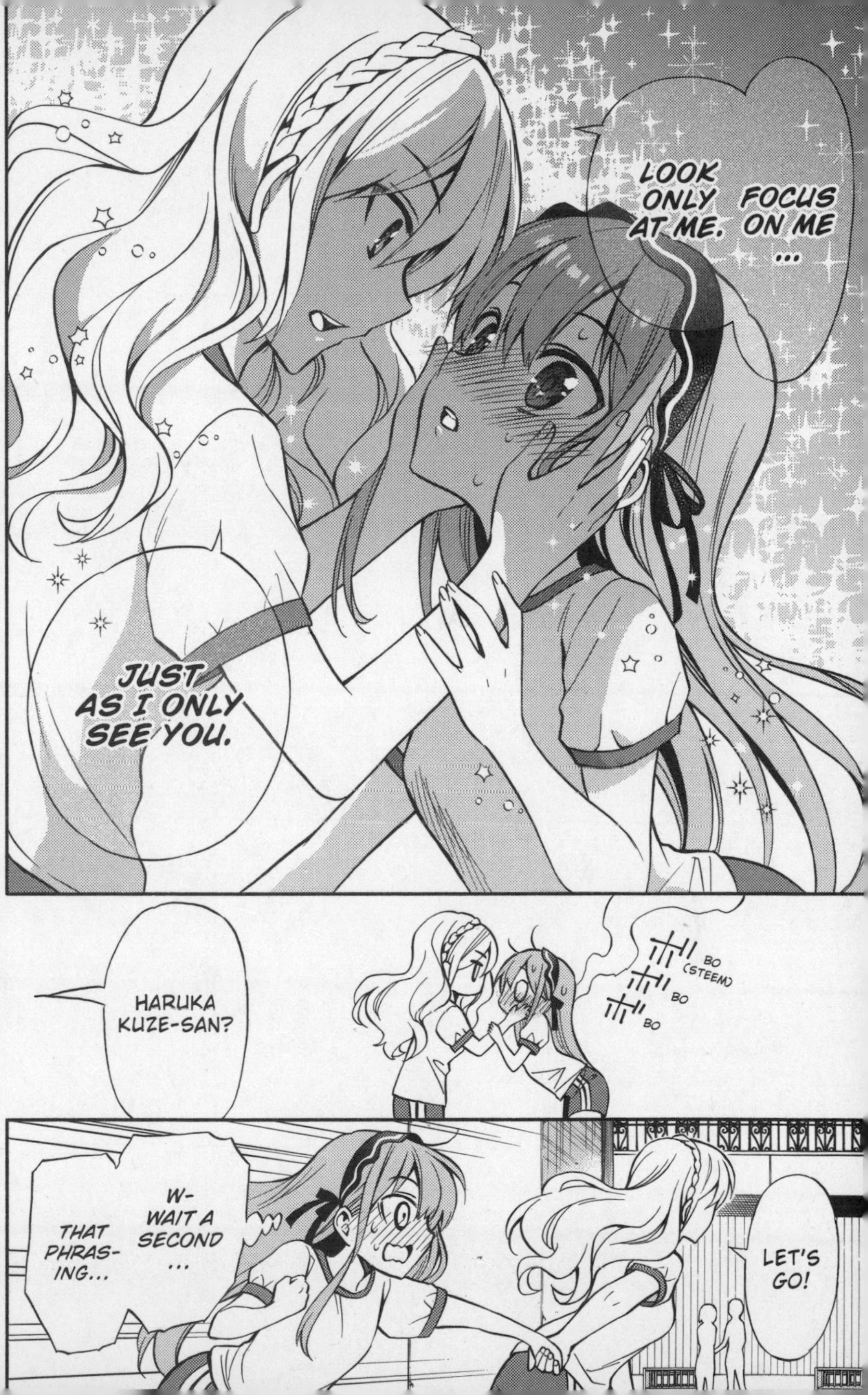
LOOK ONLY AT ME. FOCUS ON ME ...
JUST AS I ONLY SEE YOU.
ボ BO (STEEM)
ボ BO
ボ BO
HARUKA KUZE-SAN?
LET'S GO!
W-WAIT A SECOND ...
THAT PHRAS-ING...

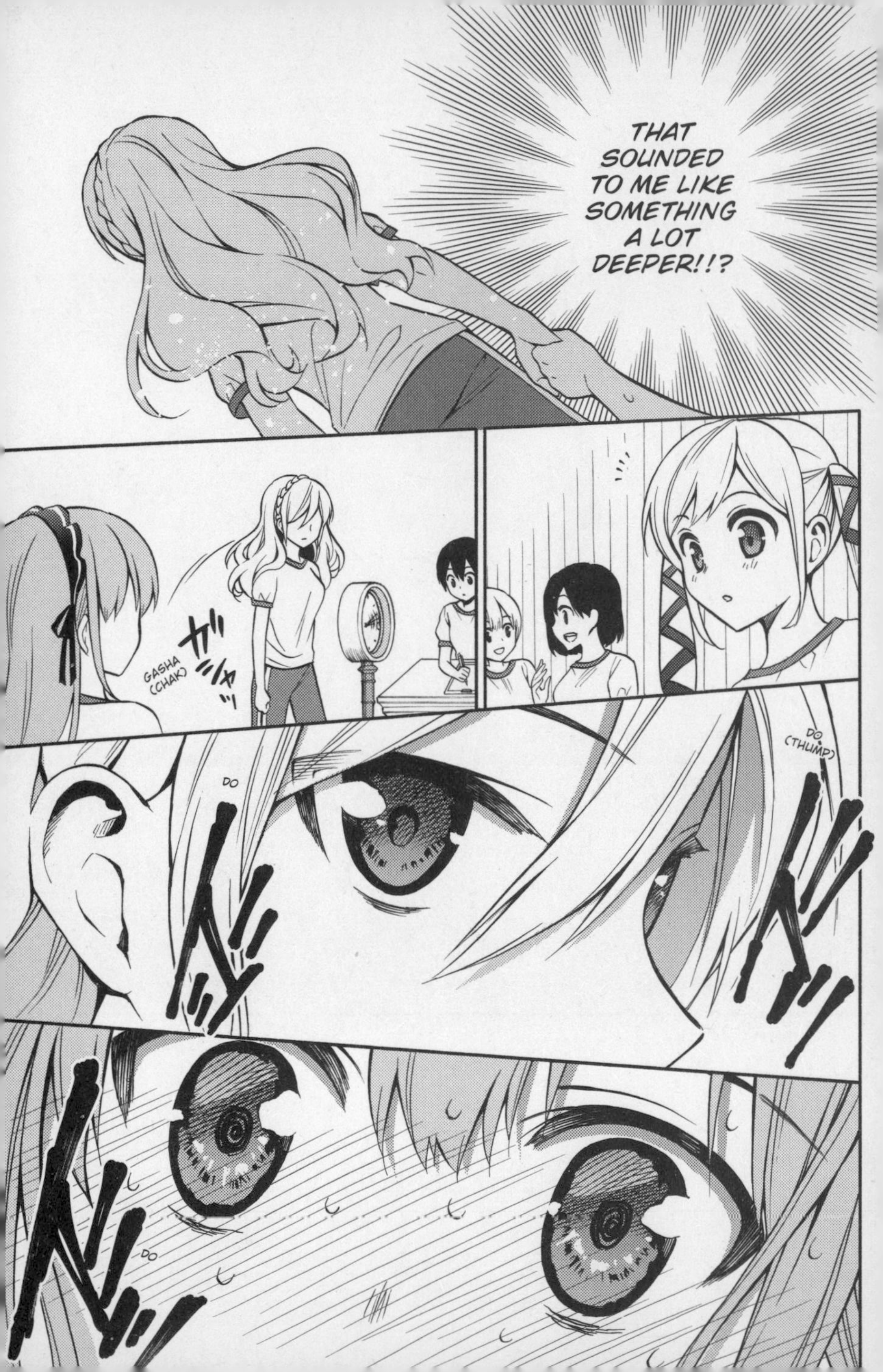
THAT SOUNDED TO ME LIKE SOMETHING A LOT DEEPER!!?
ガシャッ
GASHA (CHAK)
DO (THUMP)
DO
DO

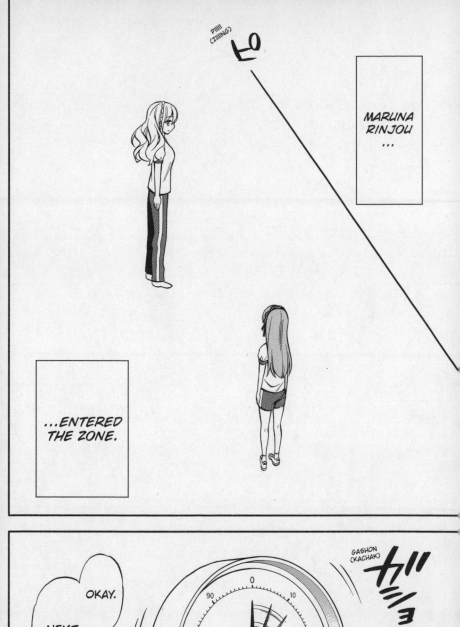

PIIII
(ZIIING)

ㄴO

MARUNA
RINJOU
...

...ENTERED
THE ZONE.

OKAY.

NEXT.

GASHON
(KACHAK)

0

90

10

80

20

70

30

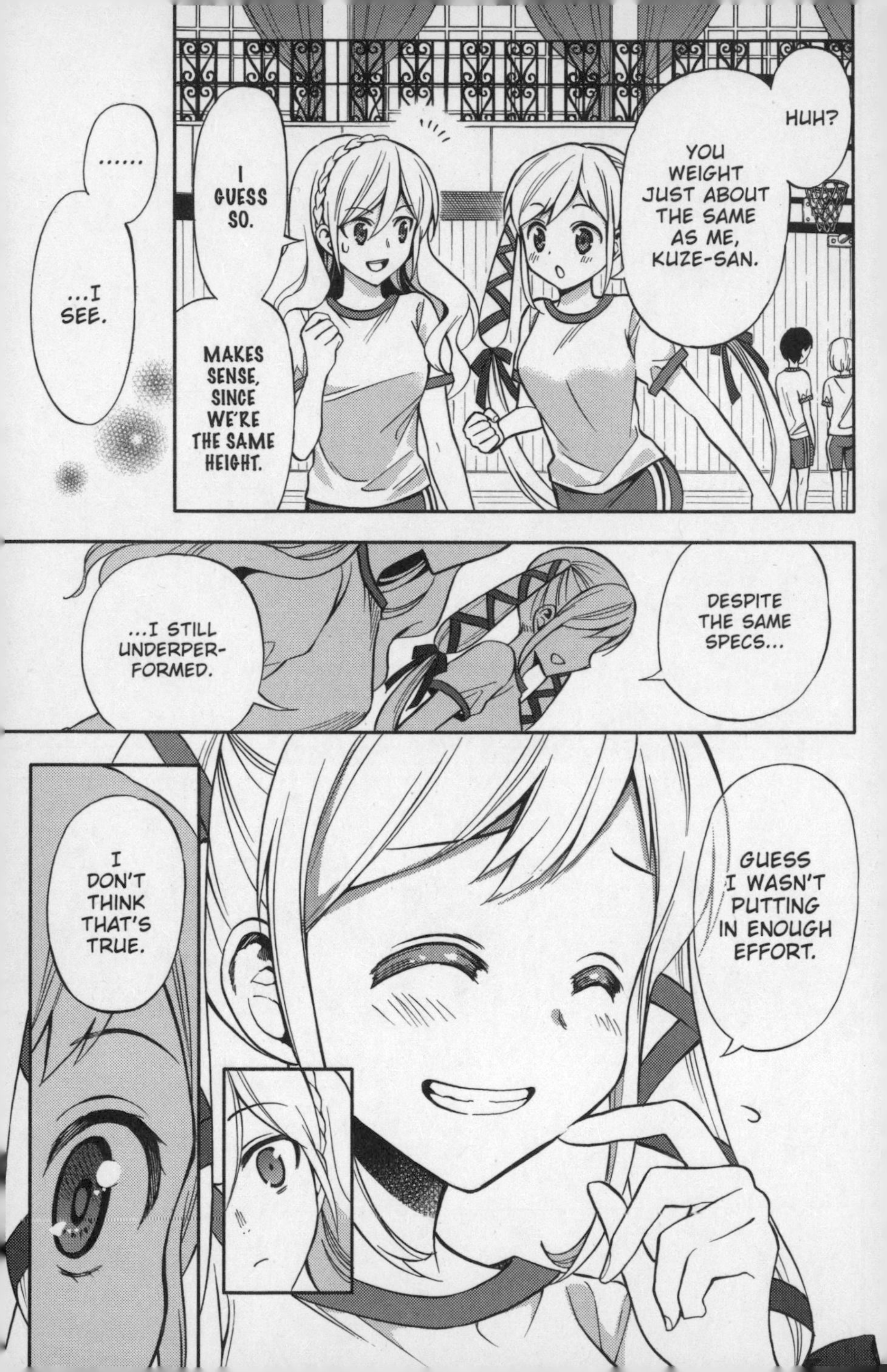
HUH?
YOU WEIGHT JUST ABOUT THE SAME AS ME, KUZE-SAN.
I GUESS SO.
MAKES SENSE, SINCE WE'RE THE SAME HEIGHT.
......
...I SEE.
DESPITE THE SAME SPECS...
...I STILL UNDERPER-FORMED.
GUESS I WASN'T PUTTING IN ENOUGH EFFORT.
I DON'T THINK THAT'S TRUE.

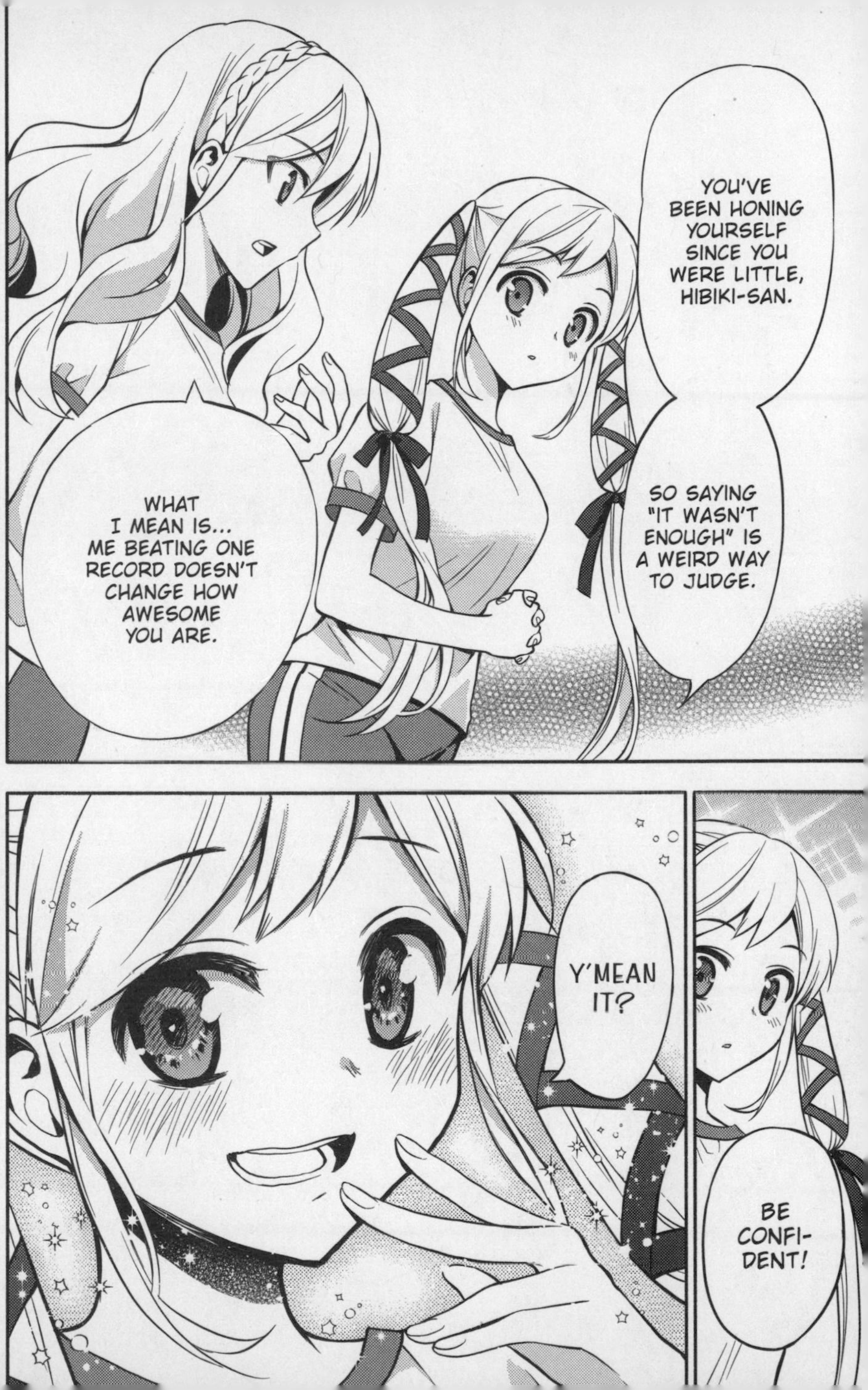
YOU'VE BEEN HONING YOURSELF SINCE YOU WERE LITTLE, HIBIKI-SAN.
SO SAYING "IT WASN'T ENOUGH" IS A WEIRD WAY TO JUDGE.
WHAT I MEAN IS... ME BEATING ONE RECORD DOESN'T CHANGE HOW AWESOME YOU ARE.
BE CONFI-DENT!
Y'MEAN IT?

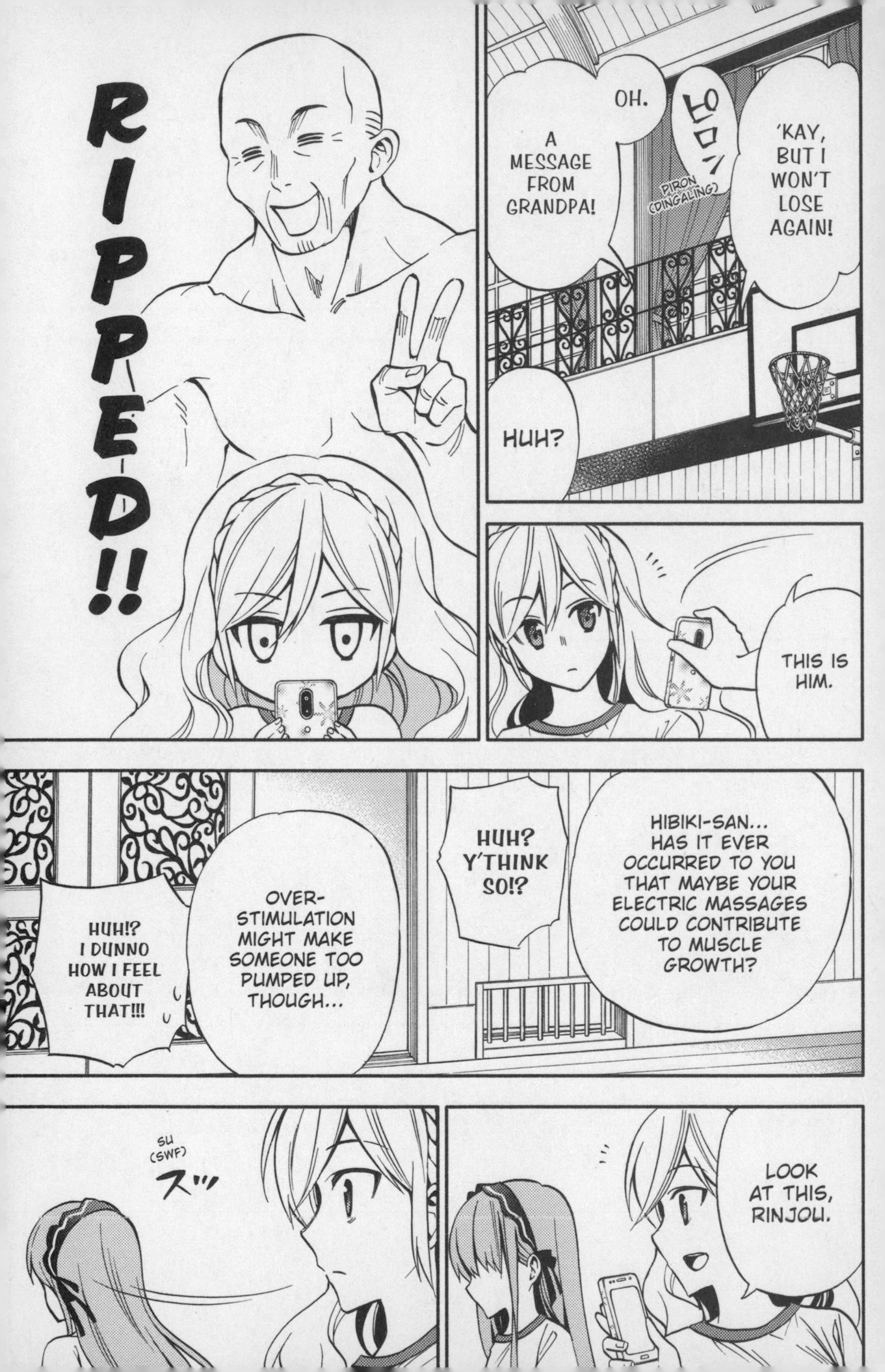
'KAY, BUT I WON'T LOSE AGAIN!
ピロン
PIRON (DINGALING)
OH. A MESSAGE FROM GRANDPA!
HUH?
THIS IS HIM.
RIPPED!!
HIBIKI-SAN... HAS IT EVER OCCURRED TO YOU THAT MAYBE YOUR ELECTRIC MASSAGES COULD CONTRIBUTE TO MUSCLE GROWTH?
HUH? Y'THINK SO!?
OVER-STIMULATION MIGHT MAKE SOMEONE TOO PUMPED UP, THOUGH...
HUH!? I DUNNO HOW I FEEL ABOUT THAT!!!
LOOK AT THIS, RINJOU.
SU (SWF)
スッ

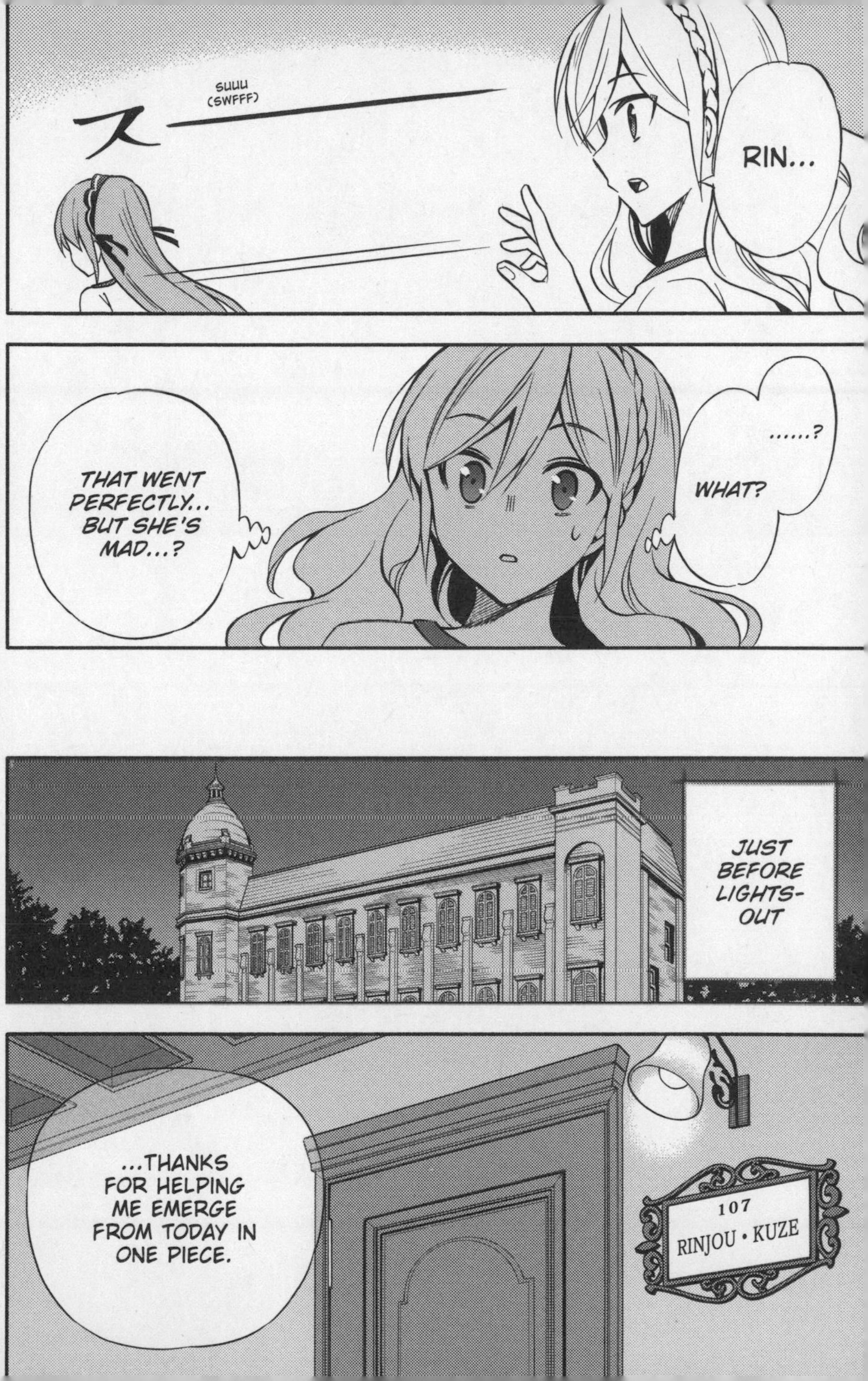
RIN...
SUUU (SWFFF)
ス
......?
WHAT?
THAT WENT PERFECTLY... BUT SHE'S MAD...?
JUST BEFORE LIGHTS-OUT
107
RINJOU • KUZE
...THANKS FOR HELPING ME EMERGE FROM TODAY IN ONE PIECE.

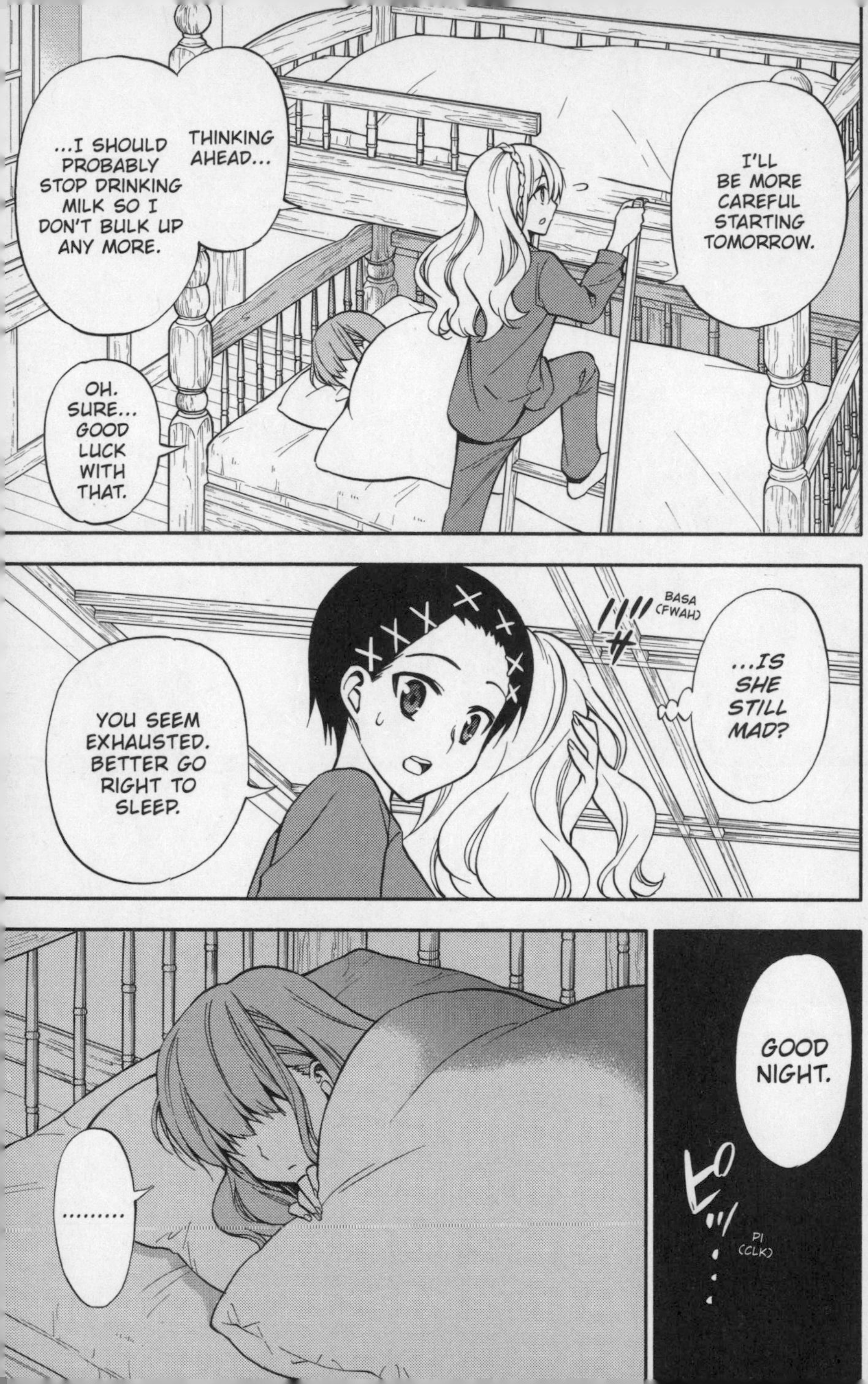
I'LL BE MORE CAREFUL STARTING TOMORROW.
THINKING AHEAD...
...I SHOULD PROBABLY STOP DRINKING MILK SO I DON'T BULK UP ANY MORE.
OH. SURE... GOOD LUCK WITH THAT.
BASA (FWAH)
...IS SHE STILL MAD?
YOU SEEM EXHAUSTED. BETTER GO RIGHT TO SLEEP.
GOOD NIGHT.
PI (CLK)
....

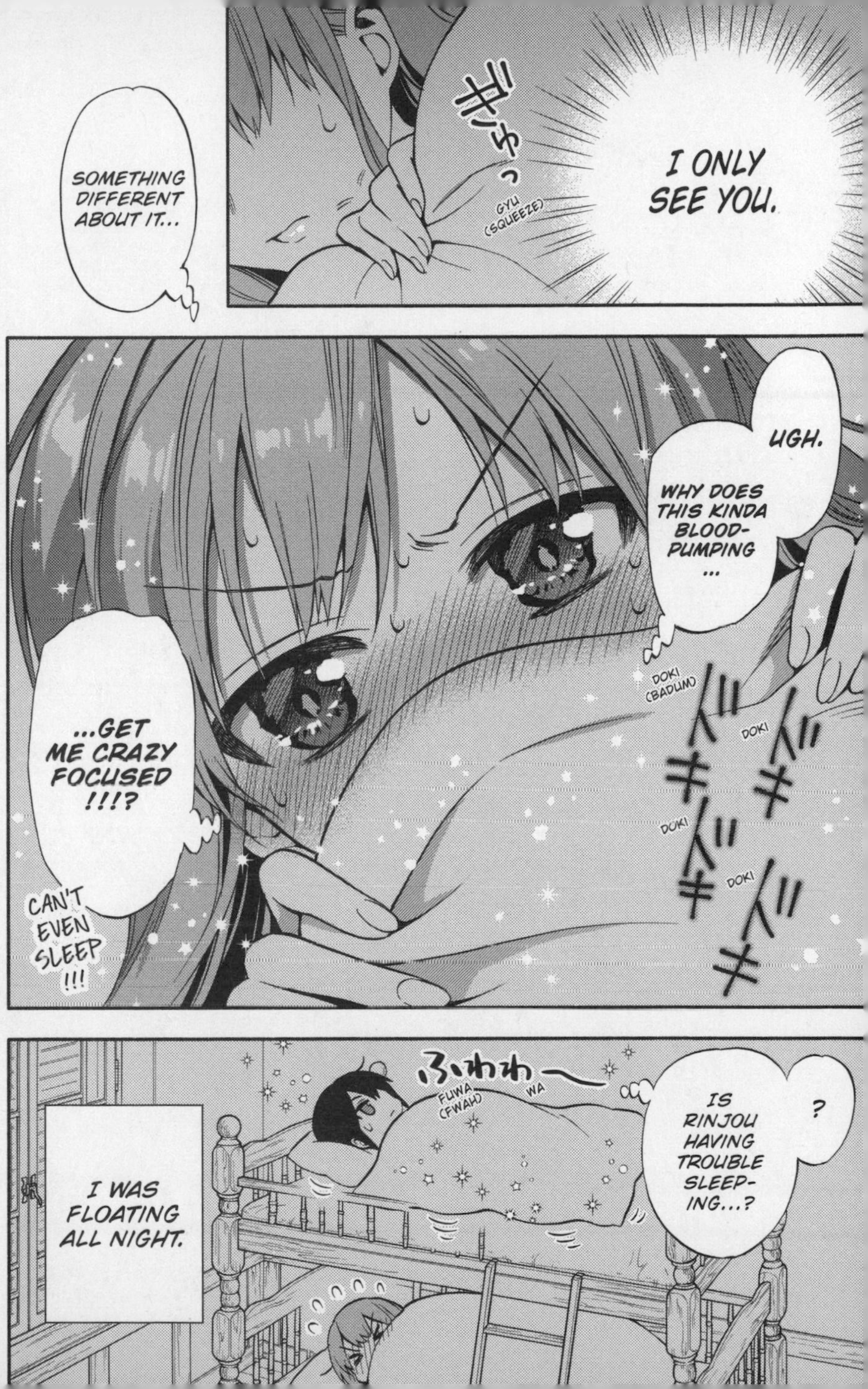

I ONLY SEE YOU.
ぎゅっ
GYU (SQUEEZE)
SOMETHING DIFFERENT ABOUT IT...
UGH.
WHY DOES THIS KINDA BLOOD-PUMPING ...
DOKI (BADUM)
DOKI
DOKI
DOKI
...GET ME CRAZY FOCUSED !!!?
CAN'T EVEN SLEEP !!!
?
IS RINJOU HAVING TROUBLE SLEEP-ING...?
ふわわ〜
FUWA (FWAH)
WA
I WAS FLOATING ALL NIGHT.

If Witch, Then Which?

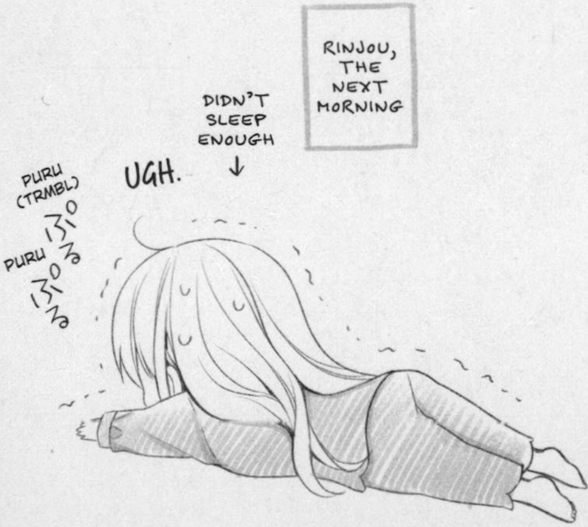
RINJOU, THE NEXT MORNING
DIDN'T SLEEP ENOUGH
UGH.
PURU (TRMBL)
ぷる
PURU
ぷる

If Witch, then Which?

SINCE HE ONCE
PUT HIMSELF
IN CHARGE OF
RINJOU'S HEALTH,
CAN ESTIMATE
A PERSON'S
WEIGHT AT A
GLANCE USING
"HARUKA EYES."

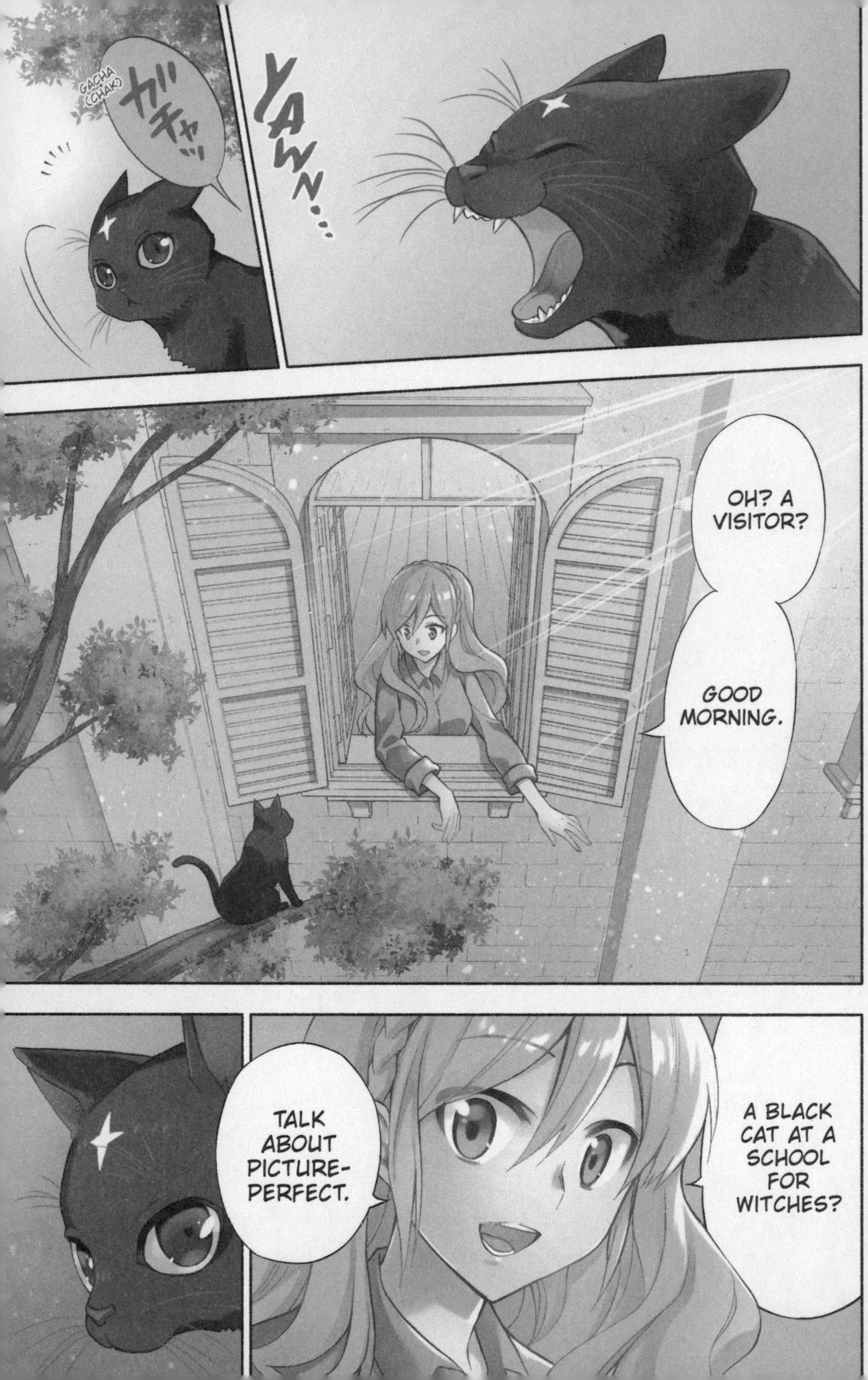
YAWN...
ガチャッ
GACHA (CHAK)
OH? A VISITOR?
GOOD MORNING.
A BLACK CAT AT A SCHOOL FOR WITCHES?
TALK ABOUT PICTURE-PERFECT.

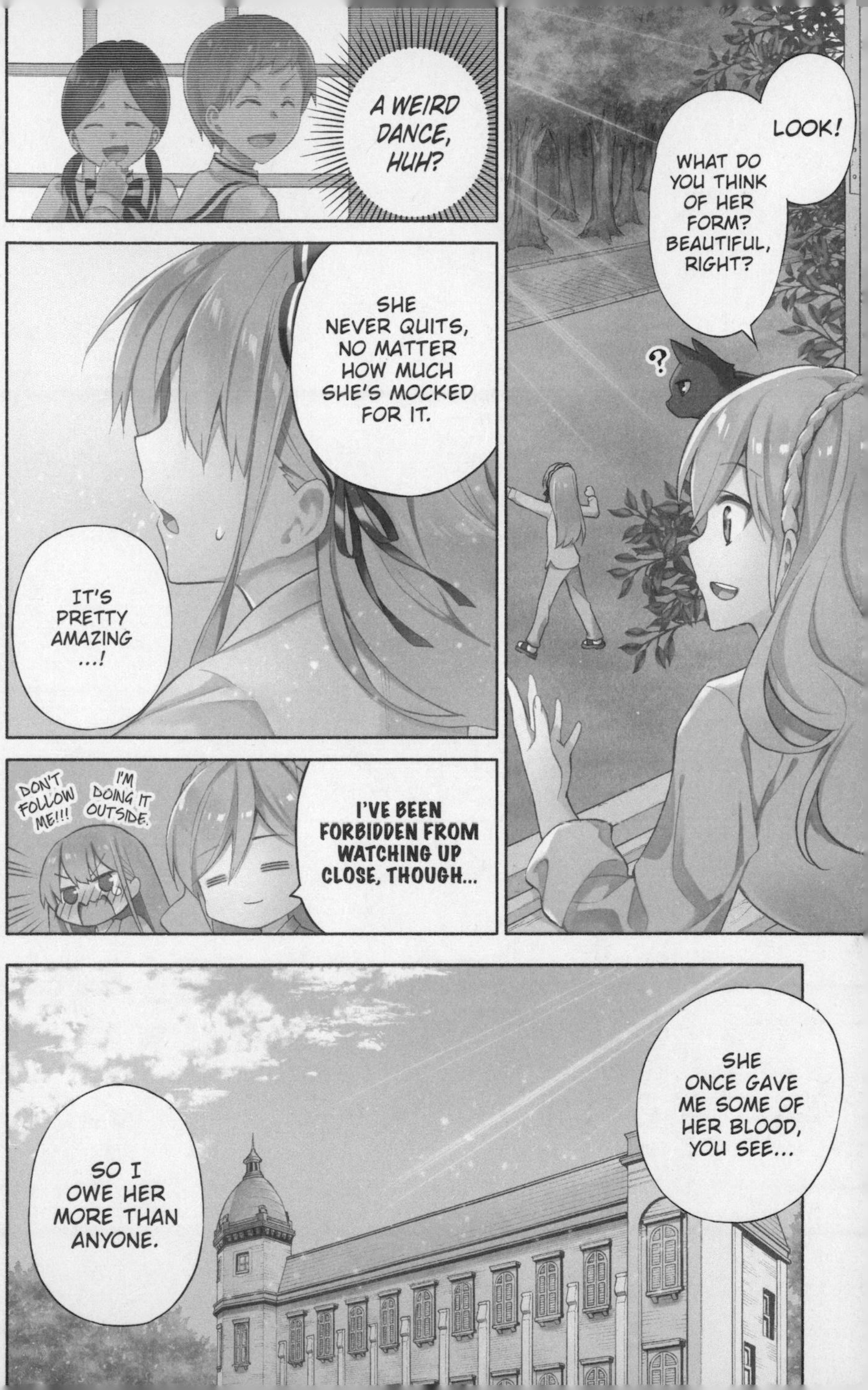
LOOK!
WHAT DO YOU THINK OF HER FORM? BEAUTIFUL, RIGHT?
A WEIRD DANCE, HUH?
SHE NEVER QUITS, NO MATTER HOW MUCH SHE'S MOCKED FOR IT.
IT'S PRETTY AMAZING...!
I'VE BEEN FORBIDDEN FROM WATCHING UP CLOSE, THOUGH...
I'M DOING IT OUTSIDE.
DON'T FOLLOW ME!!!
SHE ONCE GAVE ME SOME OF HER BLOOD, YOU SEE...
SO I OWE HER MORE THAN ANYONE.

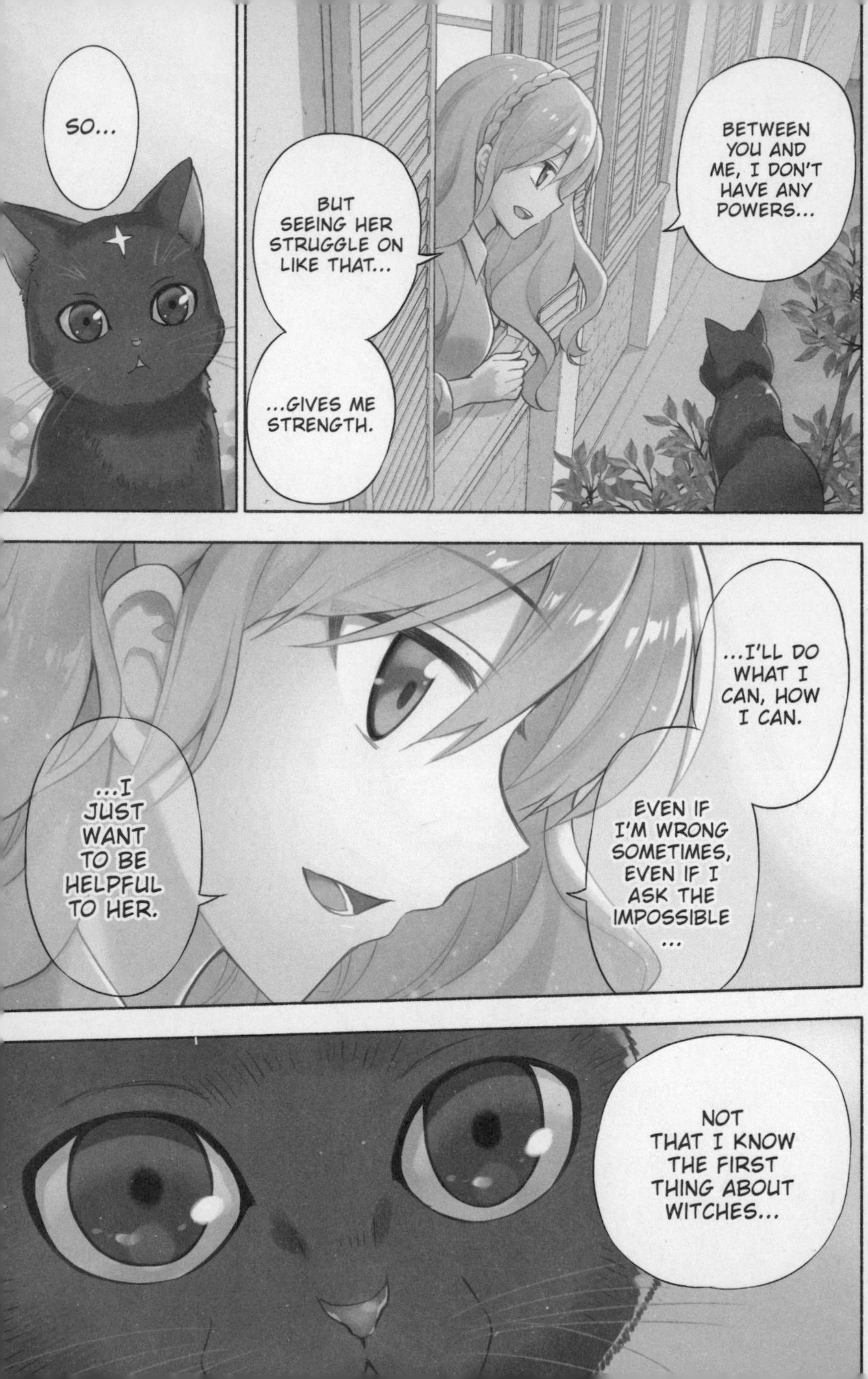
BETWEEN YOU AND ME, I DON'T HAVE ANY POWERS...
BUT SEEING HER STRUGGLE ON LIKE THAT...
...GIVES ME STRENGTH.
SO...
...I'LL DO WHAT I CAN, HOW I CAN.
EVEN IF I'M WRONG SOMETIMES, EVEN IF I ASK THE IMPOSSIBLE...
...I JUST WANT TO BE HELPFUL TO HER.
NOT THAT I KNOW THE FIRST THING ABOUT WITCHES...

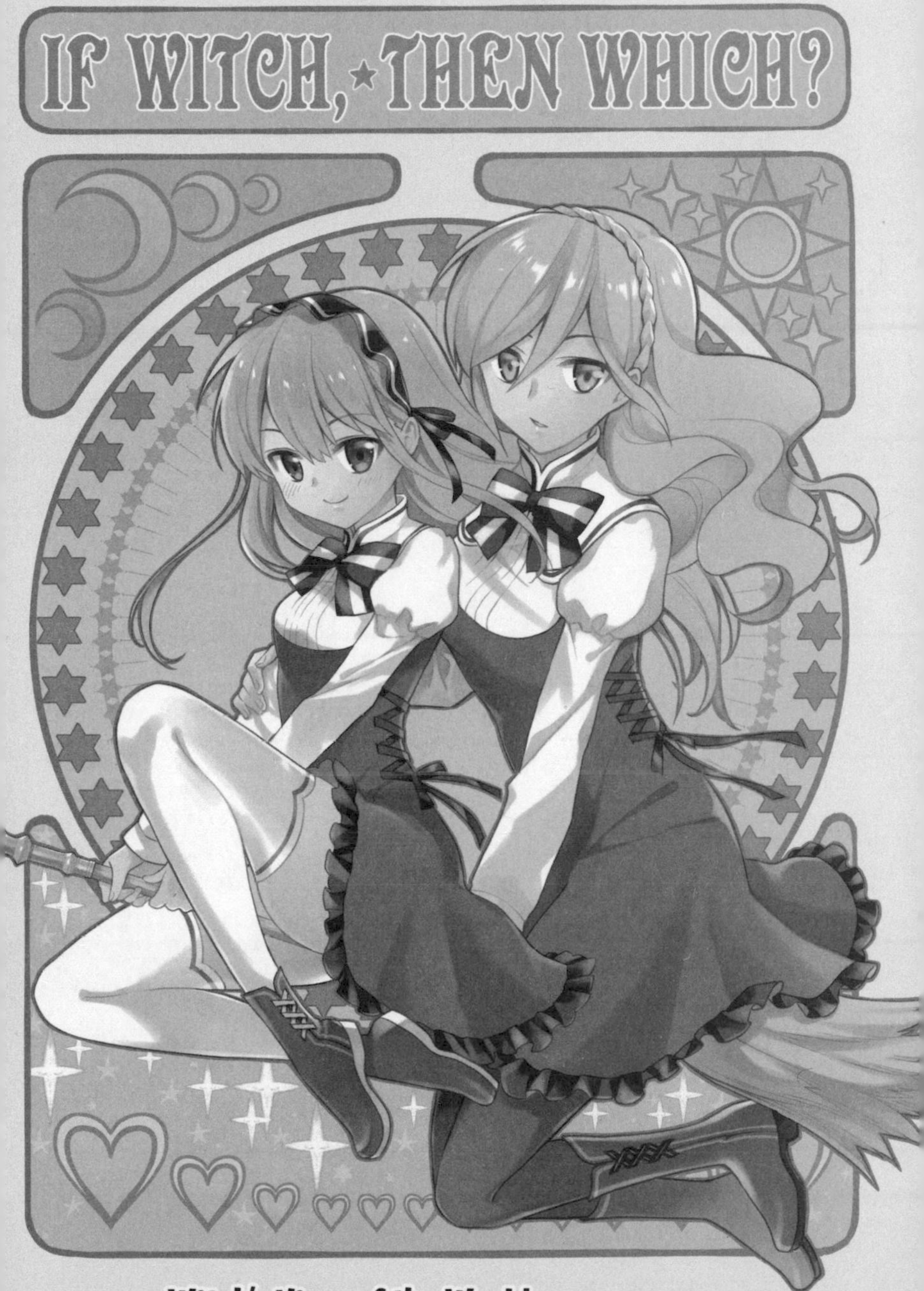
IF WITCH, THEN WHICH?

MAGIC.4 Witch's View of the World

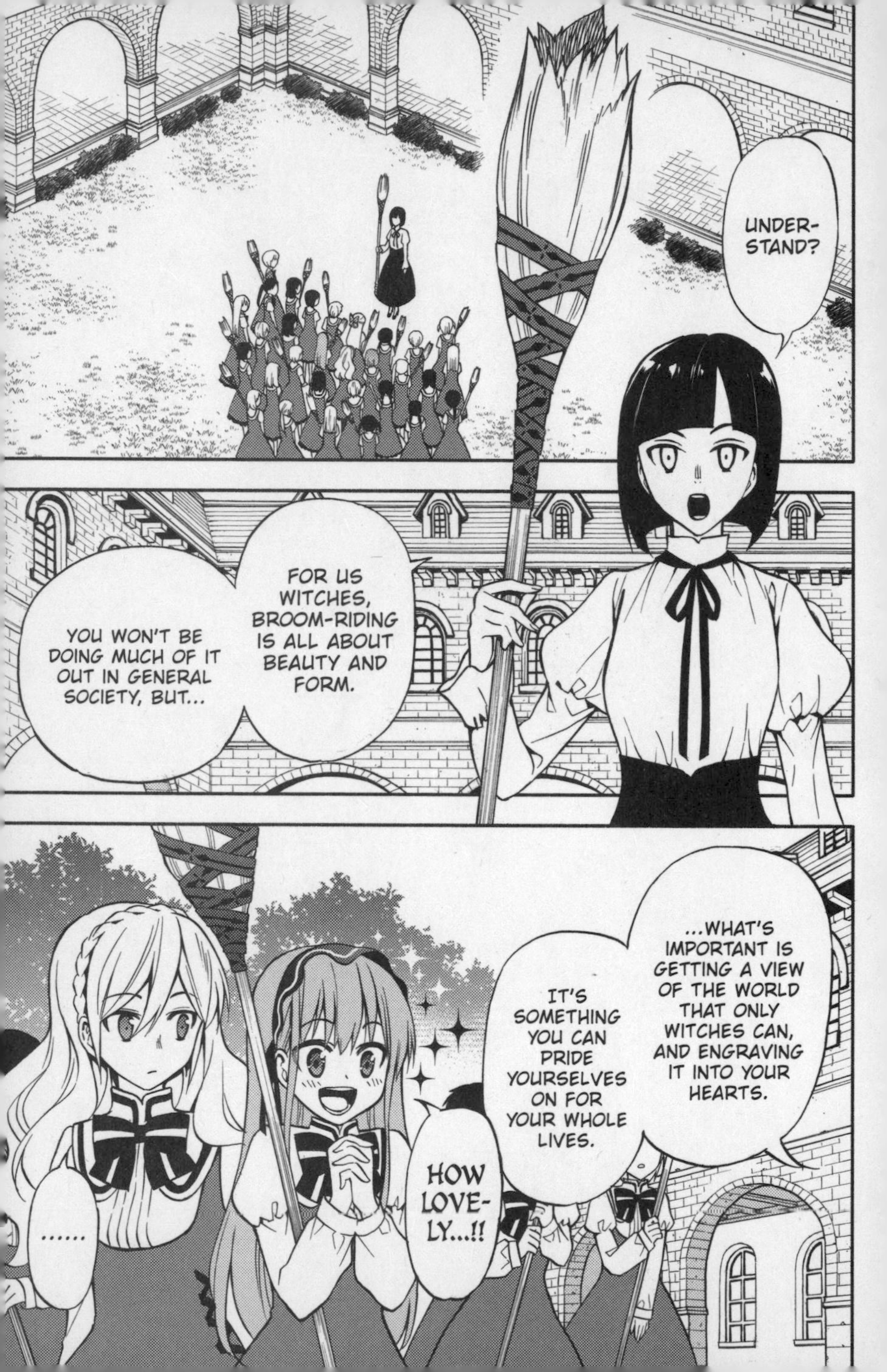
UNDER-STAND?
FOR US WITCHES, BROOM-RIDING IS ALL ABOUT BEAUTY AND FORM.
YOU WON'T BE DOING MUCH OF IT OUT IN GENERAL SOCIETY, BUT...
...WHAT'S IMPORTANT IS GETTING A VIEW OF THE WORLD THAT ONLY WITCHES CAN, AND ENGRAVING IT INTO YOUR HEARTS.
IT'S SOMETHING YOU CAN PRIDE YOURSELVES ON FOR YOUR WHOLE LIVES.
HOW LOVE-LY...!!
......

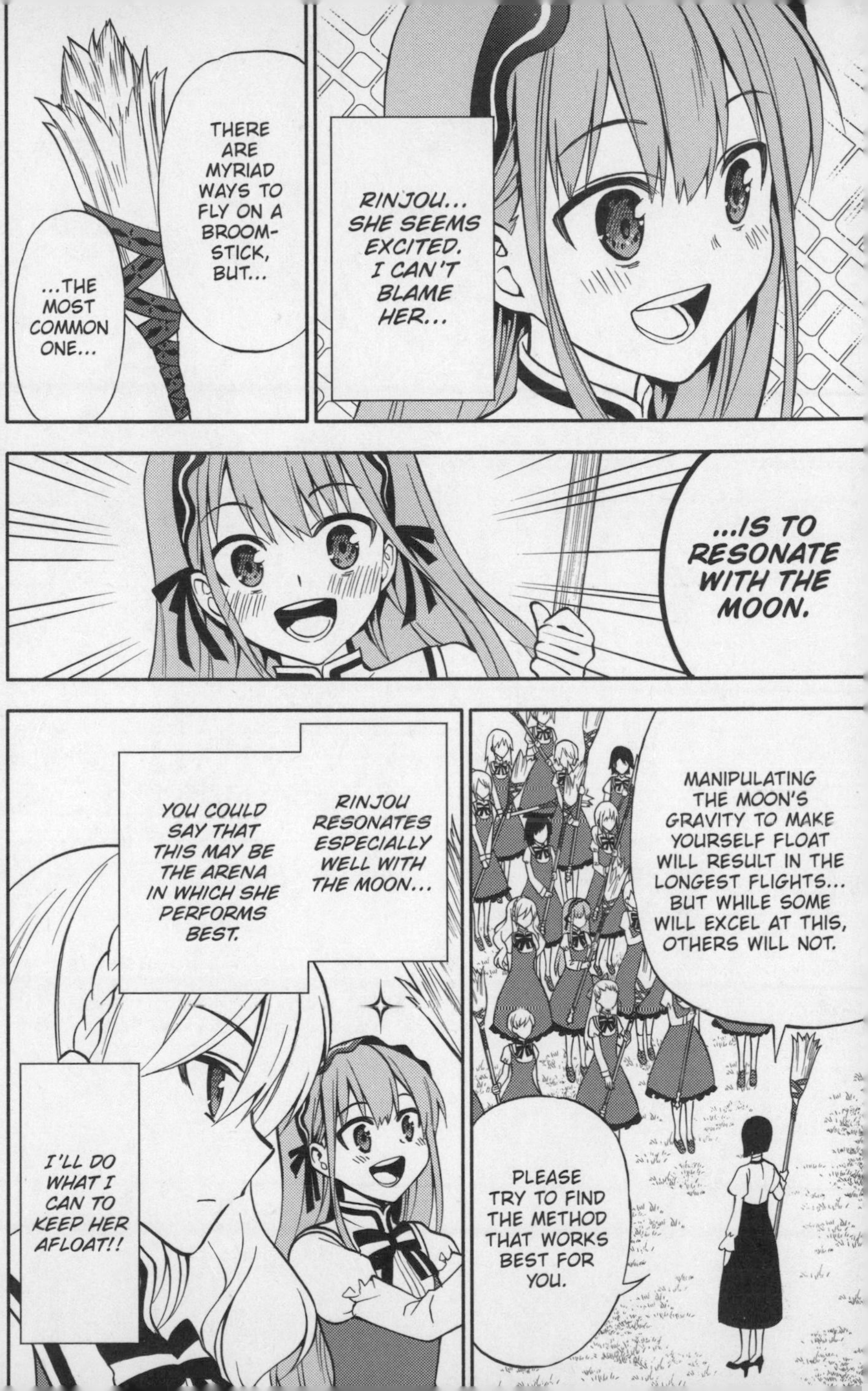
RINJOU... SHE SEEMS EXCITED. I CAN'T BLAME HER...
THERE ARE MYRIAD WAYS TO FLY ON A BROOM-STICK, BUT...
...THE MOST COMMON ONE...
...IS TO RESONATE WITH THE MOON.
MANIPULATING THE MOON'S GRAVITY TO MAKE YOURSELF FLOAT WILL RESULT IN THE LONGEST FLIGHTS... BUT WHILE SOME WILL EXCEL AT THIS, OTHERS WILL NOT.
PLEASE TRY TO FIND THE METHOD THAT WORKS BEST FOR YOU.
RINJOU RESONATES ESPECIALLY WELL WITH THE MOON...
YOU COULD SAY THAT THIS MAY BE THE ARENA IN WHICH SHE PERFORMS BEST.
I'LL DO WHAT I CAN TO KEEP HER AFLOAT!!

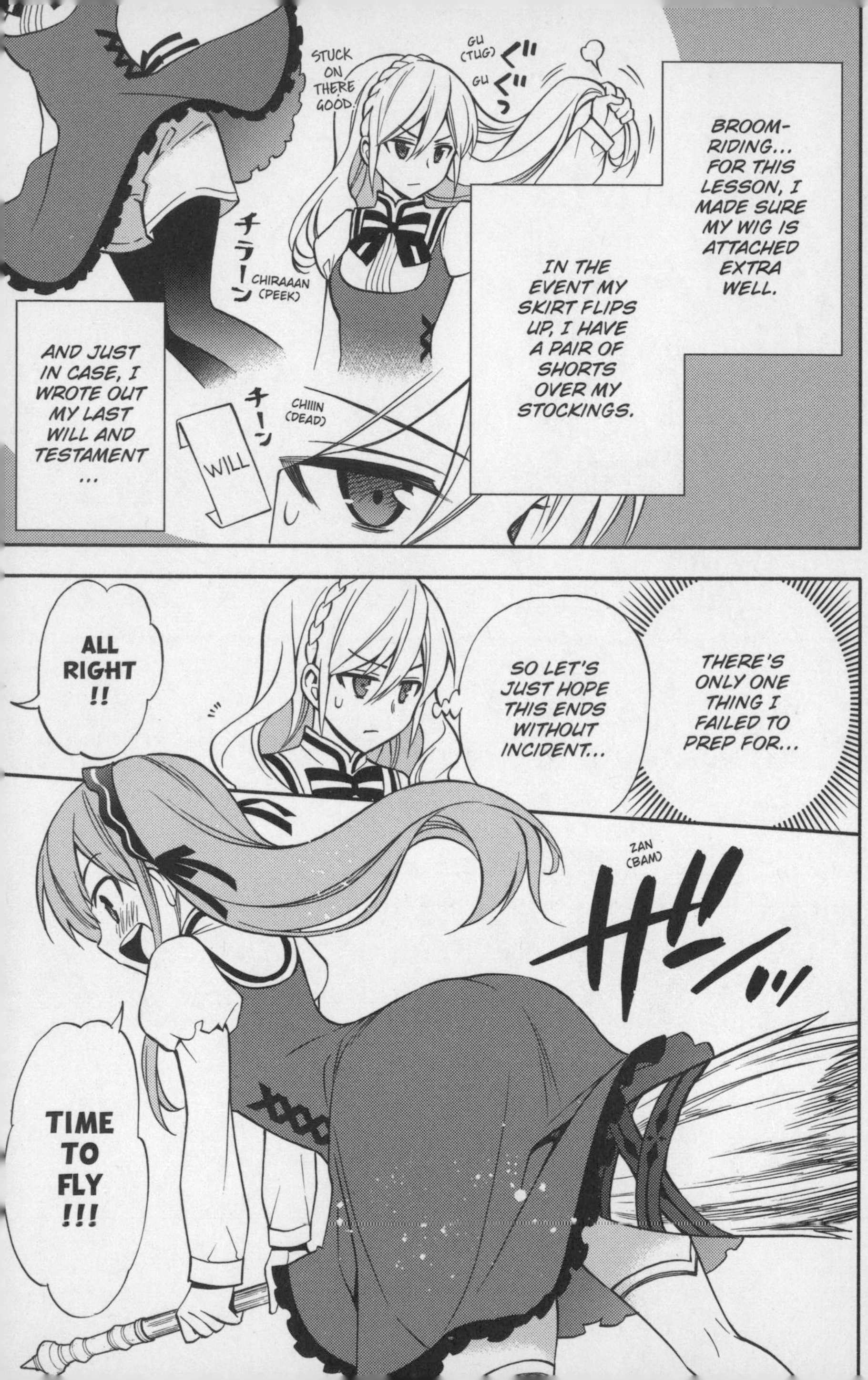
BROOM-RIDING... FOR THIS LESSON, I MADE SURE MY WIG IS ATTACHED EXTRA WELL.
GU (TUG) GU
STUCK ON THERE GOOD.
IN THE EVENT MY SKIRT FLIPS UP, I HAVE A PAIR OF SHORTS OVER MY STOCKINGS.
CHIRAAAN (PEEK)
AND JUST IN CASE, I WROTE OUT MY LAST WILL AND TESTAMENT ...
CHIIIN (DEAD)
WILL
THERE'S ONLY ONE THING I FAILED TO PREP FOR...
SO LET'S JUST HOPE THIS ENDS WITHOUT INCIDENT...
ALL RIGHT !!
ZAN (BAM)
TIME TO FLY !!!

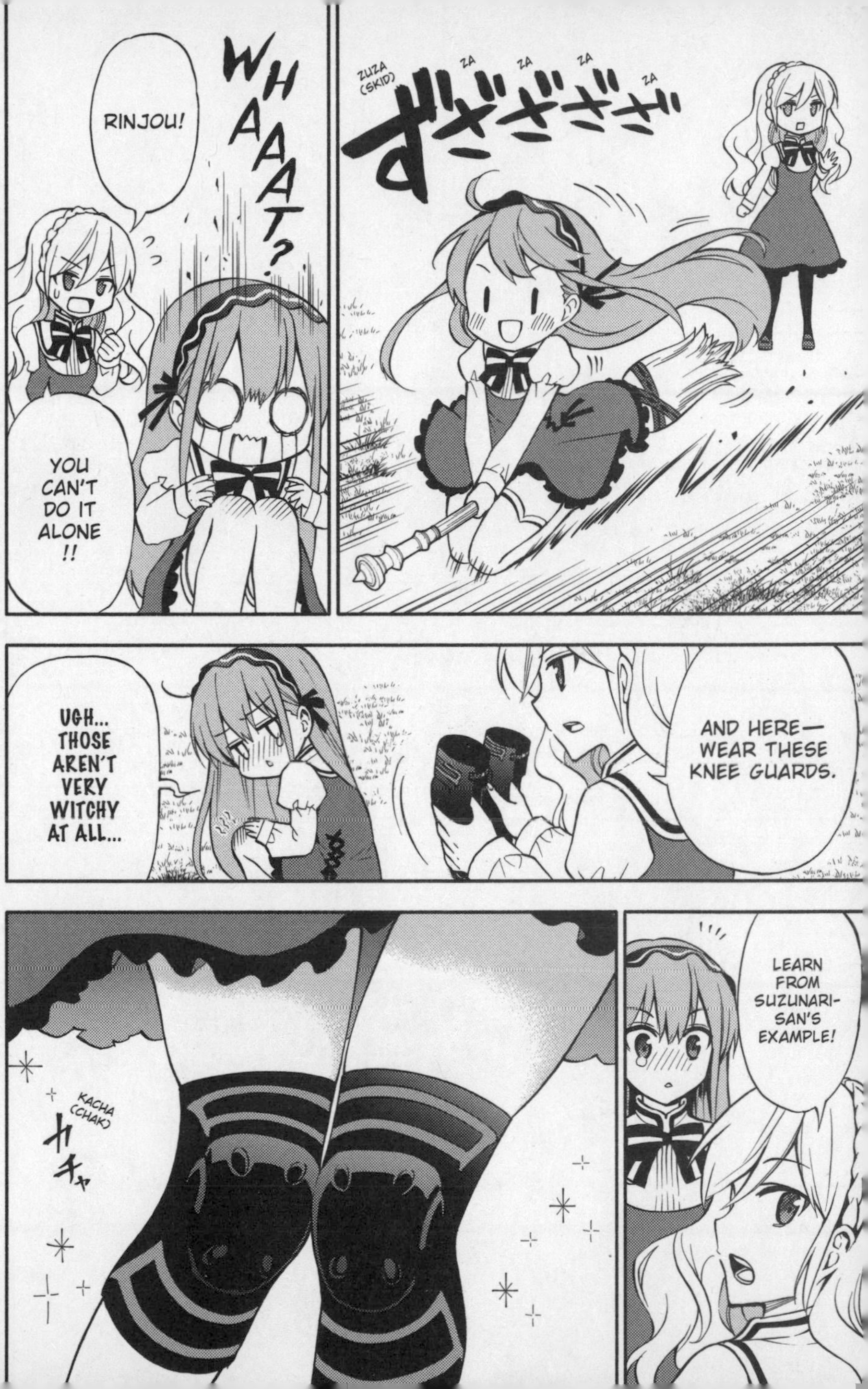

ZUZA (SKID)
ZA ZA ZA ZA
ずざざざざ
WHAAAAT?
RINJOU!
YOU CAN'T DO IT ALONE!!
AND HERE—WEAR THESE KNEE GUARDS.
UGH... THOSE AREN'T VERY WITCHY AT ALL...
LEARN FROM SUZUNARI-SAN'S EXAMPLE!
KACHA (CHAK)
カチャ

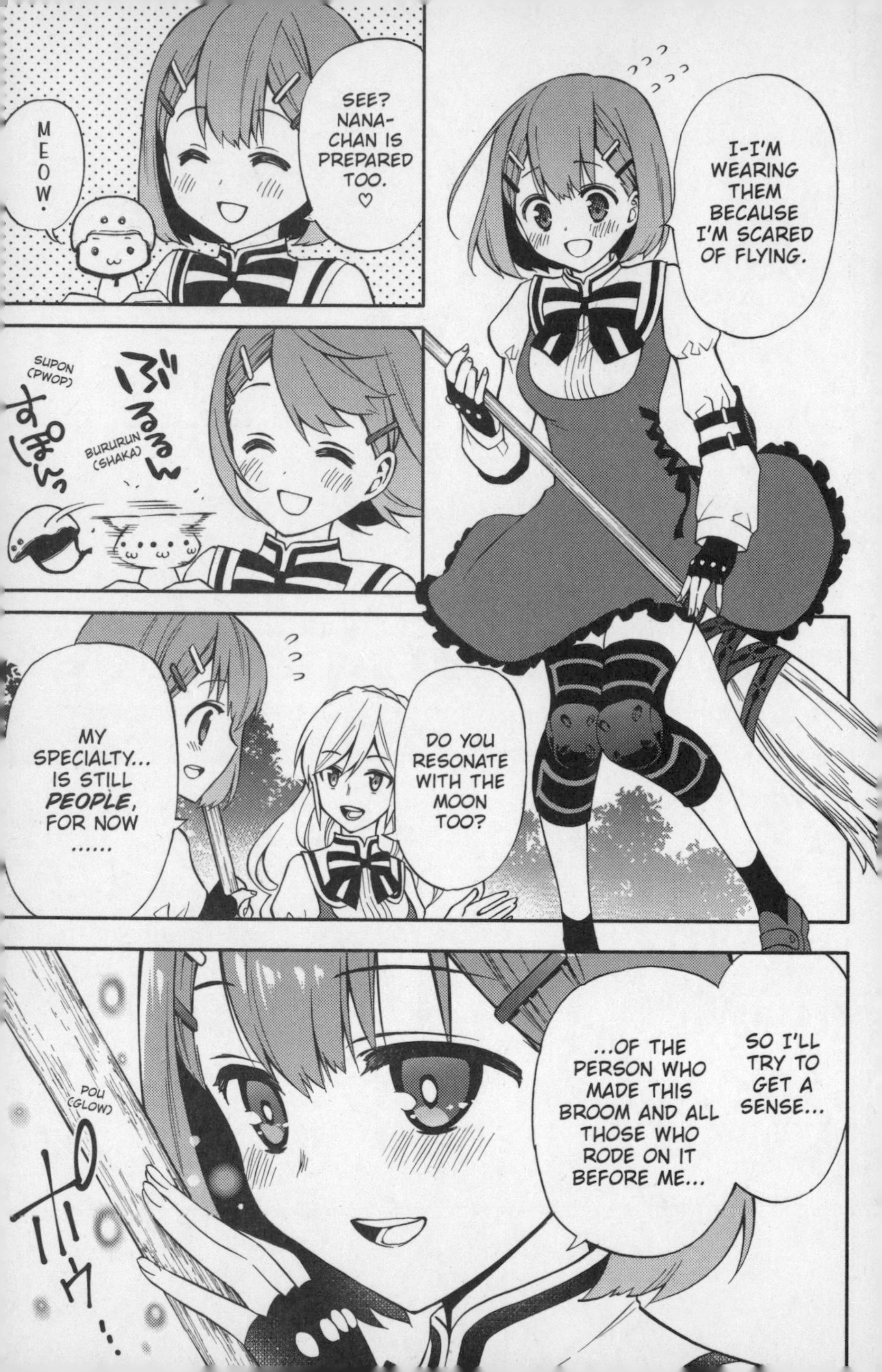
I-I'M WEARING THEM BECAUSE I'M SCARED OF FLYING.
SEE? NANA-CHAN IS PREPARED TOO. ♡
MEOW.
ぶるるん
BURURUN (SHAKA)
すぽんっ
SUPON (PWOP)
DO YOU RESONATE WITH THE MOON TOO?
MY SPECIALTY... IS STILL *PEOPLE*, FOR NOW ......
SO I'LL TRY TO GET A SENSE...
...OF THE PERSON WHO MADE THIS BROOM AND ALL THOSE WHO RODE ON IT BEFORE ME...
POU (GLOW)

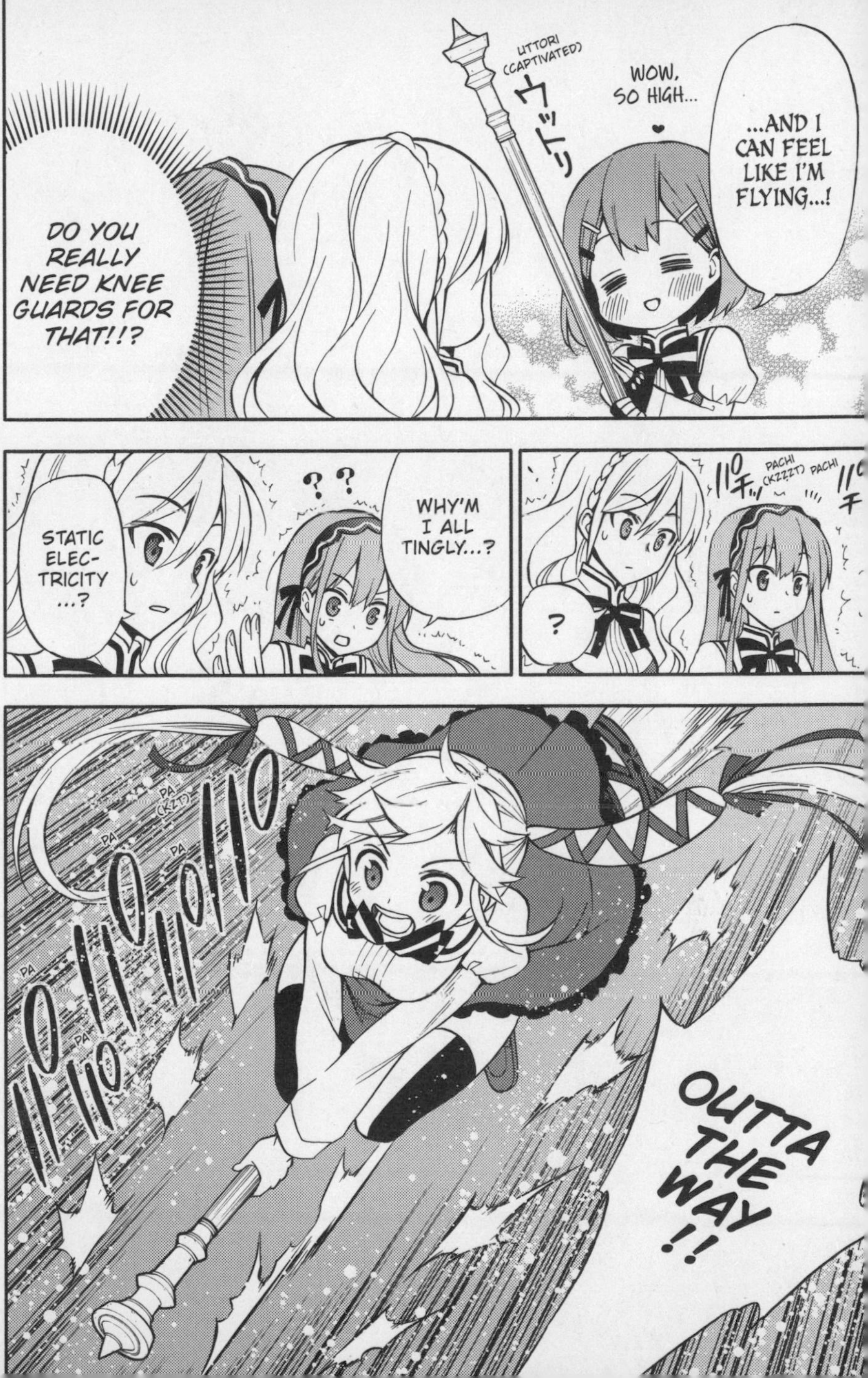
...AND I CAN FEEL LIKE I'M FLYING...!
WOW, SO HIGH...
UTTORI (CAPTIVATED)
ウットリ
DO YOU REALLY NEED KNEE GUARDS FOR THAT!!?
PACHI (KZZZT) PACHI
?
WHY'M I ALL TINGLY...?
??
STATIC ELEC-TRICITY ...?
OUTTA THE WAY!!
PA (KZT)
PA
PA
PA
PA

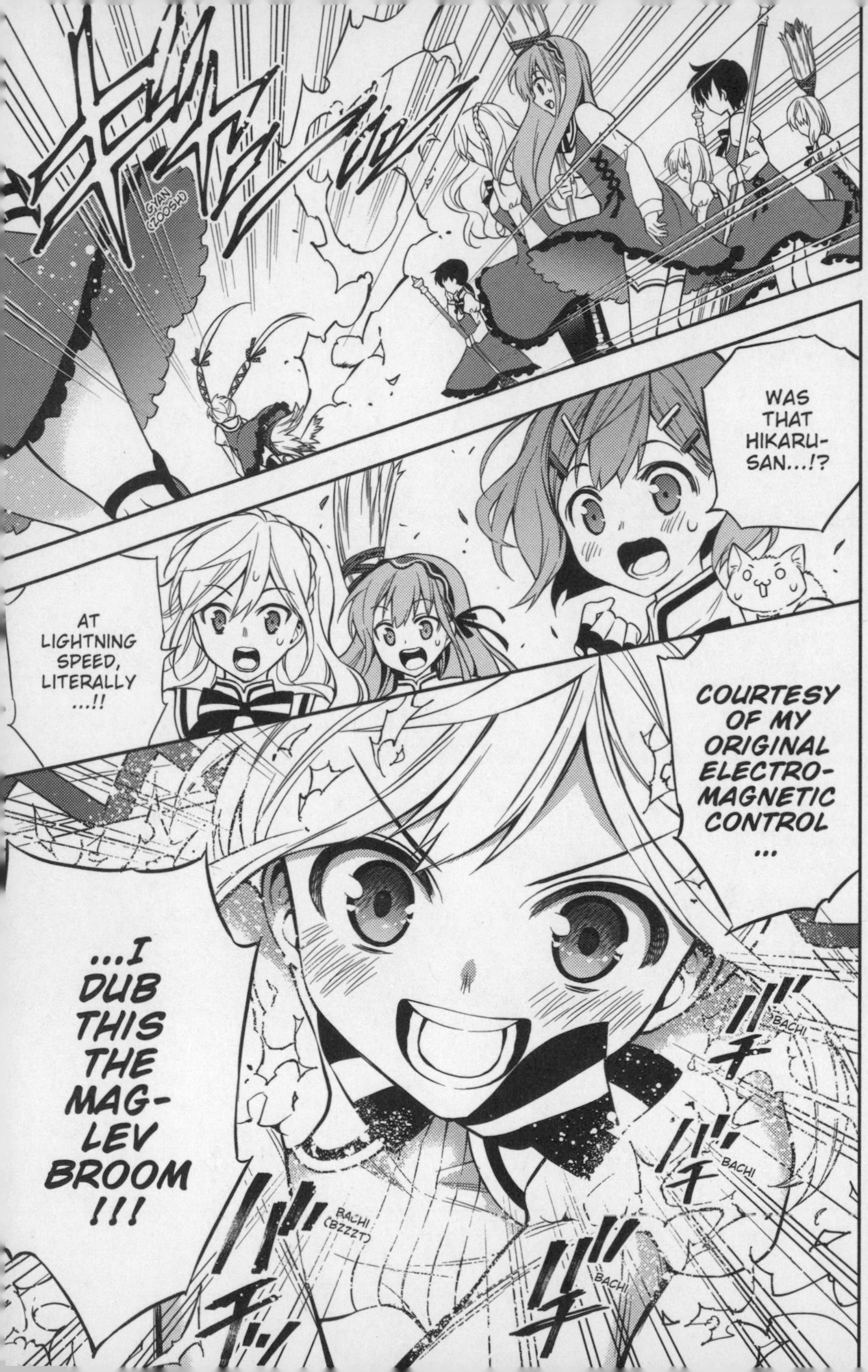
GYAN (ZOOSH)
WAS THAT HIKARU-SAN...!?
AT LIGHTNING SPEED, LITERALLY...!!
COURTESY OF MY ORIGINAL ELECTROMAGNETIC CONTROL...
...I DUB THIS THE MAG-LEV BROOM!!!
BACHI
BACHI
BACHI (BZZZT)
BACHI

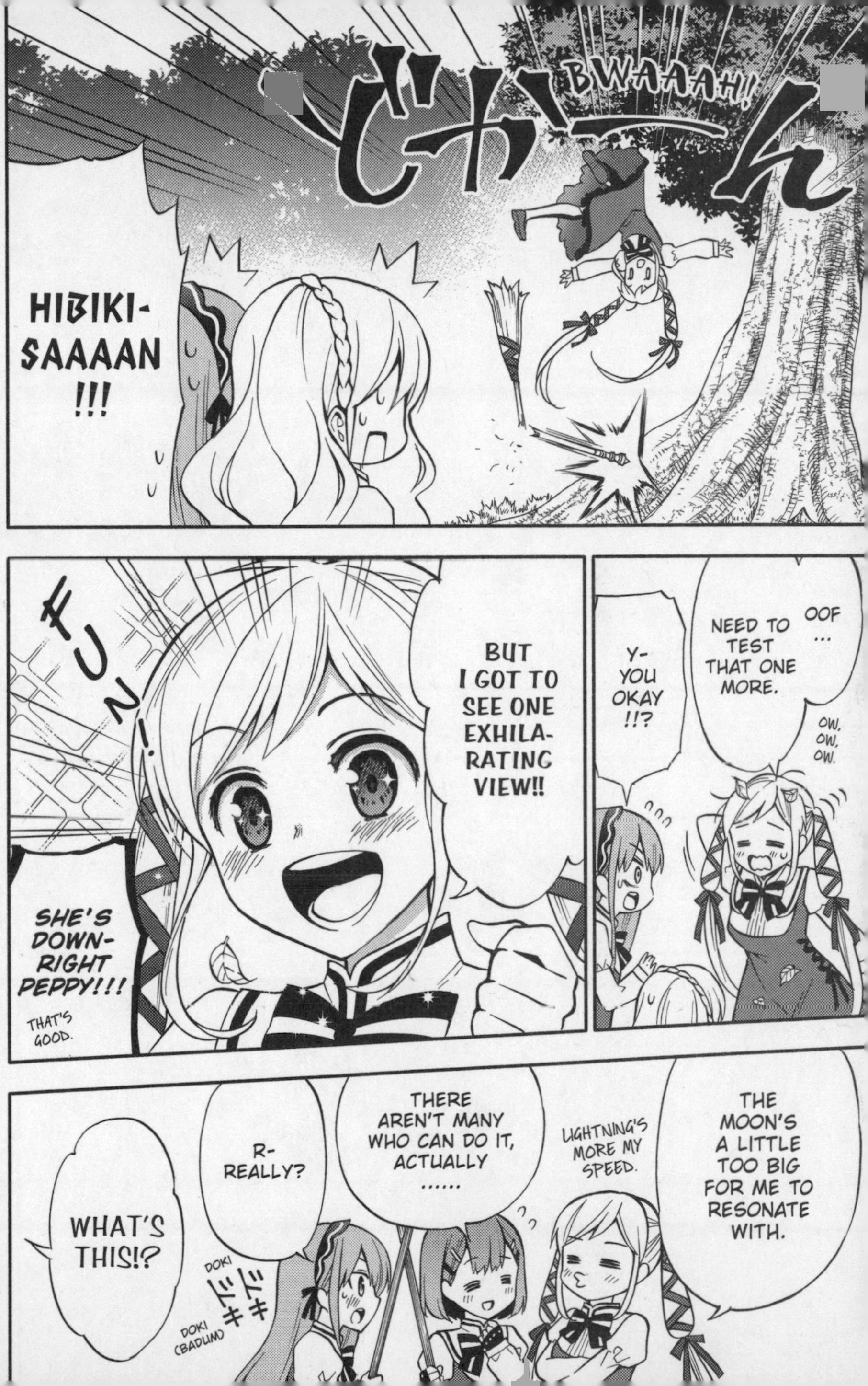
BWAAAAH!
HIBIKI-SAAAAN!!!
OOF ...
NEED TO TEST THAT ONE MORE.
OW, OW, OW.
Y-YOU OKAY!!?
FUN-!
BUT I GOT TO SEE ONE EXHILA-RATING VIEW!!
SHE'S DOWN-RIGHT PEPPY!!!
THAT'S GOOD.
THE MOON'S A LITTLE TOO BIG FOR ME TO RESONATE WITH.
LIGHTNING'S MORE MY SPEED.
THERE AREN'T MANY WHO CAN DO IT, ACTUALLY ......
R-REALLY?
WHAT'S THIS!?
DOKI
DOKI (BADUM)

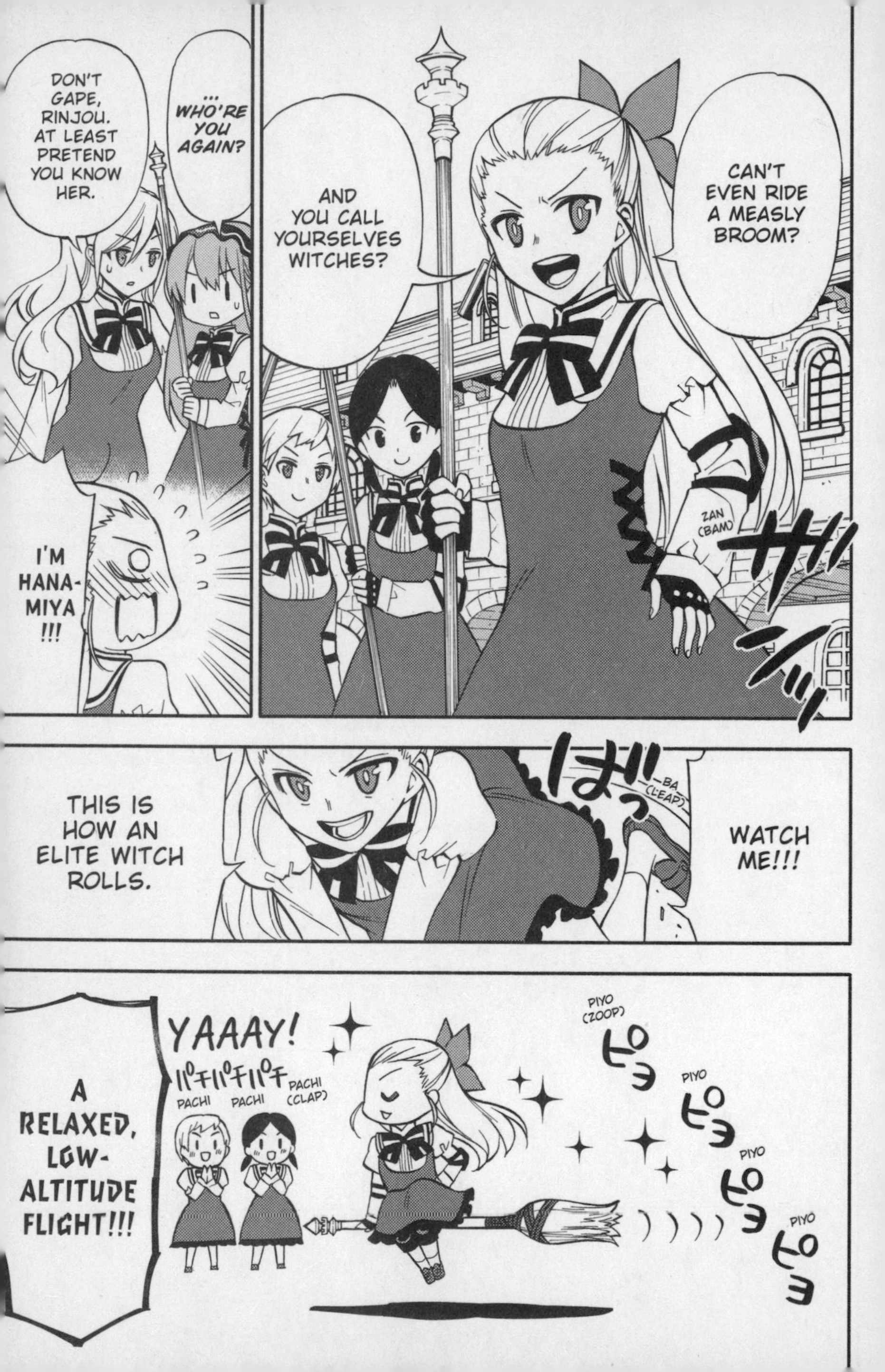
CAN'T EVEN RIDE A MEASLY BROOM?
AND YOU CALL YOURSELVES WITCHES?
ザンッ
ZAN (BAM)
...WHO'RE YOU AGAIN?
DON'T GAPE, RINJOU. AT LEAST PRETEND YOU KNOW HER.
I'M HANAMIYA!!!
WATCH ME!!!
ばっ
BA (LEAP)
THIS IS HOW AN ELITE WITCH ROLLS.
ピョ
PIYO (ZOOP)
ピョ
PIYO
ピョ
PIYO
ピョ
PIYO
YAAAY!
パチパチパチ
PACHI PACHI PACHI (CLAP)
A RELAXED, LOW-ALTITUDE FLIGHT!!!

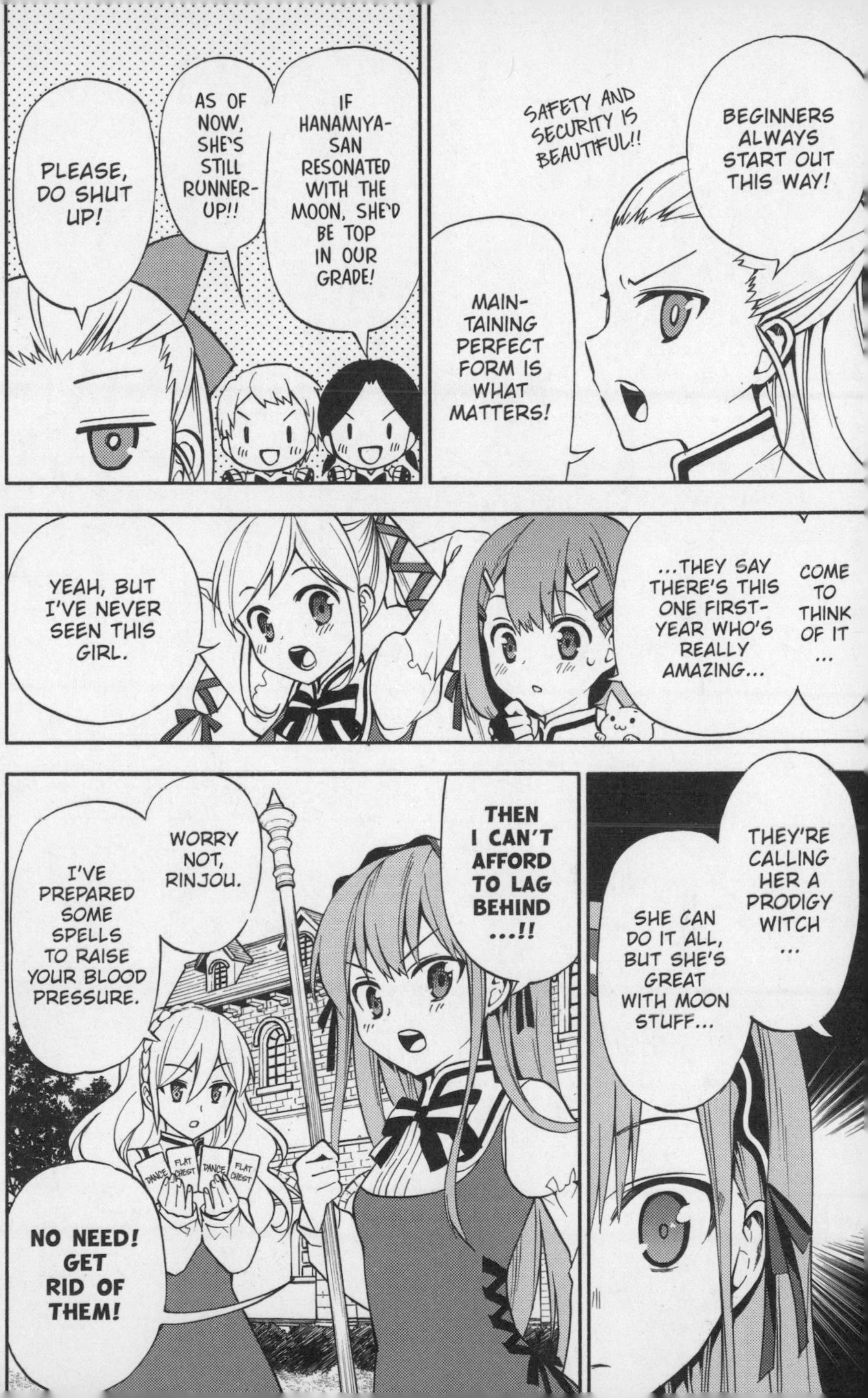
BEGINNERS ALWAYS START OUT THIS WAY!
SAFETY AND SECURITY IS BEAUTIFUL!!
MAIN-TAINING PERFECT FORM IS WHAT MATTERS!
IF HANAMIYA-SAN RESONATED WITH THE MOON, SHE'D BE TOP IN OUR GRADE!
AS OF NOW, SHE'S STILL RUNNER-UP!!
PLEASE, DO SHUT UP!
COME TO THINK OF IT ...
...THEY SAY THERE'S THIS ONE FIRST-YEAR WHO'S REALLY AMAZING...
YEAH, BUT I'VE NEVER SEEN THIS GIRL.
THEY'RE CALLING HER A PRODIGY WITCH ...
SHE CAN DO IT ALL, BUT SHE'S GREAT WITH MOON STUFF...
THEN I CAN'T AFFORD TO LAG BEHIND ...!!
WORRY NOT, RINJOU.
I'VE PREPARED SOME SPELLS TO RAISE YOUR BLOOD PRESSURE.
DANCE
FLAT CHEST
DANCE
FLAT CHEST
NO NEED! GET RID OF THEM!

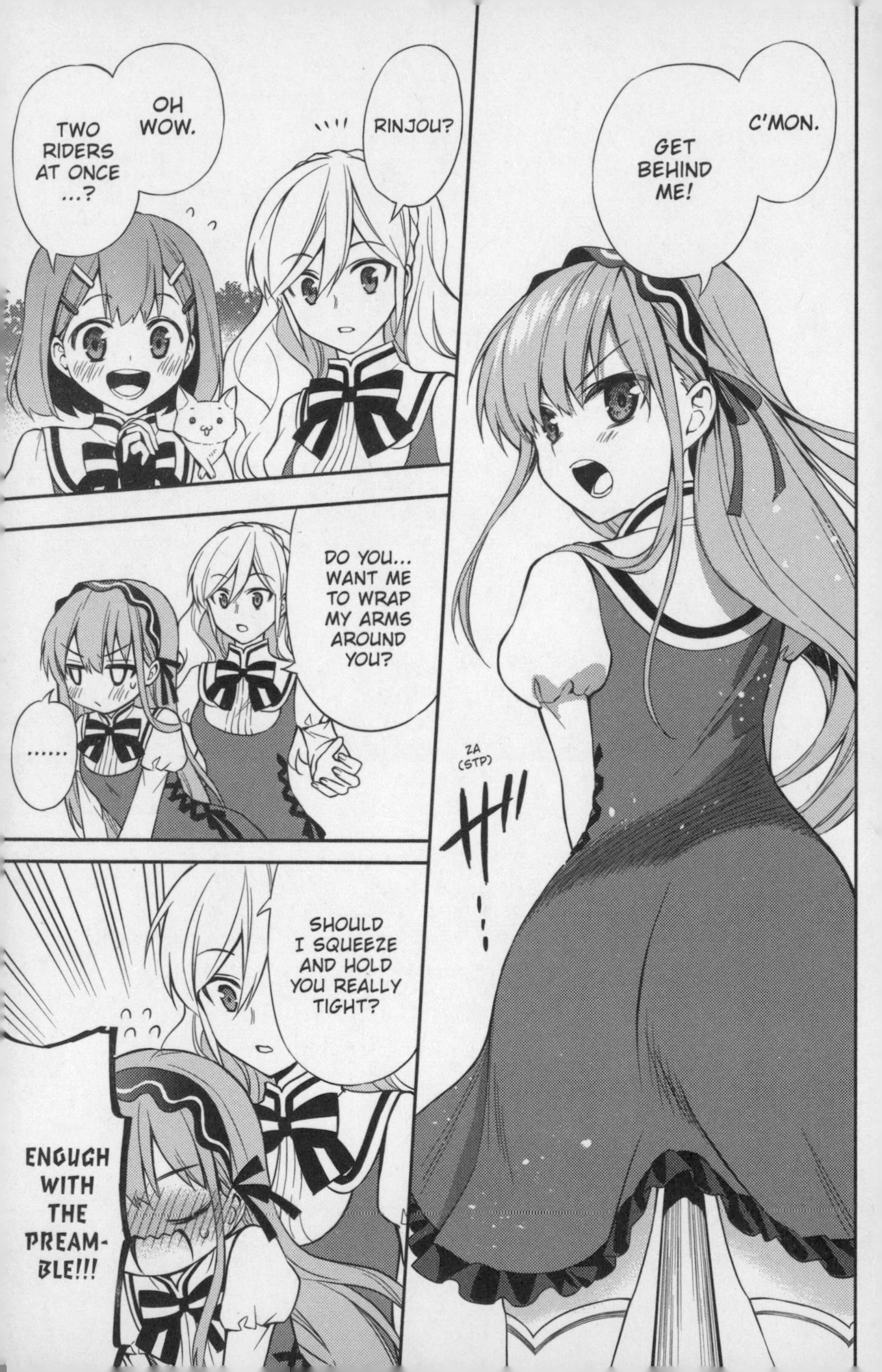
C'MON.
GET BEHIND ME!
ZA (STP)
RINJOU?
OH WOW.
TWO RIDERS AT ONCE ...?
DO YOU... WANT ME TO WRAP MY ARMS AROUND YOU?
......
SHOULD I SQUEEZE AND HOLD YOU REALLY TIGHT?
ENOUGH WITH THE PREAMBLE!!!

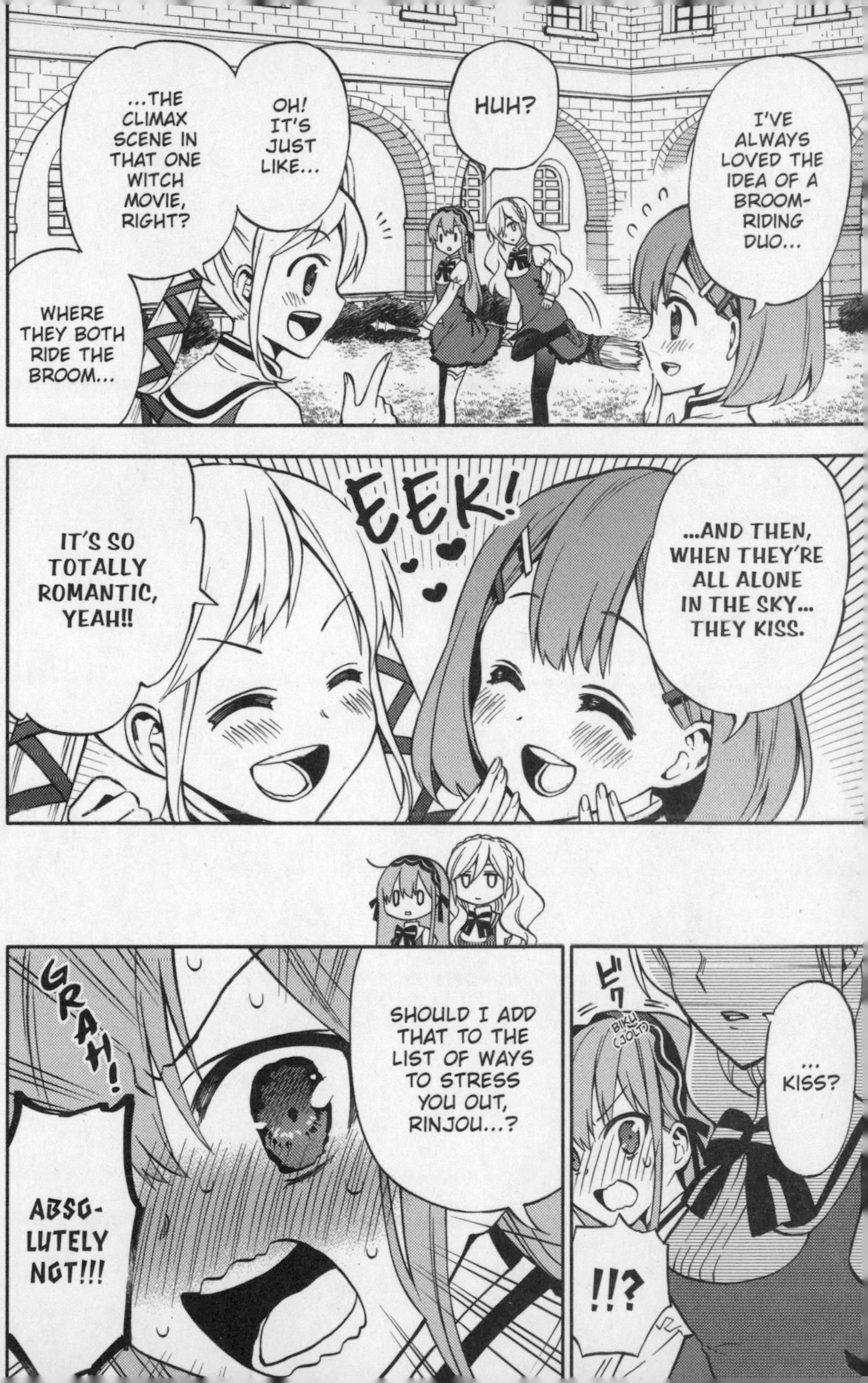
I'VE ALWAYS LOVED THE IDEA OF A BROOM-RIDING DUO...
HUH?
OH! IT'S JUST LIKE...
...THE CLIMAX SCENE IN THAT ONE WITCH MOVIE, RIGHT?
WHERE THEY BOTH RIDE THE BROOM...
...AND THEN, WHEN THEY'RE ALL ALONE IN THE SKY... THEY KISS.
EEK!
IT'S SO TOTALLY ROMANTIC, YEAH!!
BIKU (JOLT)
... KISS?
!!?
SHOULD I ADD THAT TO THE LIST OF WAYS TO STRESS YOU OUT, RINJOU...?
GRAH!
ABSO-LUTELY NOT!!!

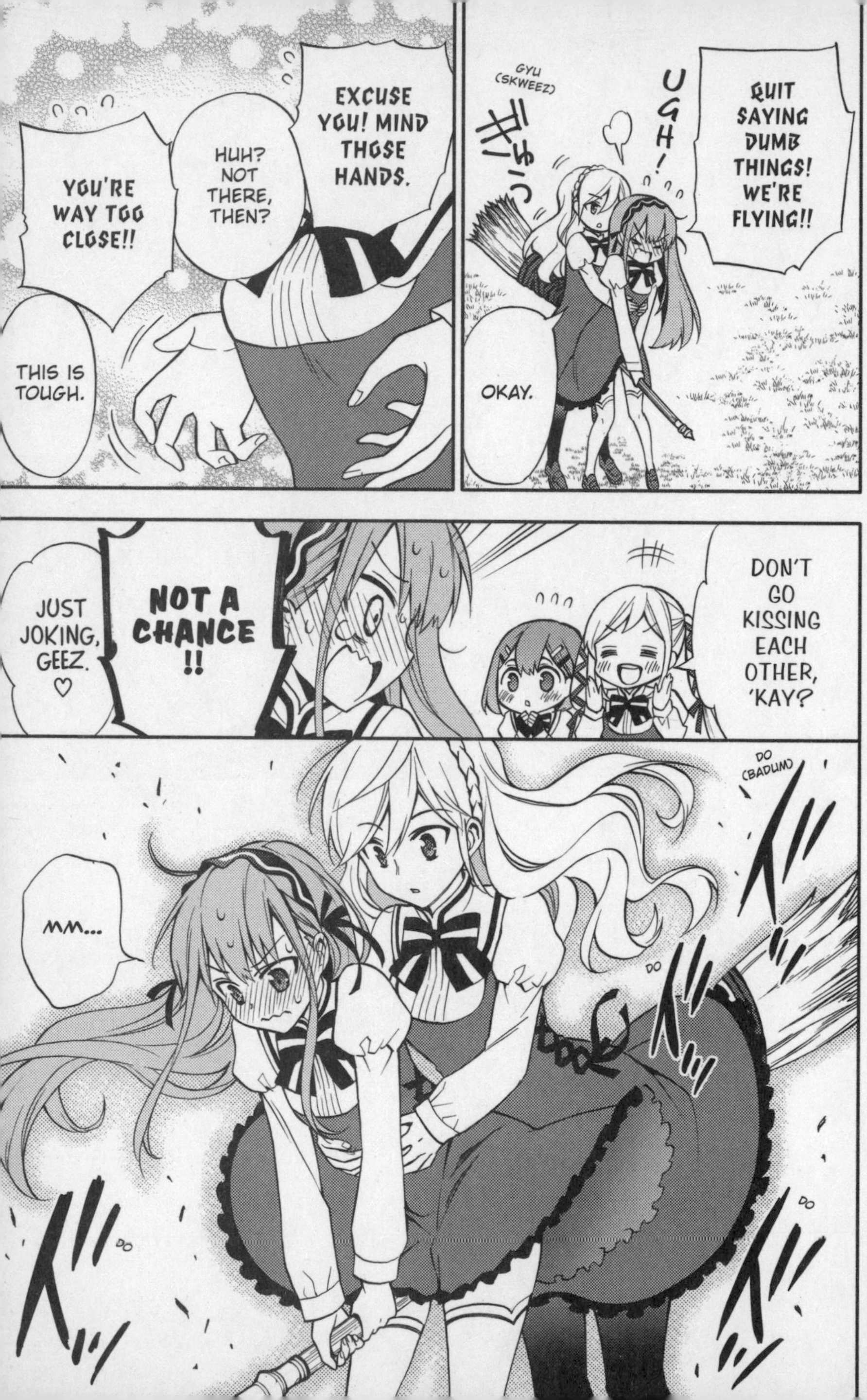
QUIT SAYING DUMB THINGS! WE'RE FLYING!!
UGH!
GYU (SKWEEZ)
OKAY.
EXCUSE YOU! MIND THOSE HANDS.
HUH? NOT THERE, THEN?
YOU'RE WAY TOO CLOSE!!
THIS IS TOUGH.
DON'T GO KISSING EACH OTHER, 'KAY?
NOT A CHANCE!!
JUST JOKING, GEEZ. ♡
DO (BADUM)
MM...
DO
DO
DO

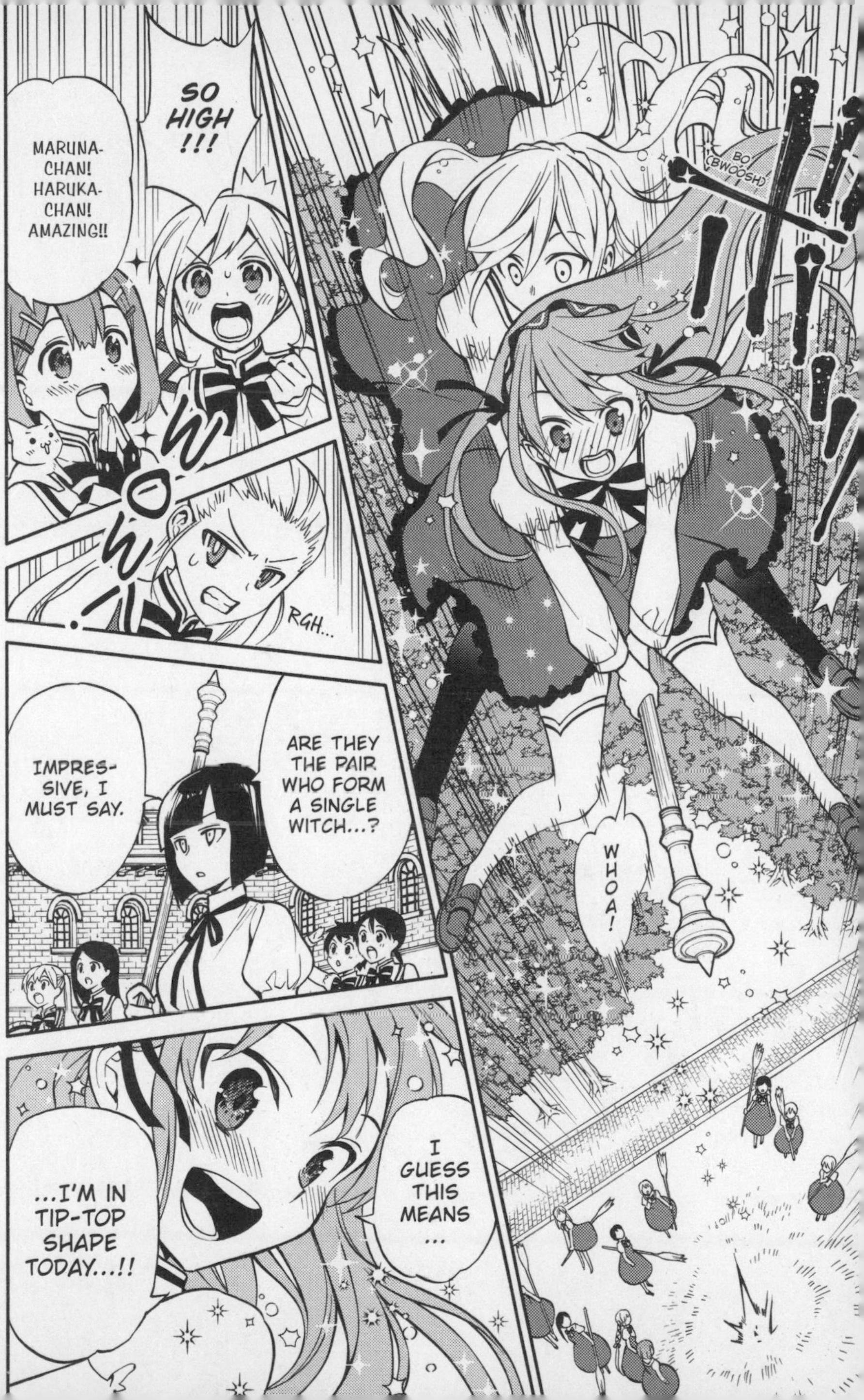
BO (BWOOSH)
WHOA!
SO HIGH!!!
MARUNA-CHAN! HARUKA-CHAN! AMAZING!!
WOW!
RGH...
ARE THEY THE PAIR WHO FORM A SINGLE WITCH...?
IMPRES-SIVE, I MUST SAY.
I GUESS THIS MEANS...
...I'M IN TIP-TOP SHAPE TODAY...!!

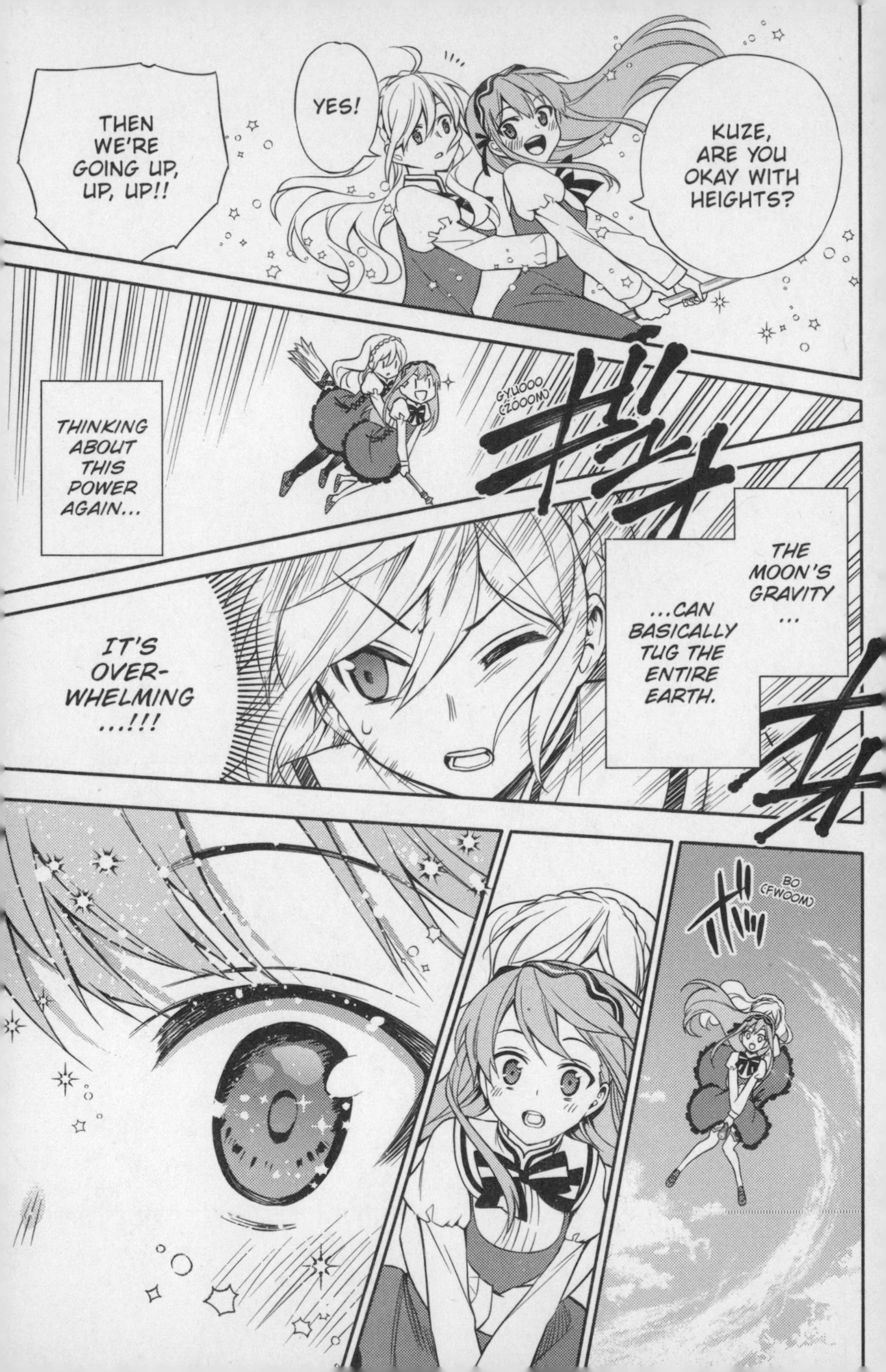
KUZE, ARE YOU OKAY WITH HEIGHTS?
YES!
THEN WE'RE GOING UP, UP, UP!!
GYUOOO (ZOOOM)
THINKING ABOUT THIS POWER AGAIN...
THE MOON'S GRAVITY...
...CAN BASICALLY TUG THE ENTIRE EARTH.
IT'S OVER-WHELMING...!!!
BO (FWOOM)

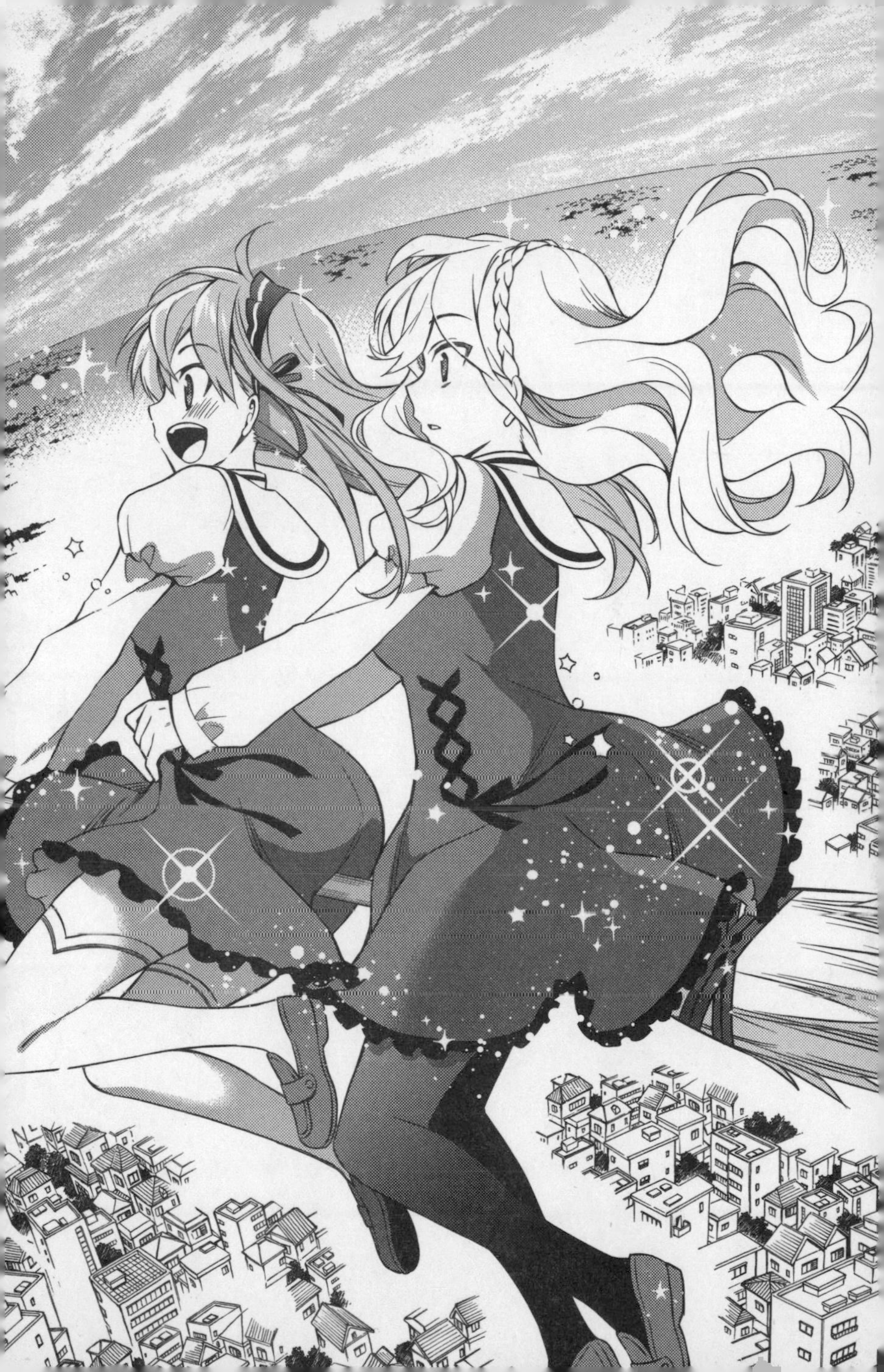

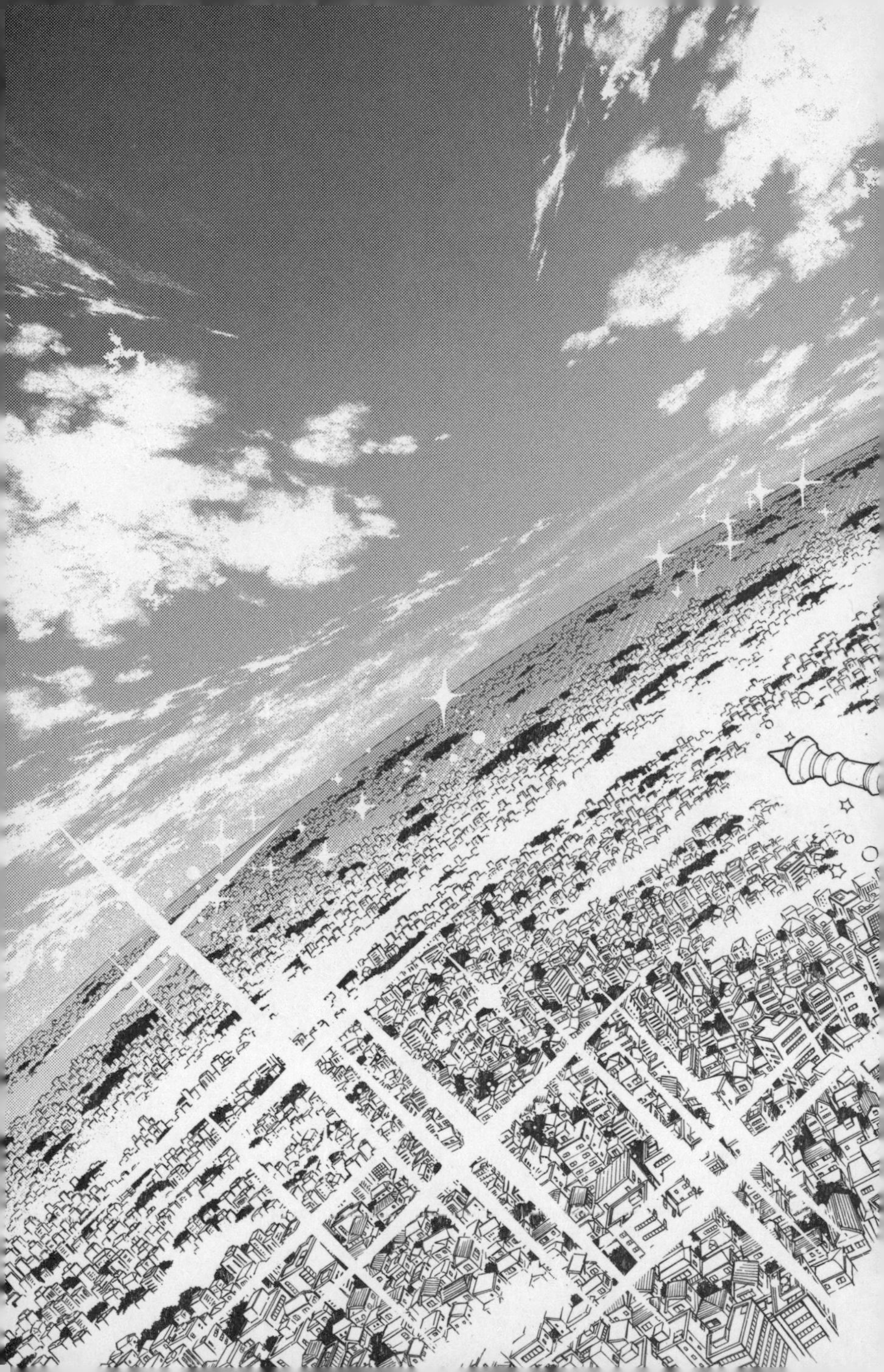

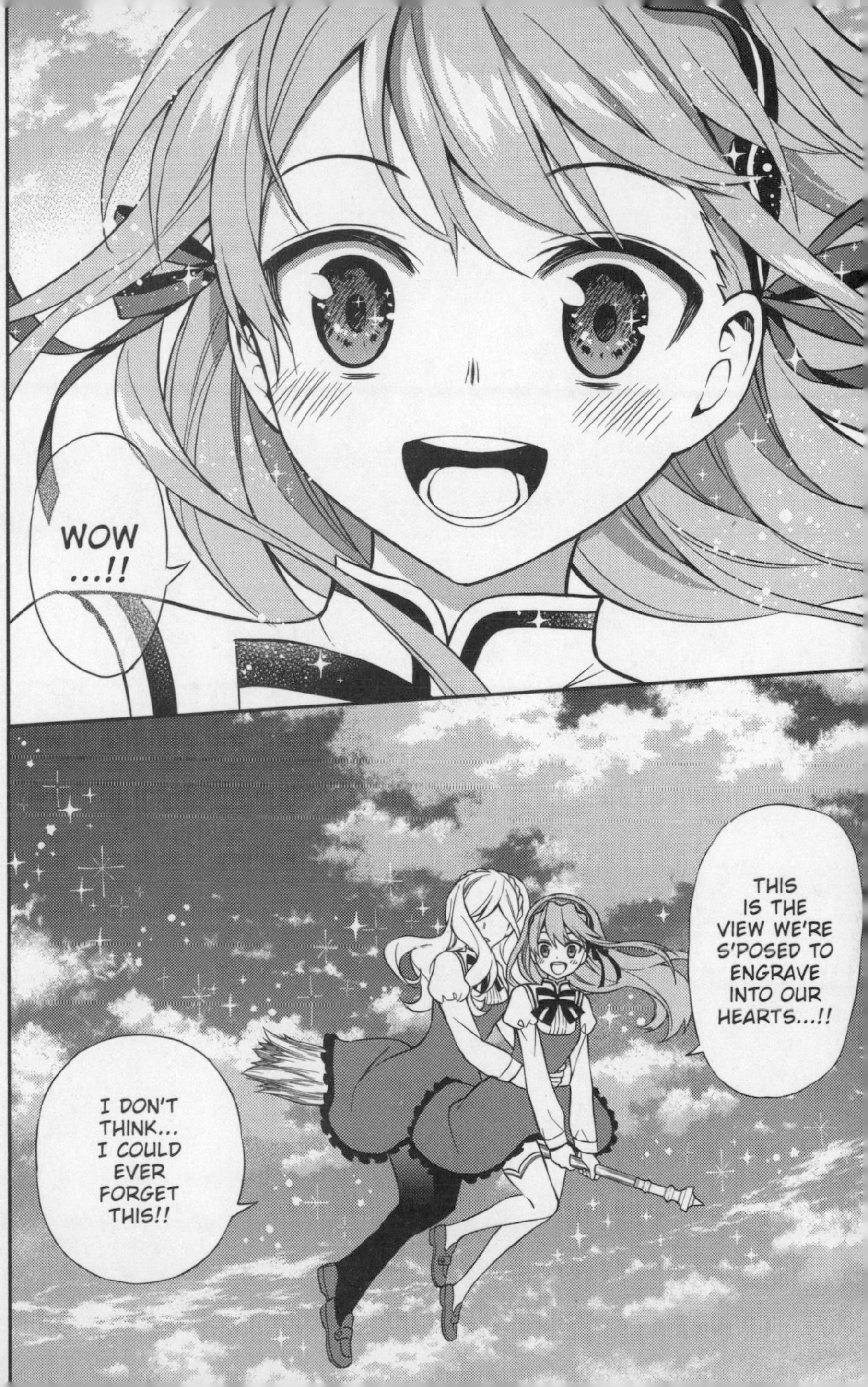
WOW ...!!
THIS IS THE VIEW WE'RE S'POSED TO ENGRAVE INTO OUR HEARTS...!!
I DON'T THINK... I COULD EVER FORGET THIS!!

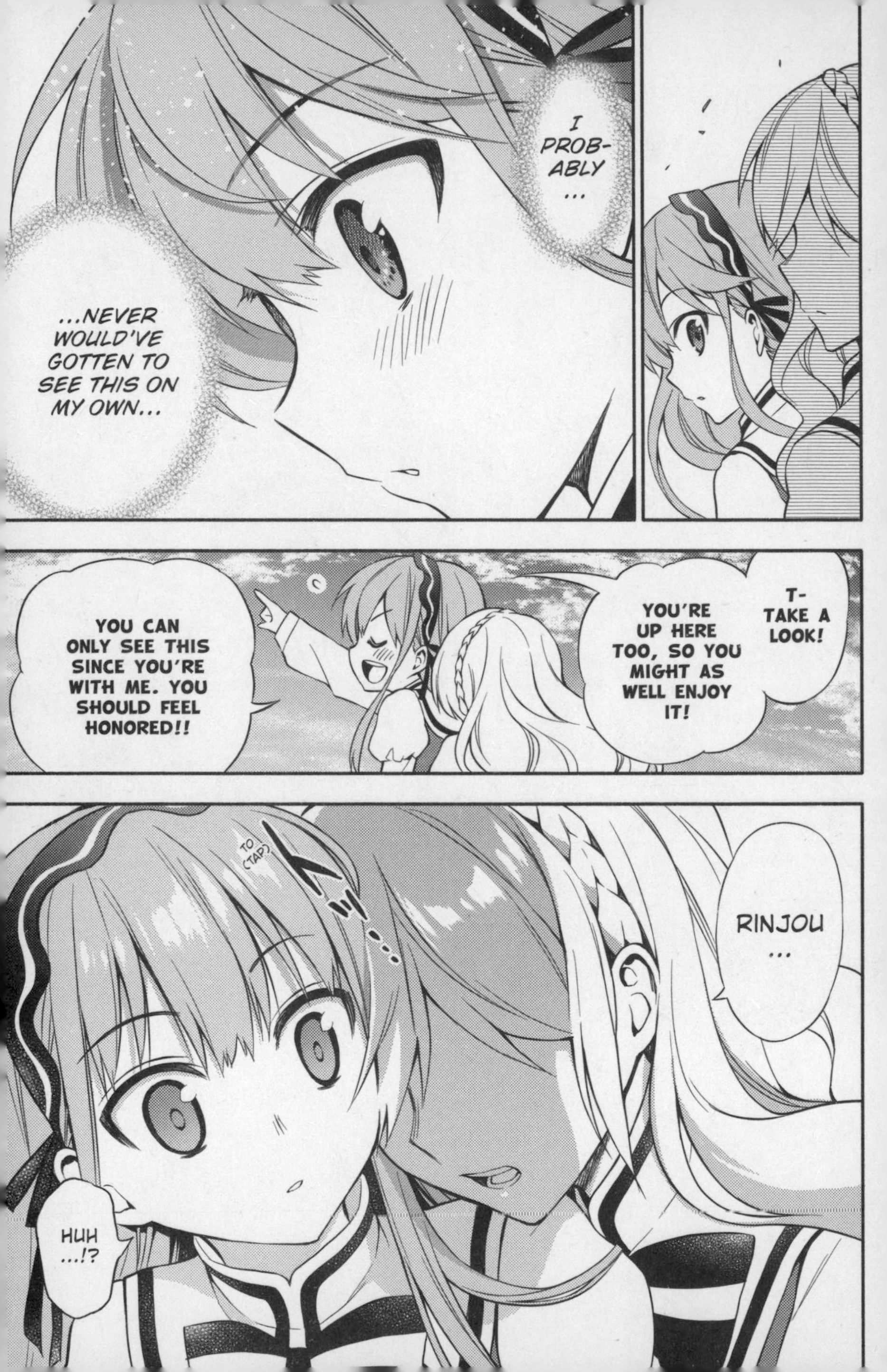
I PROBABLY...
...NEVER WOULD'VE GOTTEN TO SEE THIS ON MY OWN...
T- TAKE A LOOK!
YOU'RE UP HERE TOO, SO YOU MIGHT AS WELL ENJOY IT!
YOU CAN ONLY SEE THIS SINCE YOU'RE WITH ME. YOU SHOULD FEEL HONORED!!
RINJOU...
TO (TAP)
HUH...!?

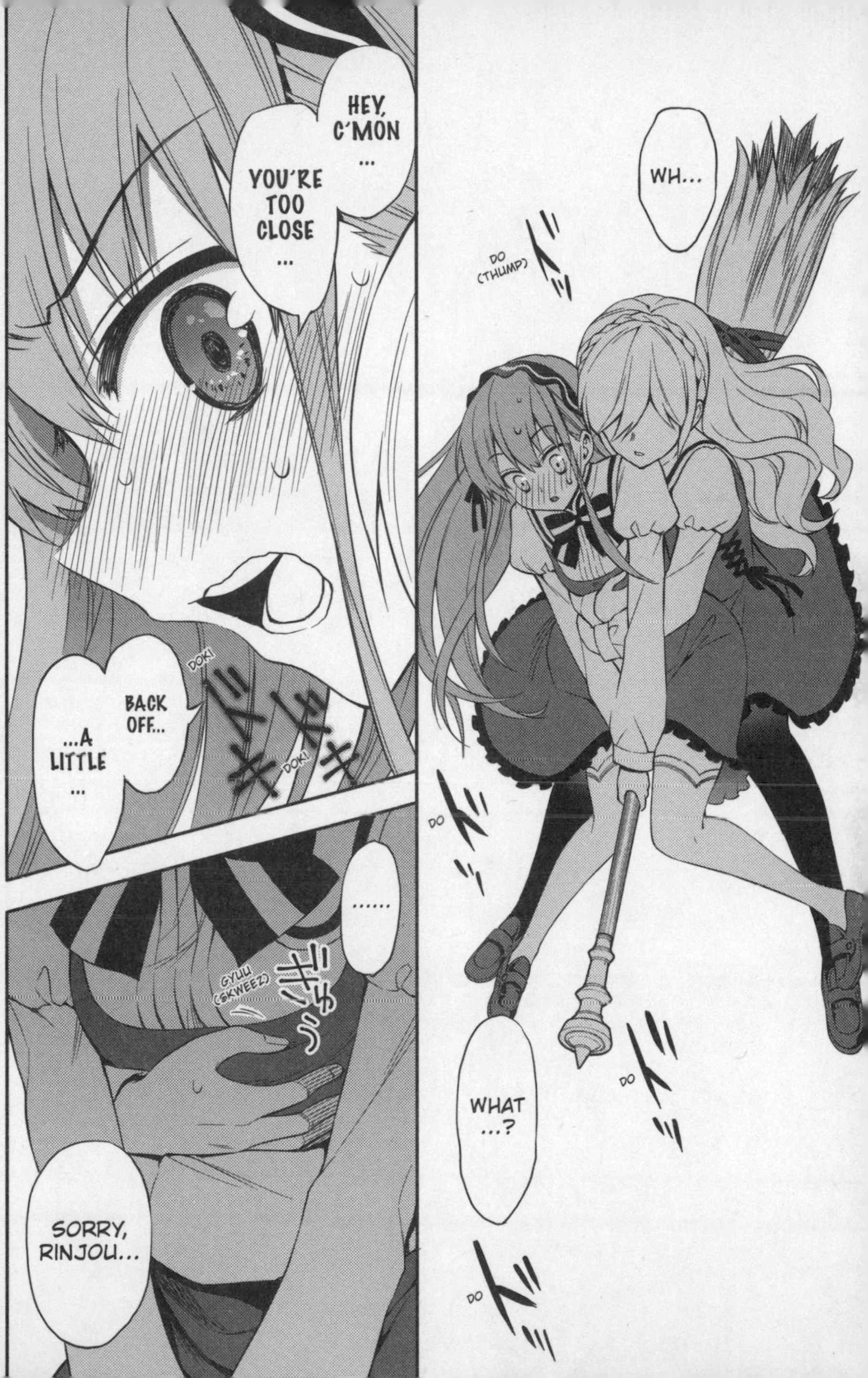
WH...
DO (THUMP)
DO
WHAT ...?
DO
DO
HEY, C'MON ... YOU'RE TOO CLOSE ...
DOK! DOK!
BACK OFF...
...A LITTLE ...
......
GYUU (SKWEEZ)
SORRY, RINJOU...

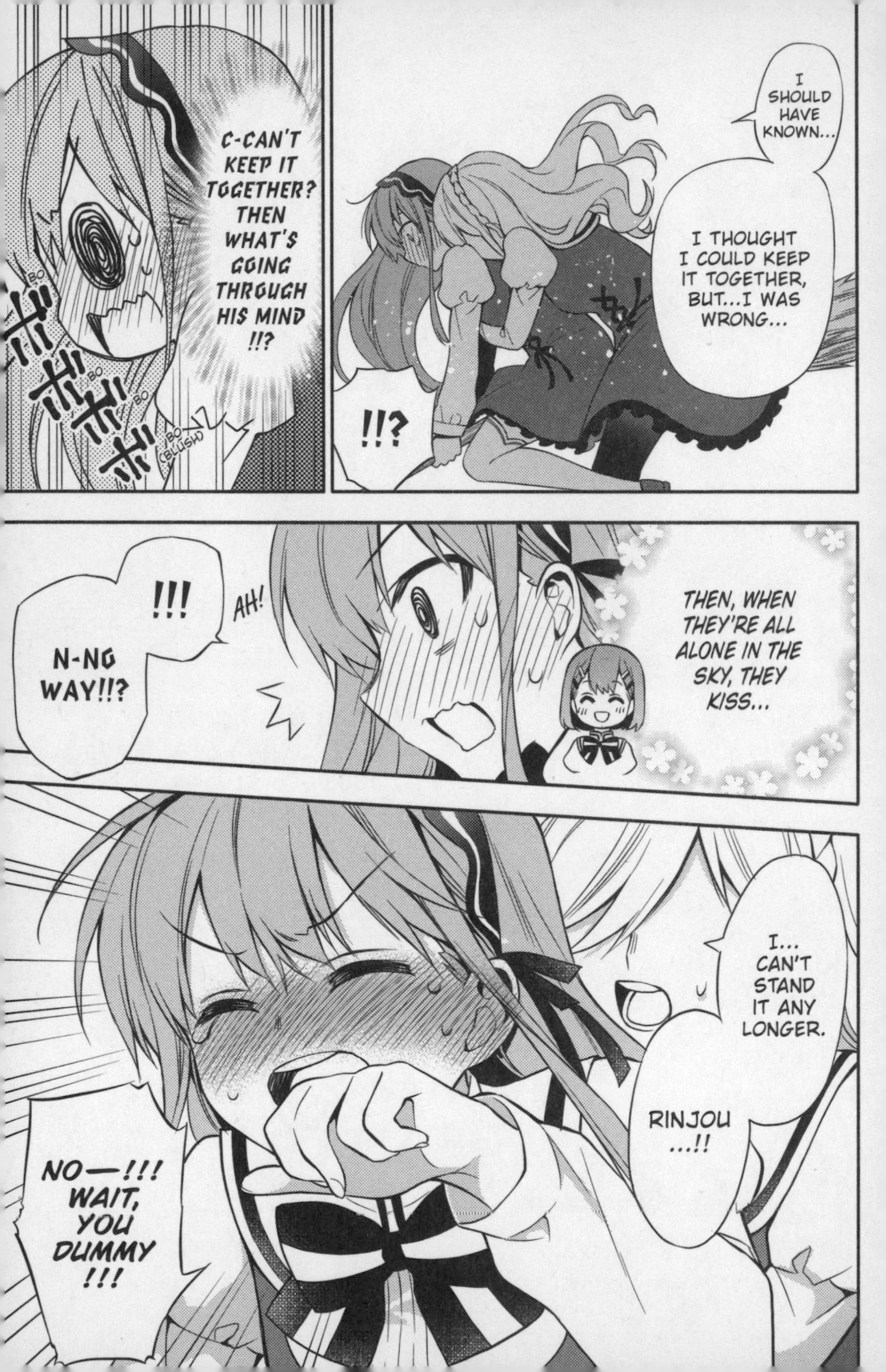
I SHOULD HAVE KNOWN...
I THOUGHT I COULD KEEP IT TOGETHER, BUT...I WAS WRONG...
!!?
C-CAN'T KEEP IT TOGETHER? THEN WHAT'S GOING THROUGH HIS MIND !!?
BO BO BO BO (BLUSH)
THEN, WHEN THEY'RE ALL ALONE IN THE SKY, THEY KISS...
AH!
!!!
N-NO WAY!!?
I... CAN'T STAND IT ANY LONGER.
RINJOU ...!!
NO—!!! WAIT, YOU DUMMY !!!

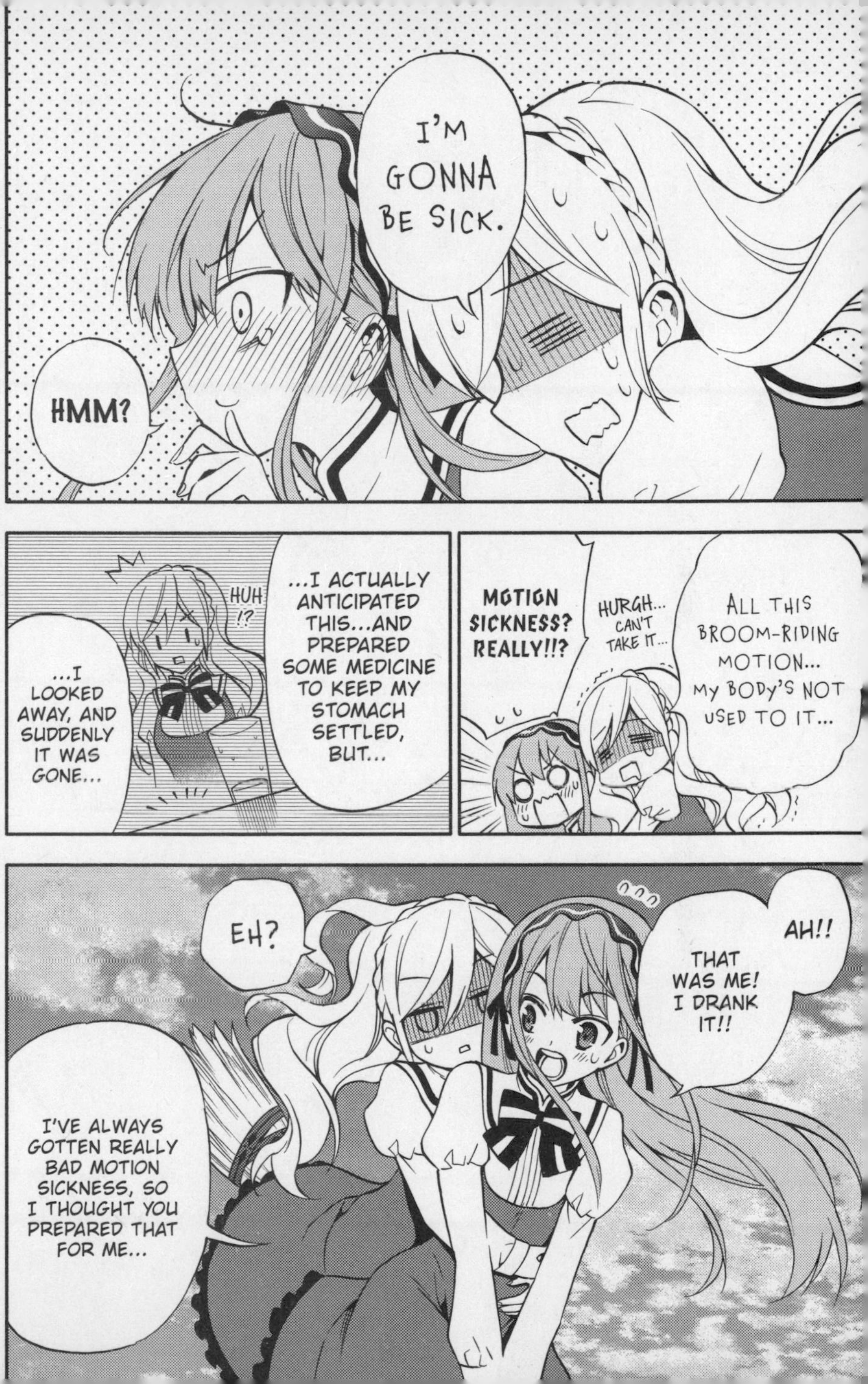
I'M GONNA BE SICK.
HMM?
ALL THIS BROOM-RIDING MOTION... MY BODY'S NOT USED TO IT...
HURGH... CAN'T TAKE IT...
MOTION SICKNESS? REALLY!!?
...I ACTUALLY ANTICIPATED THIS...AND PREPARED SOME MEDICINE TO KEEP MY STOMACH SETTLED, BUT...
HUH!?
...I LOOKED AWAY, AND SUDDENLY IT WAS GONE...
AH!!
THAT WAS ME! I DRANK IT!!
EH?
I'VE ALWAYS GOTTEN REALLY BAD MOTION SICKNESS, SO I THOUGHT YOU PREPARED THAT FOR ME...

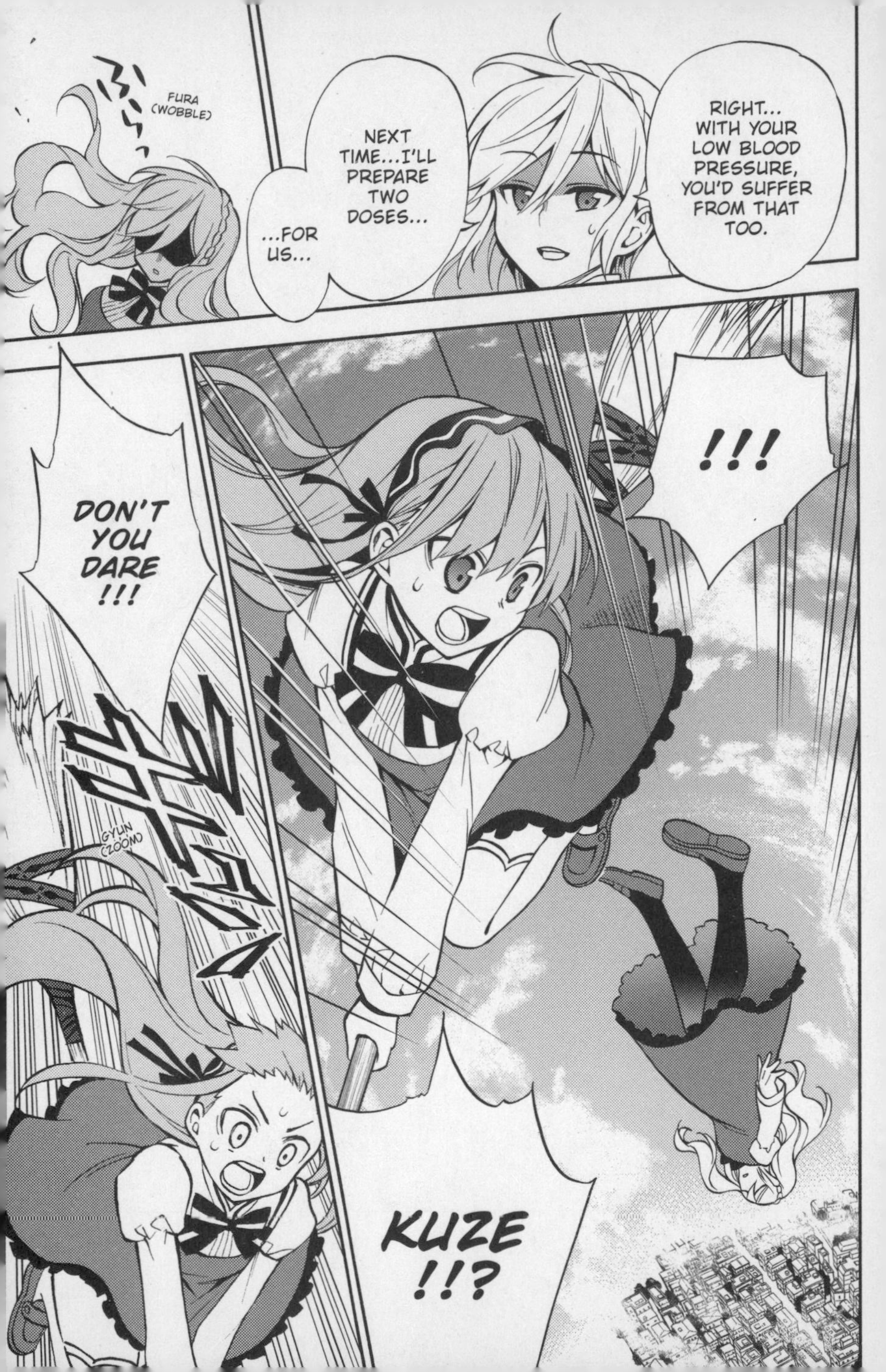
RIGHT... WITH YOUR LOW BLOOD PRESSURE, YOU'D SUFFER FROM THAT TOO.
NEXT TIME...I'LL PREPARE TWO DOSES...
...FOR US...
FURA (WOBBLE)
!!!
KUZE !!?
DON'T YOU DARE !!!
GYUN (ZOOM)

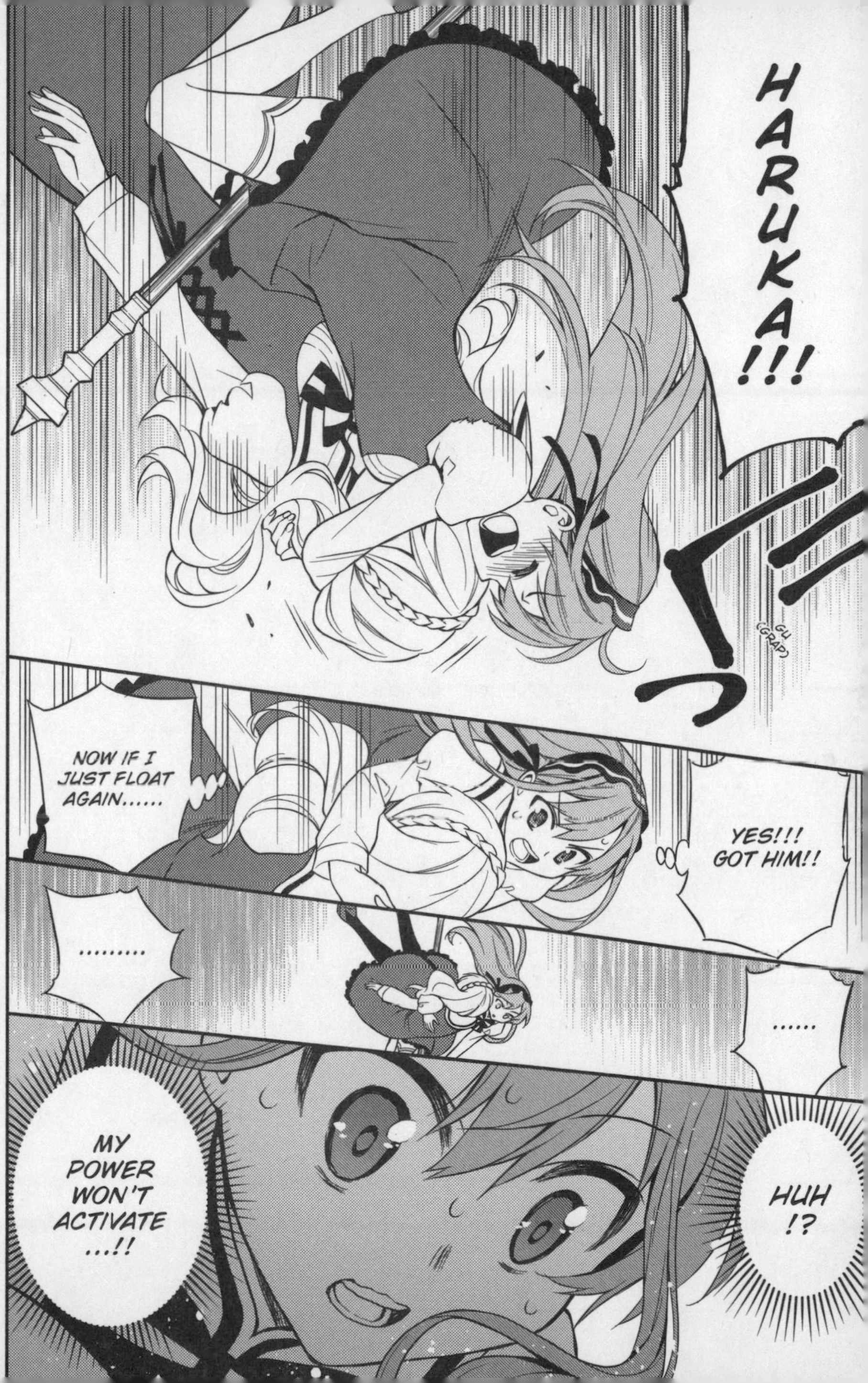
HARUKA!!!
GU (GRAP)
YES!!! GOT HIM!!
NOW IF I JUST FLOAT AGAIN......
......
....
HUH!?
MY POWER WON'T ACTIVATE ...!!

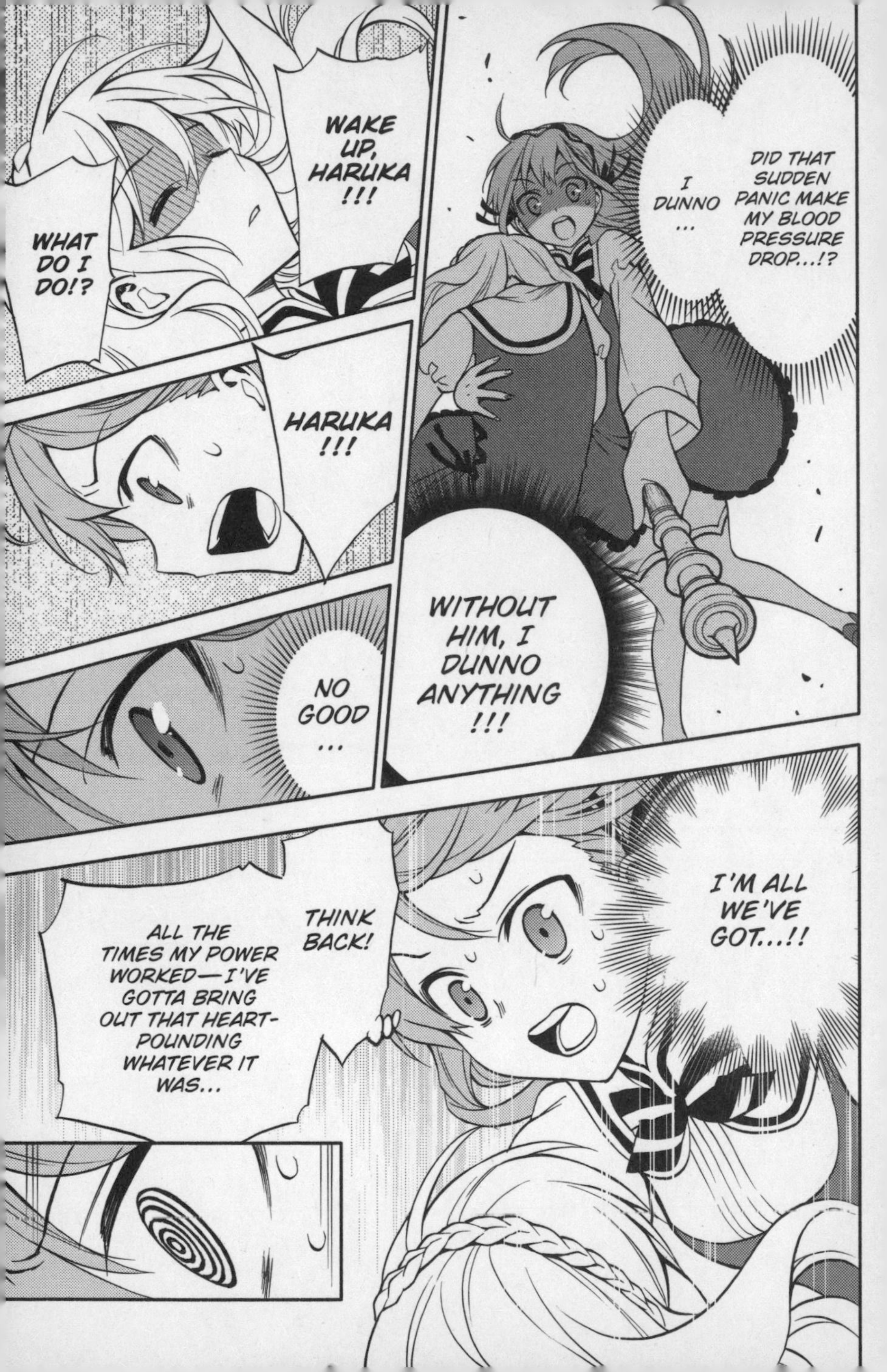
DID THAT SUDDEN PANIC MAKE MY BLOOD PRESSURE DROP...!?
I DUNNO...
WITHOUT HIM, I DUNNO ANYTHING!!!
WAKE UP, HARUKA!!!
WHAT DO I DO!?
HARUKA!!!
NO GOOD...
I'M ALL WE'VE GOT...!!
THINK BACK!
ALL THE TIMES MY POWER WORKED—I'VE GOTTA BRING OUT THAT HEART-POUNDING WHATEVER IT WAS...

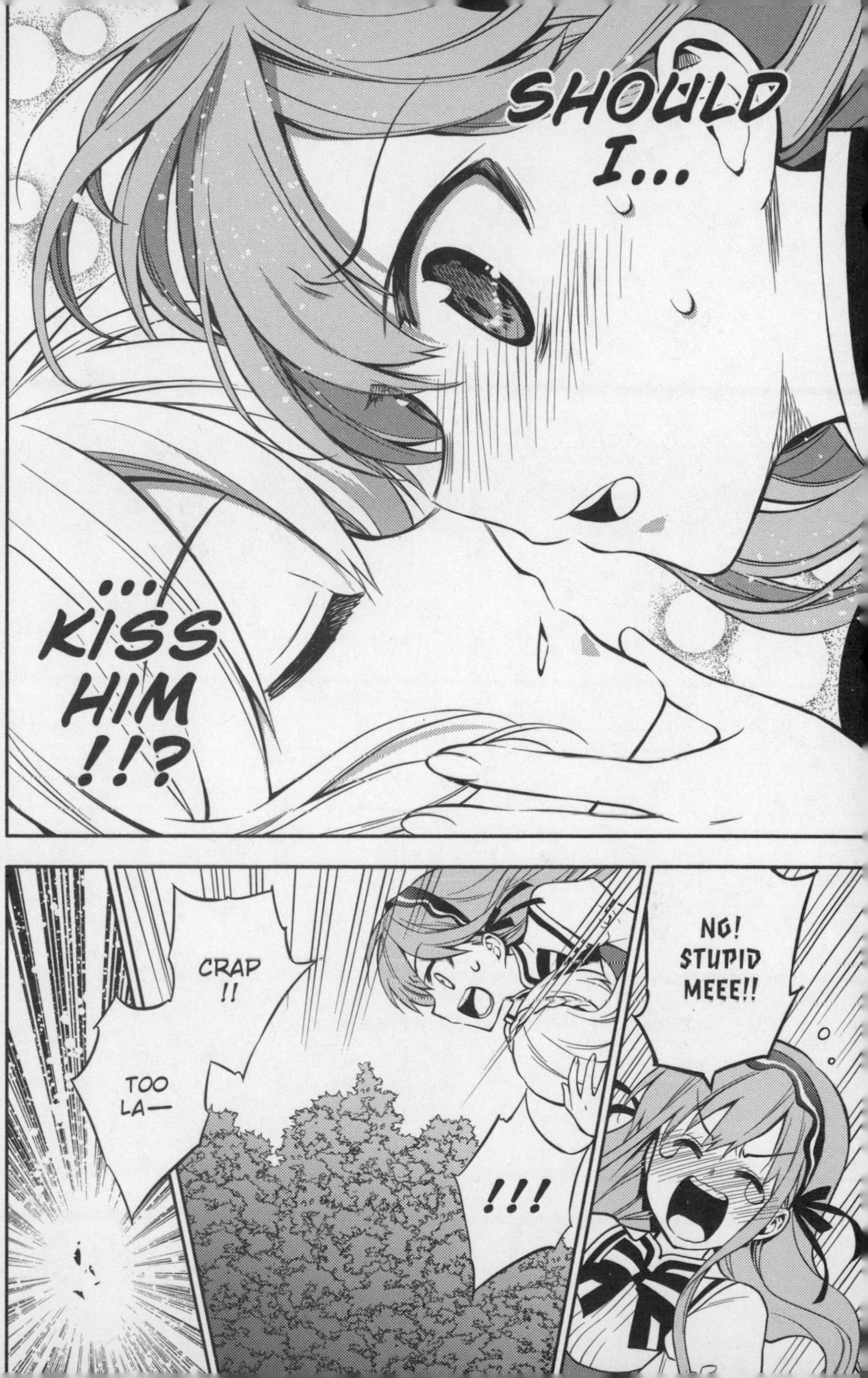
SHOULD I...
...KISS HIM!!?
NG! STUPID MEEE!!
!!!
CRAP!!
TOO LA—

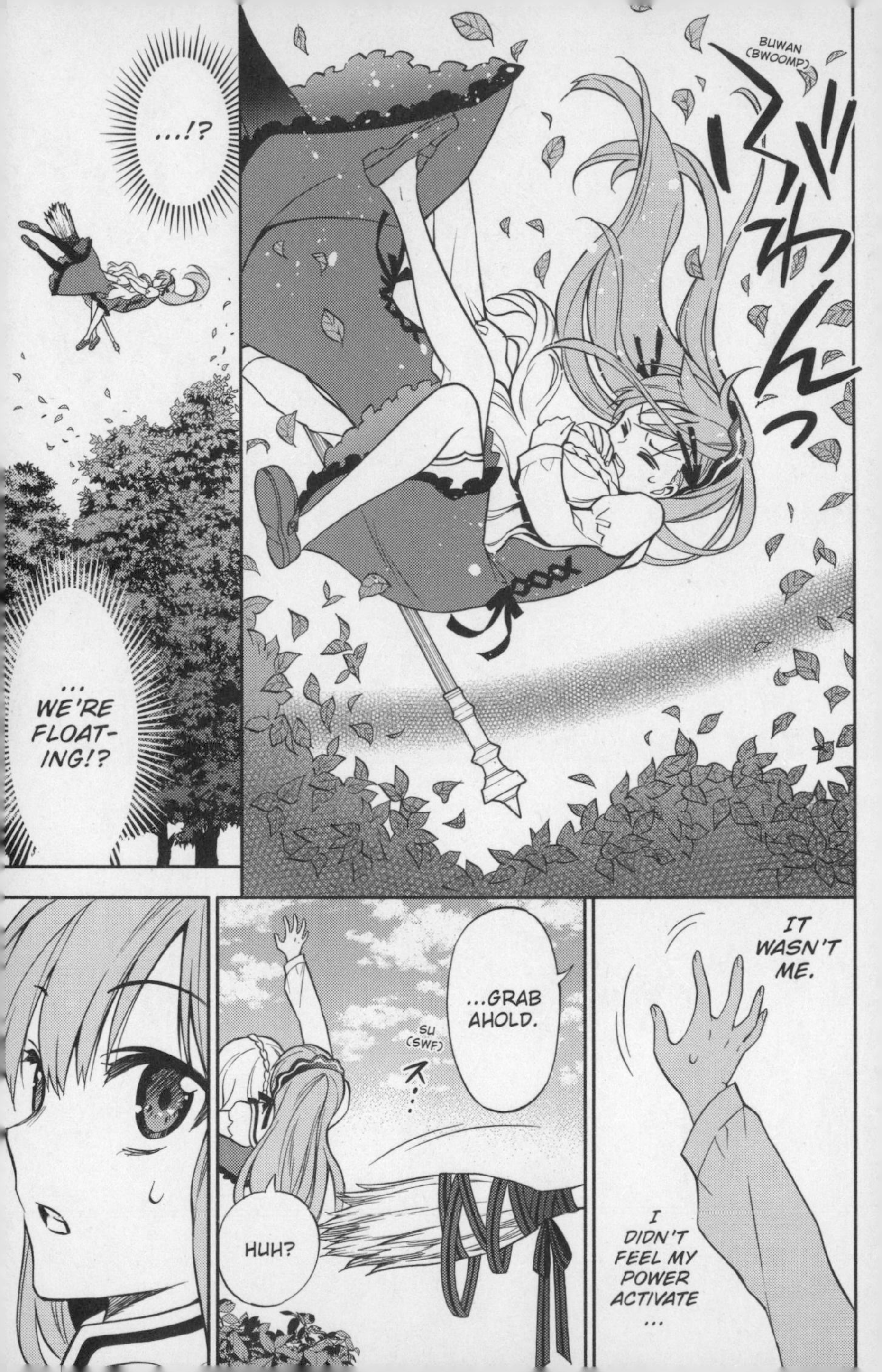

BUWAN (BWOOMP)
ぶわんっ
...!?
...WE'RE FLOATING!?
IT WASN'T ME.
I DIDN'T FEEL MY POWER ACTIVATE...
...GRAB AHOLD.
SU (SWF)
ス…
HUH?

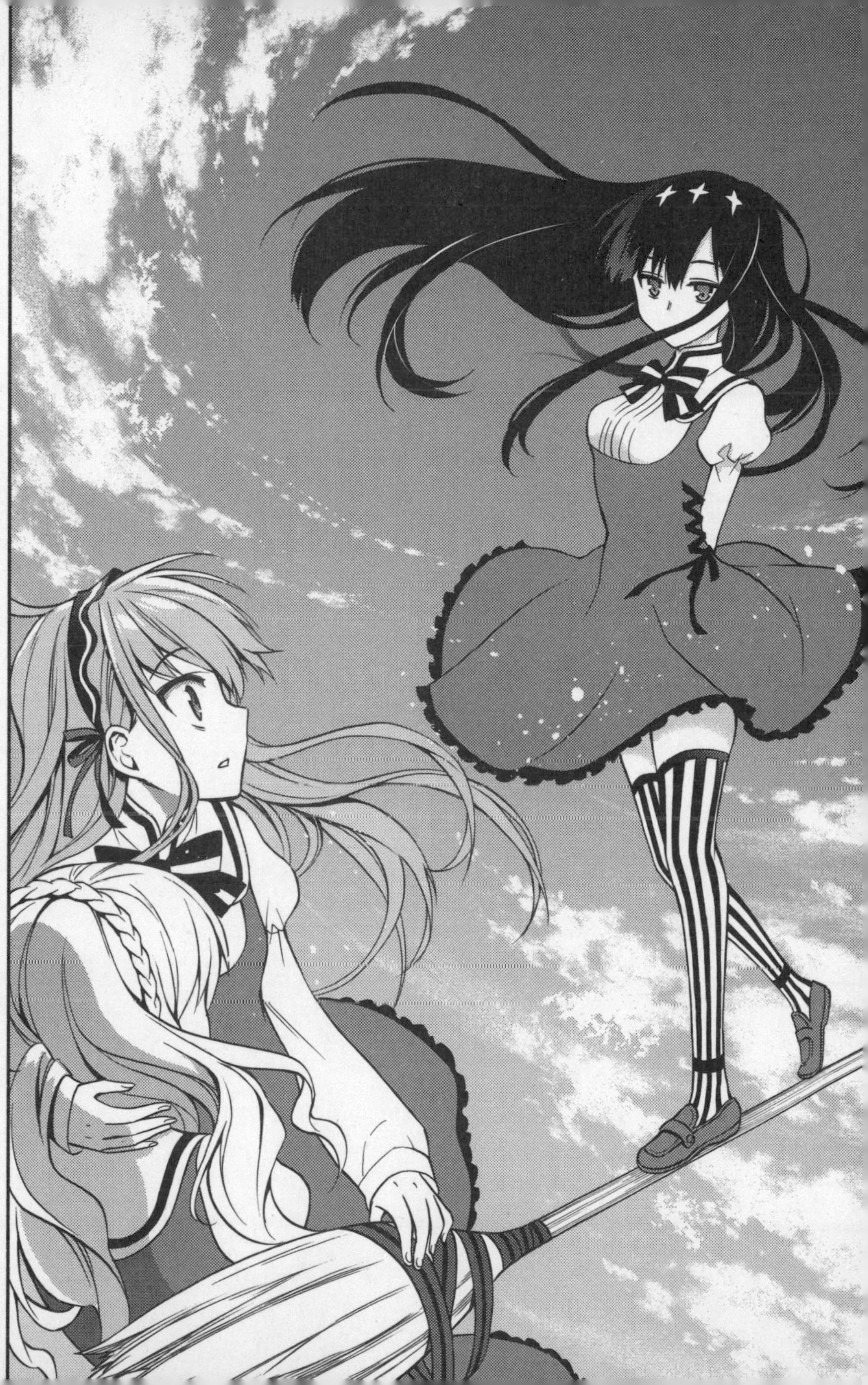

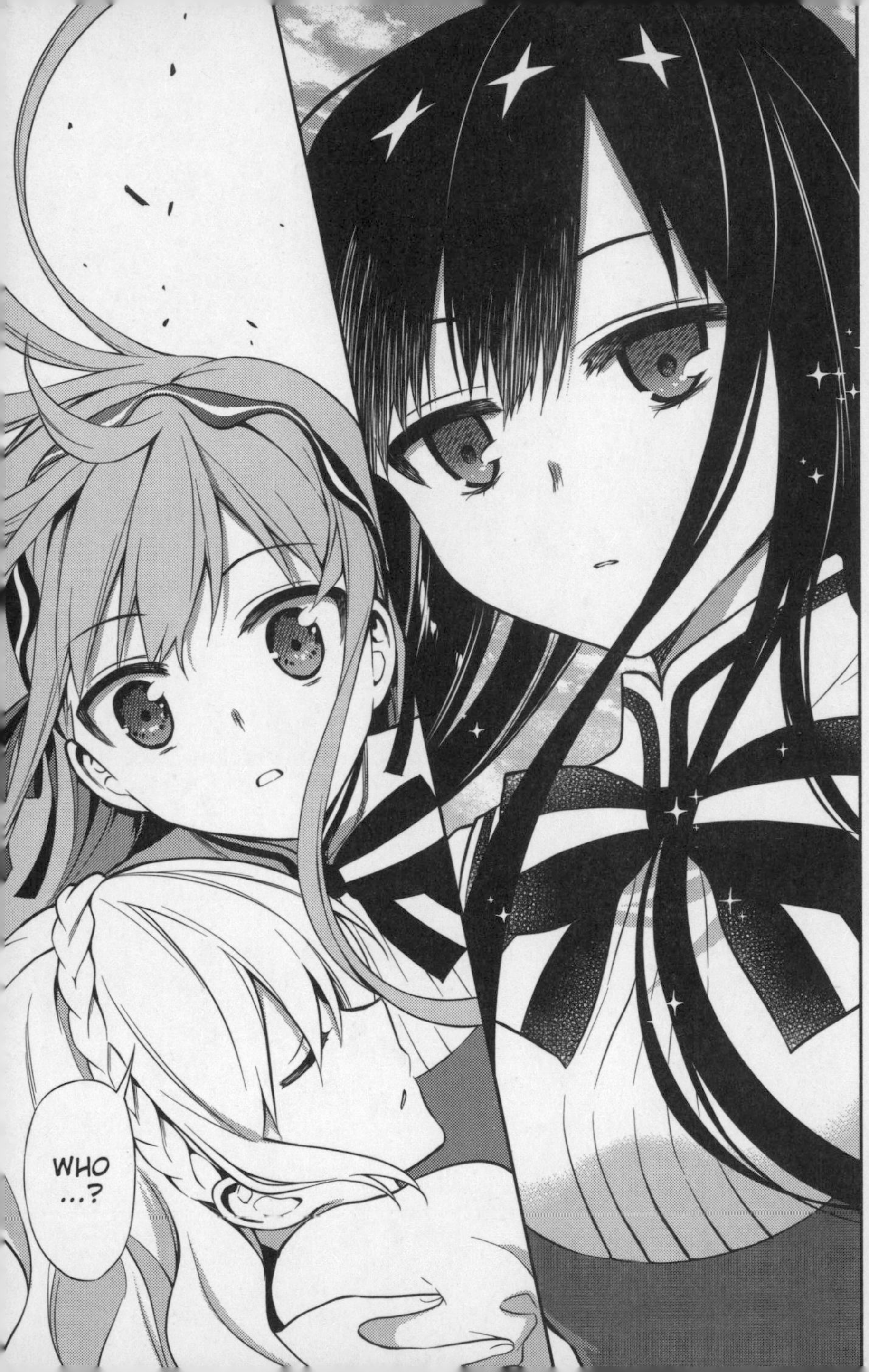
WHO
...?

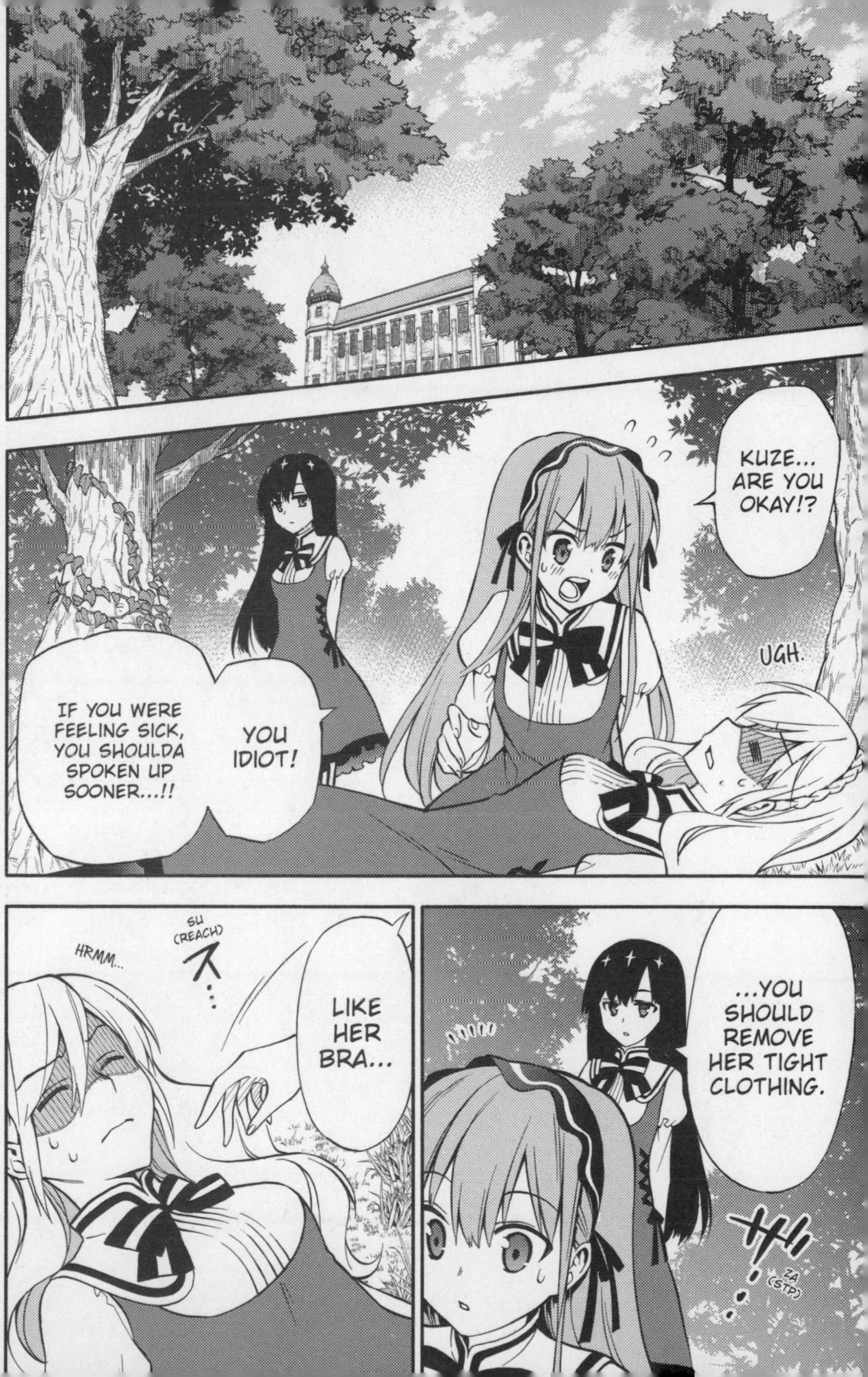
KUZE... ARE YOU OKAY!?
UGH.
YOU IDIOT!
IF YOU WERE FEELING SICK, YOU SHOULDA SPOKEN UP SOONER...!!
...YOU SHOULD REMOVE HER TIGHT CLOTHING.
ZA (STP)
LIKE HER BRA...
SU (REACH)
HRMM...

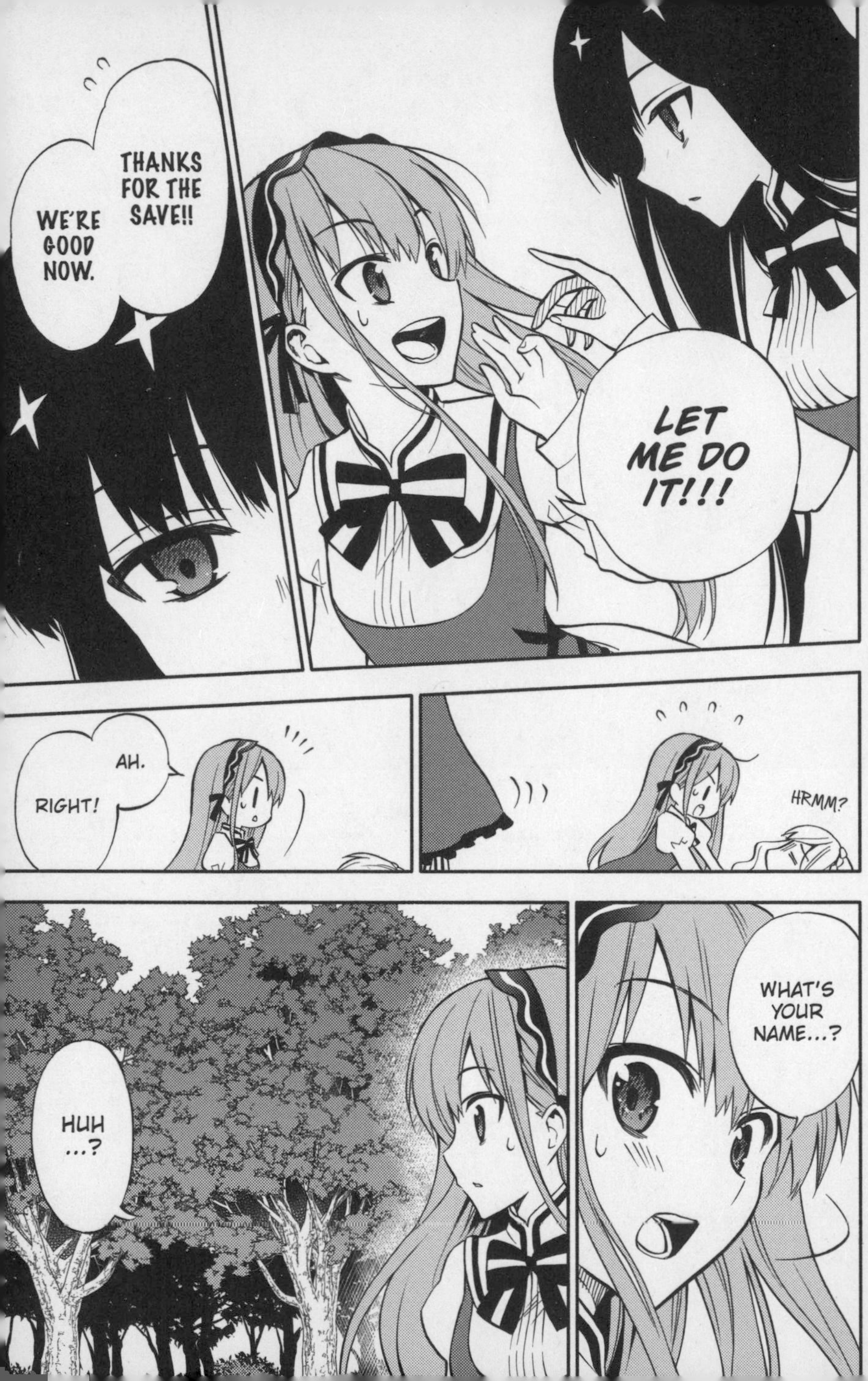
LET ME DO IT!!!
THANKS FOR THE SAVE!!
WE'RE GOOD NOW.
HRMM?
AH.
RIGHT!
WHAT'S YOUR NAME...?
HUH ...?

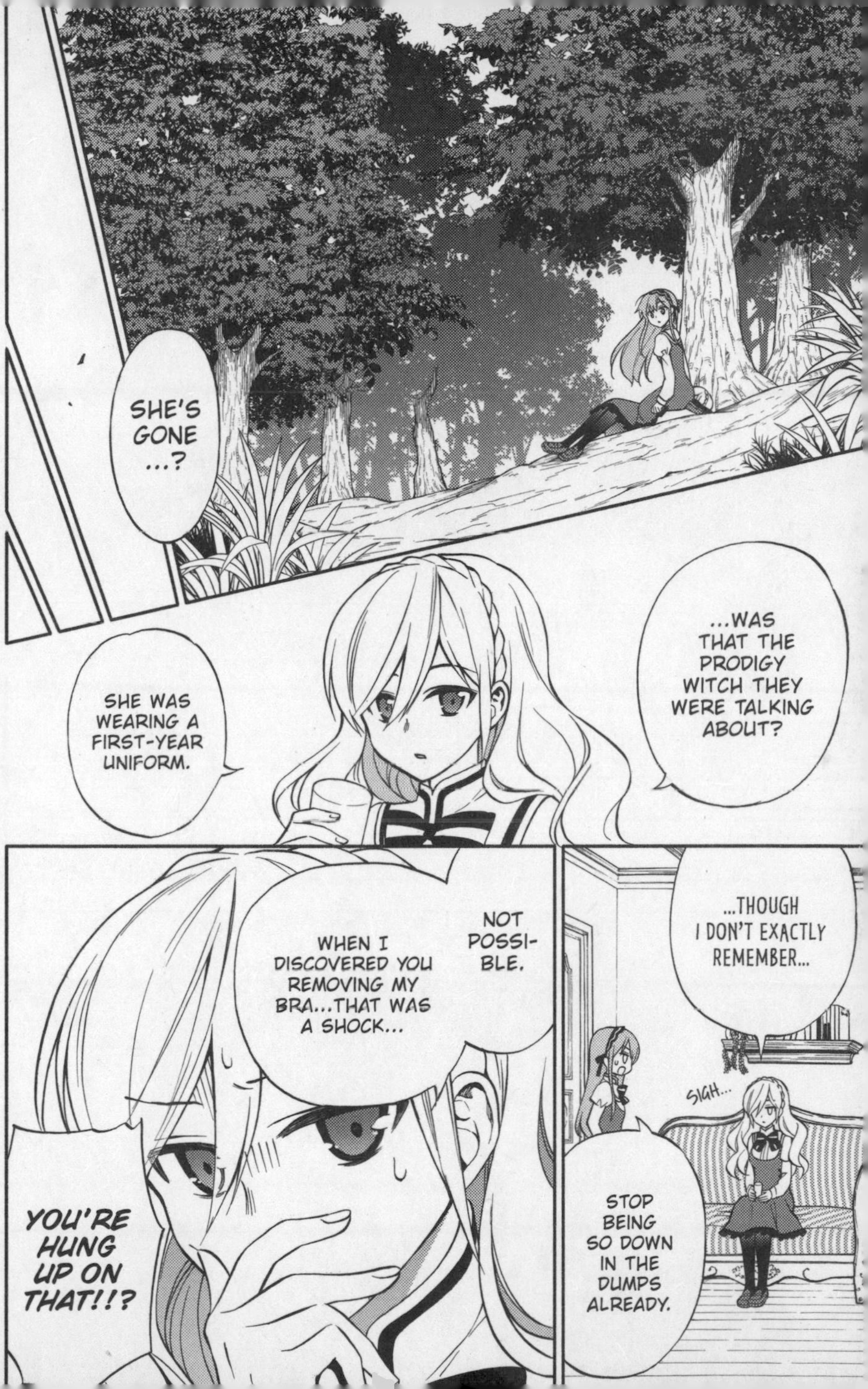
SHE'S GONE ...?
...WAS THAT THE PRODIGY WITCH THEY WERE TALKING ABOUT?
SHE WAS WEARING A FIRST-YEAR UNIFORM.
...THOUGH I DON'T EXACTLY REMEMBER...
SIGH...
STOP BEING SO DOWN IN THE DUMPS ALREADY.
NOT POSSI-BLE.
WHEN I DISCOVERED YOU REMOVING MY BRA...THAT WAS A SHOCK...
YOU'RE HUNG UP ON THAT!!?

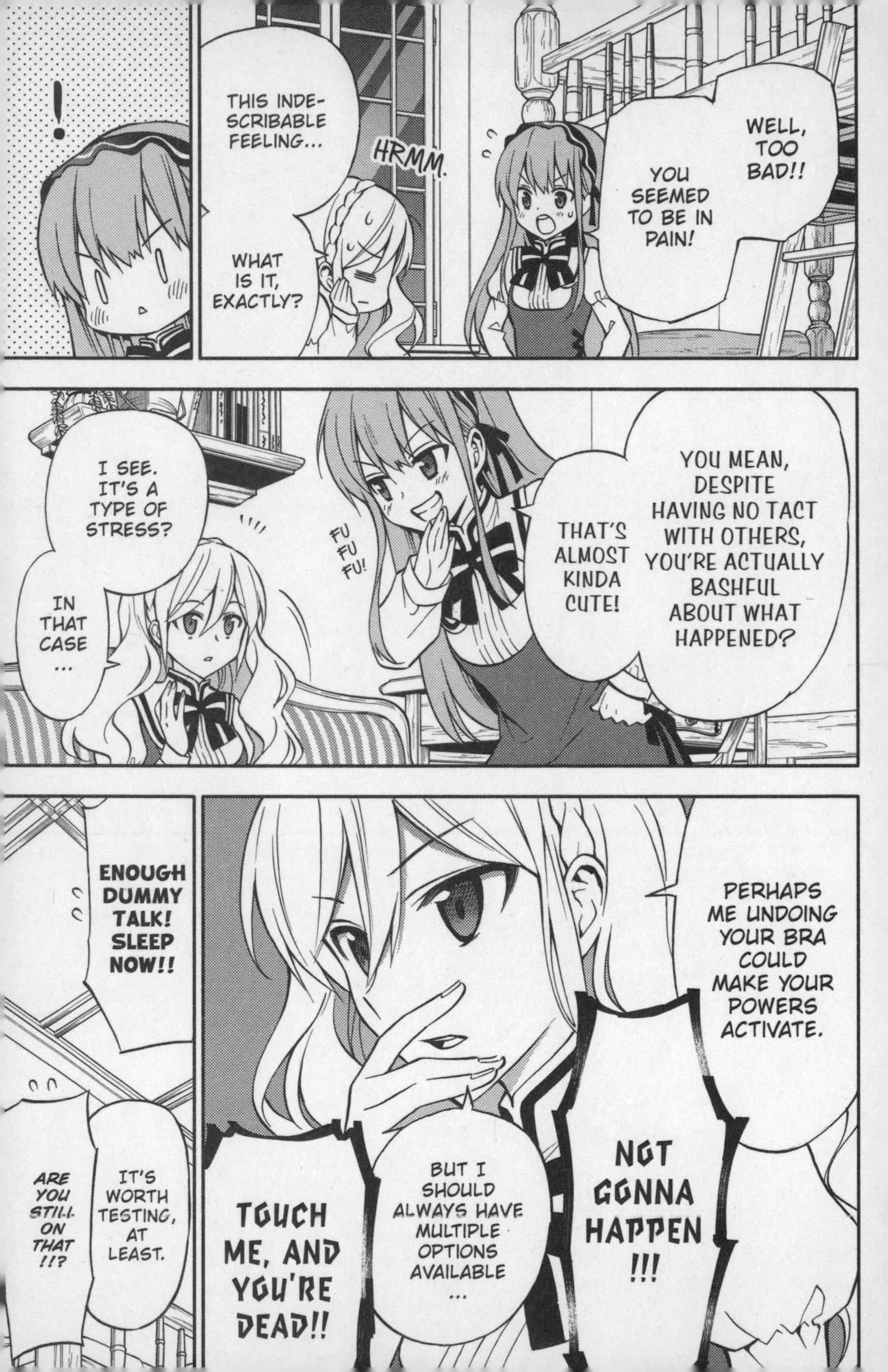
WELL, TOO BAD!!
YOU SEEMED TO BE IN PAIN!
THIS INDE-SCRIBABLE FEELING...
HRMM.
WHAT IS IT, EXACTLY?
!
YOU MEAN, DESPITE HAVING NO TACT WITH OTHERS, YOU'RE ACTUALLY BASHFUL ABOUT WHAT HAPPENED?
THAT'S ALMOST KINDA CUTE!
FU FU FU!
I SEE. IT'S A TYPE OF STRESS?
IN THAT CASE ...
PERHAPS ME UNDOING YOUR BRA COULD MAKE YOUR POWERS ACTIVATE.
NOT GONNA HAPPEN!!!
BUT I SHOULD ALWAYS HAVE MULTIPLE OPTIONS AVAILABLE ...
TOUCH ME, AND YOU'RE DEAD!!
ENOUGH DUMMY TALK! SLEEP NOW!!
IT'S WORTH TESTING, AT LEAST.
ARE YOU STILL ON THAT!!?

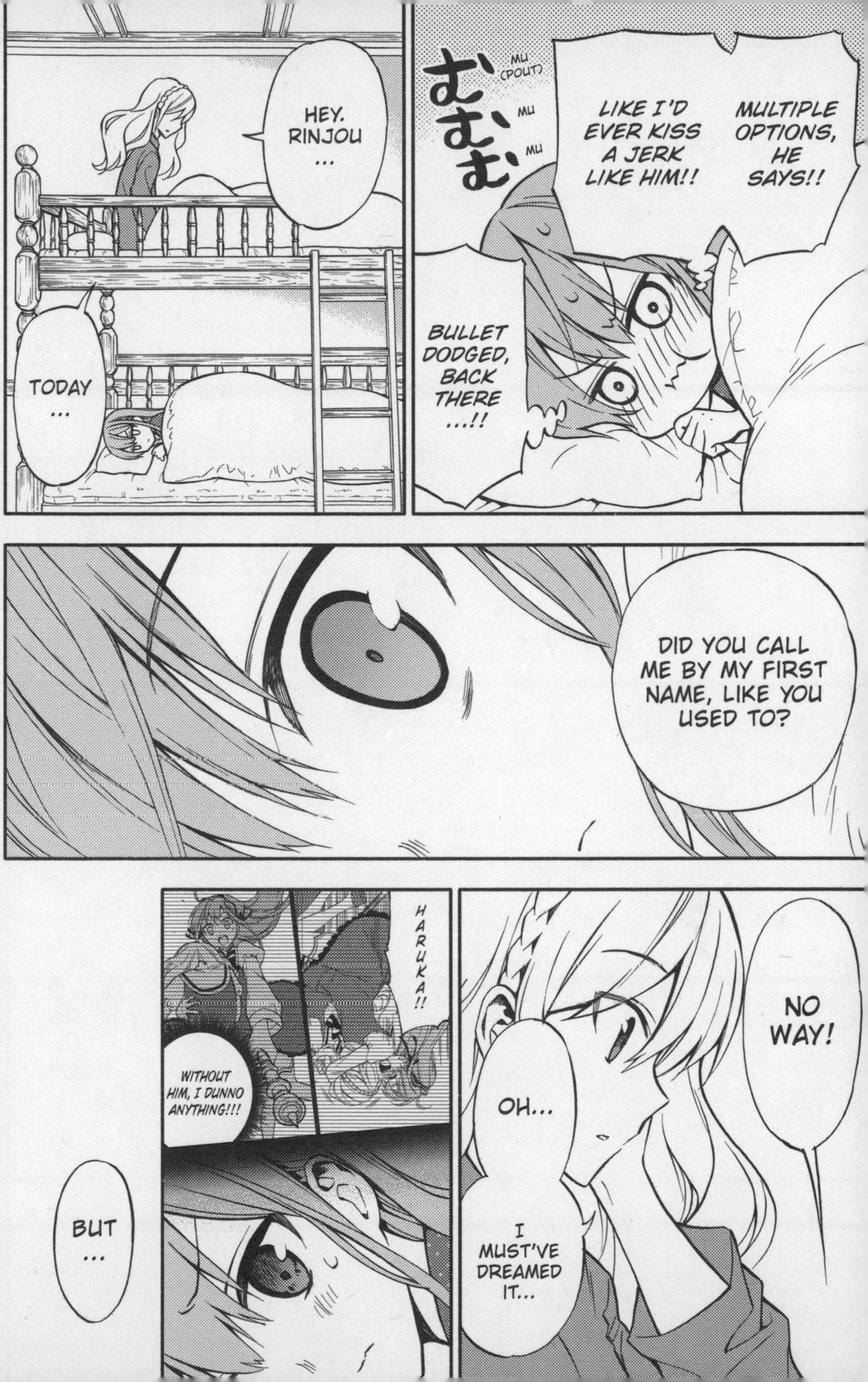

MULTIPLE OPTIONS, HE SAYS!!
LIKE I'D EVER KISS A JERK LIKE HIM!!
むむむ
MU (POUT)
MU
MU
BULLET DODGED, BACK THERE ...!!
HEY. RINJOU ...
TODAY ...
DID YOU CALL ME BY MY FIRST NAME, LIKE YOU USED TO?
NO WAY!
OH...
I MUST'VE DREAMED IT...
HARUKA!!
WITHOUT HIM, I DUNNO ANYTHING!!!
BUT ...

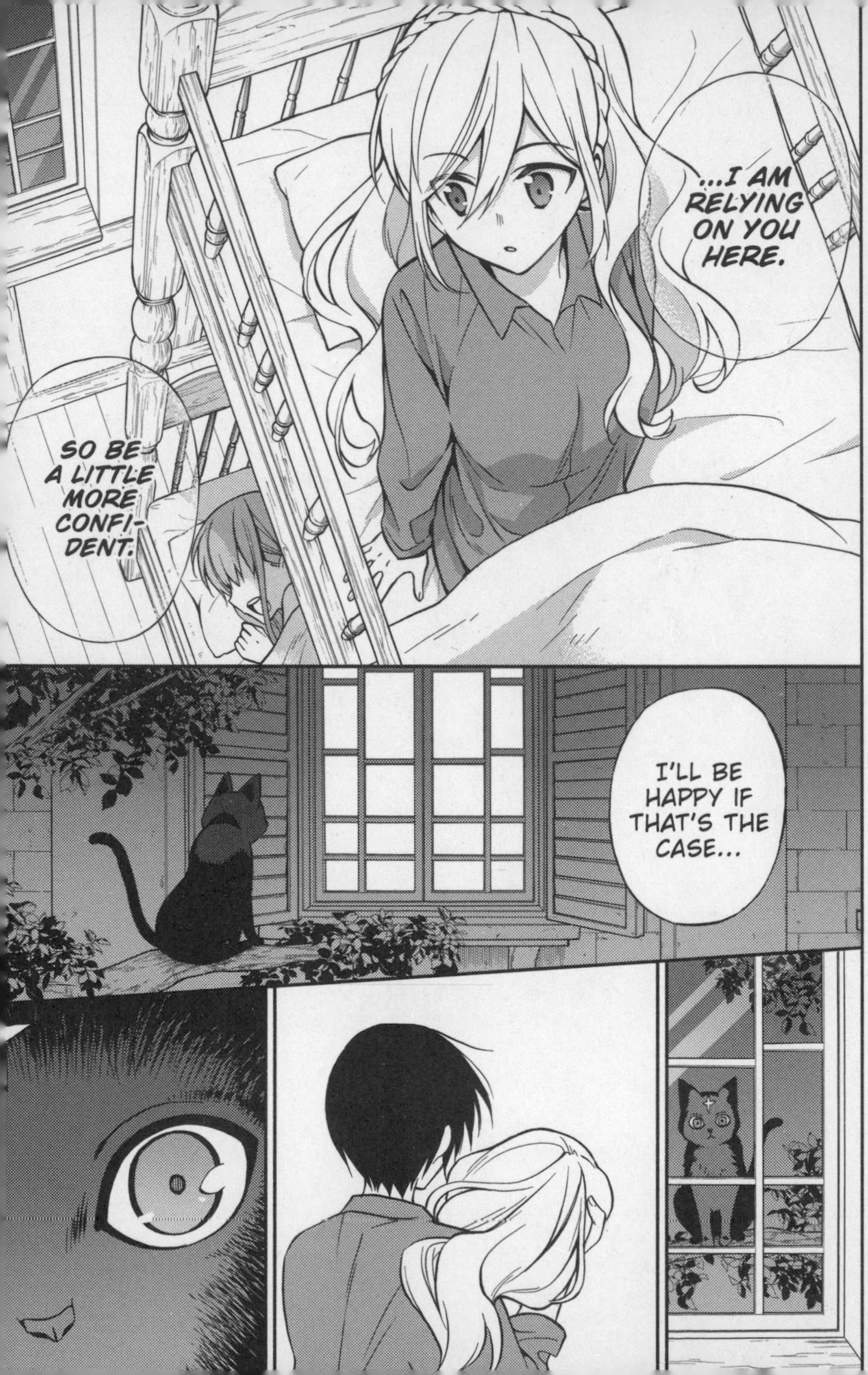
...I AM RELYING ON YOU HERE.
SO BE A LITTLE MORE CONFI-DENT.
I'LL BE HAPPY IF THAT'S THE CASE...

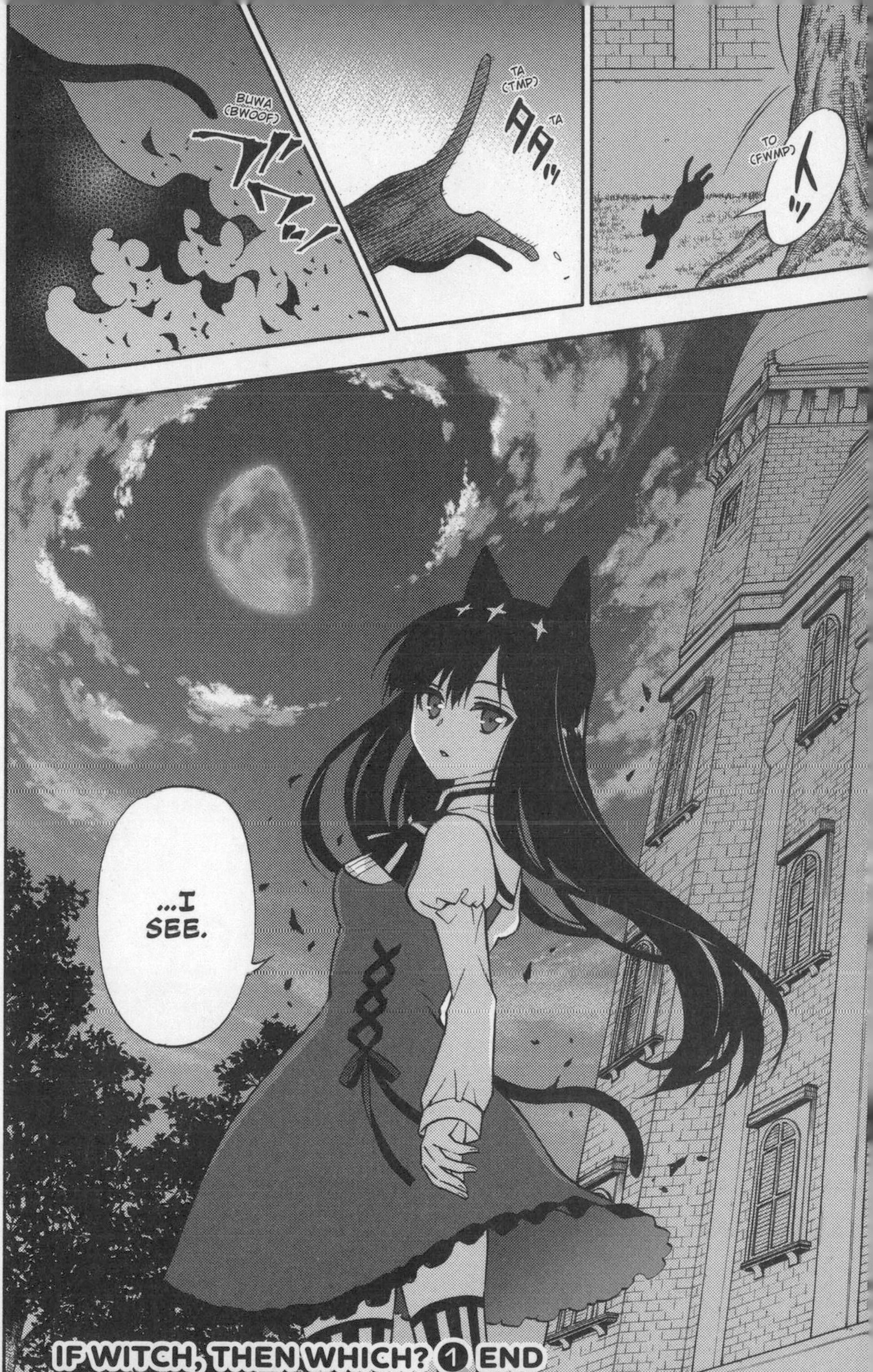
TO
(FWMP)
TA
(TMP)
TA
BUWA
(BWOOF)
...I SEE.
IF WITCH, THEN WHICH? 1 END

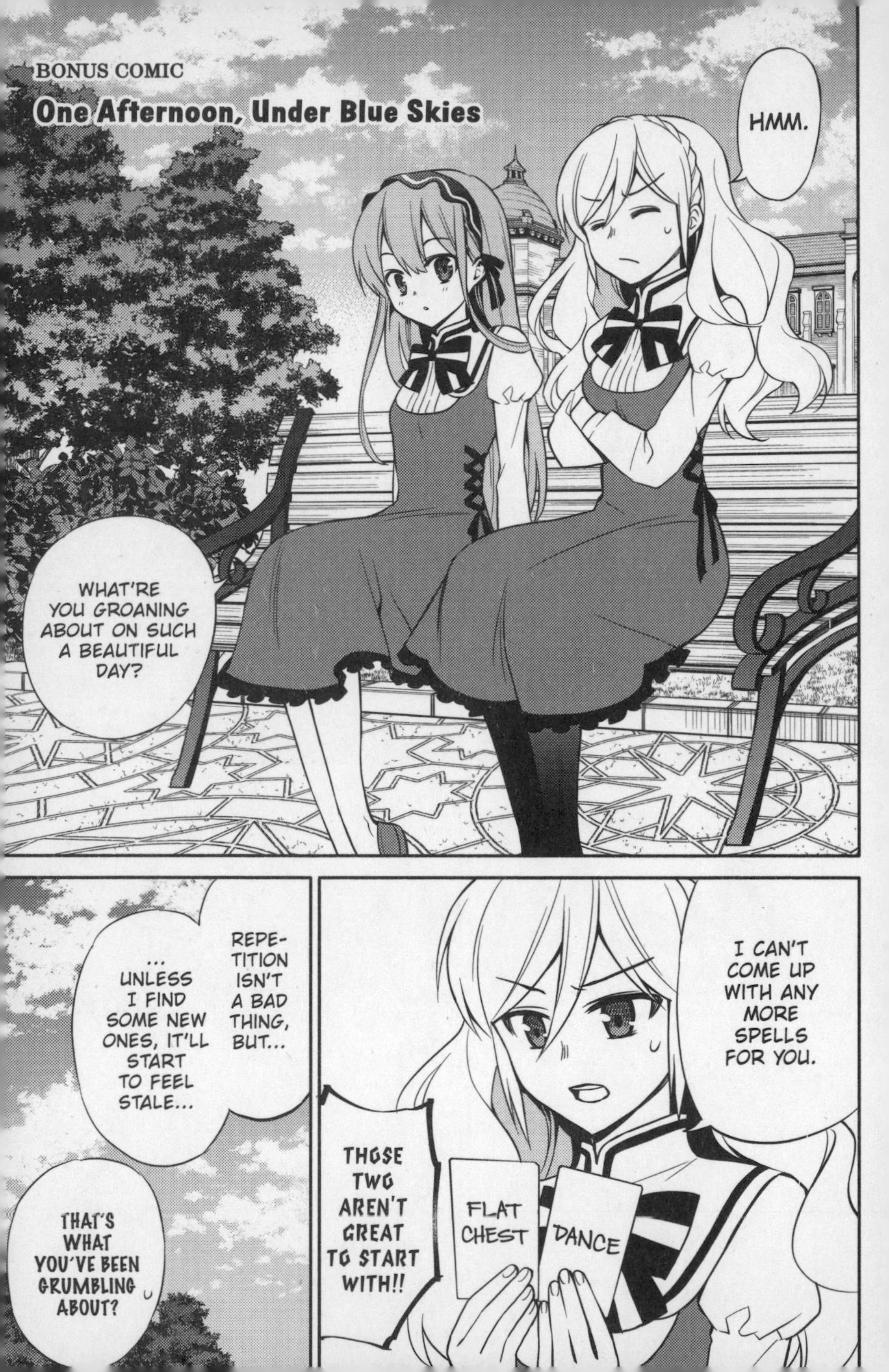
BONUS COMIC
One Afternoon, Under Blue Skies
HMM.
WHAT'RE YOU GROANING ABOUT ON SUCH A BEAUTIFUL DAY?
I CAN'T COME UP WITH ANY MORE SPELLS FOR YOU.
THOSE TWO AREN'T GREAT TO START WITH!!
DANCE
FLAT CHEST
REPETITION ISN'T A BAD THING, BUT...
...UNLESS I FIND SOME NEW ONES, IT'LL START TO FEEL STALE...
THAT'S WHAT YOU'VE BEEN GRUMBLING ABOUT?

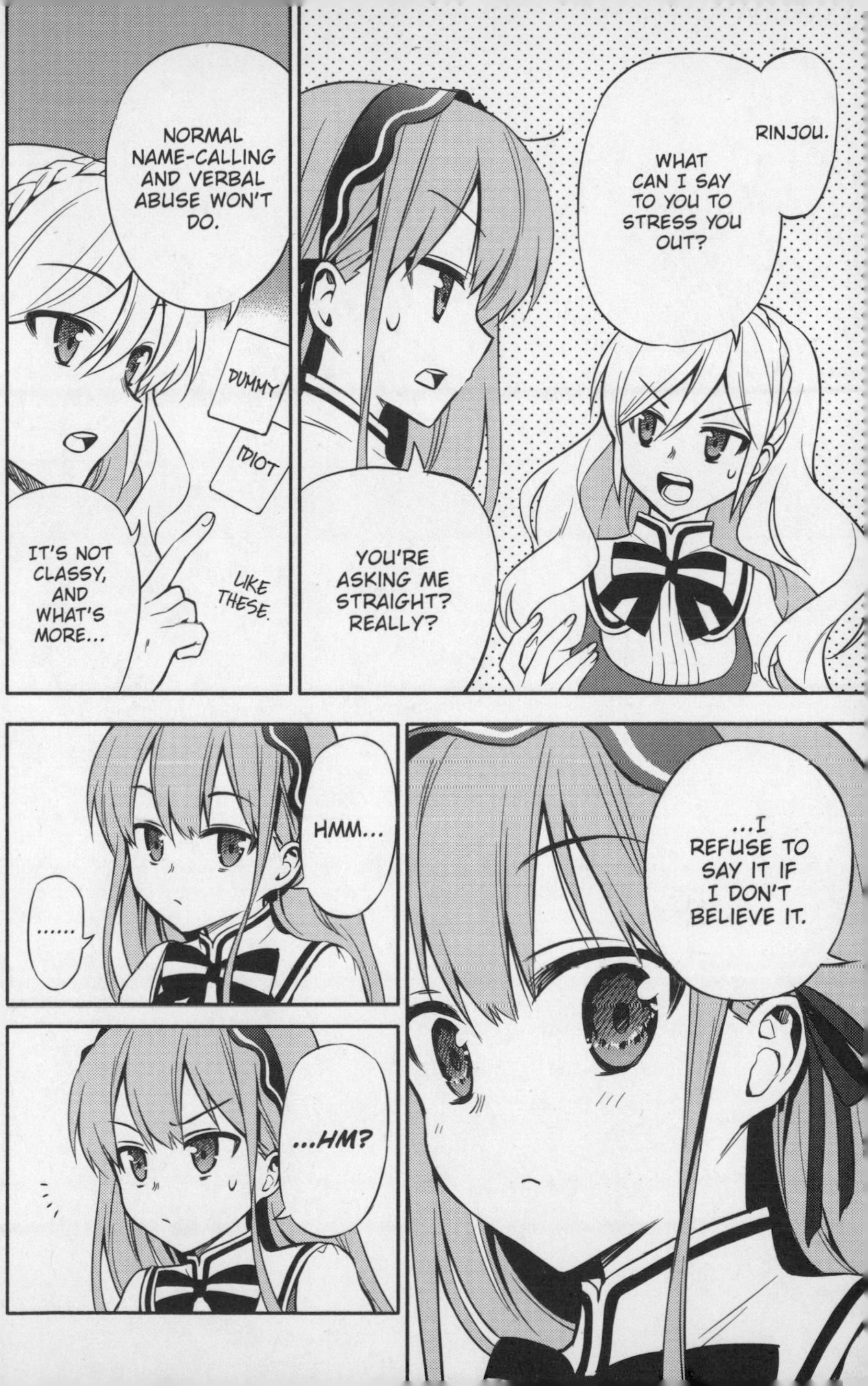
RINJOU.
WHAT CAN I SAY TO YOU TO STRESS YOU OUT?
YOU'RE ASKING ME STRAIGHT? REALLY?
NORMAL NAME-CALLING AND VERBAL ABUSE WON'T DO.
DUMMY
IDIOT
LIKE THESE.
IT'S NOT CLASSY, AND WHAT'S MORE...
...I REFUSE TO SAY IT IF I DON'T BELIEVE IT.
HMM...
......
...HM?

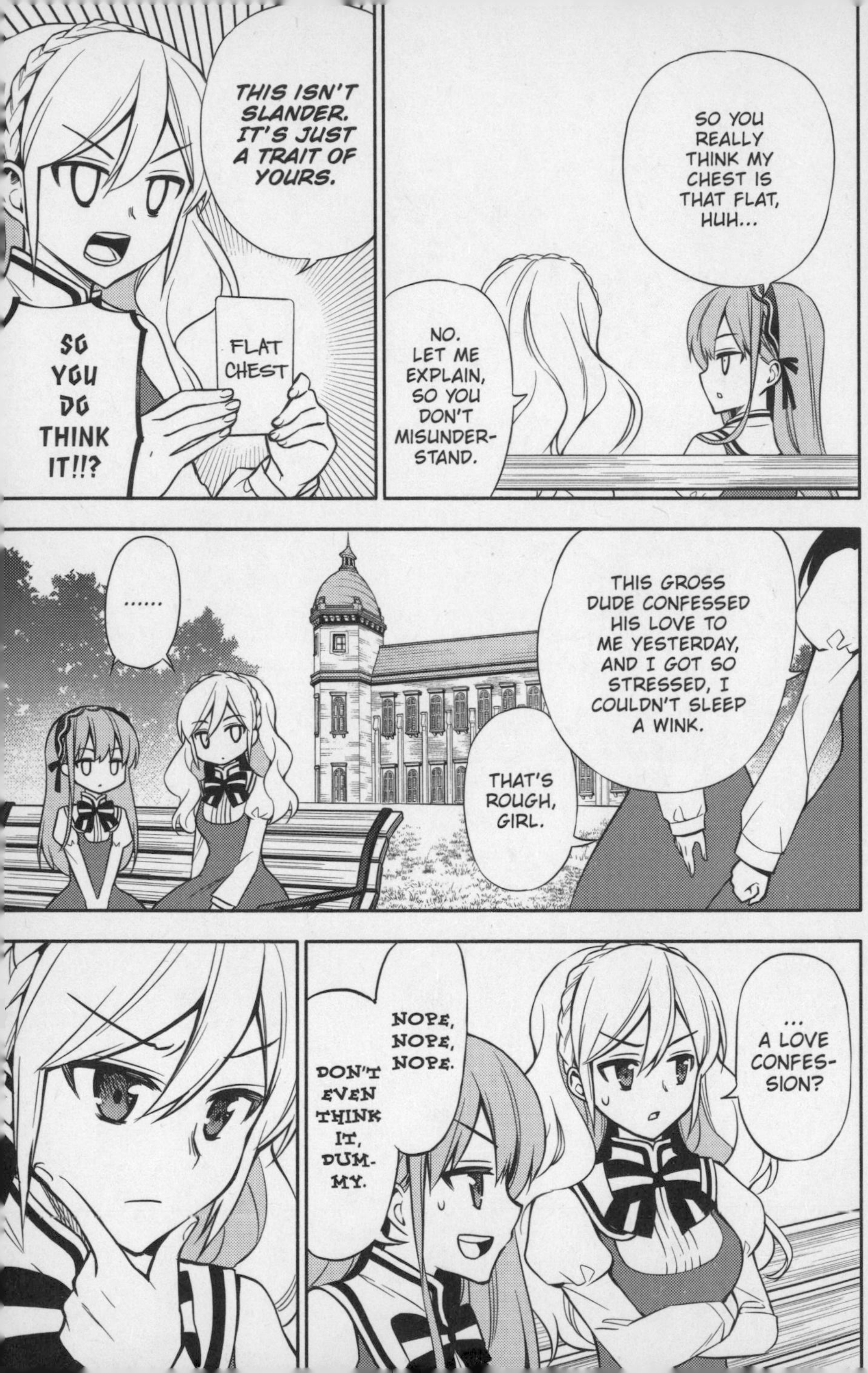
SO YOU REALLY THINK MY CHEST IS THAT FLAT, HUH...
NO. LET ME EXPLAIN, SO YOU DON'T MISUNDERSTAND.
THIS ISN'T SLANDER. IT'S JUST A TRAIT OF YOURS.
FLAT CHEST
SO YOU DO THINK IT!!?
THIS GROSS DUDE CONFESSED HIS LOVE TO ME YESTERDAY, AND I GOT SO STRESSED, I COULDN'T SLEEP A WINK.
THAT'S ROUGH, GIRL.
......
... A LOVE CONFESSION?
NOPE, NOPE, NOPE.
DON'T EVEN THINK IT, DUMMY.

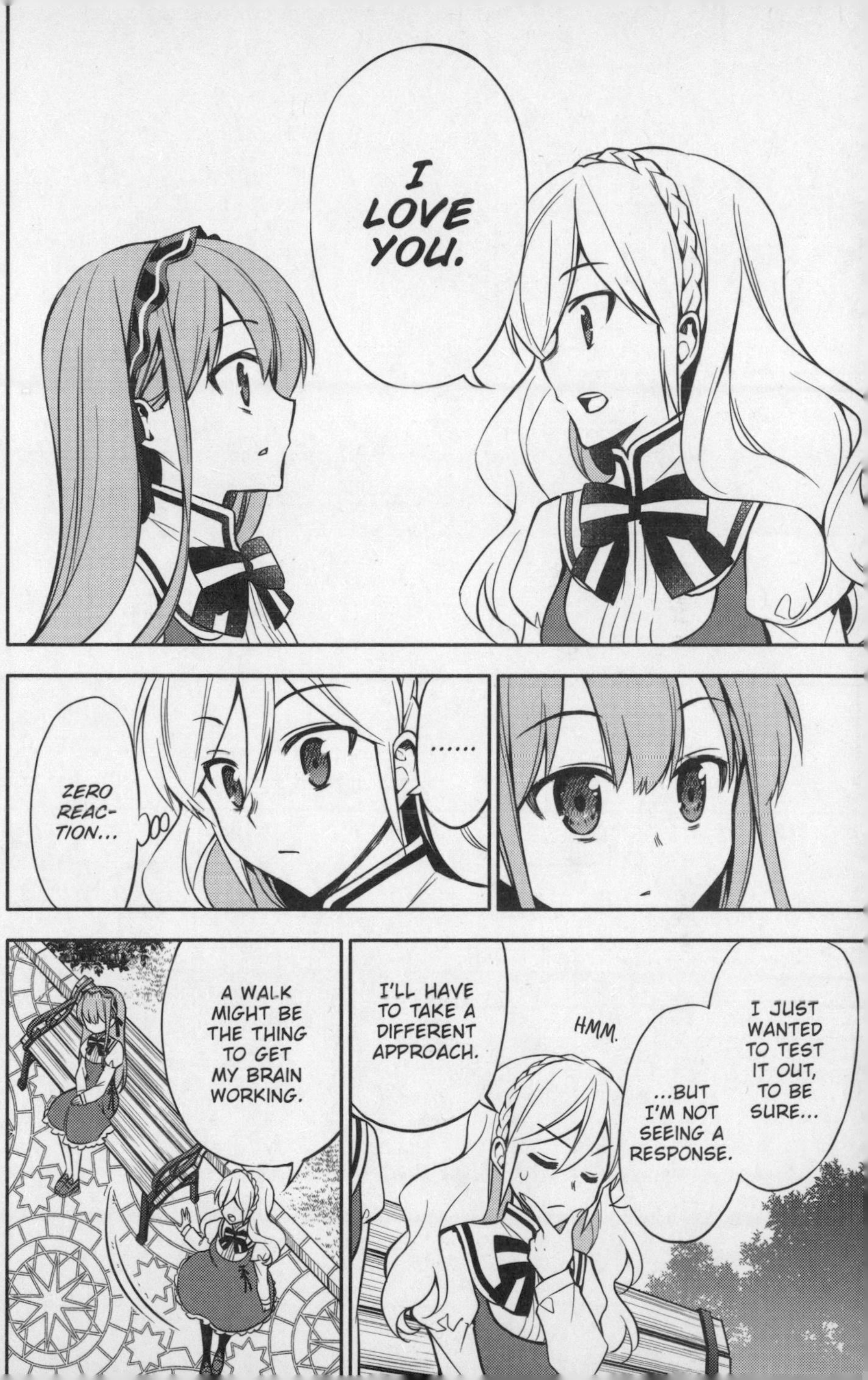
I LOVE YOU.
......
ZERO REACTION...
I JUST WANTED TO TEST IT OUT, TO BE SURE...
...BUT I'M NOT SEEING A RESPONSE.
HMM.
I'LL HAVE TO TAKE A DIFFERENT APPROACH.
A WALK MIGHT BE THE THING TO GET MY BRAIN WORKING.

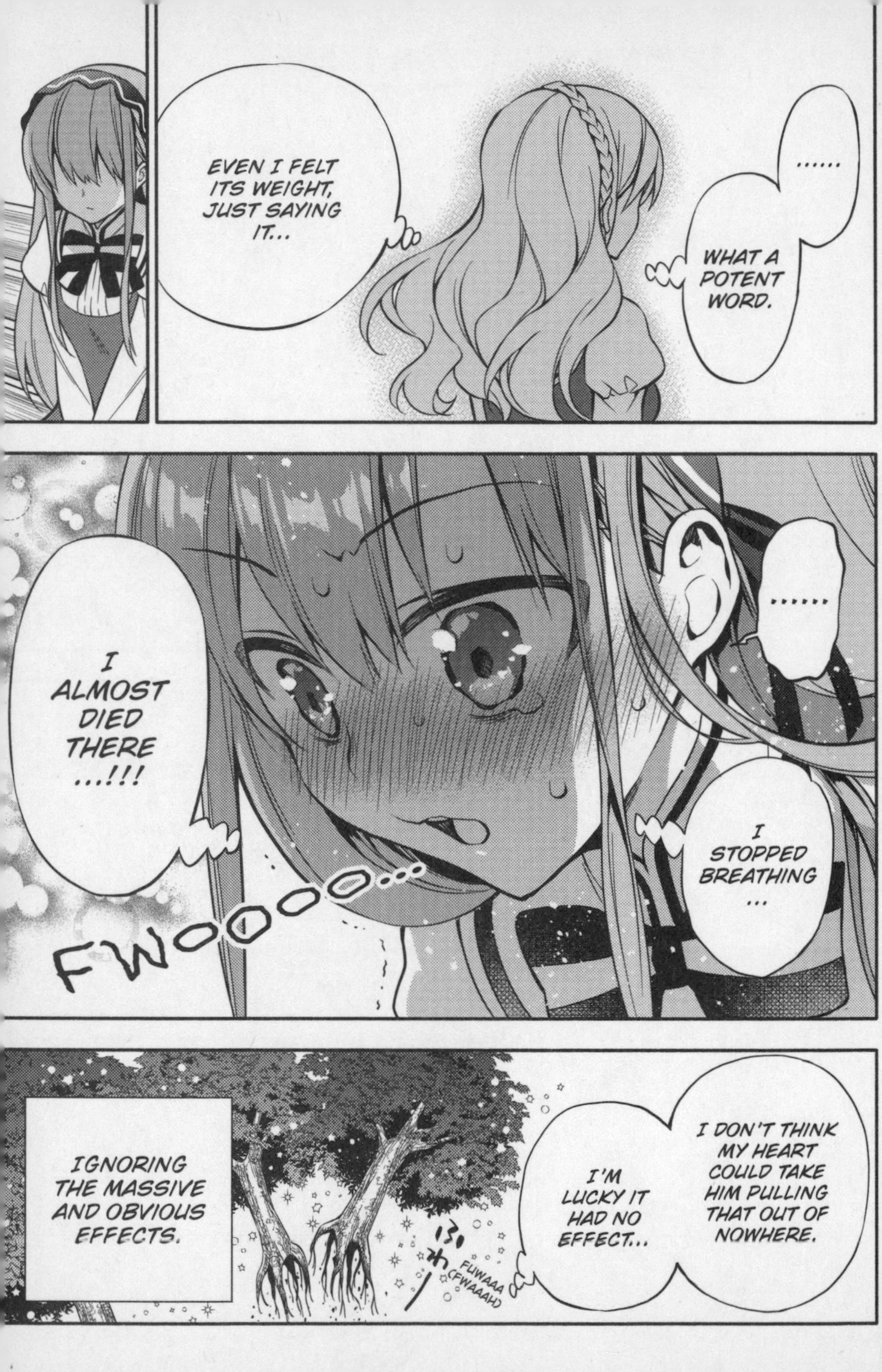
......
EVEN I FELT ITS WEIGHT, JUST SAYING IT...
WHAT A POTENT WORD.
......
I STOPPED BREATHING...
I ALMOST DIED THERE...!!!
FWOOOO...
I DON'T THINK MY HEART COULD TAKE HIM PULLING THAT OUT OF NOWHERE.
I'M LUCKY IT HAD NO EFFECT...
ふわっ
FUWAAA (FWAAAH)
IGNORING THE MASSIVE AND OBVIOUS EFFECTS.

SPRING BREAK FOR THESE TWO

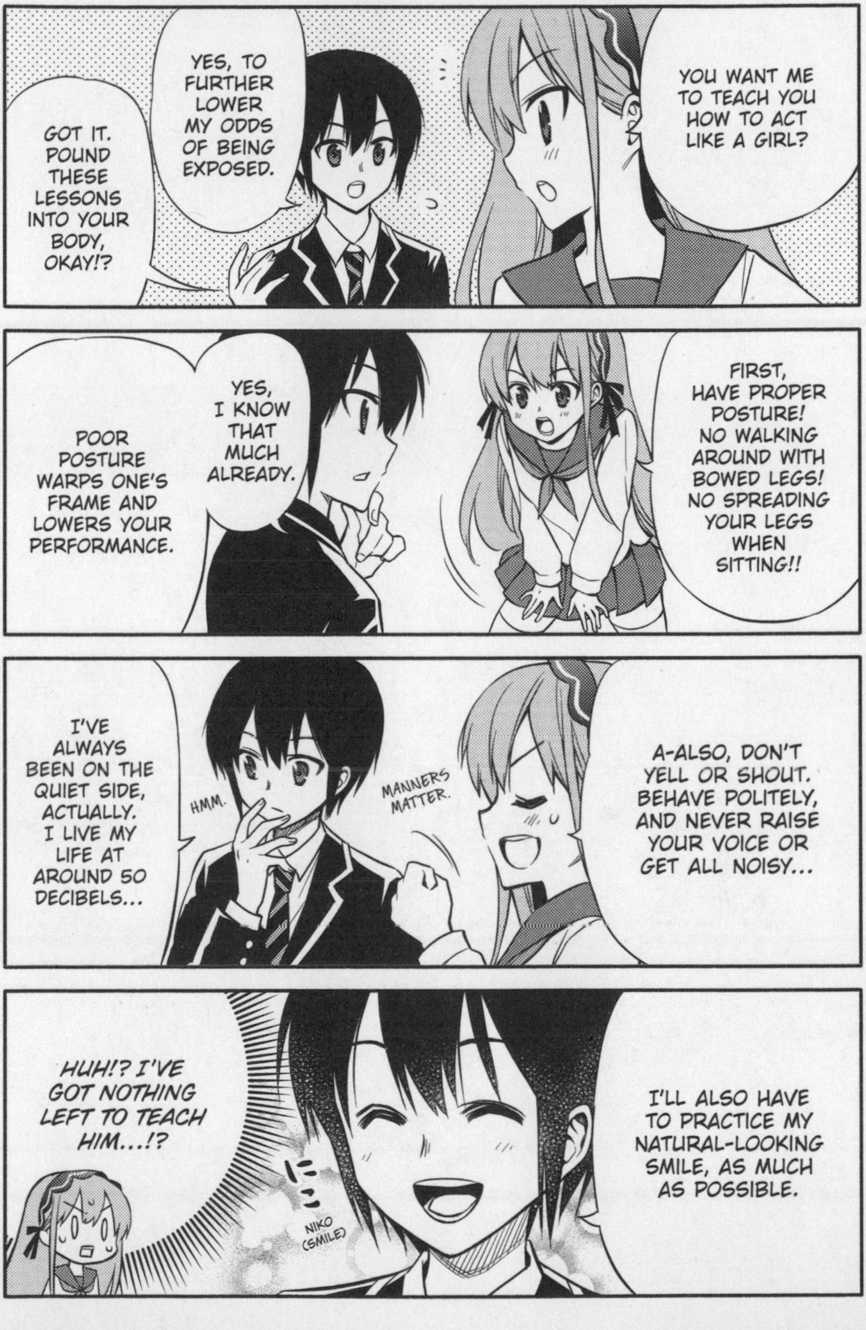
YOU WANT ME TO TEACH YOU HOW TO ACT LIKE A GIRL?
YES, TO FURTHER LOWER MY ODDS OF BEING EXPOSED.
GOT IT. POUND THESE LESSONS INTO YOUR BODY, OKAY!?
FIRST, HAVE PROPER POSTURE! NO WALKING AROUND WITH BOWED LEGS! NO SPREADING YOUR LEGS WHEN SITTING!!
YES, I KNOW THAT MUCH ALREADY.
POOR POSTURE WARPS ONE'S FRAME AND LOWERS YOUR PERFORMANCE.
A-ALSO, DON'T YELL OR SHOUT. BEHAVE POLITELY, AND NEVER RAISE YOUR VOICE OR GET ALL NOISY...
MANNERS MATTER.
HMM.
I'VE ALWAYS BEEN ON THE QUIET SIDE, ACTUALLY. I LIVE MY LIFE AT AROUND 50 DECIBELS...
I'LL ALSO HAVE TO PRACTICE MY NATURAL-LOOKING SMILE, AS MUCH AS POSSIBLE.
にこ
NIKO (SMILE)
HUH!? I'VE GOT NOTHING LEFT TO TEACH HIM...!?